370.4
T14
cop2

GREAT PEDAGOGICAL ESSAYS

PLATO TO SPENCER

BY

F. V. N. PAINTER, A. M., D.D.

PROFESSOR OF MODERN LANGUAGES IN ROANOKE COLLEGE, AUTHOR OF A HISTORY OF EDUCATION, HISTORY OF ENGLISH LITERATURE, INTRODUCTION TO AMERICAN LITERATURE, ETC.

NEW YORK ∴ CINCINNATI ∴ CHICAGO
AMERICAN BOOK COMPANY

COPYRIGHT, 1905, BY
F. V. N. PAINTER.

Entered at Stationers' Hall, London.

Painter's Ped. Ess.

W. P. I

PREFACE.

This volume is intended to introduce the student to the principal documents of educational history. With growth in scholarship there comes a desire to be acquainted with the original sources of information. It is to meet this demand among students of educational history that the present work has been compiled.

The idea of the present compilation, which had long been in the writer's mind, assumed definite shape a year ago, while he was making some investigations in the library of the Bureau of Education. With the original documents in his hands, it became apparent that a collection of them, either in their entirety or in satisfactory selections, could be brought within the compass of a single convenient volume. It seems strange that the attempt had not previously been made.

In preparing this volume, existing translations have been utilized as far as possible. Bohn's Classical Library has been the main dependence for Greek and Latin authors. The principal works of the great educational reformers of the Continent — Comenius, Pestalozzi, Froebel, and others — are accessible in good English versions. In a few cases, among which may be mentioned Rhabanus Maurus, Luther, Fénelon, and the *Ratio Studiorum* of the Jesuits, the author found it necessary to make the translations here used.

The brief biographical sketches will be found to throw more or less light upon the selections. For a critical estimate of the various educators, which it has been thought best not to attempt here, the student is referred to the author's "History of Education," or to any other of the excellent educational histories now on the market. It is hoped that the present work will be found an acceptable and useful volume supplementary to them all.

The successive topics discussed in each selection are given in the index under the author's name. This arrangement shows at a glance the scope of the selections. As will be seen, there is scarcely any important phase of education that has not received consideration.

F. V. N. PAINTER.

CONTENTS

(For analysis of each author, see Index)

Chapter		Page
I.	PLATO, Biographical Sketch,	7
	Selection from the "Laws,"	9
II.	ARISTOTLE, Biographical Sketch,	33
	Selection from the "Politics,"	34
III.	XENOPHON, Biographical Sketch,	61
	Selection from the "Cyropædia,"	62
	Selection from the "Economics,"	68
IV.	CICERO, Biographical Sketch,	83
	Selection from "De Oratore,"	85
V.	SENECA, Biographical Sketch,	97
	1. "On the Education of Children,"	98
	2. "Philosophy,"	100
VI.	QUINTILIAN, Biographical Sketch	103
	Selection from "The Institutes of Oratory,"	104
VII.	PLUTARCH, Biographical Sketch,	125
	Selection from "Morals,"	126
VIII.	JEROME, Biographical Sketch,	143
	"Letter to Laeta,"	144
IX.	APOSTOLICAL CONSTITUTIONS, Historical Sketch,	150
	Selections from the "Apostolical Constitutions,"	150
X.	CHARLEMAGNE, Biographical Sketch,	155
	"Capitulary of 787,"	156
XI.	RHABANUS MAURUS, Biographical Sketch,	158
	"Education of the Clergy,"	159
XII.	MARTIN LUTHER, Biographical Sketch,	169
	"Letter to the Mayors and Aldermen of all the Cities of Germany in behalf of Christian Schools,"	171
XIII.	THE JESUITS, Historical Sketch,	187
	Selection from the "Ratio Studiorum,"	188

Chapter		Page
XIV.	MONTAIGNE, Biographical Sketch,	203
	"Of the Education of Children,"	204
XV.	ROGER ASCHAM, Biographical Sketch,	228
	Selection from "The Scholemaster,"	230
XVI.	JOHN MILTON, Biographical Sketch,	240
	"A Tractate on Education,"	242
XVII.	JOHN AMOS COMENIUS, Biographical Sketch,	255
	Selection from "The Great Didactic,"	258
XVIII.	JOHN LOCKE, Biographical Sketch,	278
	"Some Thoughts Concerning Education,"	280
XIX.	FÉNELON, Biographical Sketch,	291
	"The Education of Girls,"	294
XX.	CHARLES ROLLIN, Biographical Sketch,	303
	"General Instructions upon the Education of Youth,"	304
XXI.	JEAN JACQUES ROUSSEAU, Biographical Sketch,	321
	Selections from "Émile,"	323
XXII.	IMMANUEL KANT, Biographical Sketch,	340
	"Pedagogy,"	341
XXIII.	JOHN HENRY PESTALOZZI, Biographical Sketch,	351
	1. "Diary, 1774,"	353
	2. "The Evening Hour of a Hermit, 1780,"	355
	3. "Swiss News, 1782,"	357
	4. "Letter on His Work at Stanz, 1799,"	359
	5. "The Song of the Swan, 1826,"	364
XXIV.	FREDERICK FROEBEL, Biographical Sketch,	369
	"The Education of Man,"	372
XXV.	HORACE MANN, Biographical Sketch,	383
	"Physical, Intellectual, Moral, and Religious Education,"	385
XXVI.	HERBERT SPENCER, Biographical Sketch,	399
	"What Knowledge is of Most Worth?"	400
INDEX		419

GREAT PEDAGOGICAL ESSAYS.

I. PLATO.

BIOGRAPHICAL SKETCH.

Plato is the earliest of the Greek philosophers whose writings have been transmitted to us. Unlike his great pupil Aristotle, he was a speculative philosopher who sought behind the changing phenomena of nature the absolute and eternal. His thoughts are often astonishingly profound, and he has exerted a far-reaching influence upon the Fathers of the Church and upon the mystics of mediæval and modern times. "Out of Plato," says Emerson in his "Representative Men," "come all things that are still written and debated among men of thought. Great havoc makes he with our originalities."

Unlike his distinguished teacher Socrates, who sprang from the artisan class, Plato descended from a noble family; on his mother's side he was related to Solon, and on his father's side to Codrus, one of the ancient kings of Athens. Perhaps it was the influence of his descent and early training that made him aristocratic in his sympathies. When he came to theorize about an ideal "Republic," he placed the government in the hands of an aristocratic class.

Plato was born in Athens about 427 B. C., and no doubt received the best education in gymnastics and music that his native city afforded. His imaginative intellect first turned him to poetry, in which he probably might have achieved distinction; but at the age of twenty he came under the influence of Socrates, and henceforth devoted his great powers to philosophy. He spent some years in travel. He resided for a time with Euclid at Megara; he visited Italy, where he came under the influence of the Pythagorean school of philosophy. In 386 B. C., in the full maturity of manhood and with a mind richly stored with learning, he began to teach philosophy in the Academy at Athens. For nearly half a century he lectured to a circle of disciples drawn not only from his native city but also from distant parts of Greece.

It was during this long period of philosophizing and teaching that his series of famous dialogues was produced. Among them may be mentioned "Protagoras," or the Socratic doctrine of virtue; "Timæus," or concerning the origin and nature of the world; "Phædo," or concerning the immortality of the soul; the "Republic," or concerning the state that realizes justice; and the "Laws," which deals with the state, but is less speculative than the "Republic." In three of these writings — "Protagoras," the "Republic" and the "Laws" — he discusses education; in the first briefly, and in the last two elaborately. In the "Republic" his views are purely speculative and Utopian; in the "Laws," which was written in his old age, and which may be regarded as representing his most matured views, he is more practical. He remains in closer sympathy with the prevailing system at Athens, though here and there he gives us interesting glimpses of education in Egypt and Sparta. The following selection is from Book VII. of the "Laws," the translation being that of Bohn's Classical Library. It treats of gymnastics and of music, the two main branches of Athenian education.

SELECTION FROM THE "LAWS" OF PLATO.

PERSONS OF THE DIALOGUE.

AN ATHENIAN STRANGER. CLEINIAS, *a Cretan.*
MEGILLUS, *a Lacedæmonian.*

BOOK VII.

ATH. Up to the age of three years, whether of boy or girl, if a person strictly carries out our previous regulations and makes them a principal aim, he will do much for the advantage of the young creatures. But at three, four, five, and six years the childish nature will require sports; now is the time to get rid of self-will in him, punishing him, not so as to disgrace him. As we were saying about slaves, that we ought neither to punish them in hot blood or so as to anger them, nor yet to leave them unpunished lest they become self-willed, a like rule is to be observed in the case of the free-born. Children at that age have certain natural modes of amusement which they find out for themselves when they meet. And all the children who are between the ages of three and six ought to meet at the temples of the villages, several families of a village uniting on one spot, and the nurses seeing that the children behave properly and orderly,— they themselves and their whole company being under the care of one of the twelve women aforesaid annually appointed out of their number by the guardians of the law to inspect and order each company. Let the twelve be appointed by the women who have authority over marriage, one out of each tribe and all of the same age; and when appointed, let them hold office and go to the temples every day, punishing all offenders, male or female, who are slaves or strangers, by the help of some of the public servants; but if any citizen disputes the punishment, let her bring him before the wardens of the city; or, if there be no dispute, let her punish him herself. After the age of six years the time has arrived for the separation of the sexes,— let boys live with boys, and girls in like manner with girls. Now they must begin to learn — the boys going to teachers of horsemanship and the use of the bow, the javelin, and sling; and if they do not object, let women also go to learn if not to practice; above all, they ought to know the use of arms; for I may note, that the practice which now almost universally prevails is due to ignorance.

CLE. In what respect?

ATH. In this respect, that the right and left hand are supposed to differ by nature when we use them; whereas no difference is found in the use of the feet and the lower limbs; but in the use of the hands we are in a manner lame, by reason of the folly of nurses and mothers; for although our several limbs are by nature balanced, we create a difference in them by bad habit. In some cases this is of no consequence, as, for example, when we hold the lyre in the left hand, and the plectrum in the right, but it is downright folly to make the same distinction in other cases. The custom of the Scythians proves our error; for they not only hold the bow from them with the left hand and draw the arrow to them with their right, but use either hand for both purposes. And there are many similar examples in charioteering and other things, from which we may learn that those who make the left side weaker than the right act contrary to nature. In the case of the plectrum, which is of horn only, and similar instruments, as I was saying, it is of no consequence, but makes a great difference, and may be of very great importance to the warrior who has to use iron weapons, bows and javelins, and the like; above all, when in heavy armor, he has to fight against heavy armor. And there is a very great difference between one who has learnt and one who has not, and between one who has been trained in gymnastic exercises and one who has not been. For as he who is perfectly skilled in the Pancratium or boxing or wrestling, is not unable to fight from his left side, and does not limp and draggle in confusion when his opponent makes him change his position, so in heavy-armed fighting, and in all other things, if I am not mistaken, the like holds — he who has these double powers of attack and defense ought not in any case to leave them either unused or untrained; and if a person had the nature of Geryon or Briareus he ought to be able with his hundred hands to throw a hundred darts. Now, the rulers, male and female, should see to all these things; the women superintending the nursing and amusements of the children, and the men superintending their education, that all of them, boys and girls alike, may be sound in hand and foot, and may not, if they can help, spoil the gifts of nature by bad habits.

Education has two branches,— one of gymnastic, which is concerned with the body, and the other of music, which is designed for the improvement of the soul. And gymnastics has also two parts — dancing and wrestling; and one sort of dancing imitates musical recitation, and aims at preserving dignity and freedom; the other aims at producing health, agility, and beauty of the limbs and parts of the body, giving the proper flexion and extension to each of them, diffusing and accompanying the harmonious motion of the dance everywhere. As regards wrestling, the tricks which Antæus and Cercyon devised in their systems out of a vain spirit of competition, or the tricks of boxing which Epeius or Amycus invented, are useless for war, and do not deserve to have much said about them; but the art of wrestling erect and keeping free the neck and hands and sides, working with energy and constancy, with a composed strength, and for the sake of health — these are always useful, and are not to be neglected, but to be enjoined alike on masters and scholars, when we reach that part of legislation; and we will desire the one to give their instructions freely, and the others to receive them thankfully. Nor, again, must we omit suitable imitations of war in our dances; in Crete there are the armed sports of the Curetes, and in Lacedæmon of the Dioscori. And our virgin lady, delighting in the sports of the dance, thought it not fit to dance with empty hands; she must be clothed in a complete suit of armor, and in this attire go through the dance; and youths and maidens should in every respect imitate her example, honoring the Goddess both with a view to the actual necessities of war, and to festive amusements; it will be right also for the boys until such time as they go out to war to make processions and supplications to the Gods in goodly array, armed and on horseback, in dances and marches, fast or slow, offering up prayers to the Gods and to the sons of Gods; and also engaging in contests and preludes of contests, if at all, with these objects. For this sort of exercises, and no others, are useful both in peace and war, and are beneficial both to states and to private houses. But other labors and sports and excessive training of the body are unworthy of freemen, O Megillus and Cleinias.

I have now completely described the kind of gymnastic which I said at first ought to be described; if you know of any better, will you communicate your thoughts?

CLE. It is not easy, Stranger, to put these principles of gymnastic aside and to enunciate better ones.

ATH. Next in order follow the gifts of the Muses and of Apollo: before, we fancied that we had said all, and that gymnastics alone remained to be discussed; but now we see clearly what points have been omitted, and should be first proclaimed; of these, then, let us proceed to speak.

CLE. By all means.

ATH. Hear me once more, although you have heard me say the same before — that caution must be always exercised, both by the speaker and by the hearer, about anything that is singular and unusual. For my tale is one which many a man would be afraid to tell, and yet I have a confidence which makes me go on.

CLE. What have you to say, Stranger?

ATH. I say that in states generally no one has observed that the plays of childhood have a great deal to do with the permanence or want of permanence in legislation. For when plays are ordered with a view to children having the same plays and amusing themselves after the same manner, and finding delight in the same playthings, the more solemn institutions of the state are allowed to remain undisturbed. Whereas if sports are disturbed and innovations are made in them, and they constantly change, and the young never speak of their having the same likings, or the same established notions of good and bad taste, either in the bearing of their bodies or in their dress, but he who devises something new and out of the way in figures and colors and the like is held in special honor, we may truly say that no greater evil can happen in a state; for he who changes the sports is secretly changing the manners of the young, and making the old to be dishonored among them and the new to be honored. And I affirm that there is nothing which is a greater injury to all states than saying or thinking thus. Will you hear me tell how great I deem it to be?

CLE. You mean the evil of blaming antiquity in states?

ATH. Exactly.

CLE. If you are speaking of that, you will find in us hearers who are disposed to receive what you say not unfavorably but most favorably.

ATH. I should expect so.

CLE. Proceed.

ATH. Well, then, let us give all the greater heed to one another's words. The argument says that to change from anything except the bad is the most dangerous of all things; this is true in the case of the seasons and of the winds, in the management of our bodies and the habits of our minds — true of all things except, as I said before, of the bad. He who looks at the constitution of individuals accustomed to eat any sort of meat or drink any drink or do any work which they could get, may see that they are at first disordered but afterwards, as time goes on, their bodies grow adapted to them, and they learn to know and like variety, and have good health and enjoyment of life; and if ever afterwards they are confined again to a superior diet, at first they are troubled with disorders, and with difficulty become habituated to their new food. A similar principle we may imagine to hold good about the minds of men and the nature of their souls. For when they have been brought up in certain laws, which by some Divine Providence have remained unchanged during long ages, so that no one has any memory or tradition of their ever having been otherwise than they are, then every one is afraid and ashamed to change that which is established. The legislator must somehow find a way of implanting this reverence for antiquity, and I would propose the following way: — People are apt to fancy, as I was saying before, that when the plays of children are altered they are merely plays, not seeing that the most serious and detrimental consequences arise out of the change; and they readily comply with the child's wishes instead of deterring him, not considering that these children who make innovations in their games, when they grow up to be men will be different from the last generation of children, and, being different, will desire a different sort of life, and under the influence of this desire will want other institutions and laws; and no one ever apprehends that there will follow what I just now called the greatest of evils to states. Changes in bodily fashions are no such serious evils, but frequent changes in the praise and censure of manners are the greatest of evils, and require the utmost prevision.

CLE. To be sure.

ATH. And now do we still hold to our former assertion, that rhythms and music in general are imitations of good and evil characters in men? What say you?

CLE. That is the only doctrine which I can admit.

ATH. Must we not, then, try in every possible way to prevent our youth desiring imitations and novelties either in dance or song? Nor must any one be allowed to offer them varieties of pleasures.

CLE. Most true.

ATH. Can any better mode of effecting this object be imagined by any of us than that of the Egyptians?

CLE. What is their method?

ATH. They consecrate every sort of dance or melody, first ordaining festivals,— calculating for the year what they ought to be, and at what time, and in honor of what Gods, sons of Gods, and heroes they ought to be celebrated; and, in the next place, what hymns ought to be sung at the several sacrifices, and with what dances the particular festival is to be honored. This is to be arranged at first by certain persons, and, when arranged, the whole assembly of the citizens are to offer sacrifices and libations to the Fates and all the other Gods, and to consecrate the several odes to Gods and heroes; and if any one offers any other hymns or dances to any one of the Gods, the priests and priestesses, with the consent of the guardians of the law, shall religiously and lawfully exclude him, and he who is excluded, if he do not submit, shall be liable all his life long to have a suit of impiety brought against him by any one who likes.

CLE. Very good.

ATH. In the consideration of this subject, let us remember what is due to ourselves.

CLE. To what are you referring?

ATH. I mean that any young man, and much more any old one, when he sees or hears anything strange or unaccustomed, does not at once run to embrace the paradox, but he stands considering, like a person who is at a place where three ways meet, and does not very well know his way — he may be alone or he may be walking with others, and he will say to himself and them, "Which is the way?" and will not move forward until he is satisfied that he is going right. And this is our case, for a strange discussion on the subject of law has arisen, which requires the utmost consideration, and we should not at our age be too ready to speak about such great matters, or be confident that we can say anything certain all in a moment.

CLE. Most true.

ATH. Then we will allow time for reflection, and decide when we have given the subject sufficient consideration. But that we may not be hindered from completing the natural arrangement of our laws, let us proceed to the conclusion of them in due order; for very possibly, if God will, the exposition of them, when completed, may throw light on our present perplexity.

CLE. Excellent, Stranger; let us do as you propose.

ATH. Let us then affirm the paradox that strains of music are our laws, and this latter being the name which the ancients gave to lyric songs, they probably would not have very much objected to our proposed application of the word. Some one, either asleep or awake, must have had a dreamy suspicion of their nature. And let our decree be as follows:— No one in singing or dancing shall offend against public and consecrated models, and the general fashion among the youth, any more than he would offend against any other law. And he who observes this law shall be blameless; but he who is disobedient, as I was saying, shall be punished by the guardians of the laws, and by priests and priestesses: suppose that we imagine this to be our law.

CLE. Very good.

ATH. Can any one who makes such laws escape ridicule? Let us see. I think that our only safety will be in first framing certain models for them. One of these models shall be as follows:— If when a sacrifice is going on, and the victims are being burnt according to law,— if, I say, any one who may be a son or brother, standing by another at the altar and over the victims, horribly blasphemes, will he not inspire despondency and evil omens and forebodings in the mind of his father and of his other kinsmen?

CLE. Of course.

ATH. And this is just what takes place in almost all our cities. A magistrate offers a public sacrifice, and there come in not one but many choruses, who stand by themselves a little way from the altar, and from time to time pour forth all sorts of horrible blasphemies on the sacred rites, exciting the souls of the audience with words and rhythms, and melodies most sorrowful to hear; and he who can at the instant the city is sacrificing make the citizens weep most, carries away the palm of victory. Now, ought we not to forbid such strains as these? And if ever our citizens must hear such lamentations, then on some unblest and inauspicious day let there be choruses of foreign and hired minstrels, like those who accompany the departed at funerals with barbarious Carian chants. That is the sort of thing which will be appropriate if we have such strains at all; and let the apparel of the singers be not circlets and ornaments of gold, but the reverse. Enough of the description. And now I will ask once more whether we shall lay down as one of our principles of song —

CLE. What?

ATH. That we should avoid every evil word. I need hardly ask again, but shall assume that you agree with me.

CLE. By all means; that law is approved by the suffrage of all of us.

ATH. But what shall be our next musical law or type? Ought not prayers to be offered up to the Gods when we sacrifice?

CLE. Certainly.

ATH. And our third law, if I am not mistaken, will be to the effect, that our poets understanding prayers to be requests which we make to the Gods, will take especial heed that they do not by mistake ask for evil instead of good. To make such a prayer would surely be too ridiculous.

CLE. Very true.

ATH. Were we not a little while ago quite determined that no silver or golden Plutus should dwell in our state?

CLE. To be sure.

ATH. And what did this illustration mean? Did we not imply that the poets are not always quite capable of knowing what is good or evil? And if one of them utters a mistaken prayer in song or words, he will make our citizens pray for the opposite of what is good in matters of the highest import; than which, as I was saying, there can be few greater mistakes. Shall we then propose as one of our laws and models relating to the Muses —

CLE. What? — will you explain the law more precisely?

ATH. Shall we make a law that the poet shall compose nothing contrary to the ideas of the lawful, or just, or beautiful, or good, which are allowed in the state? Nor shall he be permitted to communicate his compositions to any private individuals, until he shall have shown them to the appointed judges, and the guardians of the law, and they are satisfied with them. As to the persons whom we appoint to be our legislators about music and directors of education, they have been already indicated. Once more then, as I have asked more than once, shall this be our third law, and type, and model — What do you say?

CLE. Yes, by all means.

ATH. Next it will be proper to have hymns and praises of the Gods, intermingled with prayers; and after the Gods prayers and praises should be offered in like manner to demigods and heroes, suitable to their several characters.

CLE. Certainly.

ATH. In the third place there will be no objection to a law, that citizens who are departed and have done good and energetic deeds, either with their souls or with their bodies, and have been obedient to the laws, should receive eulogies; this will be very fitting.

CLE. Quite true.

ATH. But to honor with hymns and panegyrics those who are still alive is not safe; a man should run his course, and make a fair ending, and then we will praise him; and let praise be given equally to women as well as men who have been distinguished in virtue. The order of songs and dances shall be as follows: — There are many ancient musical compositions and dances which are excellent, and from these the government may freely select what is proper and suitable; and they shall choose judges of not less than fifty years of age, who shall make the selection, and any of the old poems which they deem sufficient they shall include; any that is deficient or altogether unsuitable, they shall either utterly throw aside, or examine and amend, taking into their counsel poets and musicians, and making use of their poetical genius; but explaining to them the wishes of the legislator in order that they may regulate dancing, music, and all choral strains, according to his mind; and not allowing them to indulge, except in some minor matters, their individual pleasures and fancies. Now, the irregular strain of music is always made ten thousand times better by attaining to law and order, and rejecting the honied Muse — not however that we mean wholly to exclude pleasure, which is the characteristic of all music. And if a man be brought up from childhood to the age of discretion and maturity in the use of the orderly and severe music, when he hears the opposite he detests it, and calls it illiberal; but if trained in the sweet and vulgar music, he deems the opposite cold and displeasing. So that, as I was saying before, while he who hears them gains no more pleasure from the one than from the other, the one has the advantage of making those who are trained in it better men, whereas the other makes them worse.

CLE. Very true.

ATH. Again, we must distinguish and determine on some general principle what songs are suitable to women, and what to men, and must assign to them their proper melodies and rhythms. It is shocking for a whole harmony to be inharmonical, or for a rhythm to be unrhythmical, and this will happen when the melody is inappropriate to them. And, therefore, the legislator must assign to them also their forms. Now, both sexes have melodies and rhythms which of necessity belong to them; and those of women are clearly enough indicated by their natural difference. The grand, and that which tends to courage, may be fairly called manly; but that which inclines to moderation and temperance, may be declared both in law and in ordinary speech to be the more womanly quality: this, then, will be the general order of them.

Let us now speak of the manner of teaching and imparting them, and the persons to whom, and the time when, they are severally to be imparted. As the shipwright first lays down the lines of the keel, and draws the design in outline, so do I seek to distinguish the patterns of life, and lay down their keels according to the nature of different men's souls; seeking truly to consider by what means, and in what ways, we may go through the voyage of life best. Now, human affairs are hardly worth considering in earnest, and yet we must be in earnest about them,— a sad necessity constrains us. And having got thus far, there will be a fitness in our completing the matter, if we can only find some suitable means of doing so. But what am I saying? And yet very probably there may be a meaning latent in these very words.

CLE. To be sure.

ATH. I say, that about serious matters a man should be serious, and about a matter which is not serious he should not be serious; and that God is the natural and worthy object of a man's most serious and blessed endeavors; who, as I said before, is made to be the plaything of God, and that this, truly considered, is the best of him; wherefore every man and woman should walk seriously, and pass life in the noblest of pastimes, and be of another mind from what they now are.

CLE. In what respect?

ATH. Now they think that their serious pursuits should

be for the sake of their sports, for they deem war a serious pursuit, which must be managed well for the sake of peace; but the truth is, that there neither is, nor has been, nor ever will be, either amusement or instruction in any degree worth speaking of in war, which is nevertheless deemed by us to be the most serious of our pursuits. And therefore, as we say, every one of us should live the life of peace as long and as well as he can. And what is the right way of living? Are we to live in sports always? If so, in what kind of sports? We ought to live sacrificing, and singing, and dancing, and then a man will be able to propitiate the Gods, and to defend himself against his enemies and conquer them in battle. The type of song or dance by which he will propitiate them has been described, and the paths along which he is to proceed have been cut for him. He will go forward in the spirit of the poet:—

"Telemachus, some things thou wilt thyself find in thy heart, but other things God will suggest; for I deem that thou wast not born or brought up without the will of the Gods."

And this ought to be the view of our alumni; they ought to think that what has been said is enough for them, and that any other things some God or a demigod will suggest to them — he will tell them to whom, and when, and to what Gods severally they are to sacrifice and perform dances, and how they may propitiate the deities, and live according to the appointment of nature; being for the most part puppets, but having some little share of reality.

MEG. You have a low opinion of mankind, Stranger.

ATH. Nay, Megillus, I was only comparing them with the Gods; and under that feeling I spoke. Let us grant, if you wish, that the human race is not to be despised, but is worthy of some consideration.

Next follow the buildings for gymnasia and schools open to all; these are to be in three places in the midst of the city; and outside the city and in the surrounding country there shall be schools for horse exercise, and open spaces also in three places, arranged with a view to archery and the throwing of missiles, at which young men may learn and practice. Of these mention has already been made; and if the mention be not sufficiently explicit, let us speak further of them and embody them in laws. In these several schools let there be dwellings for teachers, who shall be brought from foreign parts by pay, and let them teach the frequenters of the school the art of war and the art of music, and the children shall come, not only if their parents please, but if they do not please; and if their education is neglected, there shall be compulsory education, as the saying is, of all and sundry, as far as this is possible; and the pupils shall be regarded as belonging to the state rather than to their parents. My law would apply to females as well as males; they shall both go through the same exercises. I assert without fear of contradiction that gymnastic and horsemanship are as suitable to women as to men. Of the truth of this I am persuaded from ancient tradition, and at the present day there are said to be myriads of women in the neighborhood of the Black Sea, called Sauromatides, who not only ride on horseback like men, but have enjoined upon them the use of bows and other weapons equally with the men. And I further affirm, that if these things are possible, nothing can be more absurd than the practice which prevails in our own country of men and women not following the same pursuits with all their strength and with one mind, for thus the state, instead of being a whole, is reduced to a half, and yet has the same imposts to pay and the same toils to undergo; and what can be a greater mistake for any legislator to make?

CLE. Very true; and much of what has been asserted by us, Stranger, is contrary to the custom of states; still, in saying that the discourse should be allowed to proceed, and that when the discussion is completed, we should choose what seems best, you have spoken very properly, and have made me feel compunction for what I said. Tell me, then, what you would next wish to say.

ATH. I should wish to say, Cleinias, as I said before, that if the possibility of these things were not sufficiently proven in fact, then there might be an objection to the argument, but the fact being as I have said, he who rejects the law must find some other ground of objection; and, failing this, our exhortation will still hold good, nor will any one deny that women ought to share as far as possible in education and in other ways with men, for consider;— if women do not share in their whole life with men, then they must have some other order of life.

CLE. Certainly.

ATH. And what arrangement of life to be found anywhere is preferable to this community which we are now assigning to them? Shall we prefer that which is adopted by the Thracians and many other races who use their women to till the ground and to be shepherds of their herds and flocks, and to minister to them like slaves? Or shall we do as we and people in our part of the world do? getting together, as the phrase is, all our goods and chattels into one dwelling — these we entrust to our women, who are the stewards of them; and who also preside over the shuttles and the whole art of spinning. Or shall we take a middle course, as in Lacedæmon, Megillus, letting the girls share in gymnastic and music, while the grown-up women, no longer employed in spinning wool, are actively engaged in weaving the web of life, which will be no cheap or mean employment, and in the duty of serving and taking care of the household and bringing up children in which they will observe a sort of mean, not participating in the toils of war; and if there were any necessity that they should fight for their city and families, unlike the Amazons, they would be unable to take part in archery or any other skilled use of missiles, nor could they, after the example of the Goddess, carry shield or spear, or stand up nobly for their country when it was being destroyed, and strike terror into their enemies, if only because they were seen in regular order? Living as they do, they would never dare at all to imitate the Sauromatides, whose women, when compared with ordinary women, would appear to be like men. Let him who will, praise your legislators, but I must say what I think. The legislator ought to be whole and perfect, and not half a man only; he ought not to let the female sex live softly and waste money and have no order of life, while he takes the utmost care of the male sex, and leaves half of life only blest with happiness, when he might have made the whole state happy.

MEG. What shall we do, Cleinias? Shall we allow a stranger to run down Sparta in this fashion?

CLE. Yes; for as we have given him liberty of speech we must let him go on until we have perfected the work of legislation.

MEG. Very true.

ATH. Then now I may proceed?

CLE. By all means.

ATH. What will be the manner of life among men who may be supposed to have their food and clothing provided for them in moderation, and who have entrusted the practice of the arts to others, and whose husbandry, committed to slaves paying a part of the produce, brings them a return sufficient for men living temperately; who, moreover, have common tables in which the men are placed apart, and near them are the common tables of their families, of their daughters and mothers, which day by day, the rulers, male and female, are to inspect and look to their mode of life and so dismiss them; after which the magistrate and his attendants shall honor with libations those Gods to whom that day and night are dedicated, and then go home? To men whose lives are thus ordered, is there no work to be done which is necessary and fitting, but shall each one of them live fattening like a beast? Such a life is neither just nor honorable, nor can he who lives it fail of meeting his due; and the due reward of the idle fatted beast is that he should be torn in pieces by some other valiant beast whose fatness is worn down by labors and toils. These regulations, if we duly consider them, will never perfectly take effect under present circumstances, nor as long as women and children and houses and all other things are the private property of individuals; but if we can attain the second-best form of polity, with that we may be satisfied. And to men living under this second polity there remains a work to be accomplished which is far from being small or insignificant, but is the greatest of all works, and ordained by the appointment of righteous law. For a life which is wholly concerned with the virtue of body and soul may truly be said to be twice, or more than twice, as full of toil and trouble as the pursuit after Pythian and Olympic victories, which debars a man from every employment of life. For there ought to be no bye-work interfering with the greater work of providing the necessary exercise and nourishment for the body, and instruction and education for the soul. Night and day are not long enough for the accomplishment of their perfection and consummation; and therefore to this end all freemen ought to arrange the time of their employments during the whole course of the twenty-four hours, from morning to evening and from evening to the morning of the next sunrise. There may seem to be some impropriety in the legislator determining minutely the little details of the management of the house, including such particulars as the duty of wakefulness in those who are to be perpetual watchmen of the whole city; for that any citizen should continue during the whole night in sleep, instead of being seen by all his servants, always the first to awake and the first to rise — this, whether the regulation is to be called a law or only a practice, should be deemed base and unworthy of a freeman; also that the mistress of the house should be awakened by her hand-maidens instead of herself first awakening them, is what her slaves, male and female, and her children, and, if that were possible, everything in the house should regard as base. If they rise early, they may all of them do much of their public and of their household business, as magistrates in the city, and masters and mistresses in their private houses, before the sun is up. Much sleep is not required by nature, either for our souls or bodies, or for the actions in which they are concerned. For no one who is asleep is good for anything, any more than if he were dead; but he of us who has the most regard for life and reason keeps awake as long as he can, reserving only so much time for sleep as is expedient for health; and much sleep is not required, if the habit of not sleeping be once formed. Magistrates in states who keep awake at night are terrible to the bad, whether enemies or citizens, and are honored and reverenced by the just and temperate, and are useful to themselves and to the whole state.

A night which is short and devoted to work, in addition to all the above-mentioned advantages, infuses a sort of courage into the minds of the citizens. When the day breaks, the time has arrived for youth to go to their schoolmasters. Now, neither sheep nor any other animals can live without a shepherd, nor can children be left without tutors, or slaves without masters. And of all animals the boy is the most unmanageable, inasmuch as he has the fountain of reason in him not yet regulated; he is the most insidious, sharp-witted, and insubordinate of animals. Wherefore he must be bound with many bridles; in the first place, when he gets away from mothers and nurses, he must be under the control of tutors on account of his childishness and foolishness; then, again, being a freeman, he must have teachers and be educated by them in anything which they teach, and must learn what he has to learn; but he is also a slave, and in that regard any freeman who comes in his way may punish him and his tutor and his instructor, if any of them does anything wrong; and he who comes across him and does not inflict upon him the punishment which he deserves, shall incur the greatest disgrace; and let the guardian of the law, who is the director of education, see to him who coming in the way of the offenses which we have mentioned, does not chastise them when he ought, or chastises them in a way which he ought not; let him keep a sharp look-out, and take especial care of the training of our children, directing their natures, and always turning them to good according to the law.

And how can our law sufficiently train the director of education himself; for as yet all has been imperfect, and nothing has been said either clear or satisfactory? Now, as far as possible, the law ought to leave nothing to him, but to explain everything, that he may be the interpreter and tutor of others. About dances and music and choral strains, I have already spoken both as to the character of the selection of them, and the manner in which they are to be improved and consecrated. But we have not yet spoken, O illustrious guardian of education, of the manner in which your pupils are to use those strains which are written in prose, although you have been informed what martial strains they are to learn and practice; what relates in the first place to the learning of letters, and secondly, to the lyre, and also to calculation, which, as we were saying, is needful for them all to learn, and any other things which are required with a view to war and the management of house and city, and, looking to the same object, what is useful in the revolutions of the heavenly bodies — the stars and sun and moon, and the various regulations about these matters which are necessary for the whole state — I am speaking of the arrangements of days in periods of months, and of months in years, which are to be observed, in order that times and sacrifices and festivals may proceed in regular and natural order, and keep the city alive and awake, the Gods receiving the honors due to them, and men having a better understanding about them; all these things, O my friend, have not yet been sufficiently declared by the legislator. Attend, then, to what I am now going to say: We were telling you, in the first place, that you were not sufficiently informed about letters, and the objection made was to this effect,— " That you were never told whether he who was meant to be a respectable citizen should apply himself in detail to that sort of learning, or not apply himself at all;" and the same remark was made about the lyre. But now we say that he ought to attend to them. A fair time for a boy of ten years old to spend in letters is three years; at thirteen years he should begin to handle the lyre, and he may continue at this for another three years, neither more nor less, and whether his father or himself like or dislike the study, he is not to be allowed to spend more or less time in learning music than the law allows. And let him who disobeys the law be deprived of those youthful honors of which we shall hereafter speak. Hear, however, first of all, what the young ought to learn in the early years of life, and what their instructors ought to teach them. They ought to be occupied with their letters until they are able to read and write; but the acquisition of perfect beauty or quickness in writing, if nature has not stimulated them to acquire these accomplishments in the given number of years, they should let alone. And as to the learning of compositions committed to writing which are unaccompanied by song, whether metrical or without rhythmical divisions, compositions in prose, as they are termed, having no rhythm or harmony — seeing how dangerous are the writings handed down to us by many writers of this class — what will you do with them, O most excellent guardians of the law? or how can the lawgiver rightly direct you about them? I believe that he will be in great difficulty.

CLE. What troubles you, Stranger? and why are you so perplexed in your mind?

ATH. You naturally ask, Cleinias, and to you, who are my partners in the work of education, I must state the difficulties of the case.

CLE. To what do you refer in this instance?

ATH. I will tell you. There is a difficulty in opposing many myriads of mouths.

CLE. Well, and have we not already opposed the popular voice in many important enactments?

ATH. That is quite true; and you mean to imply that the road which we are taking may be disagreeable to some but is agreeable to as many others, or if not to as many, at any rate to persons not inferior to the others, and in company with them you bid me, at whatever risk, proceed along the path of legislation which has opened out of our present discourse, and to be of good cheer, and not to faint.

CLE. Certainly.

ATH. And I do not faint; I say, indeed, that we have a great many poets writing in hexameter, trimeter, and all sorts of measures — some who are serious, others who aim only at raising a laugh — and all mankind declare that the youth who are rightly educated should be brought up and saturated with them; they should be constantly hearing them read at recitations, and some would have them learn by heart entire poets; while others select choice passages and long speeches, and make compendiums of them, saying that these shall be committed to memory, and that in this way only can a man be made good and wise by experience and learning. And you want me to say plainly in what they are right and in what they are wrong.

CLE. Yes, I do.

ATH. But how can I in one word rightly comprehend all of them? I am of opinion, and, if I am not mistaken, there is a general agreement, that every one of these poets has said many things well and many things the reverse of well; and if this be true, then I do affirm that much learning brings danger to youth.

CLE. Then how would you advise the guardian of the law to act?

ATH. In what respect?

CLE. I mean to what pattern should he look as his guide in permitting the young to learn some things and forbidding them to learn others? Do not shrink from answering.

ATH. My good Cleinias, I rather think that I am fortunate.

CLE. In what?

ATH. I think that I am not wholly in want of a pattern, for when I consider the words which we have spoken from early dawn until now, and which, as I believe, have been inspired by Heaven, they appear to me to be quite like a poem. When I reflected upon all these words of ours, I naturally felt pleasure, for of all the discourses which I have ever learnt or heard, either in poetry or prose, this seemed to me to be the justest, and most suitable for young men to hear; I cannot imagine any better pattern than this which the guardian of the law and the educator can have. They cannot do better than advise the teachers to teach the young these and the like words, and if they should happen to find writings, either in poetry or prose, or even unwritten discourses like these of ours, and of the same family, they should certainly preserve them, and commit them to writing. And, first of all, they shall constrain the teachers themselves to learn and approve them, and any of them who will not, shall not be employed by them, but those whom they find agreeing in their judgment, they shall make use of and shall commit to them the instruction and education of youth. And here and on this wise let my fanciful tale about letters and teachers of letters come to an end.

II. ARISTOTLE.

BIOGRAPHICAL SKETCH.

By common consent Aristotle ranks as one of the greatest thinkers of classical antiquity. His influence in the philosophic world, though far less at the present time than it was formerly, has been almost unbroken for more than two thousand years. He was born at Stagira, in Macedonia, 384 B. C., springing from a family in which the practice of medicine, such as it was in that day, was hereditary. His father was physician to Amyntas, King of Macedonia, and grandfather of Alexander the Great. Aristotle himself was probably intended for the medical profession, and to this fact was due no doubt his interest in anatomy. But in early manhood he gave up medicine for philosophy. He became a disciple of Plato, and by his penetration of mind gained the distinction of being called "the intellect of the school."

In 342 B. C., when his fame as a philosopher had become established, he was appointed teacher of Alexander the Great, then a lad of fourteen. The course of instruction he followed with his illustrious pupil is not known in its details, but was presumably that which prevailed at Athens. He enjoyed the highest confidence of both Philip and Alexander, and during his three or four years of service as tutor, he received many marks of favor at their hands. Among these may be mentioned the restoration of his native town Stagira, which had been destroyed by war, and the erection there of a gymnasium for his philosophical lectures.

When Alexander entered upon his great expedition of conquest into Asia, Aristotle returned to Athens and established a school in the Lyceum. He lectured to a circle of disciples as he walked about the shady avenues; and this fact has given to his school of philosophy the name Peripatetic. His scholarship embraced the whole range of knowledge. Unlike his great theorizing teacher, Aristotle was a careful and practical investigator; he invented the science of logic, and made valuable contributions to many other departments of learning.

Aristotle has treated of education more or less fully in several works. His "Rhetoric" and "Poetics" are profound treatises that may still be studied with great profit. His "Nichomachean Ethics" touches repeatedly but briefly on education. It is in his "Politics" that he has treated the subject most fully; but his discussion is unfortunately incomplete, and it is greatly to be regretted that he never fulfilled his promise to return to it. The following extract is taken from the translation in Bohn's Classical Library. It includes part of Book VII. and the whole of Book VIII. of the "Politics."

SELECTION FROM THE "POLITICS" OF ARISTOTLE.

BOOK VII.

13. It follows then from what has been said that some things the legislator must find ready to his hand in a state, others he must provide. And therefore we can only say: May our state be constituted in such a manner as to be blessed with the goods of which fortune disposes (for we acknowledge her power): whereas virtue and goodness in the state are not a matter of chance but the result of knowledge and purpose. A city can be virtuous only when the

citizens who have a share in the government are virtuous, and in our state all the citizens share in the government; let us then inquire how a man becomes virtuous. For even if we could suppose all the citizens to be virtuous, and not each of them, yet the latter would be better, for in the virtue of each the virtue of all is involved.

There are three things which make men good and virtuous: these are nature, habit, reason. In the first place, every one must be born a man and not some other animal; in the second place, he must have certain character, both of body and soul. But some qualities there is no use in having at birth, for they are altered by habit, and there are some gifts of nature which may be turned by habit to good or bad. Most animals lead a life of nature, although in lesser particulars some are influenced by habit as well. Man has reason, in addition, and man only. Wherefore nature, habit, reason must be in harmony with one another (for they do not always agree); men do many things against habit and nature, if reason persuades them that they ought. We have already determined what natures are likely to be most easily molded by the hands of the legislator. All else is the work of education; we learn some things by habit and some by instruction.

14. Since every political society is composed of rulers and subjects, let us consider whether the relations of one to the other should interchange or be permanent. For the education of the citizens will necessarily vary with the answer given to this question. Now, if some men excelled others in the same degree in which gods and heroes are supposed to excel mankind in general, having in the first place a great advantage even in their bodies, and secondly in their minds, so that the superiority of the governors over their subjects was patent and undisputed, it would clearly be better that once for all the one class should rule

and the others serve. But since this is unattainable, and kings have no marked superiority over their subjects, such as Scylax affirms to be found among the Indians, it is obviously necessary on many grounds that all the citizens alike should take their turn in governing and being governed. Equality consists in the same treatment of similar persons, and no government can stand which is not founded upon justice. For (if the government be unjust) every one in the country unites with the governed in the desire to have a revolution, and it is an impossibility that the members of the government can be so numerous as to be stronger than all their enemies put together. Yet that governors should excel their subjects is undeniable. How all this is to be effected, and in what way they will respectively share in the government, the legislator has to consider. The subject has been already mentioned. Nature herself has given the principle of choice when she made a difference between old and young (though they are really the same in kind), of whom she fitted the one to govern and the others to be governed. No one takes offense at being governed when he is young, nor does he think himself better than his governors, especially if he will enjoy the same privilege when he reaches the required age.

We conclude that from one point of view governors and governed are identical, and from another different. And therefore their education must be the same and also different. For he who would learn to command well must, as men say, first of all learn to obey. As I observed in the first part of this treatise, there is one rule which is for the sake of the rulers and another rule which is for the sake of the ruled; the former is a despotic, the latter a free government. Some commands differ not in the thing commanded, but in the intention with which they are imposed. Wherefore, many apparently menial offices are an honor to the free youth by whom they are performed; for actions do not differ as honorable or dishonorable in themselves so much as in the end and intention of them. But since we say that the virtue of the citizen and ruler is the same as that of the good man, and that the same person must first be a subject and then a ruler, the legislator has to see that they become good men, and by what means this may be accomplished, and what is the end of the perfect life.

Now the soul of man is divided into two parts, one of which has reason in itself, and the other, not having reason in itself, is able to obey reason. And we call a man good because he has the virtues of these two parts. In which of them the end is more likely to be found is no matter of doubt to those who adopt our division; for in the world both of nature and of art the inferior always exists for the sake of the better or superior, and the better or superior is that which has reason. The reason too, in our ordinary way of speaking, is divided into two parts for there is a practical and a speculative reason, and there must be a corresponding division of actions; the actions of the naturally better principle are to be preferred by those who have it in their power to attain to both or to all, for that is always to every one the most eligible which is the highest attainable by him. The whole of life is further divided into two parts, business and leisure, war and peace, and all actions into those which are necessary and useful, and those which are honorable. And the preference given to one or the other class of actions must necessarily be like the preference given to one or other part of the soul and its actions over the other; there must be war for the sake of peace, business for the sake of leisure, things useful and necessary for the sake of things honorable. All these points the statesman should keep in view when he frames his laws; he should consider the parts of the soul and their functions, and above all the better and the end; he should also remember the diversities of human lives and actions. For men must engage in business and go to war, but leisure and peace are better; they must do what is necessary and useful, but what is honorable is better. In such principles children and persons of every age which requires education should be trained. Whereas even the Hellenes of the present day, who are reputed to be best governed, and the legislators who gave them their constitutions, do not appear to have framed their governments with a regard to the best end, or to have given them laws and education with a view to all the virtues, but in a vulgar spirit have fallen back on those which promised to be more useful and profitable. Many modern writers have taken a similar view: they commend the Lacedæmonian constitution, and praise the legislator for making conquest and war his sole aim, a doctrine which may be refuted by argument and has long ago been refuted by facts. For most men desire empire in the hope of accumulating the goods of fortune; and on this ground Thibron and all those who have written about the Lacedæmonian constitution have praised their legislator, because the Lacedæmonians, by a training in hardships, gained great power. But surely they are not a happy people now that their empire has passed away, nor was their legislator right. How ridiculous is the result, if, while they are continuing in the observance of his laws and no one interferes with them, they have lost the better part of life. These writers further err about the sort of government which the legislator should approve, for the government of freemen is noble, and implies more virtue than despotic government. Neither is a city to be deemed happy nor a legislator to be praised because he trains his citizens to conquer and obtain dominion over their neighbors, for there is great evil in this. On a similar principle any citizen who could, would obviously try to obtain the power in his own state, — the crime which the Lacedæmonians accuse king Pausanias of attempting, although he had so great honor already. No such principle and no law having this object is either statesmanlike or useful or right. For the same things are best both for individuals and for states, and these are the things which the legislator ought to implant in the minds of his citizens. Neither should men study war with a view to the enslavement of those who do not deserve to be enslaved; but first of all they should provide against their own enslavement, and in the second place obtain empire for the good of the governed, and not for the sake of exercising a general despotism, and in the third place they should seek to be masters only over those who deserve to be slaves. Facts, as well as arguments, prove that the legislator should direct all his military and other measures to the provision of leisure and the establishment of peace. For most of these military states are safe only while they are at war, but fall when they have acquired their empire; like unused iron they rust in time of peace. And for this the legislator is to blame, he never having taught them how to lead the life of peace.

15. Since the end of individuals and of states is the same, the end of the best man and of the best state must also be the same; it is therefore evident that there ought to exist in both of them the virtues of leisure; for peace, as has often been repeated, is the end of war, and leisure of toil. But leisure and cultivation may be promoted, not only by those virtues which are practiced in leisure, but also by some of those which are useful to business. For many necessaries of life have to be supplied before we can have leisure. Therefore a city must be temperate and brave, and able to endure; for truly, as the proverb says, "There

is no leisure for slaves," and those who cannot face danger like men are the slaves of any invader. Courage and endurance are required for business and philosophy for leisure, temperance and justice for both, more especially in times of peace and leisure, for war compels men to be just and temperate, whereas the enjoyment of good fortune and the leisure which comes with peace tends to make them insolent. Those then, who seem to be the best off and to be in the possession of every good, have special need of justice and temperance,— for example, those (if such there be, as the poets say) who dwell in the Islands of the Blest; they above all will need philosophy and temperance and justice, and all the more the more leisure they have, living in the midst of abundance. There is no difficulty in seeing why the state that would be happy and good ought to have these virtues. If it be disgraceful in men not to be able to use the goods of life, it is peculiarly disgraceful not to be able to use them in time of peace,— to show excellent qualities in action and war, and when they have peace and leisure to be no better than slaves. Wherefore we should not practice virtue after the manner of the Lacedæmonians. For they, while agreeing with other men in their conception of the highest goods, differ from the rest of mankind in thinking that they are to be obtained by the practice of a single virtue. And since these goods and the enjoyment of them are clearly greater than the enjoyment derived from the virtues of which they are the end, we must now consider how and by what means they are to be attained.

We have already determined that nature and habit and reason are required, and what should be the character of the citizens has also been defined by us. But we have still to consider whether the training of early life is to be that of reason or habit, for these two must accord, and when in accord they will then form the best of harmonies.

Reason may make mistakes and fail in attaining the highest ideal of life, and there may be a like evil influence of habit. Thus much is clear in the first place, that, as in all other things, birth implies some antecedent principle, and that the end of anything has a beginning in some former end. Now, in men reason and mind are the end towards which nature strives, so that the birth and moral discipline of the citizens ought to be ordered with a view to them. In the second place, as the soul and body are two, we see also that there are two parts of the soul, the rational and the irrational, and two corresponding states — reason and appetite. And as the body is prior in order of generation to the soul, so the irrational is prior to the rational. The proof is that anger and will and desire are implanted in children from their very birth, but reason and understanding are developed as they grow older. Wherefore, the care of the body ought to precede that of the soul, and the training of the appetitive part should follow: none the less our care of it must be for the sake of the reason, and our care of the body for the sake of the soul.

* * * * *

17. After the children have been born, the manner of rearing them may be supposed to have a great effect on their bodily strength. It would appear from the example of animals, and of those nations who desire to create the military habit, that the food which has most milk in it is best suited to human beings; but the less wine the better, if they would escape diseases. Also all the motions to which children can be subjected at their early age are very useful. But in order to preserve their tender limbs from distortion, some nations have had recourse to mechanical appliances which straighten their bodies. To accustom children to the cold from their earliest years is also an excellent practice, which greatly conduces to health, and

hardens them for military service. Hence many barbarians have a custom of plunging their children at birth into a cold stream; others, like the Celts, clothe them in a light wrapper only. For human nature should be early habituated to endure all which by habit it can be made to endure; but the process must be gradual. And children, from their natural warmth, may be easily trained to bear cold. Such care should attend them in the first stage of life.

The next period lasts to the age of five; during this no demand should be made upon the child for study or labor, lest its growth be impeded; and there should be sufficient motion to prevent the limbs from being inactive. This can be secured, among other ways, by amusement, but the amusement should not be vulgar or tiring or riotous. The Directors of Education, as they are termed, should be careful what tales or stories the children hear, for the sports of children are designed to prepare the way for the business of later life, and should be for the most part imitations of the occupations which they will hereafter pursue in earnest. Those are wrong who (like Plato) in the Laws attempt to check the loud crying and screaming of children, for these contribute towards their growth, and, in a manner, exercise their bodies. Straining the voice has an effect similar to that produced by the retention of the breath in violent exertions. Besides other duties, the Directors of Education should have an eye to their bringing up, and should take care that they are left as little as possible with slaves. For until they are seven years old they must live at home; and therefore, even at this early age, all that is mean and low should be banished from their sight and hearing. Indeed, there is nothing which the legislator should be more careful to drive away than indecency of speech; for the light utterance of shameful words is akin to shameful actions. The young especially should never be allowed to repeat or hear anything of the sort. A freeman who is fond of saying or doing what is forbidden, if he be too young as yet to have the privilege of a place at the public tables, should be disgraced and beaten, and an elder person degraded as his slavish conduct deserves. And since we do not allow improper language, clearly we should also banish pictures or tales which are indecent. Let the rulers take care that there be no image or picture representing unseemly actions, except in the temples of those Gods at whose festivals the law permits even ribaldry, and whom the law also permits to be worshiped by persons of mature age on behalf of themselves, their children, and their wives. But the legislator should not allow youth to be hearers of satirical iambic verses or spectators of comedy until they are of an age to sit at the public tables and to drink strong wine; by that time education will have armed them against the evil influences of such representations.

We have made these remarks in a cursory manner,—they are enough for the present occasion; but hereafter we will return to the subject and after a fuller discussion determine whether such liberty should or should not be granted, and in what way granted, if at all. Theodorus, the tragic actor, was quite right in saying that he would not allow any other actor, not even if he were quite second-rate, to enter before himself, because the spectators grew fond of the voices which they first heard. And the same principle of association applies universally to things as well as persons, for we always like best whatever comes first. And therefore youth should be kept strangers to all that is bad, and especially to things which suggest vice or hate. When the five years have passed away, during the two following years they must look on at the pursuits which they are hereafter to learn. There are two periods of life into which education has to be divided, from seven to the age of puberty, and onwards to the age of one and twenty. The poets, who divide ages by sevens are not always right; we should rather adhere to the divisions actually made by nature; for the deficiencies of nature are what art and education seek to fill up.

Let us then first inquire if any regulations are to be laid down about children, and secondly, whether the care of them should be the concern of the state or the private individuals, which latter is in our own day the common custom, and in the third place, what these regulations should be.

BOOK VIII.

1. No one will doubt that the legislator should direct his attention above all to the education of youth, or that the neglect of education does harm to states. The citizen should be molded to suit the form of government under which he lives. For each government has a peculiar character which originally formed and which continues to preserve it. The character of democracy creates democracy, and the character of oligarchy creates oligarchy; and always the better the character, the better the government.

Now for the exercise of any faculty or art a previous training and habituation are required; clearly therefore for the practice of virtue. And since the whole city has one end, it is manifest that education should be one and the same for all, and that it should be public, and not private,— not as at present, when every one looks after his own children separately, and gives them separate instruction of the sort which he thinks best; the training in things which are of common interest should be the same for all. Neither must we suppose that any one of the citizens belongs to himself, for they all belong to the state, and are each of them a part of the state, and the care of each part is inseparable from the care of the whole. In this particular the Lacedæmonians are to be praised, for they take the greatest pains about their children, and make education the business of the state.

2. That education should be regulated by law and should be an affair of state is not to be denied, but what should be the character of this public education, and how young persons should be educated, are questions which remain to be considered. For mankind are by no means agreed about the things to be taught, whether we look to virtue or the best life.

Neither is it clear whether education is more concerned with intellectual or with moral virtue. The existing practice is perplexing; no one knows on what principle we should proceed — should the useful in life, or should virtue, or should the higher knowledge, be the aim of our training; all three opinions have been entertained. Again, about the means there is no agreement; for different persons, starting with different ideas about the nature of virtue, naturally disagree about the practice of it.

There can be no doubt that children should be taught those useful things which are really necessary, but not all things; for occupations are divided into liberal and illiberal; and to young children should be imparted only such kinds of knowledge as will be useful to them without vulgarizing them. And any occupation, art, or science, which makes the body or soul or mind of the freeman less fit for the practice or exercise of virtue, is vulgar; wherefore we call those arts vulgar which tend to deform the body, and likewise all paid employments, for they absorb and degrade the mind.

There are also some liberal arts quite proper for a freeman to acquire, but only in a certain degee, and if he attend to them too closely, in order to attain perfection in them, the same evil effects will follow. The object also which a man sets before him makes a great difference; if he does or learns anything for his own sake or for the sake of his friends, or with a view to excellence, the action will not appear illiberal; but if done for the sake of others, the very same action will be thought menial and servile. The received subjects of instruction, as I have already remarked, are partly of a liberal and partly of an illiberal character.

3. The customary branches of education are in number four; they are — (1) reading and writing, (2) gymnastic exercises, (3) music, to which is sometimes added (4) drawing. Of these, reading and writing and drawing are regarded as useful for the purposes of life in a variety of ways, and gymnastic exercises are thought to infuse courage. Concerning music a doubt may be raised — in our own day most men cultivate it for the sake of pleasure, but originally it was included in education, because nature herself, as has often been said, requires that we should be able, not only to work well, but to use leisure well; for, as I must repeat once and again, the first principle of all action is leisure. Both are required, but leisure is better than occupation; and therefore the question must be asked in good earnest, what ought we to do when at leisure? Clearly we ought not to be amusing ourselves, for then amusement would be the end of life. But if this is inconceivable, and yet amid serious occupations amusement is needed more than at other times (for he who is hard at work has need of relaxation, and amusement gives relaxation, whereas occupation is always accompanied with exertion and effort), at suitable times we should introduce amusements, and they should be our medicines, for the emotion which they create in the soul is a relaxation, and from the pleasure we obtain rest. Leisure of itself gives pleasure and happiness and enjoyment of life, which are experienced, not by

the busy man, but by those who have leisure. For he who is occupied has in view some end which he has not attained; but happiness is an end which all men deem to be accompanied with pleasure and not with pain. This pleasure, however, is regarded differently by different persons, and varies according to the habit of individuals; the pleasure of the best man is the best, and springs from the noblest sources.

It is clear then that there are branches of learning and education which we must study with a view to the enjoyment of leisure, and these are to be valued for their own sake; whereas those kinds of knowledge which are useful in business are to be deemed necessary, and exist for the sake of other things. And therefore our fathers admitted music into education, not on the ground either of its necessity or utility, for it is not necessary, nor indeed useful in the same manner as reading and writing, which are useful in money-making, in the management of a household, in the acquisition of knowledge and in political life, nor like drawing, useful for a more correct judgment of the works of artists, nor again like gymnastic, which gives health and strength; for neither of these is to be gained from music. There remains, then, the use of music for intellectual enjoyment in leisure; which appears to have been the reason of its introduction, this being one of the ways in which it is thought that a freeman should pass his leisure; as Homer says —

"How good it is to invite men to the pleasant feast,"

and afterwards he speaks of others whom he describes as inviting

"The bard who would delight them all." [1]

[1] *Odyssey*, XVII. 385.

And in another place Odysseus says there is no better way of passing life than when

"Men's hearts are merry and the banqueters in the hall, sitting in order, hear the voice of the minstrel."[1]

It is evident, then, that there is a sort of education in which parents should train their sons, not as being useful or necessary, but because it is liberal or noble. Whether this is of one kind only, or of more than one, and if so, what they are, and how they are to be imparted, must hereafter be determined. Thus much we are now in a position to say that the ancients witness to us; for their opinion may be gathered from the fact that music is one of the received and traditional branches of education. Further, it is clear that children should be instructed in some useful things,— for example, in reading and writing,— not only for their usefulness, but also because many other sorts of knowledge are acquired through them. With a like view they may be taught drawing, not to prevent their making mistakes in their own purchases, or in order that they may not be imposed upon in the buying or selling of articles, but rather because it makes them judges of the beauty of the human form. To be seeking always after the useful does not become free and exalted souls. Now it is clear that in education habit must go before reason, and the body before the mind; and therefore boys should be handed over to the trainer, who creates in them the proper habit of body, and to the wrestling-master, who teaches them their exercises.

4. Of these states which in our own day seem to take the greatest care of children, some aim at producing in them an athletic habit, but they only injure their forms and

[1] *Odyssey*, IX. 7.

stunt their growth. Although the Lacedæmonians have not fallen into this mistake, yet they brutalize their children by laborious exercises which they think will make them courageous. But in truth, as we have often repeated, education should not be exclusively directed to this or to any other single end. And even if we suppose the Lacedæmonians to be right in their end, they do not attain it. For among barbarians and among animals courage is found associated, not with the greatest ferocity, but with a gentle and lionlike temper. There are many races who are ready enough to kill and eat men, such as the Achæans and Heniochi, who both live about the Black Sea; and there are other inland tribes, as bad or worse, who all live by plunder, but have no courage. It is notorious that the Lacedæmonians, while they were themselves assiduous in their laborious drill, were superior to others, but now they are beaten both in war and gymnastic exercises. For their ancient superiority did not depend on their mode of training their youth, but only on the circumstance that they trained them at a time when others did not. Hence we may infer that what is noble, not what is brutal, should have the first place; no wolf or other wild animal will face a really noble danger; such dangers are for the brave man. And parents who devote their children to gymnastics while they neglect their necessary education, in reality vulgarize them; for they make them useful to the state in one quality only, and even in this the argument proves them to be inferior to others. We should judge the Lacedæmonians not from what they have been but from what they are; for now they have rivals who compete with their education; formerly they had none.

It is an admitted principle, that gymnastic exercises should be employed in education, and that for children they should be of a lighter kind, avoiding severe regimen or painful toil, lest the growth of the body be impaired. The evil of excessive training in early years is strikingly proved by the example of the Olympic victors; for not more than two or three of them have gained a prize both as boys and as men; their early training and severe gymnastic exercises exhausted their constitutions. When boyhood is over, three years should be spent in other studies; the period of life which follows may then be devoted to hard exercise and strict regimen. Men ought not to labor at the same time with their minds and with their bodies; for the two kinds of labor are opposed to one another, the labor of the body impedes the mind, and the labor of the mind the body.

5. Concerning music there are some questions which we have already raised; these we may now resume and carry further; and our remarks will serve as a prelude to this or any other discussion of the subject. It is not easy to determine the nature of music, or why any one should have a knowledge of it. Shall we say, for the sake of amusement and relaxation, like sleep or drinking, which are not good in themselves, but are pleasant, and at the same time "make care to cease," as Euripides [1] says? And therefore men rank them with music, and make use of all three,— sleep, drinking, music,— to which some add dancing. Or shall we argue that music conduces to virtue, on the ground that it can form our minds and habituate us to true pleasures as our bodies are made by gymnastic to be of a certain character? Or shall we say that it contributes to the enjoyment of leisure and mental cultivation, which is a third alternative? Now obviously youth are not to be instructed with a view to their amusement, for learning is no pleasure, but is accompanied with pain. Neither is intel-

[1] Bacchæ, 380.

lectual enjoyment suitable to boys of that age, for it is the end, and that which is imperfect cannot attain the perfect or end. But perhaps it may be said that boys learn music for the sake of the amusement which they will have when they are grown up. If so, why should they learn themselves, and not, like the Persian and Median kings, enjoy the pleasure and instruction which is derived from hearing others? (for surely skilled persons who have made music the business and profession of their lives will be better performers than those who practice only to learn). If they must learn music, on the same principle they should learn cookery, which is absurd. And even granting that music may form the character, the objection still holds: why should we learn ourselves? Why cannot we attain true pleasure and form a correct judgment from hearing others, like the Lacedæmonians? For they, without learning music, nevertheless can correctly judge, as they say, of good and bad melodies. Or again, if music should be used to promote cheerfulness and refined intellectual enjoyment, the objection still remains — why should we learn ourselves instead of enjoying the performance of others? We may illustrate what we are saying by our conception of the Gods; for in the poets Zeus does not himself sing or play on the lyre. Nay, we call professional performers vulgar; no freeman would play or sing unless he were intoxicated or in jest. But these matters may be left for the present.

The first question is whether music is or is not to be a part of education. Of the three things mentioned in our discussion, which is it? — Education or amusement or intellectual enjoyment, for it may be reckoned under all three, and seems to share in the nature of all of them. Amusement is for the sake of relaxation, and relaxation is of necessity sweet, for it is the remedy of pain caused by toil, and intellectual enjoyment is universally acknowledged to contain an element not only of the noble but of the pleasant, for happiness is made up of both. All men agree that music is one of the pleasantest things, whether with or without song; as Musæus says,

> "Song is to mortals of all things the sweetest."

Hence and with good reason it is introduced into social gatherings and entertainments, because it makes the hearts of men glad: so that on this ground alone we may assume that the young ought to be trained in it. For innocent pleasures are not only in harmony with the perfect end of life, but they also provide relaxation. And whereas men rarely attain the end, but often rest by the way and amuse themselves, not only with a view to some good, but also for the pleasure's sake, it may be well for them at times to find a refreshment in music. It sometimes happens that men make amusement the end, for the end probably contains some element of pleasure, though not any ordinary or lower pleasure; but they mistake the lower for the higher, and in seeking for the one find the other, since every pleasure has a likeness to the end of action. For the end is not eligible, nor do the pleasures which we have described exist, for the sake of any future good but of the past, that is to say, they are the alleviation of past toils and pains. And we may infer this to be the reason why men seek happiness from common pleasures. But music is pursued, not only as an alleviation of past toil, but also as providing recreation. And who can say whether, having this use, it may not also have a nobler one? In addition to this common pleasure, felt and shared in by all (for the pleasure given by music is natural, and therefore adapted to all ages and characters), may it not have also some influence over the character and the soul? It must have such an influence if characters are affected by it. And that they are so affected is proved by the power which the songs of Olympus and of many others exercise; for beyond question they inspire enthusiasm, and enthusiasm is an emotion of the ethical part of the soul. Besides, when men hear imitations, even unaccompanied by melody or rhythm, their feelings move in sympathy. Since then music is a pleasure, and virtue consists in rejoicing and loving and hating aright, there is clearly nothing which we are so much concerned to acquire and to cultivate as the power of forming right judgments, and of taking delight in good dispositions and noble actions. Rhythm and melody supply imitations of anger and gentleness, and also of courage and temperance and of virtues and vices in general, which hardly fall short of the actual affections, as we know from our own experience, for in listening to such strains our souls undergo a change. The habit of feeling pleasure or pain at mere representations is not far removed from the same feeling about realities; for example, if any one delights in the sight of a statue for its beauty only, it necessarily follows that the sight of the original will be pleasant to him. No other sense, such as taste or touch, has any resemblance to moral qualities; in sight only there is a little, for figures are to some extent of a moral character, and (so far) all participate in the feeling about them. Again, figures and colors are not imitations, but signs of moral habits, indications which the body gives of states of feeling. The connection of them with morals is slight, but in so far as there is any, young men should be taught to look, not at the works of Pauson, but at those of Polygnotus, or any other painter or statuary who expresses moral ideas. On the other hand, even in mere melodies there is an imitation of character, for the musical modes differ essentially from one another, and those who hear them are differently affected by each.

Some of them make men sad and grave, like the so-called Mixolydian, others enfeeble the mind, like the relaxed harmonies, others, again, produce a moderate and settled temper, which appears to be the peculiar effect of the Dorian; the Phrygian inspires enthusiasm. The whole subject has been well treated by philosophical writers on this branch of education, and they confirm their arguments by facts. The same principles apply to rhythms: some have a character of rest, others of motion, and of these latter again, some have a more vulgar, others a nobler movement. Enough has been said to show that music has a power of forming the character, and should therefore be introduced into the education of the young. The study is suited to the stage of youth, for young persons will not, if they can help, endure anything which is not sweetened by pleasure, and music has a natural sweetness. There seems to be in us a sort of affinity to harmonies and rhythms, which makes some philosophers say that the soul is a harmony, others, that she possesses harmony.

6. And now we have to determine the question which has been already raised, whether children should be themselves taught to sing and play or not. Clearly there is a considerable difference made in the character by the actual practice of the art. It is difficult, if not impossible, for those who do not perform to be good judges of the performance of others. Besides, children should have something to do, and the rattle of Archytas, which people give to their children in order to amuse them and prevent them from breaking anything in the house, was a capital invention, for a young thing cannot be quiet. The rattle is a toy suited to the infant mind and (musical) education is a rattle or toy for children of a larger growth. We conclude then that they should be taught music in such a way as to become not only critics but performers.

The question what is or is not suitable for different ages may be easily answered; nor is there any difficulty in meeting the objection of those who say that the study of music is vulgar. We reply (1) in the first place, that they who are to be judges must also be performers, and that they should begin to practice early, although when they are older they may be spared the execution; they must have learned to appreciate what is good and to delight in it, thanks to the knowledge which they acquired in their youth. As to (2) the vulgarizing effect which music is supposed to exercise, this is a question (of degree), which we shall have no difficulty in determining, when we have considered to what extent freemen who are being trained to political virtue should pursue the art, what melodies and what rhythms they should be allowed to use, and what instruments should be employed in teaching them to play, for even the instrument makes a difference. The answer to the objection turns upon these distinctions; for it is quite possible that certain methods of teaching and learning music do really have a degrading effect. It is evident then that the learning of music ought not to impede the business of riper years, or to degrade the body or render it unfit for civil or military duties, whether for the early practice or for the later study of them.

The right measure will be attained if students of music stop short of the arts which are practiced in professional contests, and do not seek to acquire those fantastic marvels of execution which are now the fashion in such contests, and from these have passed into education. Let the young pursue their studies until they are able to feel delight in noble melodies and rhythms, and not merely in that common part of music in which every slave or child and even some animals find pleasure.

From these principles we may also infer what instruments should be used. The flute, or any other instrument which requires great skill, as for example the harp, ought not to be admitted into education, but only such as will make intelligent students of music or of the other parts of education. Besides, the flute is not an instrument which has a good moral effect; it is too exciting. The proper time for using it is when the performance aims not at instruction, but at the relief of the passions. And there is a further objection; the impediment which the flute presents to the use of the voice detracts from its educational value. The ancients therefore were right in forbidding the flute to youths and freemen, although they had once allowed it. For when their wealth gave them greater leisure, and they had loftier notions of excellence, being also elated with their success, both before and after the Persian War, with more zeal than discernment they pursued every kind of knowledge, and so they introduced the flute into education. At Lacedæmon there was a Choragus who led the chorus with a flute, and at Athens the instrument became so popular that most freemen could play upon it. The popularity is shown by the tablet which Thrasippus dedicated when he furnished the chorus to Ecphantides. Later experience enabled men to judge what was or was not really conducive to virtue, and they rejected both the flute and several other old-fashioned instruments, such as the Lydian harp, the many-stringed lyre, the "heptagon," "triangle," "sambuca," and the like — which are intended only to give pleasure to the hearer, and require extraordinary skill of hand.[1] There is a meaning also in the myth of the ancients, which tells how Athene invented the flute and then threw it away. It was not a bad idea of theirs, that the Goddess disliked the instrument because it made the face ugly; but with still more reason may we

[1] Cf. Plato, *Republic*, III. 399.

say that she rejected it because the acquirement of flute-playing contributes nothing to the mind, since to Athene we ascribe both knowledge and art.

Thus then we reject the professional instruments and also the professional mode of education in music — and by professional we mean that which is adopted in contests, for in this the performer practices the art, not for the sake of his own improvement, but in order to give pleasure, and that of a vulgar sort, to his hearers. For this reason the execution of such music is not the part of a freeman but of a paid performer, and the result is that the performers are vulgarized, for the end at which they aim is bad. The vulgarity of the spectator tends to lower the character of the music and therefore of the performers; they look to him — he makes them what they are, and fashions even their bodies by the movements which he expects them to exhibit.

7. We have also to consider rhythms and harmonies. Shall we use them all in education or make a distinction? And shall the distinction be that which is made by those who are engaged in education, or shall it be some other? For we see that music is produced by melody and rhythm, and we ought to know what influence these have respectively on education, and whether we should prefer excellence in melody or excellence in rhythm. But as the subject has been very well treated by many musicians of the present day, and also by philosophers who have had considerable experience of musical education, to these we would refer the more exact student of the subject; we shall only speak of it now after the manner of the legislator, having regard to general principles.

We accept the division of melodies proposed by certain philosophers into ethical melodies, melodies of action, and passionate or inspiring melodies, each having, as they say, a mode or harmony corresponding to it. But we maintain further that music should be studied, not for the sake of one, but of many benefits, that is to say, with a view to (1) education, (2) purification (the word "purification" we use at present without explanation, but when hereafter we speak of poetry, we will treat the subject with more precision); music may also serve (3) for intellectual enjoyment, for relaxation and for recreation after exertion. It is clear, therefore, that all the harmonies must be employed by us, but not all of them in the same manner. In education ethical melodies are to be preferred, but we may listen to the melodies of action and passion when they are performed by others. For feelings such as pity and fear, or, again, enthusiasm, exist very strongly in some souls, and have more or less influence over all. Some persons fall into a religious frenzy, whom we see disenthralled by the use of mystic melodies, which bring healing and purification to the soul. Those who are influenced by pity or fear and every emotional nature have a like experience, others in their degree are stirred by something which specially affects them, and all are in a manner purified and their souls lightened and delighted. The melodies of purification likewise give an innocent pleasure to mankind. Such are the harmonies and the melodies in which those who perform music at the theater should be invited to compete. But since the spectators are of two kinds — the one free and educated, the other a vulgar crowd composed of mechanics, laborers, and the like — there ought to be contests and exhibitions instituted for the relaxation of the second class also. And the melodies will correspond to their minds; for as their minds are perverted from the natural state, so there are exaggerated and corrupted harmonies which are in like manner a perversion. A man receives pleasure from what is natural to him, and therefore professional musicians may be allowed to practice this lower sort of music before an audience of a lower type. But, for the purposes of education, as I have already said, those modes and melodies should be employed which are ethical, such as the Dorian; though we may include any others which are approved by philosophers who have had a musical education. The Socrates of the Republic [1] is wrong in retaining only the Phrygian mode along with the Dorian, and the more so because he rejects the flute; for the Phrygian is to the modes what the flute is to musical instruments — both of them are exciting and emotional. Poetry proves this, for Bacchic frenzy and all similar emotions are most suitably expressed by the flute, and are better set to the Phrygian than to any other harmony. The dithyramb, for example, is acknowledged to be Phrygian, a fact of which the connoisseurs of music offer many proofs, saying, among other things, that Philoxenus, having attempted to compose his Tales as a dithyramb in the Dorian mode, found it impossible, and fell back into the more appropriate Phrygian. All men agree that the Dorian music is the gravest and manliest. And whereas we say that the extremes should be avoided and the mean followed, and whereas the Dorian is a mean between the other harmonies (the Phrygian and the Lydian), it is evident that our youth should be taught the Dorian music.

Two principles have to be kept in view, what is possible, what is becoming: at these every man ought to aim. But even these are relative to age; the old, who have lost their powers, cannot very well sing the severe melodies, and nature herself seems to suggest that their songs should be of the more relaxed kind. Wherefore the musicians likewise blame Socrates, and with justice, for rejecting the relaxed harmonies in education under the idea that they

[1] Cf. Plato, *Republic*, III. 399.

are intoxicating, not in the ordinary sense of intoxication (for wine rather tends to excite men), but because they have no strength in them. And so with a view to a time of life when men begin to grow old, they ought to practice the gentler harmonies and melodies as well as the others. And if there be any harmony, such as the Lydian above all others appears to be, which is suited to children of tender age, and possesses the elements both of order and of education, clearly (we ought to use it, for) education should be based upon three principles — the mean, the possible, the becoming, these three.

III. XENOPHON.

BIOGRAPHICAL SKETCH.

Xenophon, the Greek historian and essayist, was born at Athens about 430 B. C. Early in life he came under the influence of Socrates, to whom, in the " Memorabilia," he pays an affectionate tribute. This work shows that it was the moral and practical teachings of the philosopher, rather than his metaphysical speculations, that made a deep impression on the disciple.

In 401 B. C. Xenophon joined the expedition of the younger Cyrus against his brother Artaxerxes II. of Persia. After the battle of Cunaxa, in which Cyrus was killed, Xenophon directed the retreat of the Greeks, of which he has left a detailed account in his " Anabasis." It was chiefly due to his courage and skill that the Grecian force, after numerous dangers and hardships, finally made its escape.

After his return to Greece, Xenophon made his home in Sparta. He admired the institutions of that country, and had his children educated under the Spartan system. While living in retirement near Olympia he wrote his principal works. His " Cyropædia," from which the first of the following selections is taken, is a historical romance rather than sober history. Xenophon uses the Persian king to illustrate his own views of education, which do not essentially differ from the system of Sparta.

In his " Economics," which treats of the management of the household and farm, Xenophon presents a pleasing picture of the Greek wife and of her domestic duties. Unlike his "Cyropædia," it is Athenian in spirit, and limits the sphere of woman to domestic duties. It is from this work, which clearly brings before us the education of Athenian women, that the second selection is taken.

SELECTION FROM THE "CYROPÆDIA" OF XENOPHON.

CHAPTER II.

1. Cyrus is said to have had for his father Cambyses, king of the Persians. Cambyses was of the race of Perseidæ, who were so called from Perseus. It is agreed that he was born of a mother named Mandane; and Mandane was the daughter of Astyages, king of the Medes. Cyrus is described, and is still celebrated by the Barbarians, as having been most handsome in person, most humane in disposition, most eager for knowledge, and most ambitious of honor; so that he would undergo any labor and face any danger for the sake of obtaining praise. 2. Such is the constitution of mind and body that he is recorded to have had; and he was educated in conformity with the laws of the Persians.

These laws seem to begin with a provident care for the common good; not where they begin in most other governments; for most governments, leaving each individual to educate his children as he pleases, and the advanced in age to live as they please, enjoin their people not to steal, not to plunder, not to enter a house by violence, not to strike any one whom it is wrong to strike, not to be adulterous, not to disobey the magistrates, and other such things in like manner; and, if people transgress any of these precepts, they impose punishments upon them. 3. But the Persian laws, by anticipation, are careful to provide from the beginning, that their citizens shall not be such as to be inclined to any action that is bad and mean. This care they take in the following manner. They have an Agora, called the Free, where the king's palace and other houses for magistrates are built; all things for sale, and the dealers in them, their cries and coarsenesses, are banished from hence to some other place; that the disorder of these may not interfere with the regularity of those who are under instruction. 4. This Agora, round the public courts, is divided into four parts; of these, one is for the boys, one for the youth, one for the full-grown men, and one for those who are beyond the years for military service. Each of these divisions, according to the law, attend in their several quarters; the boys and full-grown men as soon as it is day; the elders when they think convenient, except upon appointed days, when they are obliged to be present. The youth pass the night round the courts, in their light arms, except such as are married; for these are not required to do so, unless orders have been previously given them; nor is it becoming in them to be often absent. 5. Over each of the classes there are twelve presidents, for there are twelve distinct tribes of the Persians. Those over the boys are chosen from amongst the elders, and are such as are thought likely to make them the best boys; those over the youth are chosen from amongst the full-grown men, and are such as are thought likely to make them the best youth; and over the full-grown men, such as are thought likely to render them the most expert in performing their appointed duties, and in executing the orders given by the chief magistrate. There are likewise chosen presidents over the elders, who take care that these also perform their duties. What it is prescribed to each age to do, we shall relate, that it may be the better understood how the Persians take precautions that excellent citizens may be produced.

6. The boys attending the public schools, pass their time in learning justice; and say that they go for this purpose, as those with us say who go to learn to read. Their presidents spend the most part of the day in dispensing justice amongst them; for there are among the boys, as among the men, accusations for theft, robbery, violence, deceit, calumny, and other such things as naturally occur; and such as they convict of doing wrong, in any of these respects, they punish. 7. They punish likewise, such as they find guilty of false accusation; they appeal to justice also in the case of a crime for which men hate one another excessively, but for which they never go to law, that is, ingratitude; and whomsoever they find able to return a benefit, and not returning it, they punish severely. For they think that the ungrateful are careless with regard to the gods, their parents, their country, and their friends; and upon ingratitude seems closely to follow shamelessness, which appears to be the principal conductor of mankind into all that is dishonorable.

8. They also teach the boys self-control; and it contributes much towards their learning to control themselves, that they see every day their elders behaving themselves with discretion. They teach them also to obey their officers; and it contributes much to this end, that they see their elders constantly obedient to their officers. They teach them temperance with respect to eating and drinking; and it contributes much to this object, that they see that their elders do not quit their stations to satisfy their appetites, until their officers dismiss them, and that the boys themselves do not eat with their mothers, but with their teachers, and when the officers give the signal. They bring from home with them bread, and a sort of cresses to eat with it; and a cup to drink from, that, if any are thirsty, they may take water from the river. They learn,

besides, to shoot with the bow, and to throw the javelin. These exercises the boys practice until they are sixteen or seventeen years of age, when they enter the class of young men.

9. The young men pass their time thus: For ten years after they go from the class of boys, they pass the night round the courts, as I have said before, both for the security and guard of the city, and for the sake of practicing self-restraint; for this age seems most to need superintendence. During the day they keep themselves at the command of their officers, in case they want them for any public service; and when it is necessary they all wait at the courts. But whenever the king goes out to hunt, he takes half the guard out with him, and leaves half of it behind; and this he does several times every month. Those that go out must have their bow, with a quiver, a bill or small sword in a sheath, a light shield, and two javelins, one to throw, and the other, if necessary, to use at hand.

10. They attend to hunting as a matter of public interest, and the king, as in war, is their leader, hunting himself, and seeing that others do so; because it seems to them to be the most efficient exercise for all such things as relate to war. It accustoms them to rise early in the morning, and to bear heat and cold; it exercises them in long marches, and in running; it necessitates them to use their bow against the beast that they hunt, and to throw their javelin, wherever he falls in their way, their courage must, of necessity, be often sharpened in the hunt, when any of the strong and vigorous beasts present themselves; for they must come to blows with the animal if he comes up to them, and must be upon their guard as he approaches; so that it is not easy to find what single thing, of all that is practiced in war, is not to be found in hunting. 11. They go out to hunt provided with a dinner, larger, indeed, as is but right,

than that of the boys, but in other respects the same; and during the hunt perhaps they may not eat it; but if it be necessary to remain on the ground to watch for the beast, or if for any other reason they wish to spend more time in the hunt, they sup upon this dinner, and hunt again the next day till supper time, and reckon these two days as but one, because they eat the food of but one day. This abstinence they practice to accustom themselves to it, so that, should it be necessary in war, they may be able to observe it. Those of this age have what they catch for meat with their bread; or, if they catch nothing, their cresses. And, if any one think that they eat without pleasure when they have cresses only with their bread, and that they drink without pleasure when they drink only water, let him recollect how pleasant barley cake or bread is to eat to one who is hungry, and how pleasant water is to drink to one who is thirsty.

12. The parties that remain at home pass their time in practicing what they learned while they were boys, as well as other things, such as using the bow and throwing the javelin; and they pursue these exercises with mutual emulation, as there are public contests in their several accomplishments, and prizes offered; and in whichsoever of the tribes there are found the most who excel in skill, in courage, and in obedience, the citizens applaud and honor, not only the present commander of them, but also the person who had the instruction of them when they were boys. The magistrates likewise make use of the youth that remain at home, if they want them, to keep guard upon any occasion, to search for malefactors, to pursue robbers, or for any other business that requires strength and agility. In these occupations the youth are exercised.

But when they have completed their ten years, they enter into the class of full-grown men; 13. who, from the time they leave the class of youth, pass five and twenty years in the following manner. First, like the youth, they keep themselves at the command of the magistrates, that they may use their services, if it should be necessary, for the public good, in whatever employments require the exertions of such as have discretion, and are yet in vigor. If it be necessary to undertake any military expedition, they who are in this state of discipline do not march out with bows and javelins, but with what are called arms for close fight, a corslet over the breast, a shield in the left hand, such as that with which the Persians are painted, and, in the right, a large sword or bill. All the magistrates are chosen from this class, except the teachers of the boys; and, when they have completed five and twenty years in this class, they will then be something more than fifty years of age, and pass into the class of such as are elders, and are so called. 14. These elders no longer go on any military service abroad, but, remaining at home, have the dispensation of public and private justice; they take cognizance of matters of life and death, and have the choice of all magistrates; and, if any of the youth or full-grown men fail in anything enjoined by the laws, the several magistrates of the tribes, or any one that chooses, gives information of it, when the elders hear the cause, and pass sentence upon it; and the person that is condemned remains infamous for the rest of his life.

15. But that the whole Persian form of government may be shown more clearly, I shall go back a little; for, from what has been already said, it may now be set forth in a very few words. The Persians are said to be in number about a hundred and twenty thousand; of these no individual is excluded by law from honors and magistracies, but all are at liberty to send their boys to the public schools of justice. Those who are able to maintain their children without putting them to work, send them to these

schools; they who are unable, do not send them. Those who are thus educated under the public teachers, are at liberty to pass their youth in the class of young men; they who are not so educated, have not that liberty. They who pass their term among the young men, discharging all things enjoined by the law, are allowed to be incorporated amongst the full-grown men, and to partake of all honors and magistracies; but they who do not complete their course in the class of youth, do not pass into that of full-grown men. Those who make their progress through the order of full-grown men unexceptionably, are then enrolled among the elders; so that the order of elders stands composed of men who have pursued their course through all things good and excellent. Such is the form of government among the Persians, and such the care bestowed upon it, by the observance of which they think that they become the best citizens. 16. . . .

These particulars I had to state concerning the Persians in general. I will now relate the actions of Cyrus, upon whose account this narrative was undertaken, beginning from his boyhood.

SELECTION FROM THE "ECONOMICS" OF XENOPHON.

SPEAKERS.

SOCRATES AND ISCHOMACHUS.

CHAPTER VII. THE EDUCATION OF WOMEN.

4. "But," said I, "Ischomachus, I would very gladly be permitted to ask you whether you instructed your wife yourself, so that she might be qualified as she ought to be, or whether, when you received her from her father and mother, she was possessed of sufficient knowledge to manage

what belongs to her." 5. "And how, my dear Socrates," said he, "could she have had sufficient knowledge when I took her, since she came to my house when she was not fifteen years old, and had spent the preceding part of her life under the strictest restraint, in order that she might see as little, hear as little, and ask as few questions as possible? 6. Does it not appear to you to be quite sufficient, if she did but know, when she came, how to take wool and make a garment, and had seen how to apportion the tasks of spinning among the maid servants? For as to what concerns the appetite, Socrates," added he, "which seems to me a most important part of instruction both for a man and for a woman, she came to me extremely well instructed." 7. "But as to other things, Ischomachus," said I, "did you yourself instruct your wife, so that she should be qualified to attend to the affairs belonging to her?" "Not, indeed," replied Ischomachus, "until I had offered sacrifice, and prayed that it might be my fortune to teach, and hers to learn, what would be best for both of us." 8. "Did your wife, then," said I, "join with you in offering sacrifice, and in praying for these blessings?" "Certainly," answered Ischomachus, "and she made many vows to the gods that she would be such as she ought to be, and showed plainly that she was not likely to disregard what was taught her." 9. "In the name of the gods, Ischomachus, tell me," said I, "what you began to teach her first; for I shall have more pleasure in hearing you give this account, than if you were to give me a description of the finest gymnastic or equestrian games." 10. "Well, then, Socrates," returned Ischomachus, "when she grew familiarized and domesticated with me, so that we conversed freely together, I began to question her in some such way as this: 'Tell me, my dear wife, have you ever considered with what view I married you, and with what object your parents gave you to me? 11. For that there was no want of other persons with whom we might have shared our respective beds must, I am sure, be evident to you as well as to me. But when I considered for myself, and your parents for you, whom we might select as the best partner for a house and children, I preferred you, and your parents, as it appears, preferred me, out of those who were possible objects of choice. 12. If, then, the gods should ever grant children to be born to us, we shall then consult together, with regard to them, how we may bring them up as well as possible; for it will be a common advantage to both of us to find them of the utmost service as supporters and maintainers of our old age. 13. At present, however, this is our common household; for I deposit all that I have as in common between us, and you put everything that you have brought into our common stock. Nor is it necessary to consider which of the two has contributed the greater share; but we ought to feel assured that whichsoever of us is the better manager of our common fortune will give the more valuable service.' 14. To these remarks, Socrates, my wife replied, 'In what respect could I coöperate with you? What power have I? Everything lies with you. My duty, my mother told me, was to conduct myself discreetly.' 15. 'Yes, by Jupiter, my dear wife,' replied I, 'and my father told me the same. But it is the part of discreet people, as well husbands as wives, to act in such a manner that their property may be in the best possible condition, and that as large additions as possible may be made to it by honorable and just means.' 16. 'And what do you see,' said my wife, 'that I can do to assist in increasing our property?' 'Endeavor by all means,' answered I, 'to do in the best possible manner those duties which the gods have qualified you to do, and which custom approves.' 17. 'And what are they?' asked she.

'I consider,' replied I, 'that they are duties of no small importance, unless indeed the queen bee in a hive is appointed for purposes of small importance. 18. For to me,'" continued he, "'the gods, my dear wife,' said I, 'seem certainly to have united that pair of beings, which is called male and female, with the greatest judgment, that they may be in the highest degree serviceable to each other in their connection. 19. In the first place, the pair are brought together to produce offspring, that the races of animals may not become extinct; and to human beings, at least, it is granted to have supporters for their old age from this union. 20. For human beings, also, their mode of life is not, like that of cattle, in the open air; but they have need, we see, of houses. It is accordingly necessary for those who would have something to bring into their houses to have people to perform the requisite employments in the open air; for tilling, and sowing, and planting, and pasturage are all employments for the open air; and from these employments the necessaries of life are procured. 21. But when these necessaries have been brought into the house, there is need of some one to take care of them, and to do whatever duties require to be done under shelter. The rearing of young children also demands shelter, as well as the preparation of food from the fruits of the earth, and the making of clothes from wool. 22. And as both these sorts of employments, alike those without doors, and those within, require labor and care, the gods, as it seems to me,' said I, 'have plainly adapted the nature of the woman for works and duties within doors, and that of the man for works and duties without doors. 23. For the divinity has fitted the body and mind of the man to be better able to bear cold, and heat, and traveling, and military exercises, so that he has imposed upon him the work without doors; and by having formed the body of the woman to be less able to bear such exertions, he appears to me to have laid upon her,' said I, 'the duties within doors. 24. But knowing that he had given the woman by nature, and laid upon her, the office of rearing young children, he has also bestowed upon her a greater portion of love for her newly-born offspring than on the man. 25. Since, too, the divinity has laid upon the woman the duty of guarding what is brought into the house, he, knowing that the mind, by being timid, is not less adapted for guarding, has given a larger share of timidity to the woman than to the man; and knowing also that if any one injures him who is engaged in the occupations without, he must defend himself, he has on that account given a greater portion of boldness to the man. 26. But as it is necessary for both alike to give and to receive, he has bestowed memory and the power of attention upon both impartially, so that you cannot distinguish whether the female or the male has the larger portion of them. 27. The power of being temperate also in what is necessary he has conferred in equal measure upon both, and has allowed that whichsoever of the two is superior in this virtue, whether the man or the woman, shall receive a greater portion of the benefit arising from it. 28. But as the nature of both is not fully adapted for all these requirements, they in consequence stand in greater need of aid from one another, and the pair are of greater service to each other, when the one is able to do those things in which the other is deficient. 29. As we know, then, my dear wife,' continued I, 'what is appointed to each of us by Providence, it is incumbent on us to discharge as well as we can that which each of us has to do."

30. "'The law, too,' I told her," he proceeded, "' gives its approbation to these arrangements, by uniting the man and the woman; and as the divinity has made them part-

ners, as it were, in their offspring, so the law ordains them to be sharers in household affairs. The law also shows that those things are more becoming to each which the divinity has qualified each to do with greater facility; for it is more becoming for the woman to stay within doors than to roam abroad, but to the man it is less creditable to remain at home than to attend to things out of doors. 31. And if any one acts contrary to what the divinity has fitted him to do, he will, while he violates the order of things, possibly not escape the notice of the gods, and will pay the penalty whether of neglecting his own duties or of interfering with those of his wife. 32. The queen of the bees,' I added, 'appears to me to discharge such duties as are appointed to her by the divinity.' 'And what duties,' inquired my wife, 'has the queen bee to perform, that she should be made an example for the business which I have to do?' 33. 'She, remaining within the hive,' answered I, 'does not allow the bees to be idle, but sends out to their duty those who ought to work abroad; and whatever each of them brings in, she takes cognizance of it and receives it, and watches over the store until there is occasion to use it; and when the time for using it is come, she dispenses to each bee its just due. 34. She also presides over the construction of the cells within, that they may be formed beautifully and expeditiously. She attends, too, to the rising progeny, that they may be properly reared; and when the young bees are grown up, and are fit for work, she sends out a colony of them under some leader taken from among the younger bees.' 35. 'Will it then be necessary for me,' said my wife, 'to do such things?' 'It will certainly be necessary for you,' said I 'to remain at home, and to send out such of the laborers as have to work abroad, to their duties; and over such as have business to do in the house you must exercise a watchful superintendence. 36. Whatever is brought into the house, you must take charge of it; whatever portion of it is required for use you must give it out; and whatever should be laid by, you must take account of it and keep it safe, so that the provision stored up for a year, for example, may not be expended in a month. Whenever wool is brought home to you, you must take care that garments be made for those who want them. You must also be careful that the dried provisions may be in a proper condition for eating. 37. One of your duties, however,' I added, 'will perhaps appear somewhat disagreeable, namely, that whoever of all the servants may fall sick, you must take charge of him, that he may be recovered.' 38. 'Nay, assuredly,' returned my wife, 'that will be a most agreeable office, if such as receive good treatment are likely to make a grateful return, and to become more attached to me than before.'" "Delighted with her answer," continued Ischomachus, "I said to her, 'Are not the bees, my dear wife, in consequence of some such care on the part of the queen of the hive, so affected toward her, that, when she quits the hive, no one of them thinks of deserting her, but all follow in her train?' 39. 'I should wonder, however,' answered my wife, 'if the duties of leader do not rather belong to you than to me; for my guardianship of what is in the house, and distribution of it, would appear rather ridiculous, I think, if you did not take care that something might be brought in from out of doors.' 40. 'And on the other hand,' returned I, 'my bringing in would appear ridiculous, unless there were somebody to take care of what is brought in. Do you not see,' said I, 'how those who are said to draw water in a bucket full of holes are pitied, as they evidently labor in vain?' 'Certainly,' replied my wife, 'for they are indeed wretched, if they are thus employed.'"

41. "'Some other of your occupations, my dear wife,' continued I, 'will be pleasing to you. For instance, when you take a young woman who does not know how to spin, and make her skilful at it, and she thus becomes of twice as much value to you. Or when you take one who is ignorant of the duties of a housekeeper or servant, and, having made her accomplished, trustworthy, and handy, render her of the highest value. Or when it is in your power to do services to such of your attendants as are steady and useful, while, if any one is found transgressing, you can inflict punishment. 42. But you will experience the greatest of pleasures, if you show yourself superior to me, and render me your servant, and have no cause to fear that, as life advances, you may become less respected in your household, but may trust that, while you grow older, the better consort you prove to me, and the more faithful guardian of your house for your children, so much the more will you be esteemed by your family. 43. For what is good and honorable,' I added, 'gains increase of respect, not from beauty of person, but from merits directed to the benefit of human life.' Such were the subjects, Socrates, on which as far as I remember, I first conversed seriously with my wife."

CHAPTER VIII.

1. "Did you then observe, Ischomachus," said I, "that your wife was at all the more incited to carefulness by your remarks?" "Indeed I did," replied Ischomachus, "and I saw her on one occasion greatly concerned and put to the blush, because, when I asked for something that had been brought into the house, she was unable to give it me. 2. Perceiving that she was in great trouble, however, I said, 'Do not be cast down, my dear wife, because

you cannot give me what I am asking you for. It is indeed pure poverty not to have a thing to use when you need it; but our present want — not to be able to find a thing when you seek it — is of a less serious nature than not to seek it at all, knowing that it is not in your possession. However,' added I, 'you are not in fault on the present occasion, but I, as I did not direct you, when I gave you the articles, where each of them ought to be deposited, so that you might know how you ought to arrange them and whence to take them. 3. There is indeed nothing, my dear wife, more useful or more creditable to people than order. A chorus of singers and dancers, for instance, consists of a number of persons; but when they do whatever each of them happens to fancy, all appears confusion, and disagreeable to behold; but when they act and speak in concert, the same persons prove themselves worthy of being seen and heard. . . .'"

11. "I once saw, I think, the most beautiful and accurate arrangement of implements possible, Socrates, when I went on board that large Phœnician vessel to look over it; for I beheld a vast number of articles severally arranged in an extremely small space. 12. For the ship," continued he, "is brought into harbor and taken out again by means of various instruments of wood and tow; it pursues its voyage with the aid of much that is called suspended tackle; it is equipped with many machines to oppose hostile vessels; it carries about in it many weapons for the men; it conveys all the utensils, such as people use in a house, for each company that take their meals together; and, in addition to all this, it is freighted with merchandise, which the owner of the ship transports in it for the purpose of profit. 13. And all the things of which I am speaking," continued he, "were stowed in a space not much larger than is contained in a room that holds half a score

dinner-couches. Yet I observed that they were severally arranged in such a manner that they were not in the way of one another, nor required anybody to seek for them, nor were unprepared for use, nor difficult to remove from their places, so as to cause any delay when it was necessary to employ them suddenly. 14. The pilot's officer, too, who is called the man of the prow, I found so well acquainted with the location of them all, that he could tell, even when out of sight of them, where each severally lay, and how many there were, not less readily than a man who knows his letters can tell how many there are in the name Socrates, and where each of them stands. 15. I saw," pursued Ischomachus, "this very man inspecting, at his leisure, all the implements that it is necessary to use in a ship, and, wondering at his minute examination, I asked him what he was doing. 'I am examining, stranger,' said he, 'in case anything should happen, in what state everything in the vessel is, and whether anything is wanting, or is placed so as to be inconvenient for use. 16. For,' said he, 'there is no time, when heaven sends a storm over the sea, either to seek for what may be wanting, or to hand out what may be difficult to use; for the gods threaten and punish the negligent; and if they but forbear from destroying those who do nothing wrong, we must be very well content; while, if they preserve even those that attend to everything quite properly, much gratitude is due to them.' 17. I, therefore, having observed the accuracy of this arrangement, said to my wife, that it would be extremely stupid in us, if people in ships, which are comparatively small places, find room for their things, and, though they are violently tossed about, nevertheless keep them in order, and, even in the greatest alarm, still find out how to get what they want; and if we, who have large separate repositories in our house for everything, and our house firmly planted on the ground, should not discover excellent and easily-found places for our several articles;— how could this, I say, be anything but extreme stupidity in us?"

18. "How excellent a thing a regular arrangement of articles is, and how easy it is to find, in a house, a place such as is suitable to put everything, I have sufficiently shown. 19. But how beautiful an appearance it has, too, when shoes, for instance, of whatever kind they are, are arranged in order; how beautiful it is to see garments, of whatever kind, deposited in their several places; how beautiful it is to see bed-clothes, and brazen vessels, and table furniture, so arranged; and (what, most of all, a person might laugh at, not indeed a grave person, but a jester), I say, that pots have a graceful appearance when they are placed in regular order. 20. Other articles somehow appear, too, when regularly arranged, more beautiful in consequence; for the several sorts of vessels seem like so many choral bands; and the space that is between them pleases the eye, when every sort of vessel is set clear of it; just as a body of singers and dancers, moving in a circle, is not only in itself a beautiful sight, but the space in the middle of it, being open and clear, is agreeable to the eye. 21. Whether what I say is true, my dear wife,' said I, 'we may make trial, without suffering any loss, or taking any extraordinary trouble. Nor ought we at all to labor under the apprehension that it will be difficult to find a person who will learn the places for every article, and remember how to keep each of them separate; 22. for we know very well that the whole city contains ten thousand times as much as our house, and yet, whichsoever of the servants you order to buy anything and bring it to you from the market place, not one of them will be in perplexity, but every one will show that he knows whither he must go to fetch any article. For this,' added I, 'there is no other reason

than that each article is deposited in its appointed place. 23. But if you should seek for a person, and sometimes even for one who is on his part seeking you, you would often give up the search in despair before you find him; and for this there is no other cause, than that it is not appointed where the particular person is to await you.'"

CHAPTER IX.

1. "And what was the result," said I, "my dear Ischomachus? Did your wife appear to attend to any of the matters which you took so much pains to impress upon her?" "What else did she do but promise that she would attend to what I said, and manifest the greatest pleasure, as if she had found relief from perplexity? and she requested me to arrange the various articles, as soon as I could, in the manner which I had proposed." 2. "And how, Ischomachus," said I, "did you arrange them for her?" "What else could I do but determine upon showing her, in the first place, the capacity of the house? For it is not adorned with decorations, but the apartments in it are constructed with such a view that they may be as convenient receptacles as possible for the things that are to be placed in them; so that they themselves invite whatever is adapted for them respectively. 3. Thus the inner chamber, being in a secure part of the house, calls for the most valuable couch coverings and vessels; the dry parts of the building for the corn; the cool places for the wine; and the well-lighted portions for such articles of workmanship, and vases, as require a clear light. 4. I pointed out to her, too, that the apartments for people to live in, which are well ornamented, are cool in the summer and exposed to the sun in winter; and I made her notice as to the whole house how it lies open to the south, so that it is

plain it has plenty of sun in winter, and plenty of shade in summer. . . . 6. When we had gone through these places," he continued, " we then proceeded to classify our goods. We began by collecting, first of all, whatever we use for offering sacrifices; after this, we arranged the dresses for women, such as are suited for festival days; and then the equipments for men, as well for festivities as for warfare; and next the bed-covering in the women's apartments, the bed-coverings in the men's apartments, the shoes for the women and the shoes for the men. 7. Of utensils there were distinct collections, one of instruments for spinning, another of those for preparing corn, another of those for cooking, another of those for the bath, another of those for kneading bread, another of those for the table. These in general we divided into two sorts, such as we have to use constantly, and such as are required only at festal entertainments. 8. We also made one assortment of what would be used in a month, and another of what was computed to last for a year; for in this way it is less likely to escape our knowledge how particular things are expended. When we had thus distinguished all our goods into classes, we conveyed them severally to the places best suited for them. 9. Afterwards, whatever utensils the servants require daily, such as those for preparing corn, for cooking, for spinning, and any others of that sort, we pointed out to those who use them, the places where they were to put them, and then committed them to their keeping, charging them to keep them safely; 10. but such as we use only for festival days, for entertaining guests, or only occasionally at long intervals, we committed, after pointing out the places for them, and numbering and making lists of them, to the housekeeper, and told her to give out any of them to whatever servant needed them, to bear in mind to which of them she gave any one, and, after receiving them back, to deposit them respectively in the places from which she took them."

11. "Of the housekeeper we made choice after considering which of the female servants appeared to have most self-restraint in eating, and wine, and sleep, and converse with the male sex; and, in addition to this, which seemed to have the best memory, and which appeared to have forethought, that she might not incur punishment from us for neglect, and to consider how, by gratifying us, she might gain some mark of approbation in return. 12. We formed her to entertain feelings of affection toward us, giving her a share in our pleasure when we had an occasion of rejoicing, and consulting her, if anything troublesome occurred, with reference to it. We also led her to become desirous of increasing our property, by stimulating her to take accounts of it, and making her in some degree partaker of our prosperity. 14. We also excited in her a love of honesty, by paying more respect to the well-principled than to the unprincipled, and showing her that they lived in greater plenty and in better style. We then installed her in her appointment. 14. But in addition to all this, Socrates," said he, "I told my wife that there would be no profit in all these arrangements, unless she herself took care that the appointed order for everything should be preserved. I also instructed her that in the best-regulated political communities it is not thought sufficient by the citizens merely to make good laws, but that they also appoint guardians of the laws, who, overlooking the state, commend him who acts in conformity with the laws, and, if any one transgresses the laws, punish him. 15. I accordingly desired my wife," continued he, "to consider herself the guardian of the laws established in the house, and to inspect the household furniture, whenever she thought proper, as the commander of a garrison

inspects his sentinels; to signify her approbation if everything was in good condition, as the senate signifies its approval of the horses and horse-soldiers; to praise and honor the deserving like a queen, according to her means, and to rebuke and disgrace any one that required such treatment. 16. But I moreover admonished her," added he, "that she would have no reason to be displeased, if I imposed on her more trouble with regard to our property than I laid on the servants; remarking to her, that servants have only so far a concern with their master's property as to carry it, or keep it in order, or take care of it; but that no servant has any power of using it unless his master puts it into his hands, while it belongs all to the master himself, so that he may use any portion of it for whatever purpose he pleases. 17. To him therefore that receives the greatest benefit from its preservation, and suffers the greatest loss by its destruction, I showed her that the greatest interest in its safety must belong."

18. "Well then, Ischomachus," said I, "how did your wife, on hearing these instructions, show herself disposed to comply with your wishes?" "She assured me, Socrates," replied he, "that I did not judge rightly of her, if I thought that I was imposing on her what was disagreeable, in telling her that she must take care of the property; for she remarked," said he, "that it would have been more disagreeable to her if I had charged her to neglect her property, than if she were required to take care of the household goods. 19. For it seems to be a provision of nature," concluded he, "that as it is easier for a well-disposed woman to take care of her children than to neglect them, so it is more pleasing (as he thought, he said), for a right-minded woman to attend to her property, which, as being her own, affords her gratification, than to be neglectful of it."

IV. CICERO.

BIOGRAPHICAL SKETCH.

Marcus Tullius Cicero, the distinguished orator, statesman, and philosopher, was perhaps the best representative of the Græco-Roman culture of his day. To natural gifts of a high order he added the best culture of Rome and Athens. The numerous works that have descended to us afford ample opportunity to judge of his character and his ability. In oratory he fairly rivaled Demosthenes; and in his various philosophical treatises, written with a polished copiousness previously unknown in Rome, he has reflected the best thought of Roman and Grecian antiquity. Though lacking in force and independence of character, he was a man of keen penetration and strict integrity.

Cicero was born at Arpinum 106 B. C. of an equestrian family. At an early age he was taken to Rome by his father, a man of large influence and culture, that he might enjoy the superior educational advantages of the metropolis. He there studied under the orator Crassus and the poet Archias, the latter of whom he afterwards defended in a beautiful oration. In addition to the laws of his country and the literature of Greece and Rome, he made a careful study of the leading systems of philosophy, and thus exemplified the principles which he inculcated later, that the orator should be acquainted with the whole circle of knowledge.

At the age of twenty-six Cicero entered upon his legal career, and at once distinguished himself by his moving eloquence. Ostensibly to regain his health but really to escape the jealousy of the dictator Sulla, he withdrew to Athens, where he further devoted himself to the cultivation of his oratorical powers. Through further travel, especially in the Roman province of Asia, he stored his capacious and acquisitive mind with new treasures of learning. On returning to Rome he successfully filled several political offices, and was finally elected, by an overwhelming vote, to the consulship. While filling this office he frustrated the treasonable designs of Catiline, and was proclaimed "the father of his country."

But not long afterwards he became the victim of partisan violence, and in 58 B. C. suffered banishment from Rome. He resided for more than a year at Thessalonica. He was then recalled to Rome, where he was received with great enthusiasm. In the civil war between Cæsar and Pompey, he espoused the cause of the latter; and after Pompey's defeat and death in 48 B. C., he lived in retirement. It was during this period of enforced leisure that he wrote his principal works. He was slain 43 B. C. by the soldiers of Antony, whom he had opposed in a series of orations to which he gave the name of Philippics.

Cicero touches upon education in his oration in defense of Archias, in his dialogue on "Brutus," and in his "Orator." It is from the last named work that the following selection is taken. It is interesting as presenting the great Roman's views of what an orator's education should be. We should not forget that to Cicero's mind the orator was the highest type of the cultured and capable gentleman. He therefore presents, in this brief extract, his conception of the highest aim of a generous and complete education.

SELECTION FROM CICERO'S "DE ORATORE."

XV. "If, therefore, any one desires to define and comprehend the whole and peculiar power of an orator, that man, in my opinion, will be an orator, worthy of so great a name, who, whatever subject comes before him, and requires rhetorical elucidation, can speak on it judiciously, in set form, elegantly, and from memory, and with a certain dignity of action. But if the phrase which I have used, 'on whatever subject,' is thought by any one too comprehensive, let him retrench and curtail as much of it as he pleases; but this I will maintain, that though the orator be ignorant of what belongs to other arts and pursuits, and understands only what concerns the discussions and practice of the Forum, yet if he has to speak on those arts, he will, when he has learned what pertains to any of them from persons who understand them, discourse upon them much better than the very persons of whom those arts form the peculiar province. Thus, if our friend Sulpicius have to speak on military affairs, he will inquire about them of my kinsman Caius Marius, and when he has received information, will speak upon them in such a manner, that he shall seem to Marius to understand them better than himself. Or if he has to speak on the civil law, he will consult with you, and will excel you, though eminently wise and learned in it, in speaking on those very points which he shall have learned from yourself. Or if any subject presents itself, requiring him to speak on the nature and vices of men, on desire, on moderation, on continence, on grief, on death, perhaps, if he thinks proper (though the orator ought to have a knowledge of these things), he will consult with Sextus Pompeius, a man learned in philosophy. But this he will certainly accomplish, that, of whatever matter he gains a knowledge, or from whomsoever, he will speak upon it much more elegantly than the very person from whom he gained the knowledge. But, since philosophy is distinguished into three parts, inquiries into the obscurities of physics, the subtleties of logic, and the knowledge of life and manners, let us, if Sulpicius will listen to me, leave the two former, and consult our ease; but unless we have a knowledge of the third, which has always been the province of the orator, we shall leave him nothing in which he can distinguish himself. The part of philosophy, therefore, regarding life and manners, must be thoroughly mastered by the orator; other subjects, even if he has not learned them, he will be able, whenever there is occasion, to adorn by his eloquence, if they are brought before him and made known to him.

XVI. " For if it is allowed amongst the learned that Aratus, a man ignorant of astronomy, has treated of heaven and the constellations in extremely polished and excellent verses; if Nicander, of Colophon, a man totally unconnected with the country, has written well on rural affairs, with the aid of poetical talent, and not from understanding husbandry, what reason is there why an orator should not speak most eloquently on those matters of which he shall have gained a knowledge for a certain purpose and occasion? For the poet is nearly allied to the orator; being somewhat more restricted in numbers, but less restrained in the choice of words, yet in many kinds of embellishment his rival and almost equal; in one respect, assuredly, nearly the same, that he circumscribes or bounds his jurisdiction by no limits, but reserves to himself full right to range wherever he pleases with the same ease and liberty. For why did you say, Scævola, that you would not endure, unless you were in my domain, my assertion, that the orator ought to be accomplished in every style of speaking, and in every part of polite learning? I should certainly not have said this if I had thought myself to be the orator whom I conceive in my imagination. But, as Caius Lucilius used frequently to say (a man not very friendly to you, and on that account less familiar with me than he could wish, but a man of learning and good breeding), I am of this opinion, that no one is to be numbered among orators who is not thoroughly accomplished in all branches of knowledge requisite for a man of good breeding; and though we may not put forward such knowledge in conversation, yet it is apparent, and indeed evident, whether we are destitute of it, or have acquired it; as those who play at tennis do not exhibit, in playing, the gestures of the palæstra, but their movements indicate whether they have learned those exercises or are unacquainted with them; and as those who shape out anything, though they do not then exercise the art of painting, yet make it clear whether they can paint or not; so in orations to courts of justice, before the people, and in the senate, although other sciences have no peculiar place in them, yet is it easily proved whether he who speaks has only been exercised in the parade of declamation, or has devoted himself to oratory after having been instructed in all liberal knowledge."

* * * * *

XIX. "Certain men of eloquence at Athens, versed in public affairs and judicial pleadings, disputed on the other side; among whom was Menedemus, lately my guest at Rome; but when he had observed that there is a sort of wisdom which is employed in inquiring into the methods of settling and managing governments, he, though a ready speaker, was promptly attacked by the other, a man of abundant learning, and of an almost incredible variety and copiousness of argument; who maintained that every portion of such wisdom must be derived from philosophy, and that whatever was established in a state concerning the immortal gods, the discipline of youth, justice, patience, temperance, moderation in everything, and other matters, without which states would either not subsist at all, or be corrupt in morals, was nowhere to be found in the petty treatises of the rhetoricians. For if those teachers of rhetoric included in their art such a multitude of the most important subjects, why, he asked, were their books crammed with rules about proems and perorations, and such trifles (for so he called them), while about the modeling of states, the composition of laws, about equity, justice, integrity, about mastering the appetites, and forming the morals of mankind, not one single syllable was to be found in their pages? Their precepts he ridiculed in such a manner, as to show that the teachers were not only destitute of the knowledge which they arrogated to themselves, but that they did not even know the proper art and method of speaking; for he thought that the principal business of an orator was, that he might appear to those to whom he spoke to be such as he would wish to appear (that this was to be attained by a life of good reputation, on which those teachers of rhetoric had laid down nothing in their precepts); and that the minds of the audience should be affected in such a manner as the orator would have them to be affected, an object, also, which could by no means be attained, unless the speaker understood by what methods, by what arguments, and by what sort of language the minds of men are moved in any particular direction; but that these matters were involved and concealed in the profoundest doctrines of philosophy, which these rhetoricians had not touched even with the extremity of their lips. These assertions Menedemus endeavored to refute, but rather by *authorities* than by *arguments;* for, repeating from memory many noble passages from the orations of Demosthenes, he showed that that orator, while he swayed the minds of judges or of the people by his eloquence, was not ignorant by what means he attained his end, which Charmadas denied that any one could know without philosophy.

XX. "To this Charmadas replied, that he did not deny that Demosthenes was possessed of consummate ability and the utmost energy of eloquence; but whether he had these powers from natural genius, or because he was, as was acknowledged, a diligent hearer of Plato, it was not what Demosthenes could do, but what the rhetoricians taught, that was the subject of inquiry. Sometimes too he was carried so far by the drift of his discourse, as to maintain that there was no art at all in speaking; and having shown by various arguments that we are so formed by nature as to be able to flatter, and to insinuate ourselves, as suppliants, into the favor of those from whom we wish to obtain anything, as well as to terrify our enemies by menaces, to relate matters of fact, to confirm what we assert, to refute what is said against us, and, finally, to use entreaty or lamentation; particulars in which the whole faculties of the orator are employed; and that practice and exercise sharpened the understanding, and produced fluency of speech, he rested his cause, in conclusion, on a multitude of examples that he adduced; for first, as if stating an indisputable fact, he affirmed that no writer on the art of rhetoric was ever even moderately eloquent, going back as far as I know not what Corax and Tisias, who, he said, appeared to be the inventors and first authors of rhetorical science; and then named a vast number of the most eloquent men who had neither learned, nor cared to understand the rules of art, and amongst whom, (whether in jest, or because he thought, or had heard something to that effect,) he instanced me as one who had received none of their instructions, and yet, as he said, had some abilities as a speaker; of which two observations I readily granted the truth of one, that I had never been instructed, but thought that in the other he was either joking with me, or was under some mistake. But he denied there was any art, except such as lay in things that were known and thoroughly understood, things tending to the same object, and never misleading; but that everything treated by the orators was doubtful and uncertain; as it was uttered by those who did not fully understand it, and was heard by them to whom knowledge was not meant to be communicated, but merely false, or at least obscure notions, intended to live in their minds only for a short time. In short, he seemed bent on convincing me that there was no art of speaking, and that no one could speak skilfully, or so as fully to illustrate a subject, but one who had attained that knowledge which is delivered by the most learned of the philosophers. On which occasions Charmadas used to say, with a passionate admiration of your genius, Crassus, that I appeared to him very easy in listening, and you most pertinacious in disputation.

XXI. "Then it was that I, swayed by this opinion, remarked in a little treatise which got abroad, and into people's hands without my knowledge and against my will, that I had known many good speakers, but never yet any one that was truly eloquent; for I accounted him *a good speaker,* who could express his thoughts with accuracy and perspicuity, according to the ordinary judgment of mankind, before an audience of moderate capacity; but I considered him alone *eloquent,* who could in a more admirable and noble manner amplify and adorn whatever subjects he chose, and who embraced in thought and memory all the principles of everything relating to oratory.

* * * * * *

XXXI. . . . "In the first place, I will not deny that, as becomes a man well born and liberally educated, I learned those trite and common precepts of teachers in general; first, that it is the business of an orator to speak in a manner adapted to persuade; next, that every speech is either upon a question concerning a matter in general, without specification of persons or times, or concerning a matter referring to certain persons and times. But that, in either case, whatever falls under controversy, the question with regard to it is usually, whether such a thing has been done, or, if it has been done, of what nature it is, or by what name it should be called; or, as some add, whether it seems to have been done rightly or not. That controversies arise also on the interpretation of writing, in which anything has been expressed ambiguously, or contradictorily, or so that what is written is at variance with the writer's evident intention; and that there are certain lines of argument adapted to all these cases. But that of such subjects as are distinct from general questions, part come under the head of judicial proceedings, part under that of deliberations; and that there is a third kind which is employed in praising or censuring particular persons. That there are also certain commonplaces on which we may insist in judicial proceedings, in which equity is the object; others, which we may adopt in deliberations, all which are to be directed to the advantage of those to whom we give counsel; others in panegyric, in which all must be referred to the dignity of the persons commended. That since all the business and art of an orator is divided into five parts, he ought first to find out what he should say; next, to dispose and arrange his matter, not only in a certain order, but with a sort of power and judgment; then to clothe and deck his thoughts with language; then to secure them in his memory; and lastly, to deliver them with dignity and grace. I had learned and understood also, that before we enter upon the main subject, the minds of the audience should be conciliated by an exordium; next that the case should be clearly stated; then, that the point in controversy should be established; then, that what we maintain should be supported by proof, and that whatever was said on the other side should be refuted; and that, in the conclusion of our speech, whatever was in our favor should be amplified and enforced, and whatever made 'for our adversaries should be weakened and invalidated.'

XXXII. "I had heard also what is taught about the costume of a speech; in regard to which it is first directed that we should speak correctly and in pure Latin; next, intelligibly and with perspicuity; then gracefully; then suitably to the dignity of the subject, and as it were becomingly; and I had made myself acquainted with the rules relating to every particular. Moreover, I had seen art applied to those things which are properly endowments of nature; for I had gone over some precepts concerning action, and some concerning artificial memory, which were short indeed, but requiring much exercise; matters on which almost all the learning of those artificial orators is employed; and if I should say that it is of no assistance, I should say what is not true; for it conveys some hints to admonish the orator, as it were, to what he should refer each part of his speech, and to what points he may direct his view, so as not to wander from the object which he has proposed to himself. But I consider that with regard to all precepts the case is this, not that orators by adhering to them have obtained distinction in eloquence; but that certain persons have noticed what men of eloquence practiced of their own accord, and formed rules accordingly; so that eloquence has not sprung from art, but art from eloquence; not that, as I said before, I entirely reject art, for it is, though not essentially necessary to oratory, yet proper for a man of liberal education to learn. And by you, my young friends, some preliminary exercise must be undergone; though indeed you are already on the course; but those who are to enter upon a race, and those who are preparing for what is to be done in the forum, as their field of battle, may alike previously learn, and try their powers, by practicing in sport." "That sort of exercise," said Sulpicius "is just what we wanted to understand; but we desire to hear more at large what you have briefly and cursorily delivered concerning art; though such matters are not strange even to us. Of that subject, however, we shall inquire hereafter; at present we wish to know your sentiments on exercise."

XXXIII. "I like that method," replied Crassus, "which you are accustomed to practice, namely, to lay down a case similar to those which are brought on in the forum, and to speak upon it, as nearly as possible, as if it were a real case. But in such efforts the generality of students exercise only their voice (and not even that skilfully), and try their strength of lungs, and volubility of tongue, and please themselves with a torrent of their own words; in which exercise what they have heard deceives them, *that men by speaking succeed in becoming speakers.* For it is truly said also, *That men by speaking badly make sure of becoming bad speakers.* In those exercises, therefore, although it be useful even frequently to speak on the sudden, yet it is more advantageous, after taking time to consider, to speak with greater preparation and accuracy. But the chief point of all is that which (to say the truth) we hardly ever practice (for it requires great labor, which most of us avoid); I mean, to write as much as possible. *Writing* is said to be *the best and most excellent modeler and teacher of oratory;* and not without reason; for if what is meditated and considered easily surpasses sudden and extemporary speech, a constant and diligent habit of writing will surely be of more effect than meditation and consideration itself; since all the arguments relating to the subject on which we write, whether they are suggested by art, or by a certain power of genius and understanding, will present themselves, and occur to us, while we examine and contemplate it in the full light of our intellect; and all the thoughts and words, which are the most expressive of their kind, must of necessity come under and submit to the keenness of our judgment while writing; and a fair arrangement and collocation of the words is effected by writing, in a certain rhythm and measure, not poetical, but oratorical. Such are the qualities which bring applause and admiration to good orators; nor will any man ever attain them, unless after long and great practice in writing, however resolutely he may have exercised himself in extemporary speeches; and he who comes to speak after practice in writing brings this advantage with him, that though he speak at the call of the moment, yet what he says will bear a resemblance to something written; and if ever, when he comes to speak, he brings anything with him in writing, the rest of his speech, when he departs from what is written, will flow on in a similar strain. As, when a boat has once been impelled forward, though the rowers suspend their efforts, the vessel herself still keeps her motion and course during the intermission of the impulse and force of the oars; so, in a continued stream of oratory, when written matter fails, the rest of the speech maintains a similar flow, being impelled by the resemblance and force acquired from what was written.

XXXIV. "But in my daily exercises I used, when a youth, to adopt chiefly that method which I knew that Caius Carbo, my adversary, generally practiced; which was, that, having selected some nervous piece of poetry, or read over such a portion of a speech as I could retain in my memory, I used to declaim upon what I had been reading in other words, chosen with all the judgment that I possessed. But at length I perceived that in that method there was this inconvenience, that Ennius, if I exercised myself on his verses, or Gracchus, if I laid one of his orations before me, had forestalled such words as were peculiarly appropriate to the subject, and such as were the most elegant and altogether the best; so that, if I used the same words, it profited nothing; if others, it was even prejudicial to me, as I habituated myself to use such as were less eligible. Afterwards I thought proper, and continued the practice at a rather more advanced age, to translate the orations of the best Greek orators; by fixing upon which I gained this advantage, that while I rendered into Latin what I had read in Greek, I not only used the best words, and yet such as were of common occurrence, but also formed some words by imitation, which would be new to our countrymen, taking care, however, that they were unobjectionable.

"As to the exertion and exercise of the voice, of the breath, of the whole body, and of the tongue itself, they do not so much require art as labor; but in those matters we ought to be particularly careful whom we imitate and whom we would wish to resemble. Not only orators are to be observed by us, but even actors, lest by vicious habits we contract any awkwardness or ungracefulness. The memory is also to be exercised, by learning accurately by heart as many of our own writings, and those of others, as we can. In exercising the memory, too, I shall not object if you accustom yourself to adopt that plan of referring to places and figures which is taught in treatises on the art. Your language must then be brought forth from this domestic and retired exercise, into the midst of the field, into the dust and clamor, into the camp and military array of the forum; you must acquire practice in everything; you must try the strength of your understanding; and your retired lucubrations must be exposed to the light of reality. The poets must also be studied; an acquaintance must be formed with history; the writers and teachers in all the liberal arts and sciences must be read, and turned over, and must, for the sake of exercise, be praised, interpreted, corrected, censured, refuted; you must dispute on both sides of every question; and whatever may seem maintainable on any point must be brought forward and illustrated. The civil war must be thoroughly studied; laws in general must be understood; all antiquity must be known; the usages of the senate, the nature of our government, the rights of our allies, our treaties and conventions, and whatever concerns the interests of the state, must be learned. A certain intellectual grace must also be extracted from every kind of refinement, with which, as with salt, every oration must be seasoned. I have poured forth to you all I had to say, and perhaps any citizen whom you had laid hold of in any company whatever, would have replied to your inquiries on these subjects equally well."

V. SENECA.

BIOGRAPHICAL SKETCH.

Lucius Annæus Seneca was born at Corduba, Spain, in the year 3 B. C. His father, who was a teacher of rhetoric, spent some years in Rome, where he acquired an ample property for his family. The young Seneca, after pursuing the study of eloquence, devoted himself to the Stoic philosophy under several able teachers, but subsequently, upon the urgent solicitation of his father, took up the legal profession, in which he became distinguished for his oratorical ability.

He entered public life as quæstor; but having become involved in some court intrigue, he was banished to Corsica. He remained there eight years, a period devoted to high philosophic speculation, and to fruitless appeals to the Emperor Claudius for pardon. At last he was recalled through the influence of Agrippina, whose son, afterwards the infamous Nero, became his pupil. Subsequently when Nero had become emperor, Seneca fell under suspicion, and about 63 A. D. he withdrew entirely from public life to live in retirement. Two years later he was condemned to death.

A noble spirit pervades his writings. He enjoins piety toward God, and charity toward men. Goodness seemed to him the supreme end of life; and philosophy, which teaches virtue, he regarded as the chief of liberal sciences. Beyond all other ancient writers he emphasized the moral side of education. It is unfortunate that his life did not exemplify his lofty precepts.

Among his numerous writings may be mentioned his treatises on Anger, Consolation, Providence, Tranquillity of Mind, A Happy Life, and Benefits. The first extract that follows " On the Education of Children," is a chapter in his treatise on Anger, which was written about 50 A. D. It is here taken from the translation of Aubrey Stuart, in Bohn's Classical Library. The other extract entitled " Philosophy," is taken from " The Morals of Seneca," edited by Walter Clode in the Camelot Series.

SELECTIONS FROM SENECA.

I. ON THE EDUCATION OF CHILDREN.

It is, I assure you, of the greatest service to boys that they should be soundly brought up, yet to regulate their education is difficult, because it is our duty to be careful neither to cherish a habit of anger in them, nor to blunt the edge of their spirit. This needs careful watching, for both qualities, those which are to be encouraged, and those which are to be checked, are fed by the same things; and even a careful watcher may be deceived by their likeness. A boy's spirit is increased by freedom and depressed by slavery; it rises when praised, and is led to conceive great expectations of itself; yet this same treatment produces arrogance and quickness of temper. We must, therefore, guide him between these two extremes, using the curb at one time and the spur at another. He must undergo no servile or degrading treatment; he never must beg abjectly for anything, nor must he gain anything by begging. Let him rather receive it for his own sake, for his past good behavior, or for his promises of future good conduct.

In contests with his comrades we ought not to allow him to become sulky or fly into a passion; let us see that he be on friendly terms with those whom he contends with, so that in the struggle itself he may learn to wish not to hurt his antagonist but to conquer him. Whenever he has gained the day or done something praiseworthy, we should allow him to enjoy the victory, but not to rush into transports of delight; for joy leads to exultation, and exultation leads to swaggering and excessive self-esteem.

We ought to allow him some relaxation, yet not yield him up to sloth and laziness, and we ought to keep him far beyond the reach of luxury, for nothing makes children more prone to anger than a soft and fond bringing-up, so that the more children are indulged, and the more liberty is given them, the more they are corrupted. He to whom nothing is ever denied, will not be able to endure a rebuff, whose anxious mother always wipes away his tears, whose pedagogue is made to pay for his shortcomings.

Do you not observe how a man's anger becomes more violent as he rises in station? This shows itself especially in those who are rich and noble, or in great place, when the favoring gale has roused all the most empty and trivial passions of their minds. Prosperity fosters anger, when a man's proud ears are surrounded by a mob of flatterers, saying, " That man answer you! you do not act according to your dignity, you lower yourself." And so forth, with all the language which can hardly be resisted even by healthy and originally well-principled minds. Flattery, then, must be kept well out of the way of children.

Let a child hear the truth, and sometimes fear it; let him always reverence it. Let him rise in the presence of his elders. Let him obtain nothing by flying into a passion; let him be given when he is quiet what was refused him when he cried for it. Let him behold, but not make use of his father's wealth; let him be reproved for what he does wrong.

It will be advantageous to furnish boys with even-tempered teachers and pedagogues; what is soft and unformed clings to what is near, and takes its shape. The habits of young men reproduce those of their nurses and pedagogues. Once a boy, who was brought up in Plato's house, went home to his parents, and, on seeing his father shouting with passion, said, "I never saw any one at Plato's house act like that." I doubt not that he learned to imitate his father sooner than he learned to imitate Plato.

Above all, let his food be scanty, his dress not costly, and of the same fashion as that of his comrades. If you begin by putting him on a level with many others, he will not be angry when some one is compared with him.

2. PHILOSOPHY.

It is of the bounty of nature that we live, but of philosophy that we live well, which is, in truth, a greater benefit than life itself. Not but that philosophy is also the gift of heaven, so far as to the faculty, but not to the science, for that must be the business of industry. No man is born wise, but wisdom and virtue require a tutor, though we can easily learn to be vicious without a master. It is philosophy that gives us a veneration for God, a charity for our neighbor; that teaches us our duty to heaven, and exhorts us to an agreement one with another. It unmasks things that are terrible to us, assuages our lusts, refutes our errors, restrains our luxury, reproves our avarice, and works strangely upon tender natures.

To tell you now my opinion of the liberal sciences, I have no great esteem for anything that terminates in profit or money; and yet I shall allow them to be so far beneficial, as they only prepare the understanding, without detaining it. They are but the rudiments of wisdom, and only then to be learned when the mind is capable of nothing better, and the knowledge of them is better worth the keeping than the acquiring. They do not so much as pretend to the making of us virtuous, but only to give us an aptitude of disposition to be so. The grammarian's business lies in a syntax of speech; or if he proceed to history, or the measuring of a verse, he is at the end of his line. But what signifies a congruity of periods, the computing of syllables, or the modifying of numbers, to the taming of our passions, or the repressing of our lusts?

The philosopher proves the body of the sun to be large, but for the true dimensions of it we must ask the mathematician. Geometry and music, if they do not teach us to master our hopes and fears, all the rest is to little purpose. What does it concern us which was the elder of the two, Homer or Hesiod, or which was the taller, Helen or Hecuba? We take a great deal of pains to trace Ulysses in his wanderings, but were it not time as well spent to look to ourselves, that we may not wander at all? Are not we ourselves tossed with tempestuous passions, and both assaulted by terrible monsters on the one hand, and tempted by sirens on the other? Teach me my duty to my country, to my father, to my wife, to mankind. What is it to me whether Penelope was honest or not? Teach me to know how to be so myself, and to live according to that knowledge. What am I the better for putting so many parts together in music, and raising a harmony out of so many different tones? Teach me to tune my affections, and to hold constant to myself. Geometry teaches me the art of measuring acres; teach me to measure my appetites, and to know when I have enough; teach me to divide with my brother, and to rejoice in the prosperity of my neighbor. You teach me how I may hold my own, and keep my estate; but I would rather learn how I may lose it all, and yet be contented.

He that designs the institution of human life should not be

over curious of his words; it does not stand with his dignity to be solicitous about sounds and syllables, and to debase the mind of man with small and trivial things, placing wisdom in matters that are difficult rather than great. If he be eloquent, it is his good fortune, not his business. Subtile disputations are only the sports of wits that play upon the catch, and are fitter to be contemned than resolved. Were not I a madman to sit wrangling about words, and putting of nice and impertinent questions, when the enemy has already made the breach, the town fired over my head, and the mine ready to play that shall blow me up in the air? Were this a time for fooleries? Let me rather fortify myself against death and inevitable necessities; let me understand that the good of life does not consist in the length or space, but in the use of it. . . . Let us rather study how to deliver ourselves from sadness, fear, and the burthen of all our secret lusts. Let us pass over all our most solemn levities, and make haste to a good life, which is a thing that presses us.

VI. QUINTILIAN.

BIOGRAPHICAL SKETCH.

Quintilian, the famous rhetorician of Rome, was born at Calahorra in Spain about 43 A. D. Comparatively little is known about his family and early life; but, like most other great men of his time, he was educated at the metropolis of the empire. After returning for a brief period to his native province, he established himself in Rome in 68 A. D., and soon achieved distinction as an able pleader in the forum and as a successful teacher of eloquence. Among his numerous pupils was the younger Pliny. He was invested by Vespasian with the consular dignity, and granted an allowance from the public treasury. He was the first Roman teacher that was salaried by the state and honored with the title of "professor of eloquence."

After twenty years of pleading and teaching, in which he had accumulated an ample property, he retired from public employments and devoted the later years of his life to the preparation of his "Institutes of Oratory." This celebrated work consists of twelve books, and is the most comprehensive and systematic treatise on education that has descended to us from antiquity. It has been a storehouse from which subsequent educational writers, particularly in the period of the Renaissance, have drawn copiously for materials. Of its wide scope the author says: "I shall proceed to regulate the studies of the orator from his infancy, just as if he were entrusted to me to be brought up."

"The great merit of Quintilian's treatise on oratory," says

his translator Watson, "above all works of the kind that had preceded it, was its superior copiousness of matter and felicity of embellishment. It does not offer a mere dry list of rules, but illustrates them with an abundance of examples from writers of all kinds, interspersed with observations that must interest, not only the orator, but readers of every class. It embraces a far wider field than the 'De Oratore' of Cicero, and treats of all that concerns eloquence with far greater minuteness. The orator conducts his pupil from the cradle to the utmost heights of the oratorical art." Of especial general interest are the brief but penetrating and judicious criticisms in the tenth book upon the leading Grecian and Roman writers.

The following selection is taken from the first book of the "Institutes," and presents in full Quintilian's principles and methods of primary education:

SELECTION FROM THE "INSTITUTES OF ORATORY."

BOOK I., CHAPTER I.

1. Let a father, then, as soon as his son is born, conceive, first of all, the best possible hopes of him; for he will thus grow the more solicitous about his improvement from the very beginning; since it is a complaint without foundation that "to very few people is granted the faculty of comprehending what is imparted to them, and that most, through dullness of understanding, lose their labor and their time." For, on the contrary, you will find the greater number of men both ready in conceiving and quick in learning; since such quickness is natural to man; and as birds are born to fly, horses to run, and wild beasts to show fierceness, so to us peculiarly belong activity and sagacity of understanding;

whence the origin of the mind is thought to be from heaven. 2. But dull and unteachable persons are no more produced in the course of nature than are persons marked by monstrosity and deformities; such are certainly but few. It will be a proof of this assertion, that, among boys, good promise is shown in the far greater number; and, if it passes off in the progress of time, it is manifest that it was not natural ability, but care, that was wanting. 3. But one surpasses another, you will say, in ability. I grant that this is true; but only so far as to accomplish more or less; whereas there is no one who has not gained something by study. Let him who is convinced of this truth, bestow, as soon as he becomes a parent, the most vigilant possible care on cherishing the hopes of a future orator.

4. Before all things, let the talk of the child's nurses not be ungrammatical. Chrysippus wished them, if possible, to be women of some knowledge; at any rate he would have the best, as far as circumstances would allow, chosen. To their morals, doubtless, attention is first to be paid; but let them also speak with propriety. 5. It is they that the child will hear first; it is their words that he will try to form by imitation. We are by nature most tenacious of what we have imbibed in our infant years; as the flavor, with which you scent vessels when new, remains in them; nor can the colors of wool, for which its plain whiteness has been exchanged, be effaced; and those very habits, which are of a more objectionable nature, adhere with the greater tenacity; for good ones are easily changed for the worse, but when will you change bad ones into good? Let the child not be accustomed, therefore, even while he is yet an infant, to phraseology which must be unlearned.

6. In parents I should wish that there should be as much learning as possible. Nor do I speak, indeed, merely of fathers; for we have heard that Cornelia, the mother of the

Gracchi (whose very learned writing in her letters has come down to posterity), contributed greatly to their eloquence; the daughter of Lælius is said to have exhibited her father's elegance in her conversation; and the oration of the daughter of Quintus Hortensius, delivered before the Triumviri, is read not merely as an honor to her sex. 7. Nor let those parents, who have not had the fortune to get learning themselves, bestow the less care on the instruction of their children, but let them, on this very account, be more solicitous as to other particulars.

Of the boys, among whom he who is destined to this prospect is to be educated, the same may be said as concerning nurses.

8. Of *pædagogi* this further may be said, that they should either be men of acknowledged learning, which I should wish to be the first object, or that they should be conscious of their want of learning; for none are more pernicious than those who, having gone some little beyond the first elements, clothe themselves in a mistaken persuasion of their own knowledge; since they disdain to yield to those who are skilled in teaching, and, growing imperious, and sometimes fierce, in a certain right, as it were, of exercising their authority (with which that sort of men are generally puffed up), they teach only their own folly. 9. Nor is their misconduct less prejudicial to the manners of their pupils; for Leonidas, the tutor of Alexander, as is related by Diogenes of Babylon, tinctured him with certain bad habits, which adhered to him, from his childish education, even when he was grown up and become the greatest of kings.

10. If I seem to my reader to require a great deal, let him consider that it is an orator that is to be educated; an arduous task, even when nothing is deficient for the formation of his character; and that more and more difficult labors yet remain; for there is need of constant study, the most

excellent teachers, and a variety of mental exercises. 11. The best of rules, therefore, are to be laid down; and if any one shall refuse to observe them, the fault will lie, not in the method, but in the man.

If however it should not be the good fortune of children to have such nurses as I should wish, let them at least have one attentive *pædagogus,* not unskilled in language, who, if anything is spoken incorrectly by the nurse in the presence of his pupil, may at once correct it, and not let it settle in his mind. But let it be understood that what I prescribed at first is the right course, and this only a remedy.

12. I prefer that a boy should begin with the Greek language, because he will acquire Latin, which is in general use, even though we tried to prevent him, and because, at the same time, he ought first to be instructed in Greek learning, from which ours is derived. 13. Yet I should not wish this rule to be so superstitiously observed that he should for a long time speak or learn only Greek, as is the custom with most people; for hence arise many faults of pronunciation, which is viciously adapted to foreign sounds, and also of language, in which when Greek idioms have become inherent by constant usage, they keep their place most pertinaciously even when we speak a different tongue. 14. The study of Latin ought therefore to follow at no long interval, and soon after to keep pace with the Greek; and thus it will happen, that, when we have begun to attend to both tongues with equal care, neither will impede the other.

15. Some have thought that boys, as long as they are under seven years of age, should not be set to learn, because that is the earliest age that can understand what is taught, and endure the labor of learning. Of which opinion a great many writers say that Hesiod was, at least such writers as lived before Aristophanes the grammarian, for he was the first to deny that the *Hupothækai,* in which this

opinion is found, was the work of that poet. 16. But other writers likewise, among whom is Eratosthenes, have given the same advice. Those, however, advise better, who, like Chrysippus think that no part of a child's life should be exempt from tuition; for Chrysippus, though he has allowed three years to the nurses, yet is of opinion that the minds of children may be imbued with excellent instruction even by them. 17. And why should not that age be under the influence of learning, which is now confessedly subject to moral influences? I am not indeed ignorant that, during the whole time of which I am speaking, scarcely as much can be done as one year may afterwards accomplish, yet those who are of the opinion which I have mentioned, appear with regard to this part of life to have spared not so much the learners as the teachers. 18. What else, after they are able to speak, will children do better, for they must do something? Or why should we despise the gain, how little soever it be, previous to the age of seven years? For certainly, small as may be the proficiency which an earlier age exhibits, the child will yet learn something greater during the very year in which he would have been learning something less. 19. This advancement extended through each year, is a profit on the whole; and whatever is gained in infancy is an acquisition to youth. The same rule should be prescribed as to the following years, so that what every boy has to learn, he may not be too late in beginning to learn. Let us not then lose even the earliest period of life, and so much the less, as the elements of learning depend on the memory alone, which not only exists in children, but is at that time of life even most tenacious.

20. Yet I am not so unacquainted with differences of age, as to think that we should urge those of tender years severely, or exact a full complement of work from them; for it will be necessary, above all things, to take care lest the child

should conceive a dislike to the application which he cannot yet love, and continue to dread the bitterness which he has once tasted, even beyond the years of infancy. Let his instruction be an amusement to him; let him be questioned, and praised; and let him never feel pleased that he does not know a thing; and sometimes, if he is unwilling to learn, let another be taught before him, of whom he may be envious. Let him strive for victory now and then, and generally suppose that he gains it; and let his powers be called forth by rewards, such as that age prizes.

21. We are giving small instructions, while professing to educate an orator; but even studies have their infancy; and as the rearing of the very strongest bodies commenced with milk and the cradle, so he, who was to be the most eloquent of men, once uttered cries, tried to speak at first with a stuttering voice, and hesitated at the shapes of the letters. Nor, if it is impossible to learn a thing completely, is it therefore unnecessary to learn it at all. 22. If no one blames a father, who thinks that these matters are not to be neglected in regard to his son, why should he be blamed who communicates to the public what he would practice to advantage in his own house? And this is so much the more the case, as younger minds more easily take in small things; and as bodies cannot be formed to certain flexures of the limbs unless while they are tender, so even strength itself makes our minds likewise more unyielding to most things. 23. Would Philip, king of Macedonia, have wished the first principles of learning to be communicated to his son Alexander by Aristotle, the greatest philosopher of that age, or would Aristotle have undertaken that office, if they had not both thought that the first rudiments of instruction are best treated by the most accomplished teacher, and have an influence on the whole course? 24. Let us suppose, then, that Alexander were committed to me, and laid in my lap,

an infant worthy of so much solicitude (though every man thinks his own son worthy of similar solicitude), should I be ashamed, even in teaching him his very letters, to point out some compendious methods of instruction?

For that at least, which I see practiced in regard to most children, by no means pleases me, namely, that they learn the names and order of the letters before they learn their shapes. 25. This method hinders their recognition of them, as, while, they follow their memory that takes the lead, they do not fix their attention on the forms of the letters. This is the reason why teachers, even when they appear to have fixed them sufficiently in the minds of children, in the straight order in which they are usually first written, make them go over them again the contrary way, and confuse them by variously changing the arrangement, until their pupils know them by their shape, not by their place. It will be best for children, therefore, to be taught the appearances and names of the letters at once, as they are taught those of men. 26. But that which is hurtful with regard to letters, will be no impediment with regard to syllables. I do not disapprove, however, the practice, which is well known, of giving children, for the sake of stimulating them to learn, ivory figures of letters to play with, or whatever else can be invented, in which that infantine age may take delight, and which may be pleasing to handle, look at, or name.

27. But as soon as the child shall have begun to trace the forms of the letters, it will not be improper that they should be cut for him, as exactly as possible, on a board, that his style may be guided along them as along grooves, for he will then make no mistakes, as on wax (since he will be kept in by the edge on each side, and will be unable to stray beyond the boundary); and, by following these sure traces rapidly and frequently, he will form his hand, and not require the assistance of a person to guide his hand with his

own hand placed over it. 28. The accomplishment of writing well and expeditiously, which is commonly disregarded by people of quality, is by no means an indifferent matter; for as writing itself is the principal thing in our studies, and that by which alone sure proficiency, resting on the deepest roots, is secured, a too slow way of writing retards thought, a rude and confused hand cannot be read; and hence follows another task, that of reading off what is to be copied from the writing. 29. At all times, therefore, and in all places, and especially in writing private and familiar letters, it will be a source of pleasure to us, not to have neglected even this acquirement.

30. For learning syllables there is no short way; they must all be learned throughout; nor are the most difficult of them, as is the general practice, to be postponed, that children may be at a loss, forsooth, in writing words. 31. Moreover, we must not even trust to the first learning by heart; it will be better to have syllables repeated, and to impress them long upon the memory; and in reading too, not to hurry on, in order to make it continuous or quick, until the clear and certain connection of the letters becomes familiar, without at least any necessity to stop for recollection. Let the pupil then begin to form words from syllables, and to join phrases together from words. 32. It is incredible how much retardation is caused to reading, by haste; for hence arise hesitation, interruption, and repetition, as children attempt more than they can manage; and then, after making mistakes, they become distrustful even of what they know. 33. Let reading, therefore, be at first sure, then continuous, and for a long time slow, until, by exercise, a correct quickness is gained. 34. For to look to the right, as everybody teaches, and to look forward, depends not merely on rule, but on habit, since, while the child is looking to what follows, he has to pronounce what goes before, and,

what is very difficult, the direction of his thoughts must be divided, so that one duty may be discharged with his voice, and another with his eyes.

When the child shall have begun, as is the practice, to write words, it will cause no regret if we take care that he may not waste his efforts on common words, and such as perpetually occur. 35. For he may readily learn the explanations of obscure terms, which the Greeks call *glossai,* while some other occupation is before him, and acquire, amidst his first rudiments, a knowledge of that which would afterwards demand a special time for it. Since, too, we are still attending to small matters, I would express a wish that even the lines, which are set him for his imitation in writing, should not contain useless sentences, but such as convey some moral instruction. 36. The remembrance of such admonitions will attend him to old age, and will be of use even for the formation of his character. It is possible for him, also, to learn the sayings of eminent men, and select passages, chiefly from the poets (for the reading of poets is more pleasing to the young), in his play-time; since memory (as I shall show in its proper place) is most necessary to an orator, and is eminently strengthened and nourished by exercise; and, at the age of which we are now speaking, and which cannot, as yet, produce anything of itself, it is almost the only faculty that can be improved by the aid of teachers.

37. It will not be improper, however, to require of boys of this age (in order that their pronunciation may be fuller and their speech more distinct) to roll forth, as rapidly as possible, certain words and lines of studied difficulty, composed of several syllables, and those roughly clashing together, and, as it were, rugged-sounding; the Greeks call them *Chalepoi.* This may seem a trifling matter to mention, but when it is neglected, many faults of pronunciation, unless

they are removed in the years of youth, are fixed by incorrigible ill habit for the rest of life.

CHAPTER II.

1. But let us suppose that the child now gradually increases in size, and leaves the lap, and applies himself to learning in earnest. In this place, accordingly, must be considered the question, whether it be more advantageous to confine the learner at home, and within the walls of a private house, or to commit him to the large numbers of a school, and, as it were, to public teachers. 2. The latter mode, I observe, has had the sanction of those by whom the polity of the most eminent states was settled, as well as that of the most illustrious authors.

Yet it is not to be concealed, that there are some who, from certain notions of their own, disapprove of this almost public mode of instruction. These persons appear to be swayed chiefly by two reasons: one, that they take better precautions for the morals of the young, by avoiding a concourse of human beings of that age which is most prone to vice (from which cause I wish it were falsely asserted that provocations to immoral conduct arise); the other, that whoever may be the teacher, he is likely to bestow his time more liberally on one pupil, than if he has to divide it among several. 3. The first reason indeed deserves great consideration; for if it were certain that schools, though advantageous to studies, are pernicious to morals, a virtuous course of life would seem to me preferable to one even of the most distinguished eloquence. But in my opinion, the two are combined and inseparable; for I am convinced that no one can be an orator who is not a good man; and, even if any one could, I should be unwilling that he should be. On this point, therefore, I shall speak first.

4. People think that morals are corrupted in schools; for indeed they are at times corrupted; but such may be the case even at home. Many proofs of this fact may be adduced; proofs of character having been vitiated, as well as preserved with the utmost purity, under both modes of education. It is the disposition of the individual pupil, and the care taken of him, that make the whole difference. Suppose that his mind be prone to vice, suppose that there be neglect in forming and guarding his morals in early youth, seclusion would afford no less opportunity for immorality than publicity; for the private tutor may be himself of bad character; nor is intercourse with vicious slaves at all safer than that with immodest free-born youths. 5. But if his disposition be good, and if there be not a blind and indolent negligence on the part of his parents, it will be possible for them to select a tutor of irreproachable character, (a matter to which the utmost attention is paid by sensible parents,) and to fix on a course of instruction of the very strictest kind; while they may at the same time place at the elbow of their son some influential friend or faithful freedman, whose constant attendance may improve even those of whom apprehensions may be entertained.

6. The remedy for this object of fear is easy. Would that we ourselves did not corrupt the morals of our children! We enervate their very infancy with luxuries. That delicacy of education, which we call fondness, weakens all the powers, both of body and mind. What luxury will he not covet in his manhood, who crawls about on purple! He cannot yet articulate his first words, when he already distinguishes scarlet, and wants his purple. 7. We form the palate of children before we form their pronunciation. They grow up in sedan chairs; if they touch the ground, they hang by the hands of attendants supporting them on each side. We are delighted if they utter anything im-

modest. Expressions which would not be tolerated even from the effeminate youths of Alexandria, we hear from them with a smile and a kiss. Nor is this wonderful; we have taught them; they have heard such language from ourselves.

9. But, it is said, one tutor will have more time for one pupil. First of all, however, nothing prevents that one pupil, whoever he may be, from being the same with him who is taught in the school. But if the two objects cannot be united, I should still prefer the day-light of an honorable seminary to darkness and solitude; for every eminent teacher delights in a large concourse of pupils, and thinks himself worthy of a still more numerous auditory. 10. But inferior teachers, from a consciousness of their inability, do not disdain to fasten on single pupils, and to discharge the duty as it were of *pædagogi*. 11. But supposing that either interest, or friendship, or money, should secure to any parent a domestic tutor of the highest learning, and in every respect unrivaled, will he however spend the whole day on one pupil? Or can the application of any pupil be so constant as not to be sometimes wearied, like the sight of the eyes, by continued direction to one object, especially as study requires the far greater portion of time to be solitary? 12. For the tutor does not stand by the pupil while he is writing, or learning by heart, or thinking; and when he is engaged in any of those exercises, the company of any person whatsoever is a hindrance to him. Nor does every kind of reading require at all times a prælector or interpreter; for when, if such were the case, would the knowledge of so many authors be gained? The time, therefore, during which the work as it were for the whole day may be laid out, is but short. 13. Thus the instructions which are to be given to each may reach to many. Most of them, indeed, are of such a nature that they may be communi-

cated to all at once with the same exertion of the voice. I say nothing of the topics and declamations of the rhetoricians, at which, certainly, whatever be the number of the audience, each will still carry off the whole. 14. For the voice of the teacher is not like a meal, which will not suffice for more than a certain number, but like the sun, which diffuses the same portion of light and heat to all. If a grammarian, too, discourses on the art of speaking, solves questions, explains matters of history, or illustrates poems, as many as shall hear him will profit by his instructions. 15. But, it may be said, number is an obstacle to correction and explanation. Suppose that this be a disadvantage in a number (for what in general satisfies us in every respect?) we will soon compare that disadvantage with other advantages.

Yet I would not wish a boy to be sent to a place where he will be neglected. Nor should a good master encumber himself with a greater number of scholars than he can manage; and it is to be a chief object with us, also, that the master may be in every way our kind friend, and may have regard in his teaching, not so much to duty, as to affection. Thus we shall never be confounded with the multitude. 16. Nor will any master, who is in the slightest degree tinctured with literature, fail particularly to cherish that pupil in whom he shall observe application and genius, even for his own honor. But even if great schools ought to be avoided (a position to which I cannot assent, if numbers flock to a master on account of his merit), the rule is not to be carried so far that schools should be avoided altogether. It is one thing to shun schools, another to choose from them.

17. If I have now refuted the objections which are made to schools, let me next state what opinions I myself entertain. 18. First of all, let him who is to be an orator, and

who must live amidst the greatest publicity, and in the full daylight of public affairs, accustom himself, from his boyhood, not to be abashed at the sight of men, nor pine in a solitary and as it were recluse way of life. The mind requires to be constantly excited and roused, while in such retirement it either languishes, and contracts rust, as it were, in the shade, or on the other hand, becomes swollen with empty conceit, since he who compares himself to no one else, will necessarily attribute too much to his own powers. 19. Besides, when his acquirements are to be displayed in public, he is blinded at the light of the sun, and stumbles at every new object, as having learned in solitude that which is to be done in public. 20. I say nothing of friendships formed at school, which remain in full force even to old age, as if cemented with a certain religious obligation; for to have been initiated in the same studies is a not less sacred bond than to have been initiated in the same sacred rites. That sense, too, which is called common sense, where shall a young man learn when he has separated himself from society, which is natural not to men only, but even to dumb animals? 21. Add to this, that, at home, he can learn only what is taught himself; at school, even what is taught others. 22. He will daily hear many things commended, many things corrected; the idleness of a fellow student, when reproved, will be a warning to him; the industry of any one, when commended, will be a stimulus; emulation will be excited by praise; and he will think it a disgrace to yield to his equals in age, and an honor to surpass his seniors. All these matters excite the mind; and though ambition itself be a vice, yet it is often the parent of virtues.

23. I remember a practice that was observed by my masters, not without advantage. Having divided the boys into classes, they assigned them their order in speaking in

conformity to the abilities of each; and thus each stood in the higher place to declaim according as he appeared to excel in proficiency. 24. Judgments were pronounced on the performances; and great was the strife among us for distinction; but to take the lead of the class was by far the greatest honor. Nor was sentence given on our merits only once; the thirtieth day brought the vanquished an opportunity of contending again. Thus he who was most successful, did not relax his efforts, while uneasiness incited the unsuccessful to retrieve his honor. 25. I should be inclined to maintain, as far as I can form a judgment from what I conceive in my own mind, that this method furnished stronger incitements to the study of eloquence, than the exhortations of preceptors, the watchfulness of *pædagogi,* or the wishes of parents.

26. But as emulation is of use to those who have made some advancement in learning, so, to those who are but beginning, and are still of tender age, to imitate their schoolfellows is more pleasant than to imitate their master, for the very reason that it is more easy; for they who are learning the first rudiments will scarcely dare to exalt themselves to the hope of attaining that eloquence which they regard as the highest; they will rather fix on what is nearest to them, as vines attached to a tree gain the top by taking hold of the lower branches first. 27. This is an observation of such truth, that it is the care even of the master himself, when he has to instruct minds that are still unformed, not (if he prefer at least the useful to the showy) to overburden the weakness of his scholars, but to moderate his strength, and to let himself down to the capacity of the learner. 28. For as narrow-necked vessels reject a great quantity of the liquid that is poured upon them, but are filled by that which flows or is poured into them by degrees, so it is for us to ascertain how much the minds of boys can

receive, since what is too much for their grasp of intellect will not enter their minds, as not being sufficiently expanded to admit it. 29. It is of advantage therefore for a boy to have school-fellows whom he may first imitate, and afterwards try to surpass. Thus will he gradually conceive hope of higher excellence.

To these observations I shall add, that masters themselves, when they have but one pupil at a time with them, cannot feel the same degree of energy and spirit in addressing him, as when they are excited by a large number of hearers. 30. Eloquence depends in a great degree on the state of the mind, which must conceive images of objects, and transform itself, so to speak, to the nature of the things of which we discourse. Besides, the more noble and lofty a mind is, by the more powerful springs, as it were, is it moved, and accordingly is both strengthened by praise, and enlarged by effort, and is filled with joy at achieving something great. 31. But a certain secret disdain is felt at lowering the power of eloquence, acquired by so much labor, to one auditor; and the teacher is ashamed to raise his style above the level of ordinary conversation. Let any one imagine, indeed, the air of a man haranguing, or the voice of one entreating, the gesture, the pronunciation, the agitation of mind and body, the exertion, and, to mention nothing else, the fatigue, while he has but one auditor; would not he seem to be affected with something like madness? There would be no eloquence in the world, if we were to speak only with one person at a time.

CHAPTER III.

1. Let him that is skilled in teaching, ascertain first of all, when a boy is entrusted to him, his ability and disposition. The chief symptom of ability in children is memory,

of which the excellence is twofold, to receive with ease and retain with fidelity. The next symptom is imitation; for that is an indication of a teachable disposition, but with this provision, that it express merely what it is taught, and not a person's manner or walk, for instance, or whatever may be remarkable for deformity. 2. The boy who shall make it his aim to raise a laugh by his love of mimicry, will afford me no hope of good capacity; for he who is possessed of great talent will be well disposed; else I should think it not at all worse to be of a dull, than of a bad, disposition; but he who is honorably inclined will be very different from the stupid or idle. 3. Such a pupil as I would have, will easily learn what is taught him, and will ask questions about some things, but will still rather follow than run on before. That precocious sort of talent scarcely ever comes to good fruit. 4. Such are those who do little things easily, and, impelled by impudence, show at once all that they can accomplish in such matters. But they succeed only in what is ready to their hand; they string words together, uttering them with an intrepid countenance, not in the least discouraged by bashfulness; and do little but do it readily. 5. There is no real power behind, or any that rests on deeply fixed roots; but they are like seeds which have been scattered on the surface of the ground and shoot up prematurely, and like grass that resembles corn, and grows yellow, with empty ears, before the time of harvest. Their efforts give pleasure, as compared with their years; but their progress comes to a stand and our wonder diminishes.

6. When a tutor has observed these indications, let him next consider how the mind of his pupil is to be managed. Some boys are indolent, unless you stimulate them; some are indignant at being commanded; fear restrains some, and unnerves others; continued labor forms some; with

others, hasty efforts succeed better. 7. Let the boy be given to me, whom praise stimulates, whom honor delights, who weeps when he is unsuccessful. His powers must be cultivated under the influence of ambition; reproach will sting him to the quick; honor will incite him; and in such a boy I shall never be apprehensive of indifference.

8. Yet some relaxation is to be allowed to all; not only because there is nothing that can bear perpetual labor, (and even those things that are without sense and life are unbent by alternate rest, as it were, in order that they may preserve their vigor), but because application to learning depends on the will, which cannot be forced. 9. Boys, accordingly, when re-invigorated and refreshed, bring more sprightliness to their learning, and a more determined spirit, which for the most part spurns compulsion. 10. Nor will play in boys displease me; it is also a sign of vivacity; and I cannot expect that he who is always dull and spiritless will be of an eager disposition in his studies, when he is indifferent even to that excitement which is natural to his age. 11. There must however be bounds set to relaxation, lest the refusal of it beget an aversion to study, or too much indulgence in it a habit of idleness. There are some kinds of amusement, too, not unserviceable for sharpening the wits of boys, as when they contend with each other by proposing all sorts of questions in turn. 12. In their plays, also, their moral dispositions show themselves more plainly, supposing that there is no age so tender that it may not readily learn what is right and wrong; and the tender age may best be formed at a time when it is ignorant of dissimulation, and most willingly submits to instructors; for you may break, sooner than mend, that which has hardened into deformity. 13. A child is as early as possible, therefore, to be admonished that he must do nothing too eagerly, nothing dishonestly,

nothing without self-control; and we must always keep in mind the maxim of Virgil, *Adeo in teneris consuescere multum est,* "of so much importance is the acquirement of habit in the young."

14. But that boys should suffer corporal punishment, though it be a received custom, and Chrysippus makes no objection to it, I by no means approve; first, because it is a disgrace, and a punishment for slaves, and in reality (as will be evident if you imagine the age changed) an affront; secondly, because, if a boy's disposition be so abject as not to be amended by reproof, he will be hardened, like the worst of slaves, even to stripes and lastly, because, if one who regularly exacts his tasks be with him, there will not be the least need of any such chastisement. 15. At present, the negligence of *pædagogi* seems to be made amends for in such a way that boys are not obliged to do what is right, but are punished whenever they have not done it. Besides, after you have coerced a boy with stripes, how will you treat him when he becomes a young man, to whom such terror cannot be held out, and by whom more difficult studies must be pursued? 16. Add to these considerations, that many things unpleasant to be mentioned, and likely afterwards to cause shame, often happen to boys while being whipped, under the influence of pain or fear; and such shame enervates and depresses the mind, and makes them shun people's sight and feel a constant uneasiness. 17. If, moreover, there has been too little care in choosing governors and tutors of reputable character, I am ashamed to say how scandalously unworthy men may abuse their privilege of punishing, and what opportunity also the terror of the unhappy children may sometimes afford to others. I will not dwell upon this point; what is already understood is more than enough. It will be sufficient therefore to intimate, that no man

should be allowed too much authority over an age so weak and so unable to resist ill-treatment.

18. I will now proceed to show in what studies he who is to be so trained that he may become an orator, must be instructed, and which of them must be commenced at each particular period of youth.

CHAPTER IV.

1. In regard to the boy who has attained facility in reading and writing, the next object is instruction from the grammarians. Nor is it of importance whether I speak of the Greek or Latin grammarian, though I am inclined to think that the Greek should take the precedence. 2. Both have the same method. This profession, then, distinguished as it is, most compendiously, into two parts, the art *of speaking correctly* and the *illustration of the poets,* carries more beneath the surface than it shows on its front. 3. For not only is the *art of writing* combined with that of speaking, but *correct reading* also precedes illustration, and with all these is joined the exercise of *judgment,* which the old grammarians, indeed, used with such severity, that they not only allowed themselves to distinguish certain verses with a particular mark of censure, and to remove, as spurious, certain books which had been inscribed with false titles, from their sets, but even brought some authors within their canon, and excluded others altogether from classification. 4. Nor is it sufficient to have read the poets only; every class of writers must be studied, not simply for matter, but for words, which often receive their authority from writers. Nor can grammar be complete without a knowledge of music, since the grammarian has to speak of meter and rhythm; nor if he is ignorant of astronomy, can he understand the poets, who, to say nothing of other

matters, so often allude to the rising and setting of the stars in marking the seasons; nor must he be unacquainted with philosophy, both on account of numbers of passages, in almost all poems, drawn from the most abstruse subtleties of physical investigation, and also on account of Empedocles among the Greeks, and Varro and Lucretius among the Latins, who have committed the precepts of philosophy to verse. 5. The grammarian has also need of no small portion of eloquence, that he may speak aptly and fluently on each of those subjects which are here mentioned. Those therefore are by no means to be regarded who deride this science as trifling and empty, for unless it lays a sure foundation for the future orator, whatever superstructure you raise will fall; it is a science which is necessary to the young, pleasing to the old, and an agreeable companion in retirement, and which alone, of all departments of learning, has in it more service than show.

VII. PLUTARCH.

BIOGRAPHICAL SKETCH.

Plutarch, the celebrated biographer and moralist, was born at Chæronea, in Bœotia about 50 A. D. After studying at Delphi under a distinguished teacher, he took up his residence in Rome, where during the reign of Domitian he became a popular teacher of philosophy. In later years the emperor Hadrian, his friend and pupil, appointed him magistrate in his native city, where he died about 120 A. D. He was a man of superior native ability and wide scholarship. History and philosophy were evidently his favorite studies.

He is best known for his "Parallel Lives," which has always enjoyed a high degree of popularity. The numerous authorities which he quotes, show that his work is based on elaborate research. His "Morals," a collection of philosophical and practical essays, is less widely known, though it contains his famous treatise "On Education." Though the authenticity of this essay has been questioned, there can be no reasonable doubt that it presents the views of the Greco-Roman philosopher. It is singularly modern in tone, and justly entitles Plutarch to a place among the great educational thinkers of the ancient world. Throughout his admirable discussion it will be observed that he particularly insists on moral training. With the exception of the two opening paragraphs, which recommend good birth and sobriety in parents, the essay is given, with unessential omissions, as it appears in Bohn's Classical Library.

SELECTION FROM PLUTARCH'S "MORALS."

ON EDUCATION.

1. To speak generally, what we are wont to say about the arts and sciences is also true of moral excellence, for to its perfect development three things must meet together, natural ability, theory, and practice. By theory I mean training, and by practice working at one's craft. Now the foundation must be laid in training, and practice gives facility, but perfection is attained only by the junction of all three. For if any one of these elements be wanting, excellence must be so far deficient. For natural ability without training is blind: and training without natural ability is defective, and practice without both natural ability and training is imperfect. For just as in farming the first requisite is good soil, next a good farmer, next good seed, so also here: the soil corresponds to natural ability, the training to the farmer, the seed to precepts and instruction. I should therefore maintain stoutly that these three elements were found combined in the souls of such universally famous men as Pythagoras, and Socrates, and Plato, and of all who have won undying fame. Happy at any rate and dear to the gods is he to whom any deity has vouchsafed all these elements!

But if anyone thinks that those who have not good natural ability cannot to some extent make up for the deficiencies of nature by right training and practice, let such a one know that he is very wide of the mark, if not out of it altogether. For good natural parts are impaired by sloth; while inferior ability is mended by training: and while simple things escape the eyes of the careless, difficult things are reached by painstaking. The wonderful efficacy and power of long and continuous labor you may see indeed every day in the world around you. Thus water continually dropping wears away rocks: and iron and steel are molded by the hands of the artificer: and chariot wheels bent by some strain can never recover their original symmetry: and the crooked staves of actors can never be made straight. But by toil what is contrary to nature becomes stronger than even nature itself.

2. The next point to discuss will be nutrition. In my opinion mothers ought to nurse and suckle their own children. For they will bring them up with more sympathy and care, if they love them so intimately and, as the proverb puts it, "from their first growing their nails." Whereas the affection of wet or dry nurses is spurious and counterfeit, being merely for pay. And nature itself teaches that mothers ought themselves to suckle and rear those they have given birth to. . . . For infancy is supple and easily molded, and what children learn sinks deeply into their souls while they are young and tender, whereas everything hard is softened only with great difficulty. For just as seals are impressed on soft wax, so instruction leaves its permanent mark on the minds of those still young. And divine Plato seems to me to give excellent advice to nurses not to tell their children any kind of fables, that their souls may not in the very dawn of existence be full of folly or corruption. Phocylides the poet also seems to give admirable advice when he says, "We must teach good habits while the pupil is still a boy."

3. Attention also must be given to this point, that the lads that are to wait upon and be with young people must be first and foremost of good morals, and able to speak Greek distinctly and idiomatically, that they may not by contact with foreigners of loose morals contract any of their viciousness. For as those who are fond of quoting

proverbs say not amiss, "If you live with a lame man, you will learn to halt."

4. Next, when our boys are old enough to be put into the hands of pedagogues, great care must be taken that we do not hand them over to slaves, or foreigners, or flighty persons. For what happens nowadays in many cases is highly ridiculous: good slaves are made farmers, or sailors, or merchants, or stewards, or money-lenders; but if they find a winebibbing, greedy, and utterly useless slave, to him parents commit the charge of their sons, whereas the good tutor ought to be such a one as was Phœnix, the tutor of Achilles. The point also which I am now going to speak about is of the utmost importance. The schoolmasters we ought to select for our boys should be of blameless life, of pure character, and of great experience. For a good training is the source and root of gentlemanly behavior. And just as farmers prop up their trees, so good schoolmasters prop up the young by good advice and suggestions, that they may become upright. How one must despise, therefore, some fathers, who, whether from ignorance or inexperience before putting the intended teachers to the test, commit their sons to the charge of untried and untested men. If they act so through inexperience it is not so ridiculous; but it is to the remotest degree absurd when, though perfectly aware of both the inexperience and worthlessness of some schoolmasters, they yet entrust their sons to them: some overcome by flattery, others to gratify friends who solicit their favors; acting just as if anybody ill in body, passing over the experienced physician, should, to gratify his friend, call him in and so throw away his life; or as if to gratify one's friend one should reject the best pilot and choose him instead. Zeus and all the gods! can anyone bearing the sacred name of father put obliging a petitioner before obtaining the best education for his sons?

Were they not then wise words that the time-honored Socrates used to utter and say that he would proclaim, if he could, climbing up to the highest part of the city, "Men, what can you be thinking of, who move heaven and earth to make money while you bestow next to no attention on the sons you are going to leave that money to?"[1] I would add to this that such fathers act very similarly to a person who should be very careful about his shoe but care nothing about his foot. Many persons also are so niggardly about their children, and indifferent to their interests, that for the sake of a paltry saving, they prefer worthless teachers for their children, practicing a vile economy at the expense of their children's ignorance. *Apropos* of this, Aristippus on one occasion rebuked an empty-headed parent neatly and wittily. For being asked how much money a parent ought to pay for his son's education, he answered, "A thousand drachmæ." And he replying, "Hercules, what a price! I could buy a slave for as much;" Aristippus answered, "You shall have two slaves then, your son and the slave you buy." And is it not altogether strange that you accustom your son to take his food in his right hand, and chide him if he offers his left, whereas you care very little about his hearing good and sound discourses? I will tell you what happens to such admirable fathers, when they have educated and brought up their sons so badly: when the sons grow to man's estate, they disregard a sober and well-ordered life, and rush headlong into disorderly and low vices; then at the last the parents are sorry they have neglected their education, bemoaning bitterly when it is too late their sons' debasement.

5. I say, then, to speak comprehensively (and I might be justly considered in so saying to speak as an oracle, not to be delivering a mere precept), that a good education

---

[1] Plato, "Clitophon."

and sound bringing-up is of the first and middle and last importance; and I declare it to be most instrumental and conducive to virtue and happiness. For all other human blessings compared to this are petty and insignificant. For noble birth is a great honor, but it is an advantage from our forefathers. And wealth is valuable, but it is the acquisition of Fortune, who has often taken it away from those who had it, and brought it to those who little expected it; and much wealth is a sort of mark for villainous slaves and informers to shoot at to fill their own purses; and what is a most important point, even the greatest villains have money sometimes. And glory is noble, but insecure. And beauty is highly desirable, but shortlived. And health is highly valuable, but soon impaired. And strength is desirable, but illness or age soon makes sad inroads into it. And generally speaking, if any one prides himself on his bodily strength, let him know that he is deficient in judgment. For how much inferior is the strength of a man to that of animals, as elephants, bulls, and lions! But education is of all our advantages the only one immortal and divine. And two of the most powerful agencies in man's nature are mind and reason. And mind governs reason, and reason obeys mind; and mind is irremovable by fortune, cannot be taken away by informers, cannot be destroyed by disease, cannot have inroads made into it by old age. For the mind alone flourishes in age; and while time takes away everything else, it adds wisdom to old age. Even war, that sweeps away everything else like a winter torrent, cannot take away education.

6. And as I advise parents to think nothing more important than the education of their children, so I maintain that it must be a sound and healthy education, and that our sons must be kept as far as possible from vulgar twaddle. For what pleases the vulgar displeases the wise.

I am borne out by the lines of Euripides, "Unskilled am I in the oratory that pleases the mob; but amongst the few that are my equals I am reckoned rather wise. For those who are little thought of by the wise, seem to hit the taste of the vulgar."[1] And I have myself noticed that those who practice to speak acceptably and to the gratification of the masses promiscuously, for the most part become also profligate and lovers of pleasure in their lives. Naturally enough. For if in giving pleasure to others they neglect the noble, they would be hardly likely to put the lofty and sound above a life of luxury and pleasure, and to prefer moderation to delights. Yet what better advice could we give our sons than to follow this? or to what could we better exhort them to accustom themselves? For perfection is only attained by neither speaking nor acting at random — as the proverb says, *Perfection is only attained by practice.* Whereas extempore oratory is easy and facile, mere windbag, having neither beginning nor end. And besides their other shortcomings extempore speakers fall into great disproportion and repetition, whereas a well considered speech preserves its due proportions. It is recorded by tradition that Pericles, when called on by the people for a speech, frequently refused on the plea that he was unprepared. Similarly Demosthenes, his state-rival, when the Athenians called upon him for his advice, refused to give it, saying, "I am not prepared." But this you will say, perhaps, is mere tradition without authority. But in his speech against Midias he plainly sets forth the utility of preparation, for he says, "I do not deny, men of Athens, that I have prepared this speech to the best of my ability: for I should have been a poor creature if, after suffering so much at his hands, and even still suffering, I had neglected how to plead my case." Not that I would altogether reject

[1] "Hippolytus," 986–989.

extempore oratory, or its use in critical cases, but it should be used only as one would take medicine. Up, indeed, to man's estate I would have no extempore speaking, but when anyone's powers of speech are rooted and grounded, then, as emergencies call for it, I would allow his words to flow freely. For as those who have been for a long time in fetters stumble if unloosed, not being able to walk from being long used to their fetters, so those who for a long time have used compression in their words, if they are suddenly called upon to speak off-hand, retain the same character of expression. But to let mere lads speak extempore is to give rise to the acme of foolish talk. A wretched painter once showed Apelles, they say, a picture, and said, "I have just done it." Apelles replied, "Without your telling me, I should know it was painted quickly; I only wonder you haven't painted more such in the time."

As then (for I now return from my digression), I advise to avoid stilted and bombastic language, so again do I urge to avoid a finical and petty style of speech; for tall talk is unpopular, and petty language makes no impression. And as the body ought to be not only sound but in good condition, so speech ought to be not only not feeble but vigorous. For a safe mediocrity is indeed praised, but a bold venturesomeness is also admired. I am also of the same opinion with regard to the disposition of the soul, which ought to be neither audacious nor timid and easily dejected: for the one ends in impudence and the other in servility; but to keep in all things the mean between extremes is artistic and proper. And, while I am still on this topic, I wish to give my opinion, that I regard a monotonous speech first as no small proof of want of taste, next as likely to generate disdain, and certain not to please long. For to harp on one string is always tiresome and brings satiety; whereas variety is pleasant always whether to the ear or eye.

7. Next our freeborn lad ought to go in for a course of what is called general knowledge, but a smattering of this will be sufficient, a taste as it were (for perfect knowledge of all subjects would be impossible); but he must seriously cultivate philosophy. I borrow an illustration to show my meaning: it is well to sail round many cities, but advantageous to live in the best. Philosophy, therefore, ought to be regarded as the most important branch of study. For as regards the cure of the body, men have found two branches, medicine and exercise: the former of which gives health, and the latter good condition of body; but philosophy is the only cure for the maladies and disorders of the soul. For with her as ruler and guide we can know what is honorable, what is disgraceful; what is just, what unjust; generally speaking, what is to be sought after, what to be avoided; how we ought to behave to the gods, to parents, to elders, to the laws, to foreigners, to rulers, to friends, to women, to children, to slaves: viz., that we ought to worship the gods, honor parents, reverence elders, obey the laws, submit ourselves to rulers, love our friends, be chaste in our relations with women, kind to our children, and not to treat our slaves badly; and, what is of the greatest importance, to be neither over elated in prosperity nor over depressed in adversity, nor to be dissolute in pleasures, nor fierce and brutish in anger. These I regard as the principal blessings that philosophy teaches. For to enjoy prosperity nobly shows a man; and to enjoy it without exciting envy shows a moderate man; and to conquer the passions by reason argues a wise man; and it is not everybody who can keep his temper in control. And those who can unite political ability with philosophy I regard as perfect men, for I take them to attain two of the greatest blessings, serving the state in a public capacity, and living the calm and tranquil life of philosophy. For, as there are three kinds

of life, the practical, the contemplative, and the life of enjoyment, and of these three the one devoted to enjoyment is a paltry and animal life, and the practical without philosophy an unlovely and harsh life, and the contemplative without the practical a useless life, so we must endeavor with all our power to combine public life with philosophy as far as circumstances will permit. Such was the life led by Pericles, by Archytas of Tarentum, by Dion of Syracuse, by Epaminondas the Theban, one of whom was a disciple of Plato (viz., Dion).

And as to education, I do not know that I need dwell any more on it. But in addition to what I have said, it is useful, if not necessary, not to neglect to procure old books, and to make a collection of them, as is usual in agriculture. For the use of books is an instrument in education, and it is profitable in learning to go to the fountain head.

8. Exercise also ought not to be neglected, but we ought to send our boys to the master of the gymnasium to train them duly, partly with a view to carrying the body well, partly with a view to strength. For good habit of body in boys is the foundation of a good old age. For as in fine weather we ought to lay up for winter, so in youth one ought to form good habits and live soberly so as to have a reserve stock of strength for old age. Yet ought we to husband the exertions of the body, so as not to be wearied out by them and rendered unfit for study. For, as Plato says, excessive sleep and fatigue are enemies to learning.

But why dwell on this? For I am in a hurry to pass to the most important point. Our lads must be trained for warlike encounters, making themselves efficient in hurling the javelin and darts, and in the chase. For the possessions of those who are defeated in battle belong to the conquerors as booty of war; and war is not the place for delicately brought up bodies: it is the spare warrior that makes the best combatant, who as an athlete cuts his way through the ranks of the enemies. Supposing anyone objects: "How so? As you undertook to give advice on the education of free-born children, do you now neglect the poor and plebeian ones, and give instructions only suitable to the rich?" It is easy enough to meet such critics. I should prefer to make my teaching general and suitable to all; but if any, through their poverty, shall be unable to follow up my precepts, let them blame fortune, and not the author of these hints. We must try with all our might to procure the best education for the poor as well as the rich, but if that is impossible, then we must put up with the practicable. I inserted those matters into my discourse here, that I might hereafter confine myself to all that appertains to the right education of the young.

9. And this I say that we ought to try to draw our boys to good pursuits by entreaties and exhortation, but certainly not by blows or abusive language. For that seems to be more fitting for slaves than the freeborn. For slaves try to shirk and avoid their work, partly because of the pain of blows, partly on account of being reviled. But praise or censure are far more useful than abuse to the freeborn, praise pricking them on to virtue, censure deterring them from vice. But one must censure and praise alternately: when they are too saucy we must censure them and make them ashamed of themselves, and again encourage them by praise, and imitate those nurses who, when their children sob, give them the breast to comfort them. But we must not puff them up and make them conceited with excessive praise, for that will make them vain and give themselves airs.

10. And I have ere now seen some fathers, whose excessive love for their children has turned into hatred. My meaning I will endeavor to make clearer by illustration.

While they are in too great a hurry to make their sons take the lead in everything, they lay too much work upon them, so that they faint under their tasks, and, being overburdened, are disinclined for learning. For just as plants grow with moderate rain, but are done for by too much rain, so the mind enlarges by a proper amount of work, but by too much is unhinged. We must therefore give our boys remission from continuous labor, bearing in mind that all our life is divided into labor and rest; thus we find not only wakefulness but sleep, not only war but peace, not only foul weather but fine also, not only working days but also festivals. And, to speak concisely, rest is the sauce of labor. And we can see this not only in the case of animate, but even inanimate things, for we make bows and lyres slack that we may be able to stretch them. And generally the body is preserved by repletion and evacuation, and the soul by rest and work.

We ought also to censure some fathers who, after entrusting their sons to pedagogues and preceptors, neither see nor hear how the teaching is done. This is a great mistake. For they ought after a few days to test the progress of their sons, and not to base their hopes on the behavior of a hireling; and the preceptors will take all the more pains with the boys, if they have from time to time to give an account of their progress. Hence the propriety of that remark of the groom, that nothing fats the horse so much as the king's eye.

And especial attention, in my opinion, must be paid to cultivating and exercising the memory of boys, for memory is, as it were, the storehouse of learning; and that was why they fabled Mnemosyne to be the mother of the Muses, hinting and insinuating that nothing so generates and contributes to the growth of learning as memory. And therefore the memory must be cultivated, whether boys have a good one by nature, or a bad one. For we shall so add to natural good parts, and make up somewhat for natural deficiencies, so that the deficient will be better than others, and the clever will outstrip themselves. For good is that remark of Hesiod, "If to a little you keep adding a little, and do so frequently, it will soon be a lot." And let not fathers forget, that thus cultivating the memory is not only good for education, but is also a great aid in the business of life. For the remembrance of past actions gives a good model how to deal wisely in future ones.

11. We must also keep our sons from filthy language. For, as Democritus says, language is the shadow of action. They must also be taught to be affable and courteous. For as want of affability is justly hateful, so boys will not be disagreeable to those they associate with, if they yield occasionally in disputes. For it is not only excellent to know how to conquer, but also to know how to be defeated, when victory would be injurious, for there is such a thing as a Cadmean victory. I can cite wise Euripides as a witness of the truth of what I say, who says, "When two are talking, and one of them is in a passion, he is the wiser who first gives way."

I will next state something quite as important, indeed, if anything, even more important. That is, that life must be spent without luxury, the tongue must be under control, so must the temper and the hands. All this is of extreme importance, as I will show by examples. To begin with the last case, some who have put their hands to unjust gains, have lost all the fruits of their former life, as the Lacedæmonian Gylippus, who was exiled from Sparta for embezzling the public money. To be able to govern the temper also argues a wise man. For Socrates, when a very impudent and disgusting young fellow kicked him on one occasion, seeing all the rest of his class vexed and impatient, even to the point of wanting to prosecute the young man, said, "What! If a young ass kicked me would you have me kick it back?" Not that the young fellow committed this outrage on Socrates with impunity, for as all reviled him and nicknamed him the kicker, he hung himself. And when Aristophanes brought his "Clouds" on the stage, and bespattered Socrates with his gibes and flouts, and one of the spectators said, "Aren't you vexed, Socrates, at his exhibiting you on the stage in this comic light?" he answered, "Not I, by Zeus, for I look upon the theater as only a large supper party." Very similar to this was the behavior of Archytas of Tarentum and Plato. The former, on his return from war, where he had been general, finding his land neglected, called his bailiff, and said to him, "You would have caught it, had I not been very angry." And Plato, very angry with a gluttonous and shameless slave, called his sister's son Speusippus, and said, "Go and beat him, for I am too angry."

But some one will say, these examples are difficult and hard to follow. I know it. But we must try, as far as possible, following these examples, to avoid ungovernable and mad rage. For we cannot in other respects equal those distinguished men in their ability and virtue, nevertheless we must, like initiating priests of the gods and torchbearers of wisdom, attempt as far as possible to imitate and nibble at their practice.

Then, again, if any one thinks it a small and unimportant matter to govern the tongue, another point I promised to touch on, he is very far from the reality. For silence at the proper season is wisdom, and better than any speech. And that is, I think, the reason why the ancients instituted the mysteries that we, learning therein to be silent, might transfer our secrecy from the gods to human affairs. And no one ever yet repented of his silence, while multitudes have repented of their speaking. And what has not been said is easy to say, while what has been once said can never be recalled. I have heard of myriads who have fallen into the greatest misfortunes through inability to govern their tongues. . . . Our boys must also be taught to speak the truth as a most sacred duty; for to lie is servile, and most hateful in all men, hardly to be pardoned even in poor slaves.

12. And now, as I have spoken about the good and decent behavior of boys, I shall change my subject and speak a little about youths. For I have often censured the introducers of bad habits, who have set over boys pedagogues and preceptors, but have given to youths full liberty, when they ought, on the contrary, to have watched and guarded them more than boys. For who does not know that the offenses of boys are petty and easily cured, and proceed from the carelessness of tutors or want of obedience to preceptors; but the faults of young men are often grave and serious, as gluttony, and robbing their fathers, and dice, and revelings, and drinking-bouts, and licentiousness. Such outbreaks ought to be carefully checked and curbed. For that prime of life is prodigal in pleasure, and frisky, and needs a bridle, so that those parents who do not strongly check that period, are foolishly, if unawares, giving their youths license for vice. Sensible parents, therefore, ought during all that period to guard and watch and restrain their youths, by precepts, by threats, by entreaties, by advice, by promises, by citing examples, on the one hand of those who have come to ruin by being too fond of pleasure, on the other hand, of those who by their self-control have attained to praise and good report. For these are, as it were, the two elements of virtue, hope of honor, and fear of punishment; the former inciting to good practices, the latter deterring from bad.

13. We ought, at all hazards, to keep our boys also

from association with bad men, for they will catch some of their villainy. This was the meaning of Pythagoras' enigmatical precepts, which I shall quote and explain, as they give no slight momentum towards the acquisition of virtue: as, *Do not touch black tails:* that is, do not associate with bad men. *Do not go beyond the balance:* that is, we must pay the greatest attention to justice and not go beyond it. *Do not sit on a measure:* that is, do not be lazy, but earn to-morrow's bread as well as to-day's. *Do not give every one your right hand:* that is, do not be too ready to strike up a friendship. *Do not wear a tight ring:* that is, let your life be free, do not bind yourself by a chain. *Do not poke the fire with a sword:* that is, do not provoke an angry person, but yield to such. *Do not eat the heart:* do not wear away the heart by anxiety. *Abstain from beans:* that is, do not meddle in state affairs, for the voting for offices was formerly taken by beans. *Do not put your food in the mire:* that is, do not throw your pearls before swine, for words are the food of the mind, and the villainy of men twist them to a corrupt meaning. *When you have come to the end of a journey do not look back:* that is, when people are going to die and see that their end is near, they ought to take it easily and not be dejected. But I will return from my digression. We must keep our boys, as I said, from association with all bad men, but especially from flatterers. For, as I have often said to parents, and still say, and will constantly affirm, there is no race more pestilential, nor more sure to ruin youths swiftly, than the race of flatterers, who destroy both parents and sons root and branch, making the old age of the one and the youth of the other miserable, holding out pleasure as a sure bait. The sons of the rich are by their fathers urged to be sober, but by them to be drunk; by their fathers to be chaste, by them to wax wanton; by their fathers to save, by them to spend; by their fathers to be industrious, by them to be lazy. For they say, "'Our life's but a span'; we can only live once; why should you heed your father's threats? he's an old twaddler, he has one foot in the grave; we shall soon hoist him up and carry him off to burial."

14. What I have said hitherto is *apropos* to my subject: I will now speak a word to the men. Parents must not be over harsh and rough in their natures, but must often forgive their sons' offenses, remembering that they themselves were once young. And just as doctors by infusing a sweet flavor into their bitter potions find delight a passage to benefit, so fathers must temper the severity of their censure by mildness; and sometimes relax and slacken the reins of their sons' desires, and again tighten them; and must be especially easy in respect to their faults, or if they are angry must soon cool down. For it is better for a father to be hot-tempered than sullen, for to continue hostile and irreconcilable looks like hating one's son. And it is good to seem not to notice some faults, but to extend to them the weak sight and deafness of old age, so as seeing not to see, and hearing not to hear, their doings. We tolerate the faults of our friends; why should we not that of our sons? Often even our slaves' drunken debauches we do not expose. Have you been rather near? Spend more freely. Have you been vexed? Let the matter pass. Has your son deceived you by the help of a slave? Do not be angry. Did he take a yoke of oxen from the field, did he come home smelling of yesterday's debauch? Wink at it. Is he scented like a perfume shop? Say nothing. Thus frisky youth gets broken in.

15. Those of our sons who are given to pleasure and pay little heed to rebuke, we must endeavor to marry, for marriage is the surest restraint upon youth. And we must marry our sons to wives not much richer or better born, for

the proverb is a sound one, "Marry in your own walk of life." For those who marry wives superior to themselves in rank are not so much the husbands of their wives as unawares slaves to their dowries.

16. I shall add a few remarks, and then bring my subject to a close. Before all things fathers must, by a good behavior, set a good example to their sons, that, looking at their lives as a mirror, they may turn away from bad deeds and words. For those fathers who censure their sons' faults while they themselves commit the same, are really their own accusers, if they know it not, under their sons' name; and those who live a depraved life have no right to censure their slaves, far less their sons. And besides this they will become counselors and teachers of their sons in wrongdoing; for where old men are shameless, youths will of a certainty have no modesty. We must therefore take all pains to teach our sons self-control, emulating the conduct of Eurydice, who, though an Illyrian and more than a barbarian, to teach her sons educated herself though late in life, and her love to them is well depicted in the inscription which she offered to the Muses: "Eurydice of Hierapolis made this offering to the Muses, having conceived a vast love for knowledge. For when a mother with sons full-grown she learnt letters, the preservers of knowledge."

To carry out all these precepts would be perhaps a visionary scheme; but to attain to many, though it would need a happy disposition and much care, is a thing possible to human nature.

VIII. JEROME.

BIOGRAPHICAL SKETCH.

Jerome, who was born at Stridon on the border-line between Dalmatia and Pannonia about 340 A. D., is regarded as the most learned of the Latin Fathers. After receiving an elementary education under his father, who was a Christian, he studied rhetoric and philosophy at Rome, where in 360 he was also admitted to the Church by baptism. A few years later a serious illness at Antioch deepened his religious fervor and he withdrew into the desert to lead a life of asceticism. After four years of ascetic life he returned to Antioch, where in 379 he was ordained a presbyter. He afterwards studied under Gregory Nazianzen at Constantinople, and later sojourned in Rome till the year 385. Here he worked on his famous translation of the Bible, now known as the Vulgate, and at the same time attained to great popularity by his sanctity and eloquence. He gathered a company of Christian women about him for religious instruction, among whom were the lady Paula and her daughter Eustochium. He was accompanied by them on a pilgrimage to the Holy Land and when Paula had founded several convents at Bethlehem for nuns and monks, he fixed his permanent residence there. It was in monastic retirement in the town of the nativity that Jerome completed the great literary labors of his life, and wrote the important letters and controversial treatises that compose so large a part of his published works.

The following extract is his famous letter to Laeta about

the education of her little daughter Paula. It was written in 403, and, as would naturally be expected, is pervaded by the ascetic spirit of the author and of the age in which he lived. Doubting whether the details of the child's training, as he had proposed them, could be carried out in Rome, he advises Laeta, in case of difficulty, to send Paula to the convent at Bethlehem, where she would be under the care of her grandmother, the elder Paula, and of her aunt Eustochium. Acting upon Jerome's advice Laeta subsequently sent her daughter to Bethlehem, where she eventually succeeded Eustochium as head of the nunnery founded by her grandmother.

JEROME'S LETTER TO LAETA.

Thus must a soul be educated which is to be a temple of God. It must learn to hear nothing and to say nothing but what belongs to the fear of God. It must have no understanding of unclean words, and no knowledge of the world's songs. Its tongue must be steeped while still tender in the sweetness of the Psalms. Boys with their wanton thoughts must be kept from Paula: even her maids and female attendants must be separated from worldly associates. For if they have learned some mischief they may teach more.

Get for her a set of letters made of boxwood or of ivory and called each by its proper name. Let her play with these, so that even her play may teach her something. And not only make her grasp the right order of the letters and see that she forms their names into a rhyme, but constantly disarrange their order and put the last letters in the middle and the middle ones at the beginning that she may know them all by sight as well as by sound.

Moreover, so soon as she begins to use the style upon the

wax, and her hand is still faltering, either guide her soft fingers by laying your hand upon hers, or else have simple copies cut upon a tablet; so that her efforts confined within these limits may keep to the lines traced out for her and not stray outside of these. Offer prizes for good spelling and draw her onwards with little gifts such as children of her age delight in.

And let her have companions in her lessons to excite emulation in her, that she may be stimulated when she sees them praised. You must not scold her if she is slow to learn but must employ praise to excite her mind, so that she may be glad when she excels others and sorry when she is excelled by them. Above all you must take care not to make her lessons distasteful to her, lest a dislike for them conceived in childhood may continue into her maturer years. The very words which she tries bit by bit to put together and to pronounce ought not to be chance ones, but names specially fixed upon and heaped together for the purpose, those for example of the prophets or the apostles or the list of patriarchs from Adam downwards, as it is given by Matthew and Luke. In this way while her tongue will be well trained, her memory will be likewise developed.

Again, you must choose for her a master of approved years, life, and learning. A man of culture will not, I think, blush to do for a kinswoman or a high-born virgin what Aristotle did for Philip's son when, descending to the level of an usher, he consented to teach him his letters. Things must not be despised as of small account in the absence of which great results can not be achieved. The very rudiments and first beginnings of knowledge sound differently in the mouth of an educated man and of an uneducated. Accordingly you must see that the child is not led away by the silly coaxing of women to form a habit of shortening long words or of decking herself with gold and purple. Of these habits one will spoil her conversation and the other her character. She must not therefore learn as a child what afterwards she will have to unlearn.

The eloquence of the Gracchi is said to have been largely due to the way in which from their earliest years their mother spoke to them. Hortensius became an orator while still on his father's lap. Early impressions are hard to eradicate from the mind. When once wool has been dyed purple, who can restore it to its previous whiteness? An unused jar long retains the taste and smell of that with which it is first filled. Grecian history tells us that the imperious Alexander, who was lord of the whole world, could not rid himself of the tricks of manner and gait which in his childhood he had caught from his governor Leonidas. We are always ready to imitate what is evil; and faults are quickly copied where virtues appear inattainable. Paula's nurse must not be intemperate, or loose, or given to gossip. Her bearer must be respectable, and her foster-father of grave demeanor.

* * * * *

Let her very dress and garb remind her to Whom she is promised. Do not pierce her ears or paint her face, consecrated to Christ, with white lead or rouge. Do not hang gold or pearls about her neck or load her head with jewels, or by reddening her hair make it suggest the fires of Gehenna.

* * * * *

When Paula comes to be a little older and to increase like her Spouse in wisdom and stature and in favor with God and man, let her go with her parents to the temple of her true Father but let her not come out of the temple with them. Let them seek her upon the world's highway amid the crowds and the throng of their kinsfolk, and let them find her nowhere but in the shrine of the Scriptures, questioning the prophets and the apostles on the meaning of that spiritual marriage to which she is vowed. Let her imitate the retirement of Mary whom Gabriel found alone in her chamber.

*   *   *   *   *

And let it be her daily task to bring you the flowers which she has culled from Scripture. Let her learn by heart so many verses in the Greek, but let her be instructed in the Latin also. For, if the tender lips are not from the first shaped to this, the tongue is spoiled by a foreign accent and its native speech debased by alien elements. You must yourself be her mistress, a model on which she may form her childish conduct. Never either in you or in her father let her see what she can not imitate without sin. Remember both of you that you are the parents of a consecrated virgin, and that your example will teach her more than your precepts.

Flowers are quick to fade, and a baleful wind soon withers the violet, the lily, and the crocus. Let her never appear in public unless accompanied by you. Let her never visit a church or martyr's shrine unless with her mother. Let no young man greet her with smiles, no dandy with curled hair pay compliments to her. If our little virgin goes to keep solemn eves and all-night vigils, let her not stir a hair's breadth from her mother's side.

She must not single out one of her maids to make her a special favorite or a confidante. What she says to one all ought to know. Let her choose for a companion not a handsome well-dressed girl, able to warble a song with liquid notes, but one pale and serious, sombrely attired and with the hue of melancholy. Let her take as her model some aged virgin of approved faith, character, and chastity, apt to instruct her by word and by example.

She ought to rise at night to recite prayers and psalms;

to sing hymns in the morning; at the third, sixth, and ninth hours to take her place in the line to do battle for Christ; and, lastly, to kindle her lamp and to offer her evening sacrifice. In these occupations let her pass the day, and when night comes let it find her still engaged in them. Let reading follow prayer with her, and prayer again succeed to reading. Time will seem short when employed on tasks so many and so varied.

Let her learn, too, how to spin wool, to hold the distaff, to put the basket in her lap, to turn the spinning wheel and to shape the yarn with her thumb. Let her put away with disdain silken fabrics, Chinese fleeces, and gold brocades; the clothing which she makes for herself should keep out the cold and not expose the body which it professes to cover. Let her food be herbs and wheaten bread, with now and then one or two small fishes. And that I may not waste more time in giving precepts for the regulation of appetite, let her meals always leave her hungry and able on the moment to begin reading or chanting. I strongly disapprove — especially for those of tender years — of long and immoderate fasts in which week is added to week, and even oil and apples are forbidden as food. I have learned by experience that the ass toiling along the highway makes for an inn when it is weary.

* * * * *

Let her treasures be not silks or gems, but manuscripts of the Holy Scriptures; and in these let her think less of gilding, and Babylonian parchment, and arabesque patterns, than of correctness and accurate punctuation. Let her begin by learning the Psalter, and then let her gather rules of life out of the proverbs of Solomon. From the Preacher let her gain the habit of despising the world and its vanities. Let her follow the example set in Job of virtue and patience. Then let her pass on to the Gospels, never to be laid aside when once they have been taken in hand. Let her also drink in with a willing heart the Acts of the Apostles and the Epistles. As soon as she has enriched the storehouse of her mind with these treasures, let her commit to memory the prophets, the heptateuch, the books of Kings and of Chronicles, the rolls also of Ezra and Esther. When she has done all these she may safely read the Song of Songs, but not before: for, were she to read it at the beginning, she would fail to perceive that, though it is written in fleshly words, it is a marriage song of a spiritual bridal. And not understanding this she would suffer hurt from it. Cyprian's writings let her have always in her hands. The letters of Athanasius and the treatises of Hilary she may go through without fear of stumbling. Let her take pleasure in the works and wits of all in whose books a due regard for the faith is not neglected. But if she reads the works of others, let it be rather to judge them than to follow them.

You will answer, "How shall I, a woman of the world, living at Rome, surrounded by a crowd, be able to observe all these injunctions?" In that case do not undertake a burthen to which you are not equal. When you have weaned Paula as Isaac was weaned, and when you have clothed her as Samuel was clothed, send her to her grandmother and aunt; give up this most precious of gems, to be placed in Mary's chamber and to rest in the cradle where the infant Jesus cried. Let her be brought up in a monastery, let her be one amid companies of virgins, let her learn to avoid swearing, let her regard lying as sacrilege, let her be ignorant of the world, let her live the angelic life, while in the flesh let her be without the flesh, and let her suppose that all human beings are like herself.

IX. APOSTOLICAL CONSTITUTIONS.

HISTORICAL SKETCH.

The Apostolical Constitutions, consisting of eight books, is a very ancient compilation, which was designed as a manual of instruction in Christian conduct, worship, and usage for both clergy and laity. Its name is due to the old belief or assumption that it originated with the Apostles. Not all parts of the Constitutions are of the same age. It is generally agreed that the entire compilation is to be dated not later than the fourth century. It is, therefore, a document of great value in giving us an understanding of the spirit, organization, and usages of the Church in the age of Constantine. The Constitutions treat of education in three passages, which present the attitude of the Church to pagan literature, to the training of children, and to the instruction of catechumens. These passages, which are given in full, are taken from the Anti-Nicene Fathers.

SELECTIONS FROM THE "APOSTOLICAL CONSTITUTIONS."

I. WHAT BOOKS OF SCRIPTURE WE OUGHT TO READ.

V. Or if thou stayest at home, read the books of the Law, of the Kings, with the Prophets, sing the hymns of David; and peruse diligently the Gospel, which is the completion of the other.

That we ought to abstain from all the books of those that are out of the church.

VI. Abstain from all the heathen books. For what hast thou to do with such foreign discourses, or laws, or false prophets, which subvert the faith of the unstable? For what defect dost thou find in the law of God, that thou shouldst have recourse to those heathenish fables? For if thou hast a mind to read history, thou hast the books of the Kings; if books of wisdom or poetry, thou hast those of the Prophets, of Job, and the Proverbs, in which thou wilt find greater depth of sagacity than in all the heathen poets and sophisters, because these are the words of the Lord, the only wise God. If thou desirest something to sing, thou hast the Psalms; if the origin of things, thou hast Genesis; if laws and statutes, thou hast the glorious law of the Lord God. Do thou, therefore, utterly abstain from all strange and diabolical books. Nay, when thou readest the law, think not thyself bound to observe the additional precepts; though not all of them, yet some of them. Read those barely for the sake of history, in order to the knowledge of them, and to glorify God that he has delivered thee from such great and so many bonds. Propose to thyself to distinguish what rules were from the law of nature, and what were added afterwards, or were such additional rules as were introduced and given in the wilderness to the Israelites, after the making of the calf; for the law contains those precepts which were spoken by the Lord God before the people fell into idolatry, and made a calf like the Egyptian Apis — that is, the ten commandments. But as to those bonds which were further laid upon them after they had sinned, do not thou draw them upon thyself; for our Savior came for no other reason but that he might deliver those that were obnoxious thereto from the wrath which was reserved for them, that he might fulfil the Law and the Prophets, and that he might abrogate or change those secondary bonds which were superadded to the rest of the law. For therefore did he call to us, and say, " Come unto me, all ye that labor and are heavy laden, and I will give you rest." When, therefore, thou hast read the Law, which is agreeable to the Gospel and to the Prophets, read also the books of the Kings, that thou mayest thereby learn which of the kings were righteous, and how they were prospered by God, and how the promise of eternal life continued with them from Him; but those kings which went a-whoring from God did soon perish in their apostasy by the righteous judgment of God, and were deprived of his life, inheriting, instead of rest, eternal punishment. Wherefore by reading these books thou wilt be mightily strengthened in the faith, and edified in Christ, whose body and member thou art.

2. OF PARENTS AND CHILDREN.

Ye fathers, educate your children in the Lord, bringing them up in the nurture and admonition of the Lord; and teach them such trades as are agreeable and suitable to the Word, lest they by such opportunity become extravagant, and continue without punishment from their parents, and so get relaxation before their time, and go astray from that which is good. Wherefore be not afraid to reprove them, and to teach them wisdom with severity. For your corrections will not kill them, but rather preserve them. As Solomon says somewhere in the book of Wisdom: " Chasten thy son, and he will refresh thee; so wilt thou have good hope of him. Thou verily shall smite him with the rod, and shalt deliver his soul from death." And again, says the same Solomon thus, " He that spareth his rod, hateth his son"; and afterwards, "Beat his sides whilst he is an infant, lest he be hardened and disobey thee." He, therefore, that neglects to admonish and instruct his own son, hates his own child. Do you therefore teach your children the word of the Lord. Bring them under with cutting stripes, and make them subject from their infancy, teaching them the Holy Scriptures, which are Christian and divine, and delivering to them every sacred writing, "not giving them such liberty that they get the mastery," and act against your opinion, not permitting them to club together for a treat with their equals. For so they will be turned to disorderly courses, and will fall into fornication; and if this happens by the carelessness of their parents, those that begat them will be guilty of their souls. For if the offending children get into the company of debauched persons by the negligence of those that begat them, they will not be punished alone by themselves; but their parents also be condemned on their account. For this cause endeavor, at the time when they are of an age fit for marriage, to join them in wedlock, and settle them together, lest in the heat and fervor of their age their course of life become dissolute, and you be required to give an account by the Lord God in the day of judgment.

3. HOW THE CATECHUMENS ARE TO BE INSTRUCTED.

Let him, therefore, who is to be taught the truth in regard to piety be instructed before his baptism in the knowledge of the unbegotten God, in the understanding of his only begotten Son, in the assured acknowledgment of the Holy Ghost. Let him learn the order of the several parts of the creation, the series of providence, the different dispensations of thy laws. Let him be instructed how the world was made, and why man was appointed to be a citizen therein; let him also know his own nature, of what sort it is;

let him be taught how God punished the wicked with water and fire, and did glorify the saints in every generation — I mean Seth, and Enos, and Enoch, and Noah, and Abraham and his posterity, and Melchizedek, and Job, and Moses, and Joshua, and Caleb, and Phineas the priest, and those that were holy in every generation; and how God still took care of and did not reject mankind, but called them from their error and vanity to the acknowledgment of the truth at various seasons, reducing them from bondage and impiety unto liberty and piety, from injustice to righteousness, from death eternal to everlasting life. Let him that offers himself to baptism learn these and the like things during the time that he is a catechumen; and let him who lays his hands upon him adore God, the Lord of the whole world, and thank him for his creation, for his sending Christ his only begotten Son, that he might save man by blotting out his transgressions, and that he might remit ungodliness and sins, and might "purify him from all filthiness of flesh and spirit," and sanctify man according to the good pleasure of his kindness, that he might inspire him with the knowledge of his will, and enlighten the eyes of his heart to consider of his wonderful works, and make known to him the judgments of righteousness, that so he might hate every way of iniquity, and walk in the way of truth, that he might be thought worthy of the laver of regeneration, to the adoption of sons, which is in Christ, that " being planted together in the likeness of the death of Christ," in hopes of a glorious communication, he may be mortified to sin, and may live to God, as to his mind, and word, and deed, and may be numbered together in the book of the living. And after this thanksgiving, let him instruct him in the doctrines concerning our Lord's incarnation, and in those concerning his passion, and resurrection from the dead, and assumption.

X. CHARLEMAGNE.

BIOGRAPHICAL SKETCH.

Charlemagne was king of the Franks from 768 to 814 A. D. On Christmas day, 800, he was crowned by the pope as emperor of the Romans. In spite of his almost incessant wars and his brilliant career as a conqueror, he earnestly sought to promote the material and spiritual welfare of his people. He exhibited a great thirst for knowledge, and was himself a model of diligence in study. He assiduously cultivated his mind by intercourse with learned men; and, to the time of his death, scholarly discussions remained his favorite means of recreation. In addition to his native German he spoke several other languages readily, especially the Latin. He invited to his court from all parts of Europe the most distinguished scholars, of whom Alcuin, of England, is best known. He established a model school at court, and sometimes visited it in person to note the progress of the pupils.

He sought to multiply the educational facilities of his great empire, and even went so far as to contemplate the organization of a popular school system. He endeavored to enlist the interest of the clergy and monks in education, as they were at the time the chief representatives of learning. The monasteries and bishops were urged to improve the schools already existing, and to establish new ones wherever needed. It was to this end that he issued in 787 the following capitulary addressed to the abbot Bangulfus. The translation is that of Mullinger in his "Schools of Charles the Great," and is evidently more literal than elegant.

SELECTION FROM CHARLEMAGNE'S "CAPITULARY OF 787."

Charles, by the grace of God, King of the Franks and of the Lombards, and Patrician of the Romans, to Bangulfus, abbot, and to his whole congregation and the faithful committed to his charge:

Be it known to your devotion, pleasing to God, that in conjunction with our faithful we have judged it to be of utility that, in the bishoprics and monasteries committed by Christ's favor to our charge, care should be taken that there shall be not only a regular manner of life and one conformable to holy religion, but also the study of letters, each to teach and learn them according to his ability and the divine assistance. For even as due observance of the rule of the house tends to good morals, so zeal on the part of the teacher and the taught imparts order and grace to sentences; and those who seek to please God by living aright should also not neglect to please him by right speaking. It is written, "By thine own words shalt thou be justified or condemned"; and although right doing be preferable to right speaking, yet must the knowledge of what is right precede right action. Every one, therefore, should strive to understand what it is he would fain accomplish; and this right understanding will be the sooner gained according as the utterances of the tongue are free from error. And if false speaking is to be shunned by all men, especially should it be shunned by those who have elected to be the servants of the truth.

During past years we have often received letters from different monasteries, informing us that at their sacred services the brethren offered up prayers on our behalf; and we have observed that the thoughts contained in these letters, though in themselves most just, were expressed in uncouth language, and while pious devotion dictated the sentiments, the unlettered tongue was unable to express them aright. Hence there has arisen in our minds the fear lest, if the skill to write rightly were thus lacking, so too would the power of rightly comprehending the sacred Scriptures be far less than was fitting; and we all know that though verbal errors be dangerous, errors of the understanding are yet more so. We exhort you, therefore, not only not to neglect the study of letters, but to apply yourselves thereto with perseverance and with that humility which is well pleasing to God; so that you may be able to penetrate with greater ease and certainty the mysteries of the Holy Scriptures. For as these contain images, tropes, and similar figures, it is impossible to doubt that the reader will arrive far more readily at the spiritual sense according as he is the better instructed in learning. Let there, therefore, be chosen for this work men who are both able and willing to learn, and also desirous of instructing others; and let them apply themselves to the work with a zeal equaling the earnestness with which we recommend it to them. It is our wish that you may be what it behooves the soldiers of the Church to be — religious in heart, learned in discourse, pure in act, eloquent in speech; so that all who approach your house, in order to invoke the Divine Master or to behold the excellence of the religious life, may be edified in beholding you, and instructed in hearing you discourse or chant, and may return home rendering thanks to God most high.

Fail not, as thou regardest our favor, to send a copy of this letter to all thy suffragans and to all the monasteries; and let no monk go beyond his monastery to administer justice, or to enter the assemblies and the voting-places. Adieu.

XI. RHABANUS MAURUS.

BIOGRAPHICAL SKETCH.

Rhabanus Maurus, a contemporary with Charlemagne, was born at Mainz about 766 A. D. He sprang from an honorable family. After receiving from his mother — a model of Christian womanhood — a careful training in the elements of learning, he was sent to the monastery of Fulda, where he laid a broad foundation for his subsequent scholarship. In his early manhood he became for a time a pupil of Alcuin's, and won the lasting confidence and affection of his distinguished master.

After leaving Alcuin, Rhabanus became head of the monastic school of Fulda, to which he brought additional efficiency and distinction.

From far and near this school attracted numerous pupils who were preparing themselves either for ecclesiastical service or for secular pursuits. The subjects of study embraced not only the seven liberal arts, but also physics, philosophy, and theology. Rhabanus exhibited great zeal in the work of education, and was the first to win the proud distinction of *Preceptor Germaniæ*.

In 847, after having served as abbot of Fulda for some years, he was promoted to the dignity of Archbishop of Mainz. In this new position he displayed great energy in the betterment of the religious and educational conditions of his see. He was a prolific author, and more than thirty volumes bear his name on their title pages. He was acquainted with Greek as well as with Roman literature, and he drew in some measure on the treasures of both to enrich his various treatises.

Among his numerous writings there are several that treat more or less fully of education; namely, "Education of the Clergy," "The Reckoning of Time," "On the Soul," "Book of the World," and "The Study of Wisdom and of the Divine Law" — the last being in the form of a sermon. All these treatises, which are found in the *Sammlung der bedentendsten 'pädagogischen Schriften* edited by Schultz, Gansen, and Keller, give us a clear insight into the educational theory and practice of the ninth century of our era.

The following selection is translated from the "Education of the Clergy" (*Unterweisung der Geistlichen*), and is notable for two reasons: (1) It shows us the subordination of education to ecclesiastical ends; and (2) it presents the fullest discussion of the seven liberal arts that has come to us from that period.

SELECTION FROM RHABANUS MAURUS.

EDUCATION OF THE CLERGY.

1. An ecclesiastical education should qualify the sacred office of the ministry for divine service. It is fitting that those who from an exalted station undertake the direction of the life of the Church, should acquire fulness of knowledge, and that they further should strive after rectitude of life and perfection of development. They should not be allowed to remain in ignorance about anything that appears beneficial for their own information or for the instruction of those entrusted to their care. Therefore they should endeavor to grasp and include in their knowledge the following things: An acquaintance with Holy Scripture, the unadulterated truth of history, the derivative modes of speech,

the mystical sense of words, the advantages growing out of the separate branches of knowledge, the integrity of life that manifests itself in good morals, delicacy and good taste in oral discourse, penetration in the explanation of doctrine, the different kinds of medicine, and the various forms of disease. Any one to whom all this remains unknown, is not able to care for his own welfare, let alone that of others.

2. The foundation, the content, and the perfection of all wisdom is Holy Scripture, which has taken its origin from that unchangeable and eternal Wisdom, which streams from the mouth of the Most High, which was begotten before every other creature through the Holy Spirit, which is a light incessantly beaming from the words of Holy Scripture. And when anything else deserves the name of wisdom, it goes back in its origin to this one source of the wisdom of the Church. Every truth, which is discovered by any one, is recognized as true by the truth itself through the mediation of the truth; every good thing, which is in any way traced out, is recognized and determined as good by the good itself; all wisdom, which is brought to light by any one, is found to be wisdom by wisdom itself. And all that is found of truth and wisdom in the books of the philosophers of this world, dare be ascribed to nothing else than just to truth and wisdom; for it was not originally invented by those among whose utterances it is found; it has much rather been recognized as something present from eternity, so far as wisdom and truth, which bring illumination to all with their instruction, have granted the possibility of such recognition.

3. Now the Holy Scriptures, which come to the aid of the weakness of the human will, have, in dependence upon the one perfect language in which under favorable circumstances they might have spread over the whole globe, been

widely circulated in the different languages of the translators, in order that they might be known to the nations unto salvation. Those who read them strive for nothing else than to grasp the thought and meaning of those who wrote them, in order thereby to fathom the will of God, at whose bidding and under whose direction, as we believe, they were written. But those who read superficially allow themselves to be deceived through the manifold recurring passages, the sense of which is obscure, and the meaning of which is doubtful; they assign to what is read a meaning that does not belong to it; they seek errors where no errors are to be found; they surround themselves with an obscurity, in which they can not find the right path. I have no doubt that this has been so ordered by God's providence that the pride of man may be restrained through spiritual labor; in order that the knowledge of man may be divorced from pride, to which it easily falls a prey, and then loses its value entirely.

4. Above all it is necessary that he, who aims to attain the summit of wisdom, should be converted to the fear of the Lord, in order to know what the divine will bids us strive for and shun. The fear of the Lord fills us with the thought of our mortality and future death. With mortification of the flesh it nails, as it were, the movements of pride to the martyr cross of Christ. Then it is enjoined to be lowly in piety. Therefore we are not to raise any objection to the Holy Scriptures, either when we understand them and feel ourselves smitten by their words, or when we do not understand them, and give ourselves up to the thought that we can understand and grasp something better out of our own minds. We should remember that it is better and more comfortable to truth, to believe what is written, even if the sense remains concealed from us, than to hold that for true which we are able to recognize by our own strength.

5. The first of the liberal arts is grammar, the second rhetoric, the third dialectic, the fourth arithmetic, the fifth geometry, the sixth music, the seventh astronomy.

Grammar takes its name from the written character, as the derivation of the word indicates. The definition of grammar is this: Grammar is the science which teaches us to explain the poets and historians; it is the art which qualifies us to write and speak correctly. Grammar is the source and foundation of the liberal arts. It should be taught in every Christian school, since the art of writing and speaking correctly is attained through it. How could one understand the sense of the spoken word or the meaning of letters and syllables, if one had not learned this before from grammar? How could one know about metrical feet, accent, and verses, if grammar had not given one knowledge of them? How should one learn to know the articulation of discourse, the advantages of figurative language, the laws of word formation, and the correct forms of words, if one had not familiarized himself with the art of grammar?

All the forms of speech, of which secular science makes use in its writings, are found repeatedly employed in the Holy Scriptures. Every one, who reads the sacred Scriptures with care, will discover that our (biblical) authors have used derivative forms of speech in greater and more manifold abundance than would have been supposed and believed. There are in the Scriptures not only examples of all kinds of figurative expressions, but the designations of some of them by name; as, allegory, riddle, parable. A knowledge of these things is proved to be necessary in relation to the interpretation of those passages of Holy Scripture which admit of a twofold sense; an interpretation strictly literal would lead to absurdities. Everywhere we are to consider whether that, which we do not at once understand, is to be apprehended as a figurative expression in some sense. A knowledge of prosody, which is offered in grammar, is not dishonorable, since among the Jews, as St. Jerome testifies, the Psalter resounds sometimes with iambics, sometimes with Alcaics, sometimes chooses sonorous Sapphics, and sometimes even does not disdain catalectic feet. But in Deuteronomy and Isaiah, as in Solomon and Job, as Josephus and Origen have pointed out, there are hexameters and pentameters. Hence this art, though it may be secular, has nothing unworthy in itself; it should rather be learned as thoroughly as possible.

6. According to the statements of teachers, rhetoric is the art of using secular discourse effectively in the circumstances of daily life. From this definition rhetoric seems indeed to have reference merely to secular wisdom. Yet it is not foreign to ecclesiastical instruction. Whatever the preacher and herald of the divine law, in his instruction, brings forward in an eloquent and becoming manner; whatever in his written exposition he knows how to clothe in adequate and impressive language, he owes to his acquaintance with this art. Whoever at the proper time makes himself familiar with this art, and faithfully follows its rules in speaking and writing, needs not count it as something blameworthy. On the contrary, whoever thoroughly learns it so that he acquires the ability to proclaim God's word, performs a good work. Through rhetoric anything is proved true or false. Who would have the courage to maintain that the defenders of truth should stand weaponless in the presence of falsehood, so that those, who dare to represent the false, should know how by their discourse to win the favor and sympathy of the hearers, and that, on the other hand, the friends of truth should not be able to do this; that those should know how to present falsehood briefly, clearly, and with the semblance of truth, and that the latter, on the contrary, should clothe the truth in such

an exposition, that listening would become a burden, apprehension of the truth a weariness, and faith in the truth an impossibility?

7. Dialectic is the science of the understanding, which fits us for investigations and definitions, for explanations, and for distinguishing the true from the false. It is the science of sciences. It teaches how to teach others; it teaches learning itself; in it the reason marks and manifests itself according to its nature, efforts, and activities; it alone is capable of knowing; it not only will, but can lead others to knowledge; its conclusions lead us to an apprehension of our being and of our origin; through it we apprehend the origin and activity of the good, of Creator and creature; it teaches us to discover the truth and to unmask falsehood; it teaches us to draw conclusions; it shows us what is valid in argument and what is not; it teaches us to recognize what is contrary to the nature of things; it teaches us to distinguish in controversy the true, the probable, and the wholly false; by means of this science we are able to investigate everything with penetration, to determine its nature with certainty, and to discuss it with circumspection.

Therefore the clergy must understand this excellent art and constantly reflect upon its laws, in order that they may be able keenly to pierce the craftiness of errorists, and to refute their fatal fallacies.

8. Arithmetic is the science of pure extension determinable by number; it is the science of numbers. Writers on secular science assign it, under the head of mathematics, to the first place, because it does not presuppose any of the other departments. Music, geometry, and astronomy, on the contrary, need the help of arithmetic; without it they cannot arise or exist. We should know, however, that the learned Hebrew Josephus, in his work on Antiquities, Chapter VIII. of Book I., makes the statement that Abra-

ham brought arithmetic and astronomy to the Egyptians; but that they as a people of penetrating mind, extensively developed from these germs the other sciences. The holy Fathers were right in advising those eager for knowledge to cultivate arithmetic, because in large measure it turns the mind from fleshly desires, and furthermore awakens the wish to comprehend what with God's help we can merely receive with the heart. Therefore the significance of number is not to be underestimated. Its very great value for an interpretation of many passages of Holy Scripture is manifest to all who exhibit zeal in their investigations. Not without good reason is it said in praise of God, "Thou hast ordained all things by measure, number, and weight." (Book of Wisdom XI. 21.)

But every number, through its peculiar qualities, is so definite that none of the others can be like it. They are all unequal and different. The single numbers are different; the single numbers are limited; but all are infinite.

Those with whom Plato stands in especial honor will not make bold to esteem numbers lightly, as if they were of no consequence for the knowledge of God. He teaches that God made the world out of numbers. And among us the prophet says of God, "He forms the world by number." And in the Gospel the Savior says, "The very hairs of your head are all numbered." . . . Ignorance of numbers leaves many things unintelligible that are expressed in the Holy Scripture in a derivative sense or with a mystical meaning.

9. We now come to the discussion of geometry. It is an exposition of form proceeding from observation; it is also a very common means of demonstration among philosophers, who, to adduce at once the most full-toned evidence, declare that their Jupiter made use of geometry in his works. I do not know indeed whether I should find

praise or censure in this declaration of the philosophers, that Jupiter engraved upon the vault of the skies precisely what they themselves draw in the sand of the earth.

When this in a proper manner is transferred to God, the Almighty Creator, this assumption may perhaps come near the truth. If this statement seems admissible, the Holy Trinity makes use of geometry in so far as it bestows manifold forms and images upon the creatures which up to the present day it has called into being, as in its adorable omnipotence it further determines the course of the stars, as it prescribes their course to the planets, and as it assigns to the fixed stars their unalterable position. For every excellent and well-ordered arrangement can be reduced to the special requirements of this science. . . .

This science found realization also at the building of the tabernacle and temple; the same measuring rod, circles, spheres, hemispheres, quadrangles, and other figures were employed. The knowledge of all this brings to him, who is occupied with it, no small gain for his spiritual culture.

10. Music is the science of time intervals as they are perceived in tones. This science is as eminent as it is useful. He who is a stranger to it is not able to fulfil the duties of an ecclesiastical office in a suitable manner. A proper delivery in reading and a lovely rendering of the Psalms in the church are regulated by a knowledge of this science. Yet it is not only good reading and beautiful psalmody that we owe to music; through it alone do we become capable of celebrating in the most solemn manner every divine service. Music penetrates all the activities of our life, in this sense namely, that we above all carry out the commands of the Creator and bow with a pure heart to his commands; all that we speak, all that makes our hearts beat faster, is shown through the rhythm of music united with the excellence of harmony; for music is the

science which teaches us agreeably to change tones in duration and pitch. When we employ ourselves with good pursuits in life, we show ourselves thereby disciples of this art; so long as we do what is wrong, we do not feel ourselves drawn to music. Even heaven and earth, as everything that happens here through the arrangement of the Most High, is nothing but music, as Pythagoras testifies that this world was created by music and can be ruled by it. Even with the Christian religion music is most intimately united; thus it is possible that to him, who does not know even a little music, many things remain closed and hidden.

11. There remains yet astronomy which, as some one has said, is a weighty means of demonstration to the pious, and to the curious a grievous torment. If we seek to investigate it with a pure heart and an ample mind, then it fills us, as the ancients said, with great love for it. For what will it not signify, that we soar in spirit to the sky, that with penetration of mind we analyze that sublime structure, that we, in part at least, fathom with the keenness of our logical faculties what mighty space has enveloped in mystery! The world itself, according to the assumption of some, is said to have the shape of a sphere, in order that in its circumference it may be able to contain the different forms of things. Thus Seneca, in agreement with the philosophers of ancient times, composed a work under the title, "The Shape of the Earth."

Astronomy, of which we now speak, teaches the laws of the stellar world. The stars can take their place or carry out their motion only in the manner established by the Creator, unless by the will of the Creator a miraculous change takes place. Thus we read that Joshua commanded the sun to stand still in Gibeon, that in the days of King Josiah the sun went backward ten degrees, and that at the death of the Lord the sun was darkened for three hours. We call such occurrences miracles (*Wunder*), because they contradict the usual course of things, and therefore excite wonder. . . .

That part of astronomy, which is built up on the investigation of natural phenomena, in order to determine the course of the sun, of the moon, and stars, and to effect a proper reckoning of time, the Christian clergy should seek to learn with the utmost diligence, in order through the knowledge of laws brought to light and through the valid and convincing proof of the given means of evidence, to place themselves in a position, not only to determine the course of past years according to truth and reality, but also for further times to draw confident conclusions, and to fix the time of Easter and all other festivals and holy days, and to announce to the congregation the proper celebration of them.

12. The seven liberal arts of the philosophers, which Christians should learn for their utility and advantage, we have, as I think, sufficiently discussed. We have this yet to add. When those, who are called philosophers, have in their expositions or in their writings, uttered perchance some truth, which agrees with our faith, we should not handle it timidly, but rather take it as from its unlawful possessors and apply it to our own use.

XII. MARTIN LUTHER.

BIOGRAPHICAL SKETCH.

Martin Luther, the greatest of the Protestant reformers, was born at Eisleben, Germany, November 10, 1483. His father was a miner in humble circumstances. The home-training he received was severe and hardening. At school he came under the prevalent cruel discipline, and was cruelly flogged for not accomplishing tasks that were entirely beyond his power. He was sent at the age of fourteen to the school at Magdeburg conducted by the Brethren of the Common Life. A year later he went to Eisenach, where he completed his secondary education under the learned humanist John Tribonius.

In 1501 he entered the University of Erfurt which, unlike many other universities of the time, welcomed the study of the Latin and Greek classics. He took the Master's degree there in 1505, and then entered the Augustinian convent of mendicant friars at Erfurt, where he passed through a profound religious experience. In 1507 he was ordained to the priesthood, and a year later was called to the newly founded University of Wittenberg, where he lectured first on Aristotle and then on the Scriptures. On the 31st of October, 1517, in opposition to John Tetzel, who was vending indulgences throughout Germany, Luther nailed his famous Ninety-five Theses to the door of the Castle Church at Wittenberg. This event, which led to the subsequent conflict with the Papacy, is commonly regarded as the beginning of the Protestant revolution, which in the next several decades firmly established itself among the Teutonic peoples of Europe.

The necessities of the Reformation, as well as his profound patriotism, gave Luther an intense interest in education. Apart from frequent discussions of the subject in other writings, he prepared two treatises which exhibit great breadth of view and a marvelous though unrefined energy of expression. The first of these is a "Letter to the Mayors and Aldermen of All the Cities of Germany in Behalf of Christian Schools," which was written in 1524, and the second, a "Sermon on the Duty of Sending Children to School," which was prepared in 1530. These treatises touch on nearly every important phase of education, and are admirable in their statement of principles and suggestion of methods. The commendation of Dittes, director of the Normal School in Vienna, is not unmerited: "If we survey the pedagogy of Luther in all its extent," he says, "and imagine it fully realized in practice, what a splendid picture the schools and education of the sixteenth century would present! We should have courses of study, text-books, teachers, methods, principles, and modes of discipline, schools and school regulations, that could serve as models for our own age. But, alas! Luther, like all great men, was little understood by his age and adherents; and what was understood was inadequately esteemed, and what was esteemed was only imperfectly realized."

With Luther education was not an end in itself, but a means of more effective service in church and state. If people or rulers neglect the education of the young, they inflict an injury on the cause of Christ and on the weal of the state; they advance the cause of Satan, and bring down upon themselves the wrath of heaven. This is the fundamental thought that underlies all Luther's writings on education.

The "Letter to the Mayors and Aldermen of All the Cities of Germany," which follows almost in its entirety, is translated from the Leipzig edition of Luther's works. It was written in the early years of the Protestant movement, and exhibits in more than one passage the fierce energy of a strong nature engaged in a struggle of life or death. But in spite of its outbursts of rude polemic energy, we cannot fail to recognize the breadth of view, solidity of judgment, and excellence of recommendation, that make it an educational document of great importance.[1] It is the first great contribution of Protestantism to the science and art of education — the beginning of the movement that has given Europe and America its public schools.

SELECTION FROM MARTIN LUTHER.

LETTER TO THE MAYORS AND ALDERMEN OF ALL THE CITIES OF GERMANY IN BEHALF OF CHRISTIAN SCHOOLS.

First of all, we see how the schools are deteriorating throughout Germany. The universities are becoming weak, the monasteries are declining, and, as Isaiah says, "The grass withereth, the flower fadeth, because the spirit of the Lord bloweth upon it," through the Gospel. For through the word of God the unchristian and sensual character of these institutions is becoming known. And because selfish parents see that they can no longer place their children upon the bounty of monasteries and cathedrals, they refuse to educate them. "Why should we educate our children," they say, "if they are not to become priests, monks, and nuns, and thus earn a support?"

---

[1] For a complete presentation of Luther's pedagogy, the author may be permitted to refer to his "Luther on Education" (Lutheran Publication Society, Philadelphia), which contains a translation and systematic review of nearly all that the reformer wrote on the subject.

The hollow piety and selfish aims of such persons are sufficiently evident from their own confession. For if they sought anything more than the temporal welfare of their children in monasteries and the priesthood, if they were deeply in earnest to secure the salvation and blessedness of their children, they would not lose interest in education and say, "if the priestly office is abolished, we will not send our children to school." But they would speak after this manner: "If it is true, as the Gospel teaches, that such a calling is dangerous to our children, teach us another way in which they may be pleasing to God and become truly blessed; for we wish to provide not alone for the bodies of our children, but also for their souls." Such would be the language of faithful Christian parents.

It is no wonder that the devil meddles in the matter, and influences groveling hearts to neglect the children and the youth of the country. Who can blame him for it? He is the prince and god of this world, and with extreme displeasure sees the Gospel destroy his nurseries of vice, the monasteries and priesthood, in which he corrupts the young beyond measure, a work upon which his mind is especially bent. How could he consent to a proper training of the young? Truly he would be a fool if he permitted such a thing in his kingdom, and thus consented to its overthrow; which indeed would happen, if the young should escape him, and be brought up to the service of God.

Hence he acted wisely at the time when Christians were educating and bringing up their children in a Christian way. Inasmuch as the youth of the land would have escaped him thus, and inflicted an irreparable injury upon his kingdom, he went to work and spread his nets, established such monasteries, schools, and orders, that it was not possible for a boy to escape him without the miraculous intervention of God. But now that he sees his snares exposed through the word of God, he takes an opposite course, and dissuades men from all education whatever. He thus pursues a wise course to maintain his kingdom and win the youth of Germany. And if he secures them, if they grow up under his influence and remain his adherents, who can gain any advantage over him? He retains an easy and peaceful mastery over the world. For any fatal wound to his cause must come through the young who, brought up in the knowledge of God, spread abroad the truth and instruct others.

Yet no one thinks of this dreadful purpose of the devil, which is being worked out so quietly that it escapes observation; and soon the evil will be so far advanced that we can do nothing to prevent it. People fear the Turks, wars, and floods, for in such matters they can see what is injurious or beneficial; but what the devil has in mind no one sees or fears. Yet where we would give a florin to defend ourselves against the Turks, we should give a hundred florins to protect us against ignorance, even if only one boy could be taught to be a truly Christian man; for the good such a man can accomplish is beyond all computation.

Therefore I beg you all, in the name of God and of our neglected youth, not to think of this subject lightly, as many do who do not see what the prince of this world intends. For the right instruction of youth is a matter in which Christ and all the world are concerned. Thereby are we all aided. And consider that great Christian zeal is needed to overcome the silent, secret, and artful machinations of the devil. If we must annually expend large sums on muskets, roads, bridges, dams, and the like, in order that the city may have temporal peace and comfort, why should we not apply as much to our poor, neglected youth, in order that we may have a skilful schoolmaster or two?

* * * * *

It is indeed a sin and shame that we must be aroused and incited to the duty of educating our children and of considering their highest interests, whereas nature itself should move us thereto, and the example of the heathen affords us varied instruction. There is no irrational animal that does not care for and instruct its young in what they should know, except the ostrich, of which God says, "She leaveth her eggs in the earth, and warmeth them in the dust; and is hardened against her young ones, as though they were not hers." And what would it avail if we possessed and performed all else, and became perfect saints, if we neglect that for which we chiefly live, namely, to care for the young? In my judgment there is no other outward offense that in the sight of God so heavily burdens the world, and deserves such heavy chastisement, as the neglect to educate children.

Parents neglect this duty from various causes. In the first place, there are some who are so lacking in piety and uprightness that they would not do it if they could, but, like the ostrich, harden themselves against their own offspring, and do nothing for them. In the second place, the great majority of parents are unqualified for it, and do not understand how children should be brought up and taught. In the third place, even if parents were qualified and willing to do it themselves, yet on account of other employments and household duties, they have no time for it, so that necessity requires us to have teachers for public schools, unless each parent employ a private instructor.

Therefore it will be the duty of the mayors and councils to exercise the greatest care over the young. For since the happiness, honor, and life of the city are committed to their hands, they would be held recreant before God and the world, if they did not day and night, with all their power, seek its welfare and improvement. Now the welfare of a city does not consist alone in great treasures, firm walls, beautiful houses, and munitions of war; indeed, where all these are found, and reckless fools come into power, the city sustains the greater injury. But the highest welfare, safety, and power of a city consist in able, learned, wise, upright, cultivated citizens, who can secure, preserve, and utilize every treasure and advantage.

Since, then, a city must have well-trained people, and since the greatest need, lack, and lament is that such are not to be found, we must not wait till they grow up of themselves; neither can they be hewed out of stones nor cut out of wood; nor will God work miracles, so long as men can attain their object through means within their reach. Therefore we must see to it, and spare no trouble or expense to educate and form them ourselves. For whose fault is it that in all the cities there are at present so few skilful people except the rulers, who have allowed the young to grow up like trees in the forest, and have not cared how they were reared and taught? The growth, consequently, has been so irregular that the forest furnishes no timber for building purposes, but like a useless hedge is good only for fuel.

Yet there must be civil government. For us, then, to permit ignoramuses and blockheads to rule when we can prevent it, is irrational and barbarous. Let us rather make rulers out of swine and wolves, and set them over peoples who are indifferent to the manner in which they are governed. It is barbarous for men to think thus: "We will now rule; and what does it concern us how those fare who shall come after us?" Not over human beings, but over swine and dogs should such people rule, who think only of their own interests and honor in governing. Even if we exercise the greatest care to educate able, learned, and skilled rulers, yet much care and effort are necessary in order to secure prosperity. How can a city prosper, when no effort is made?

But you say again, if we shall and must have schools, what is the use to teach Latin, Greek, Hebrew, and other liberal arts? Is it not enough to teach the Scriptures, which are necessary to salvation, in the mother tongue? To which I answer: I know, alas! that we Germans must always remain irrational brutes, as we are deservedly called by surrounding nations. But I wonder why we do not also say: of what use to us are silk, wine, spices, and other foreign articles, since we ourselves have an abundance of wine, corn, wool, flax, wood, and stone in the German states, not only for our necessities, but also for embellishment and ornament? The languages and other liberal arts, which are not only harmless, but even a greater ornament, benefit, and honor than these things, both for understanding the Holy Scriptures and carrying on the civil government, we are disposed to despise; and the foreign articles which are neither necessary nor useful, and which besides greatly impoverish us, we are unwilling to dispense with. Are we not rightly called German dunces and brutes?

Indeed, if the languages were of no practical benefit, we ought still to feel an interest in them as a wonderful gift of God, with which he has now blessed Germany almost beyond all other lands. We do not find many instances in which Satan has fostered them through the universities and cloisters; on the contrary, these institutions have fiercely inveighed and continue to inveigh against them. For the devil scented the danger that would threaten his kingdom, if the languages should be generally studied. But since he could not wholly prevent their cultivation, he aims at least to confine them within such narrow limits that they will of themselves decline and fall into disuse. They are to him no welcome guest, and consequently he shows them scant courtesy in order that they may not remain long. This malicious trick of Satan is perceived by very few.

Therefore, my beloved countrymen, let us open our eyes, thank God for his precious treasure, and take pains to preserve it and to frustrate the design of Satan. For we can not deny that, although the Gospel has come and daily comes through the Holy Spirit, it has come by means of the languages, and through them must increase and be preserved. For when God wished through the apostles to spread the Gospel abroad in all the world, he gave the languages for that purpose; and by means of the Roman empire he made Latin and Greek the language of many lands, that his Gospel might speedily bear fruit far and wide. He has done the same now. For a time no one understood why God had revived the study of the languages; but now we see that it was for the sake of the Gospel, which he wished to bring to light and thereby expose and destroy the reign of Antichrist. For the same reason he gave Greece a prey to the Turks, in order that Greek scholars, driven from home and scattered abroad, might bear the Greek tongue to other countries, and thereby excite an interest in the study of languages.

And let this be kept in mind, that we shall not preserve the Gospel without the languages. The languages are the scabbard in which the word of God is sheathed. They are the casket in which this jewel is enshrined; the cask in which this wine is kept; the chamber in which this food is stored. And, to borrow a figure from the Gospel itself, they are the baskets in which this bread and fish and fragments are preserved. If through neglect we lose the languages (which may God forbid), we shall not only lose the Gospel, but it will finally come to pass that we shall lose also the ability to speak and write either Latin or German.

* * * * *

So much for the utility and necessity of the languages, and of Christian schools for our spiritual interests and the salvation of the soul. Let us now consider the body and inquire: though there were no soul, nor heaven, nor hell, but only the civil government, would not this require good schools and learned men more than do our spiritual interests? Hitherto the Papists have taken no interest in civil government, and have conducted the schools so entirely in the interests of the priesthood, that it has become a matter of reproach for a learned man to marry, and he has been forced to hear remarks like this: "Behold, he has become a man of the world, and cares nothing for the clerical state;" just as if the priestly order were alone acceptable to God, and the secular classes, as they are called, belonged to Satan, and were unchristian. But in the sight of God, the former rather belong to Satan, while the despised masses, as happened to the people of Israel in the Babylonian captivity, remain in the land and in right relations with God.

It is not necessary to say here that civil government is a divine institution; of that I have elsewhere said so much, that I hope no one has any doubts on the subject. The question is, how are we to get able and skilful rulers? And here we are put to shame by the heathen who in ancient times, especially the Greeks and Romans, without knowing that civil government is a divine ordinance, yet instructed the boys and girls with such earnestness and industry that, when I think of it, I am ashamed of Christians, and especially of our Germans, who are such blockheads and brutes that they can say: "Pray, what is the use of schools, if one is not to become a priest?" Yet we know, or ought to know, how necessary and useful a thing it is, and how acceptable to God, when a prince, lord, counselor, or other ruler, is well-trained and skilful in discharging, in a Christian way, the functions of his office.

Even if there were no soul, as I have already said, and men did not need schools and the languages for the sake of Christianity and the Scriptures, still, for the establishment of the best schools everywhere, both for boys and girls, this consideration is of itself sufficient, namely, that society, for the maintenance of civil order and the proper regulation of the household, needs accomplished and well-trained men and women. Now such men are to come from boys, and such women from girls; hence it is necessary that boys and girls be properly taught and brought up. As I have before said, the ordinary man is not qualified for this task, and cannot and will not do it. Princes and lords ought to do it; but they spend their time in pleasure — driving, drinking, and folly, and are burdened with the weighty duties of the cellar, kitchen, and bedchamber. And though some would be glad to do it, they must stand in fear of the rest, lest they be taken for fools or heretics. Therefore, honored members of the city councils, this work must remain in your hands; you have more time and opportunity for it than princes and lords.

But each one, you say, may educate and discipline his own sons and daughters. To which I reply: we see indeed how it goes with this teaching and training. And where it is carried to the highest point, and is attended with success, it results in nothing more than that the learners, in some measure, acquire a forced external propriety of manner; in other respects they remain dunces, knowing nothing, and incapable of giving aid or advice. But were they instructed in schools or elsewhere, by thoroughly qualified male or female teachers, who taught the languages, other arts, and history, then the pupils would hear the history and maxims of the world, and see how things went with each city, kingdom, prince, man, and woman; and thus, in a short time, they would be able to comprehend, as in a mirror, the character, life, counsels, undertakings, successes, and failures, of the whole world from the beginning. From this knowledge they could regulate their views, and order their course of life in the fear of God, having become wise in judging what is to be sought and what is to be avoided in this outward life, and capable of advising and directing others. But the training which is given at home is expected to make us wise through our own experience. Before that can take place, he shall die a hundred times, and all through life act injudiciously; for much time is needed to give experience.

Now since the young must leap and jump, or have something to do, because they have a natural desire for it which should not be restrained (for it is not well to check them in everything), why should we not provide for them such schools, and lay before them such studies? By the gracious arrangement of God, children take delight in acquiring knowledge, whether languages, mathematics, or history. And our schools are no longer a hell or purgatory, in which children are tortured over cases and tenses, and in which with much flogging, trembling, anguish, and wretchedness they learn nothing.

If we take so much time and pains to teach our children to play cards, sing, and dance, why should we not take as much time to teach them reading and other branches of knowledge, while they are young and at leisure, are quick at learning, and take delight in it?

As for myself, if I had children and were able, I would have them learn not only the languages and history, but also singing, instrumental music, and the whole course of mathematics. For what is all this but mere child's play, in which the Greeks in former ages trained their children, and by this means became wonderfully skilful people, capable for every undertaking? How I regret that I did not read more poetry and history, and that no one taught me in these branches!

But you say, who can do without his children and bring them up, in this manner, to be young gentlemen? I reply: it is not my idea that we should establish schools as they have been heretofore, where a boy has studied Donatus and Alexander twenty or thirty years, and yet has learned nothing. The world has changed, and things go differently. My idea is that boys should spend an hour or two a day in school, and the rest of the time work at home, learn some trade and do whatever is desired, so that study and work may go on together, while the children are young and can attend to both. They now spend twofold as much time in shooting with crossbows, playing ball, running, and tumbling about.

In like manner, a girl has time to go to school an hour a day, and yet attend to her work at home; for she sleeps, dances, and plays away more than that. The real difficulty is found alone in the absence of an earnest desire to educate the young, and to aid and benefit mankind with accomplished citizens. The devil much prefers blockheads and drones, that men may have more abundant trials and sorrows in the world.

But the brightest pupils, who give promise of becoming accomplished teachers, preachers, and workers, should be kept longer at school, or set apart wholly for study, as we read of the holy martyrs, who brought up St. Agnes, St. Agatha, St. Lucian, and others. For this purpose also the cloisters and cathedral schools were founded, but they have been perverted into another and accursed one. There is great need for such instruction; for the tonsured crowd is rapidly decreasing, and besides, for the most part, the monks are unskilled to teach and rule, since they know nothing but to care for their stomachs, the only thing they have been taught. Hence we must have persons qualified to dispense the word of God and the Sacraments, and to be pastors of the people. But where shall we obtain them, if schools are not established on a more Christian basis, since those hitherto maintained, even if they do not go down, can produce nothing but depraved and dangerous corrupters of youth?

There is consequently an urgent necessity, not only for the sake of the young, but also for the maintenance of Christianity and of civil government, that this matter be immediately and earnestly taken hold of, lest afterwards, although we should gladly attend to it, we shall find it impossible to do so, and be obliged to feel in vain the pangs of remorse forever. For God is now graciously present, and offers his aid. Consider, for example, what great zeal Solomon manifested; for he was so much interested in the young that he took time, in the midst of his imperial duties, to write a book for them called Proverbs. And think how Christ himself took the little children in his arms! How earnestly he commends them to us, and speaks of their guardian angels, in order that he may show us how great a service it is, when we rightly bring them up; on the other hand how his anger kindles, if we offend the little ones, and let them perish.

Therefore, dear Sirs, take to heart this work, which God so urgently requires at your hands, which pertains to your office, which is necessary for the young, and which neither the world nor the Spirit can do without. We have, alas! lived and degenerated long enough in darkness; we have remained German brutes too long. Let us use our reason, that God may observe in us gratitude for his mercies, and that other lands may see that we are human beings, capable both of learning and of teaching, in order that through us, also, the world may be made better.

Finally, this must be taken into consideration by all who earnestly desire to see such schools established and the languages preserved in the German states; that no cost nor pains should be spared to procure good libraries in suitable buildings, especially in the large cities that are able to afford it. For if a knowledge of the Gospel and of every kind of learning is to be preserved, it must be embodied in books, as the prophets and apostles did, as I have already shown. This should be done, not only that our spiritual and civil leaders may have something to read and study, but also that good books may not be lost, and that the arts and languages may be preserved, with which God has graciously favored us.

All the kingdoms that have been distinguished in the world have bestowed care upon this matter, and particularly the Israelites, among whom Moses was the first to begin the work, who commanded them to preserve the book of the law in the ark of God, and put it under the care of the Levites, that any one might procure copies from them. He even commanded the king to make a copy of this book in the hands of the Levites. Among other duties God directed the Levitical priesthood to preserve and attend to the books. Afterwards Joshua increased and improved this library, as did Samuel subsequently, and David, Solomon, Isaiah, and many kings and prophets. Hence have come to us the Holy Scriptures of the Old Testament, which would not otherwise have been collected and preserved, if God had not required such diligence in regard to it.

*   *   *   *   *

Has it not been a grievous misfortune that a boy has hitherto been obliged to study twenty years or longer, in order to learn enough miserable Latin to become a priest and to read mass? And whoever has succeeded in this has been called blessed, and blessed the mother that has borne such a child! And yet he has remained a poor ignorant man all through life, and has been of no real service whatever. Everywhere we have had such teachers and masters, who have known nothing themselves, who have been able to teach nothing useful, and who have been ignorant even of the right methods of learning and teaching. How has it come about? No books have been accessible but the senseless trash of the monks and sophists. How could the pupils and teachers differ from the books they studied? A jackdaw does not hatch a dove, nor a fool make a wise man. That is the recompense of our ingratitude, in that we did not use diligence in the formation of libraries, but allowed good books to perish, and bad ones to survive.

But my advice is, not to collect all sorts of books indiscriminately, thinking only of getting a vast number together. I would have discrimination used, because it is not necessary to collect the commentaries of all the jurists, the productions of all the theologians, the discussions of all the philosophers, and the sermons of all the monks.

In the first place, a library should contain the Holy Scriptures in Latin, Greek, Hebrew, German, and other languages. Then the best and most ancient commentators in Greek, Hebrew, and Latin.

Secondly, such books as are useful in acquiring the languages, as the poets and orators, without considering whether they are heathen or Christian, Greek or Latin. For it is from such works that grammar must be learned.

Thirdly, books treating of all the arts and sciences.

Lastly, books on jurisprudence and medicine, though here discrimination is necessary.

A prominent place should be given to chronicles and histories, in whatever languages they may be obtained; for they are wonderfully useful in understanding and regulating the course of the world, and in disclosing the marvelous works of God. O how many noble deeds and wise maxims produced on German soil have been forgotten and lost, because no one at the time wrote them down; or if they were written, no one preserved the books: hence we Germans are unknown in other lands, and are called brutes that know only how to fight, eat, and drink. But the Greeks and Romans, and even the Hebrews, have recorded their history with such particularity, that even if a woman or child did anything noteworthy, all the world was obliged to read and know it; but we Germans are always Germans, and will remain Germans.

Since God has so graciously and abundantly provided us with art, scholars, and books, it is time for us to reap the harvest and gather for future use the treasures of these golden years. For it is to be feared (and even now it is beginning to take place), that new and different books will be produced, until at last, through the agency of the devil, the good books which are being printed, will be crowded out by the multitude of ill-considered, senseless, and noxious works.

Therefore, my dear Sirs, I beg you to let my labor bear fruit with you. And though there be some who think me too insignificant to follow my advice, or who look down on me as one condemned by tyrants: still let them consider that I am not seeking my own interest, but that of all Germany. And even if I were a fool, and should hit upon something good, no wise man should think it a disgrace to follow me. And even if I were a Turk and heathen, and it should yet appear that my advice was advantageous, not for myself, but for Christianity, no reasonable person would despise my counsel. Sometimes a fool has given better advice than a whole company of wise men. Moses received instruction from Jethro.

Herewith I commend you all to the grace of God. May he soften your hearts, and kindle therein a deep interest in behalf of the poor, wretched, and neglected youth; and through the blessing of God may you so counsel and aid them as to attain to a happy Christian social order in respect to both body and soul, with all fullness and abounding plenty, to the praise and honor of God the Father, through Jesus Christ our Savior. Amen.

Wittenberg, 1524.

XIII. THE JESUITS.

HISTORICAL SKETCH.

The order of the Jesuits, or the Society of Jesus, was founded in 1534 by the celebrated Ignatius of Loyola. Its members have always been characterized by a spirit of utter self-abnegation, which has given the order great influence and success in missionary and educational work. Though at various times it has encountered strong secular and ecclesiastical opposition, it still survives as a potent organization within the Roman Catholic Church.

The Constitutions of the order were begun by Ignatius himself in 1541. They consist of ten parts, of which the fourth part is devoted to education. It is divided into seventeen chapters, the subjects of which are as follows: (1) Founders and Benefactors of the Colleges; (2) Temporal Affairs of the Colleges; (3) Admission of Students to the Colleges; (4) Maintenance of Students; (5) Studies to be Pursued; (6) Means of Promoting the Progress of Students; (7) Schools of the Colleges; (8) Instruction Preparing Students to be Spiritually Helpful to Others (9) Dismission of Students; (10) Government of the Colleges; (11) Establishment of Universities; (12) Sciences to be Taught at the Universities; (13) Method and Order of the Faculties; (14) Books to be Read; (15) Courses and Degrees; (16) Moral Regulations; (17) Officials of the University.

This fourth part of the Constitutions is the foundation, upon which the famous *Ratio Studiorum,* or the pedagogical system of the Jesuits, has been built. The *Ratio Studiorum,* after fifteen years of careful elaboration, was first published in 1599; and though it underwent some slight modification in 1832, it has remained without material change for more than three centuries, and determined the administration and instruction of hundreds of colleges. It covers something more than a hundred pages, and in place of pedagogical principles, which are rarely introduced, it prescribes, in great detail, the duties of the several officers, and the subjects and methods of the various teachers.

The following translation, which is sufficiently extended, it is hoped, to give a general insight into the pedagogy of the Jesuits, has been made from Pachtler's "Monumenta Germaniæ Pedagogica," which contains the *Ratio Studiorum* both in Latin and German.

SELECTION FROM THE "RATIO STUDIORUM."

SYSTEM AND PLAN OF STUDIES OF THE SOCIETY OF JESUS.

1. Since it is one of the weightiest duties of our society to teach men all the branches of knowledge in keeping with our organization in such a manner, that they may be moved thereby to a knowledge and love of our Creator and Redeemer, let the Provincial hold it as his duty, to provide with all zeal, that the results, which the grace of our vocation demands, abundantly answer to our manifold labors in education.

2. Long before let him [the Provincial] consider whom he can take as professors in each department, and take heed to those who seem to be best fitted for the place, who are learned, diligent, and assiduous, and are zealous for the progress of their students in their lectures as well as in their other literary exercises.

3. Let him promote with great care the study of the Holy Scriptures; in which he will succeed, if he selects for this office men who are not only proficient in the languages (for that is especially necessary), but also well versed in theology and the other sciences, in history and in general learning, and also, as far as possible, in eloquence.

4. But he must especially remember that only men who are well disposed to St. Thomas are to be promoted to theological chairs. Whoever is indifferent to him or is not studious of him shall be removed from the office of teaching.

5. The professors of philosophy, except when the gravest necessity calls for an exception, must not simply complete the course in theology, but also repeat it for two years, in order that their teaching may be the safer and more serviceable to theology. Should any, however, be inclined to innovating opinions or exhibit too liberal a spirit, they must undoubtedly be removed from the office of teaching.

6. When students have entered upon the philosophical course, they must undergo a rigid examination at the end of the year given by the appointed examiners in the presence of the rector, and if possible, of the Provincial himself. No one may pass from the first to the second year of philosophy, unless he has reached mediocrity, that is, so that he understands well what he hears and can give an account of it. But no one shall be admitted to scholastic theology who has not risen above mediocrity in the philosophical course, so that he can defend and maintain philosophical theses with applause; except in the case that such mediocre displays a distinguished talent for administration or preaching, on which account the Provincial may dispose of his case otherwise, though in other things he has no power to grant dispensations.

7. These examinations, in which it is decided whether

the students of philosophy or theology shall pass to the following years, shall take place by secret ballot; and the decision arrived at, together with the judgment of the examiners, shall be entered in a book designed for that purpose; and all who were present at the examination shall maintain silence about it.

8. Schools for lower studies must not exceed five in number, namely, one for rhetoric, the second for humanity, and three for grammar. For these are five grades so intimately connected that they must not be confused or increased in number.

9. Furthermore, care must be exercised that where there are too few schools, always the higher classes, so far as possible, must be retained, and the lower classes given up.

10. In order to preserve a knowledge of classical literature and to establish a sort of nursery for gymnasium teachers, let him [the Provincial] endeavor to have in his province at least two or three men distinguished in these services and in eloquence. To this end, from the number of those who are capable and inclined to these studies, he shall set apart for that work alone a few who are sufficiently instructed in the other departments, in order that through their efforts and activity a body of good teachers may be maintained and provided for the future.

11. Let him procure as many life-long teachers of grammar and rhetoric as possible. This he will be able to do, if at the close of their ethical or even theological studies he earnestly directs and exhorts to the teacher's vocation some, from whose help he can expect in the Lord greater results in this office than in any other, that they may wholly dedicate themselves to so salutary a work for the greater service of God.

12. With all diligence let him watch and esteem it a matter of the highest importance that all books of the poets

and other writings, which might prove injurious to character and good manners, be kept from our schools, until they have been purged of impure passages and words; and should this expurgation not be possible, the books shall rather not be read, in order that their contents may not contaminate the purity of the soul.

13. Let still greater care be exercised in the case of native writers, where the reading of such authors is customary in the schools. These authors shall be carefully selected, and none shall ever be read or praised, in whom the young may not take an interest without danger to their faith and morals. Therefore, men well versed in the native literature shall be consulted, in order to determine what may be done in this matter without injury, and then see to it that what has been determined, be also conscientiously observed by the prefects and teachers of the schools.

14. Let him [the Rector] see to it that the use of the Latin language is diligently maintained among the students; from this requirement of speaking Latin only holidays and recreation hours are to be excepted, unless the Provincial finds it advisable in certain localities to retain the use of Latin also on such days. He may also insist that our students, who have not yet completed their course of study, write their letters to other brethren of the order in Latin. Besides this our philosophical and theological students, two or three times a year, at the opening of a session or the renewal of their vows, shall compose and publicly post some poetical production.

15. The subject-matter of tragedies and comedies, which however shall be only in Latin and seldom acted, shall be of a sacred and pious character; the interludes also shall be in Latin and of due decorum; female roles and costumes are prohibited.

16. Prizes may be publicly distributed once a year, pro-

vided they be of moderate cost, according to the number of students and the grade of the college. But if any one provides the necessary cost for this purpose, his name must be honorably mentioned at the distribution of prizes.

17. The lower schools shall have a weekly recess of a whole day or a half day, according to the custom of the locality.

18. At all disputations, at which the professors of theology or philosophy are present, the Prefect must preside; he must give the disputants the sign to begin, and divide the time in such a manner that each one may have his turn in the discussion. He must let no difficulty which comes into the discussion be bandied about so that it remains just as obscure afterwards as it was before; but when it has been sufficiently discussed on both sides, let him have it carefully explained by the first defendant. For he himself shall not answer objections, but rather direct the advocates and defendants; an office which he will fulfil with more dignity, if he helps, not through arguments (which however he may sometimes make) but through questions, to solve the difficulty.

19. Nothing shall be publicly delivered in the House or out of it, either by those who are promoted to degrees or by those who hold general or particular disputations or by the students of rhetoric, unless it has first been examined and approved.

20. Let him [the Prefect] exercise care that the students have neither a lack of useful books nor a superfluity of useless books. Therefore, he shall early remind the rector, that our students, and those residing out of the House, may not suffer a lack of the books which they need daily or for the coming year.

21. He shall not grant to the students of theology and philosophy all the books they may desire, but with the

knowledge of the rector and the advice of the teachers, suitable books: namely, to the theologues, besides the author read in the school, the *Summa* of St. Thomas [Aquinas] and a commentary thereto or another select author, further the Council of Trent together with a Bible, in the reading of which he shall be at home. Whether they shall have a holy Father or a writer of Church history, he may consider with the rector.

To the students of philosophy, besides the text-book he may assign, if it seems good to him, another approved author. Besides, let him give to every theological and philosophical student a book from classic literature, and admonish them not to neglect the reading of the same at certain suitable hours.

22. The special aim of the teacher, in his lectures on suitable occasion and elsewhere, should be to inspire his pupils to the service and love of God and to the exercise of the virtues through which we may please him, and to lead them to recognize this as the sole end of their studies.

23. In those questions which are left free to personal judgment, let him defend his own opinion in such a manner as modestly and benevolently to consider the reputation of the other party and still more of his predecessor in case the latter taught differently. If the different authors can be brought into agreement, it is desirable that this should not be neglected. Finally, let him be modest in naming or confuting authors.

24. Even when no danger to faith and piety is involved, no one, in subjects of any importance, shall bring forward, without previous consultation with the authorities, new questions or any opinion which is not held by some reputable author, nor present any views contrary to the teachings of the doctors and against the general view of the existing schools. Rather shall they all follow carefully the ap-

proved teachers, and cling to that which through long years has been especially accepted in Catholic academies.

25. Let him not bring forward useless, obsolete, absurd, or manifestly false opinions, nor continue too long in mentioning and refuting them. Let him seek to establish his conclusions not so much by the number as by the weight of his arguments. Let him not digress to foreign materials nor use his own too diffusely or in a wrong connection. Let him not heap up a mass of possible objections, but only bring forward briefly the weightiest of them, unless their refutation is easily manifest from the fundamental principles already laid down.

26. In quoting learned authorities he shall not go to excess; but if he adduces the testimony of distinguished authors to confirm his position, let him briefly and faithfully cite, if possible, the very words; this he must do especially in passages from the Sacred Scriptures, Councils, and the holy Fathers. But for the sake of his dignity hardly any author is to be cited that he has not read himself.

27. Let him often question his pupils about the lecture, and insist on repetition. But after the lecture let him remain in or near the school, that his hearers may be able to question him.

28. Also in the House, except on Saturdays, holidays, and festival days, an hour must be assigned our students for repetition and disputation in order that in this manner the mind may be exercised and the occurring difficulties cleared up. Therefore, one or two should be designated to repeat the lesson by heart in not more than a quarter of an hour; then one or two shall assail the conclusion, while just as many defend it; and if afterwards there is sufficient time, all sorts of doubts may be proposed. But in order that there may be time, the professor must insist strenuously upon the syllogistic form in disputation, and when nothing

new is any longer brought forward, he must at once cut off the discussion.

29. Toward the end of the school year reviews are to be so arranged that, if possible, all the lessons may be repeated before the beginning of vacation.

30. Finally let him [the professor] with the help of divine grace be diligent and assiduous in all things, and seek the progress of his students not only in their lessons but also in their other exercises; and let him not be more familiar with one student than with another; let him despise none, and let him care for the studies of the poor as of the rich; let him promote the progress of each student individually.

31. Let him [the professor of Holy Scripture] recognize it as his principal duty, piously, learnedly, and thoroughly to explain the books given of God, according to their genuine and liberal sense, which confirms the right faith in God and the principles of good morals. Among other ends which he is to pursue, let this stand as chief, that he is to defend the translation (Vulgate) approved by the Church.

32. As to other translations, whether later Latin or vernacular . . . let him undertake the refutation only of weighty and easily corrupting errors; on the other hand let him not pass over what is favorable to the Latin Vulgate and the mysteries of our faith, especially when it is found in the Septuagint, which is always to be spoken of reverently.

33. When the canons of the popes or councils, especially the general councils, indicate the literal sense of a passage of Scripture as the true one, let him also by all means defend it and adduce no other literal sense, except where special reasons exist. When they employ a text expressly as proof of an article of faith, let him teach likewise that this is the indubitable sense, whether literal or mystical.

34. Let him reverently follow in the footsteps of the

holy Fathers; when they are agreed about the literal or allegorical sense of a passage, especially when they expressly say so and purposely treat of passages of Scripture or articles of faith, let him not depart from that sense; but where they are not agreed, let him choose from their different expositions what the Church for years and with great unanimity has preferred.

35. When he comes upon a text, over which we are in controversy with heretics, or which is quoted on both sides in theological discussions, let him expound it simply, yet thoroughly and vigorously, especially against heretics, and point out what weight is in the passage for deciding the question at issue; all the rest let him lay aside, in order that he, mindful of his vocation, may be simply an expounder of the Holy Scriptures.

36. Let him [the professor of theology] regard it as his function so to unite thorough subtlety of investigation with the true faith and with piety, that it may be subordinate and serviceable to them.

37. In scholastic theology our members shall follow the doctrine of St. Thomas, consider him as their true teacher, and take great pains that our students develop the utmost fondness for him. Yet it must not be thought that they are so bound to St. Thomas, that they may not deviate from him in any point; for even those who especially profess to be followers of St. Thomas, sometimes deviate from him; and it would not be right to bind our people to St. Thomas more strictly than the Thomists themselves.

38. In teaching, confirmation of faith and growth in piety must above all be considered. Therefore in questions, which St. Thomas has not expressly handled, no one shall teach anything that does not well harmonize with the views of the Church and the generally received traditions, and that in any way disturbs the foundation of genuine piety.

39. If it is known that certain views of any author would seriously offend the Catholics in a province or academy, let them not be taught and defended there. For where neither the doctrine of faith nor the purity of morals is in danger, a wise charity demands that our people accommodate themselves to those with whom they dwell.

40. Let him [the professor of Church history] treat the history of the Church with the view and with such skill, that he may render the study of theology more easy for his students, and more deeply impress upon their minds the dogmas of faith and the canons.

41. Let him clearly demonstrate that the rights of the Church and of its head rest upon antiquity, and let him show that the statements of innovators about the late origin of such rights are pure inventions.

42. Let him draw his exposition of history from unadulterated sources, and when it can be easily done, let him use the words of the authors themselves; let him show how the innovators have often corrupted the original statements.

43. Questions of doctrine and ecclesiastical law he must not treat himself, but hand them over to the proper professors; but at the same time he must consider it his duty to go over them historically and to establish them by facts themselves.

44. Inasmuch as philosophy prepares the mind for theology and other departments of study, contributes to their perfect comprehension and practical application, and promotes in itself the culture of the understanding and consequently the perfection of the will, let the teacher present it with due clearness, and honestly seek in all things the honor and glory of God, so that he may prepare his students for other sciences, but especially for theology, equip them with the weapons of truth against the errors of the inno-

vators, and encourage them above all to a recognition of their Creator.

45. In all important questions he must not deviate from the teaching everywhere accepted in the academies. Let him defend the orthodox faith with his might, and seek thoroughly to refute the philosophical systems and arguments directed against it. Finally let him not forget in the choice of different opinions that theology must light the way.

46. Those philosophers who have been unfriendly to the Christian religion he must not read without great discrimination or discuss them in the school; let him beware lest his pupils conceive an affection for them. If he quotes anything good from them, let him do so without praise, and show, if possible, that they have borrowed it elsewhere.

47. On the contrary let him always speak reverently of St. Thomas; let him follow him gladly, as often as possible, and deviate from him only unwillingly and respectfully, when he finds less pleasure in him.

48. Monthly disputations shall be held, at which the defendant shall briefly and philosophically establish one or two theses, and besides a professor invited to advocate the affirmative, the students of the higher class shall debate with those of the lower class, and then the students of the same class shall debate with one another.

49. From the beginning of logic on, the students shall be so instructed that in their disputations they may be ashamed of nothing more than of a departure from syllogistic form. The teacher shall insist on nothing more than on an observance of the laws of disputation and the proper alternation between attack and defense. Therefore, let the defendant first repeat the whole argumentation without any reply to the separate propositions; then let him repeat again the propositions, and add to each one " I grant it," or " I deny the major or minor premise or the conclusion." Let

him also sometimes draw distinctions, but not urge upon any one against his will the explanation or reasons which one is accustomed to introduce.

50. Finally he [the professor of physics] shall not forget that he is to pursue the secular sciences in a religious manner, in order that "the invisible things of God may be made known through those things which are made" [Rom. 1:20]; therefore let him seek, as occasion presents itself, to confirm the truths of faith also through physical science, yet without going aside to theological, metaphysical, or Scriptural exposition.

51. There shall be three examiners [in the lower gymnasium studies]: one of them must ordinarily be the Prefect; the other two must be learned in the humanities, and be appointed by the rector together with the Prefect. A majority of the three shall decide. But where the number of students is large, two or more such triumvirates may be appointed.

52. The order of the examination is as follows: first each student, when he is called on, shall read a part of his composition; then let him correct his mistakes and explain them, with a citation of the rule which he has failed to observe. Afterwards the grammar students shall immediately translate into Latin an exercise assigned them in the vernacular; all shall be interrogated about the rules and subjects of their class. Finally, when it is necessary, a brief interpretation of any passage from those books, which have been read in class, may be required of them.

53. When three students have been examined, and while the recollection of the examiners is still clear, the vote shall be taken, in which the composition, the notes of the teacher, and the oral examination shall all be considered.

54. The list of promoted students shall be announced publicly either in the separate classes or in the assembly

room. When any students have greatly distinguished themselves, they shall first receive honorable mention; with the rest the order of the alphabet or of studies must be observed.

55. Let him [the Prefect] have great care that the students give public proof of their progress and of the good standing of our schools with due solemnity; to this end let him timely admonish the teachers and personally examine those students who are to appear publicly before they are allowed to do so.

56. In every class, according to the custom of the place, let him appoint a student as public censor, or if this name is displeasing, an upper decurion or prætor; who, that he may be in honor among his fellow-students, must be distinguished through some privilege, and have the right, with the approval of the teacher, of petitioning in behalf of his fellow-students for the remission of lighter punishments. Let him observe whether any of his fellow-pupils before the signal for school wanders around in the yard or enters another school, or leaves his own school or place. He must also inform the Prefect every day, who has been absent from school, whether any one not a student has entered the classroom, and finally whether in the presence or absence of the teacher any fault has been committed in the school.

57. On account of those who are lacking in diligence and good morals, and for whom kind words and admonitions are not alone sufficient, a corrector must be appointed who does not belong to the Society. Where such a person can not be had, another way should be devised (either through one of the students themselves or otherwise), by which the guilty may receive proper chastisement.

58. When neither words nor the office of the corrector is sufficient, when no improvement in the student is to be hoped for, and moral contamination for others is to be

feared, it is better to remove him from the school than to keep him there, where he makes no progress himself and injures others. But that all may be done, as is fitting, to the glory and service of God, the decision of the matter must be left to the rector.

59. Christian doctrine must be learned by heart in all the classes; and in the three grammar classes, and if necessary, in the other classes, it must be repeated Fridays or Saturdays. According to the grade of each class more ample explanations shall be given and required.

60. On Friday or Saturday let him [the Professor of the lower classes] deliver for half an hour a pious exhortation or explanation of the catechism; but especially let him exhort to daily prayer to God, to a daily reciting of the rosary or office of the Blessed Virgin, to an examination of the conscience every evening, to a frequent and worthy reception of the sacraments of penance and the altar, to an avoidance of evil habits, to a detestation of vice, and finally to a practice of all the virtues becoming a Christian.

61. Especial care must be exercised that the students acquire the habit of speaking Latin. Therefore the teacher, at least from the upper grammar grade, must speak in Latin, and require also that the students speak Latin, especially in the explanation of rules, the correction of Latin exercises, in disputations, and in their daily intercourse. In the translation of authors he must himself have great regard for the purity and correct pronunciation of the mother tongue, and strictly require the same from the students.

62. The class-match (concertatio) is usually so arranged that either the teacher questions and the contestants (æmuli) correct the answers, or the contestants question one another. This exercise is to be highly esteemed and, as often as possible, engaged in, in order that a proper emulation (honesta æmulatio), which is a great incentive to study, may be cul-

tivated. This contest may take place between two students only, or between several on each side, especially from the officers of the class. Let a private student attack another, and an officer another; sometimes also let a private attack an officer, and in case of victory let him take the officer's post of honor, or any other prize or mark of victory that the dignity of the school and the usage of the locality may demand.

XIV. MONTAIGNE.

BIOGRAPHICAL SKETCH.

The distinguished French essayist Montaigne was born in Perigord the last day of February, 1533. His father was a man of prominence, who filled, among other offices, that of mayor of Bordeaux for several years. His son speaks of him, in one of his essays, as "a man of austere probity," who had "a particular regard for honor."

The young Montaigne received a careful though somewhat unconventional education. He was awakened in the morning by the sound of agreeable music, and by means of a German tutor, who used only Latin in conversing with his pupil, he learned that language without the use of the rod. He attended the College of Guienne at Bordeaux, where at the remarkably early age of thirteen he completed the course of instruction. He afterwards studied law, and in 1554 received the appointment of councillor in the parliament of Bordeaux. He maintained intimate relations with the French court, and received from Henry II. the title of Gentleman in Ordinary to the King.

But a life of courtly service and martial activity did not suit the tastes of Montaigne, and accordingly, on reaching the age of thirty-eight, he resolved to dedicate the remainder of his life to study and contemplation. In connection with miscellaneous reading he acquired the habit of setting down the choice thoughts that occurred to him. At length these thoughts, revised and re-arranged, grew into the book of essays, which first appeared at Bordeaux in 1580.

During his absence in Italy Montaigne was elected mayor of Bordeaux, an office which he accepted from a sense of civic duty and which he filled with eminent ability. But along with his municipal duties he continued to prosecute his literary studies and to make from time to time important additions to his essays. New editions appeared at intervals until his death in 1592.

In his Essays, which have given him an honorable place in French literature, he has repeatedly touched upon education. He generally displays sound judgment and fine independence. He drew freely, as he confesses, from the ancients, particularly from Plutarch and Seneca. He entertained liberal views of education, and more than any one else led the reaction against the harsh discipline and narrow course of study prevalent in his day. The following selection is his essay, "Of the Education of Children," the essential parts of which are given entire. As will be seen, the essay is in the form of a letter addressed to Montaigne's friend, the Countess of Gurson, and it embodies the substance of all that he has elsewhere written.

SELECTION FROM MONTAIGNE.

OF THE EDUCATION OF CHILDREN.

To Madame Diane de Foix, Countess de Gurson:

For a boy of quality then, who pretends to letters not upon the account of profit (for so mean an object as that is unworthy of the grace and favor of the Muses, and moreover, in it a man directs his service to and depends upon others), nor so much for outward ornament, as for his own proper and peculiar use, and to furnish and enrich himself within, having rather a desire to come out an accomplished cavalier than a mere scholar or learned man; for such a one,

I say, I would, also, have his friends solicitous to find him out a tutor, who has rather a well-made than a well-filled head; seeking, indeed, both the one and the other, but rather of the two to prefer manners and judgment to mere learning, and that this man should exercise his charge after a new method.

'Tis the custom of pedagogues to be eternally thundering in their pupil's ears, as they were pouring into a funnel, while the business of the pupil is only to repeat what the others have said: now I would have a tutor to correct this error, and, that at the very first, he should, according to the capacity he has to deal with, put it to the test, permitting his pupil himself to taste things, and of himself to discern and choose them, sometimes opening the way to him, and sometimes leaving him to open it for himself; that is, I would not have him alone to invent and speak, but that he should also hear his pupil speak in turn. Socrates, and since him Arcesilaus, made first their scholars speak, and then they spoke to them.[1] *"Obest plerumque iis, qui discere volunt, auctoritas eorum, qui docent."*[2] It is good to make him, like a young horse, trot before him that he may judge of his going and how much he is to abate of his own speed, to accommodate himself to the vigor and capacity of the other. For want of which due proportion we spoil all; which also to know how to adjust, and to keep within an exact and due measure, is one of the hardest things I know, and 'tis the effect of a high and well-tempered soul to know how to condescend to such puerile motions and to govern and direct them. I walk firmer and more secure up hill than down.

Such as, according to our common way of teaching, un-

---

[1] Diogenes Laertius, iv. 36.
[2] "The authority of those who teach, is very often an impediment to those who desire to learn."— CICERO, *De Natura Deor.*, i. 5.

dertake, with one and the same lesson, and the same measure of direction, to instruct several boys of differing and unequal capacities, are infinitely mistaken; and 'tis no wonder, if in a whole multitude of scholars, there are not found above two or three who bring away any good account of their time and discipline. Let the master not only examine him about the grammatical construction of the bare words of his lesson, but about the sense and substance of them, and let him judge of the profit he has made, not by the testimony of his memory, but by that of his life. Let him make him put what he has learned into a hundred several forms, and accommodate it to so many several subjects, to see if he yet rightly comprehends it, and has made it his own, taking instruction of his progress by the pedagogic institutions of Plato. 'Tis a sign of crudity and indigestion to disgorge what we eat in the same condition it was swallowed; the stomach has not performed its office unless it have altered the form and condition of what was committed to it to concoct. Our minds work only upon trust, when bound and compelled to follow the appetite of another's fancy, enslaved and captivated under the authority of another's instruction; we have been so subjected to the trammel, that we have no free, nor natural pace of our own; our own vigor and liberty are extinct and gone: "*Nunquam tutelæ suæ fiunt.*" [1]

Let him make him examine and thoroughly sift everything he reads, and lodge nothing in his fancy upon simple authority and upon trust. Aristotle's principles will then be no more principles to him, than those of Epicurus and the Stoics: let this diversity of opinions be propounded to, and laid before him; he will himself choose, if he be able; if not, he will remain in doubt.

---

[1] "They are ever in wardship."—SENECA, *Ep.*, 33.

"Che, non men che saper, dubbiar m' aggrata,"[1]

for, if he embrace the opinions of Xenophon and Plato, by his own reason, they will no more be theirs, but become his own. Who follows another, follows nothing, finds nothing, nay, is inquisitive after nothing. *"Non sumus sub rege; sibi quisque se vindicet."*[2] Let him at least, know that he knows. It will be necessary that he imbibe their knowledge, not that he be corrupted with their precepts; and no matter if he forgot where he had his learning, provided he know how to apply it to his own use. Truth and reason are common to everyone, and are no more his who spake them first, than his who speaks them after: 'tis no more according to Plato, than according to me, since both he and I equally see and understand them. Bees cull their several sweets from this flower and that blossom, here and there where they find them, but themselves afterward make the honey, which is all and purely their own, and no more thyme and marjoram: so the several fragments he borrows from others, he will transform and shuffle together to compile a work that shall be absolutely his own; that is to say, his judgment: his instruction, labor and study, tend to nothing else but to form that. . . . The advantages of our study are to become better and more wise. " 'Tis," says Epicharmus, " the understanding that sees and hears, 'tis the understanding that improves everything, that orders everything, and that acts, rules, and reigns: all other faculties are blind, and deaf, and without soul." And certainly we render it timorous and servile, in not allowing it the liberty and privilege to do anything of itself. Whoever asked his pupil what he thought of grammar or rhetoric, and of such and such a sentence of Cicero? Our masters

---

[1] "I love to doubt, as well to know."—DANTE, *Inferno,* xi. 93.
[2] "We are under no king; let each look to himself."—SENECA, *Ep.*, 33.

stick them, full feathered, in our memories, and there establish them like oracles, of which the letters and syllables are of the substance of the thing. To know by rote, is no knowledge, and signifies no more but only to retain what one has intrusted to our memory. That which a man rightly knows and understands, he is the free disposer of at his own full liberty, without any regard to the author from whence he had it or fumbling over the leaves of his book. A mere bookish learning is a poor, paltry learning; it may serve for ornament, but there is yet no foundation for any superstructure to be built upon it, according to the opinion of Plato, who says that constancy, faith, and sincerity, are the true philosophy, and the other sciences, that are directed to other ends, mere adulterate paint. I could wish that Paluel or Pompey, those two noted dancers of my time, could have taught us to cut capers, by only seeing them do it, without stirring from our places, as these men pretend to inform the understanding, without ever setting it to work; or that we could learn to ride, handle a pike, touch a lute, or sing, without the trouble of practice, as these attempt to make us judge and speak well, without exercising us in judging or speaking. Now in this initiation of our studies and in their progress, whatsoever presents itself before us is book sufficient; a roguish trick of a page, a sottish mistake of a servant, a jest at the table, are so many new subjects.

And for this reason, conversation with men is of very great use and travel into foreign countries; not to bring back (as most of our young monsieurs do) an account only of how many paces Santa Rotonda [1] is in circuit; or of the richness of Signora Liviá's petticoats; or, as some others, how much Nero's face, in a statue in such an old ruin, is longer and broader than that made for him on some medal; but to be able chiefly to give an account of the humors,

[1] The Pantheon of Agrippa.

manners, customs and laws of those nations where he has been, and that we may whet and sharpen our wits by rubbing them against those of others. I would that a boy should be sent abroad very young, and first, so as to kill two birds with one stone, into those neighboring nations whose language is most differing from our own, and to which, if it be not formed betimes, the tongue will grow too stiff to bend.

And also 'tis the general opinion of all, that a child should not be brought up in his mother's lap. Mothers are too tender, and their natural affection is apt to make the most discreet of them all so overfond, that they can neither find in their hearts to give them due correction for the faults they commit, nor suffer them to be inured to hardships and hazards, as they ought to be. They will not endure to see them return all dust and sweat from their exercise, to drink cold drink when they are hot, nor see them mount an unruly horse, nor take a foil in hand against a rude fencer, or so much as to discharge a carbine. And yet there is no remedy; whoever will breed a boy to be good for anything when he comes to be a man, must by no means spare him when young, and must very often transgress the rules of physic:

> "Vitamque sub dio, et trepidis agat
> In rebus." [1]

It is not enough to fortify his soul: you are also to make his sinews strong; for the soul will be oppressed if not assisted by the members, and would have too hard a task to discharge two offices alone. . . .

And yet, even in this conversing with men I spoke of but now, I have observed this vice, that instead of gather-

---

[1] "Let him live in the open air, and ever in movement about something." — HORACE, *Od.*, ii. 3, 5.

ing observations from others, we make it our whole business to lay ourselves upon them, and are more concerned how to expose and set out our own commodities, than how to increase our stock by acquiring new. Silence, therefore, and modesty are very advantageous qualities in conversation. One should, therefore, train up this boy to be sparing and a husband of his knowledge when he has acquired it; and to forbear taking exceptions at or reproving every idle saying or ridiculous story that is said or told in his presence; for it is a very unbecoming rudeness to carp at everything that is not agreeable to our own palate. Let him be satisfied with correcting himself, and not seem to condemn everything in another he would not do himself, nor dispute it as against common customs. "*Licet sapere sine pompa, sine invidia.*"[1] Let him avoid these vain and uncivil images of authority, this childish ambition of coveting to appear better bred and more accomplished, than he really will, by such carriage, discover himself to be. And, as if opportunities of interrupting and reprehending were not to be omitted, to desire thence to derive the reputation of something more than ordinary. For as it becomes none but great poets to make use of the poetical license, so it is intolerable for any but men of great and illustrious souls to assume privilege above the authority of custom; "*si quid Socrates aut Aristippus contra morem et consuetudinem fecerunt, idem sibi ne arbitretur licere: magnis enim illi et divinis bonis hanc licentiam assequebantur.*"[2] Let him be instructed not to engage in discourse or dispute but with a champion worthy of him, and, even then, not to

---

[1] "Let him be wise without ostentation, without envy."— SENECA, *Ep.*, 103.

[2] "If Socrates and Aristippus have transgressed the rules of good conduct or custom, let him not imagine that he is licensed to do the same; for it was by great and sovereign virtues that they obtained this privilege."—CICERO, *De Offic.*, i. 41.

make use of all the little subtleties that may seem pat for his purpose, but only such arguments as may best serve him. Let him be taught to be curious in the election and choice of his reasons, to abominate impertinence, and, consequently, to affect brevity; but, above all, let him be lessoned to acquiescence and submit to truth so soon as ever he shall discover it, whether in his opponent's argument, or upon better consideration of his own; for he shall never be preferred to the chair for a mere clatter of words and syllogisms, and is no further engaged to any argument whatever, than as he shall in his own judgment approve it: nor yet is arguing a trade, where the liberty of recantation and getting off upon better thoughts, are to be sold for ready money: "*Neque, ut omnia, quæ præscripta et imperata sint, defendat, necessitate ulla cogitur.*" [1]

*　　*　　*　　*　　*

Let his conscience and virtue be eminently manifest in his speaking, and have only reason for their guide. Make him understand, that to acknowledge the error he shall discover in his own argument, though only found out by himself, is an effect of judgment and sincerity, which are the principal things he is to seek after; that obstinacy and contention are common qualities, most appearing in mean souls; that to revise and correct himself, to forsake an unjust argument in the height and heat of dispute, are rare, great, and philosophical qualities. Let him be advised; being in company, to have his eye and ear in every corner, for I find that the places of greatest honor are commonly seized upon by men that have least in them, and that the greatest fortunes are seldom accompanied with the ablest parts. I have been present when, while they at the upper end of the chamber have only been commending the beauty

---

[1] "Neither is there any necessity upon him, that he should defend all things that are recommended to and enjoined him."— CICERO, *Acad.*, ii. 3.

of the arras, or the flavor of the wine, many things that have been very finely said at the lower end of the table have been lost or thrown away. Let him examine every man's talent; a peasant, a bricklayer, a passenger: one may learn something from every one of these in their several capacities, and something will be picked out of their discourse whereof some use may be made at one time or another; nay, even the folly and impertinence of others will contribute to his instruction. By observing the graces and manners of all he sees, he will create to himself an emulation of the good, and a contempt of the bad.

Let an honest curiosity be suggested to his fancy of being inquisitive after everything; whatever there is singular and rare near the place where he is, let him go and see it; a fine house, a noble fountain, an eminent man, the place where a battle has been anciently fought, the passages of Cæsar and Charlemagne:

> "Quæ tellus sit lenta gelu, quæ putris ab æstu,
> Ventus in Italiam quis bene vela ferat."[1]

Let him inquire into the manners, revenues and alliances of princes, things in themselves very pleasant to learn, and very useful to know.

In this conversing with men, I mean also and principally, those who only live in the records of history; he shall, by reading those books, converse with the great and heroic souls of the best ages. 'Tis an idle and vain study to those who make it by so doing it after a negligent manner, but to those who do it with care and observation, 'tis a study of inestimable fruit and value; and the only study, as Plato reports, that the Lacedæmonians reserved to themselves.[2]

---

[1] "What country is bound in frost, what land is friable with heat, what wind serves fairest for Italy."— PROPERTIUS, iv. 3, 39.

[2] Hippias Major.

What profit shall he not reap as to the business of men, by reading the lives of Plutarch? But, withal, let my governor remember to what end his instructions are principally directed, and that he do not so much imprint in his pupil's memory the date of the ruin of Carthage, as the manners of Hannibal and Scipio; nor so much where Marcellus died, as why it was unworthy of his duty that he died there. Let him not teach him so much the narrative parts of history as to judge them; the reading of them, in my opinion, is a thing that of all others we apply ourselves unto with the most differing measure. I have read a hundred things in Livy that another has not, or not taken notice of at least; and Plutarch has read a hundred more there than ever I could find, or than, peradventure, that author ever wrote; to some it is merely a grammar study, to others the very anatomy of philosophy, by which the most abstruse parts of our human nature penetrate.

This great world which some do yet multiply as several species under one genus, is the mirror wherein we are to behold ourselves, to be able to know ourselves as we ought to do in the true bias. In short, I would have this to be the book my young gentleman should study with the most attention. So many humors, so many sects, so many judgments, opinions, laws and customs, teach us to judge aright of our own, and inform our understanding to discover its imperfection and natural infirmity, which is no trivial speculation. So many mutations of states and kingdoms, and so many turns and revolutions of public fortune, will made us wise enough to make no great wonder of our own. So many great names, so many famous victories and conquests drowned and swallowed in oblivion, render our hopes ridiculous of eternizing our names by the taking of half-a-score of light horse, or a henroost, which only derives its memory from its ruin. The pride and arrogance of so many foreign pomps and ceremonies, the tumorous majesty of so many courts and grandeurs, accustom and fortify our sight without astonishment or winking to behold the lustre of our own; so many millions of men, buried before us, encourage us not to fear to go seek such good company in the other world: and so of all the rest. Pythagoras was wont to say,[1] that our life resembles the great and populous assembly of the Olympic games, wherein some exercise the body, that they may carry away the glory of the prize; others bring merchandise to sell for profit; there are, also, some (and those none of the worst sort) who pursue no other advantage than only to look on, and consider how and why everything is done, and to be spectators of the lives of other men, thereby the better to judge of and regulate their own.

To examples may fitly be applied all the profitable discourses of philosophy, to which all human actions, as to their best rule, ought to be especially directed: a scholar shall be taught to know —

"Quid fas optare, quid asper
Utile nummus habet; patriæ carisque propinquis
Quantum elargiri deceat; quem te Deus esse
Jussit, et humana qua parte locatus es in re;
Quid sumus, aut quidnam victuri gignimur,"[2]

what it is to know, and what to be ignorant; what ought to be the end and design of study; what valor, temperance and justice are; the difference between ambition and avarice, servitude and subjection, license and liberty; by what token

---

[1] Cicero, Tusc. Quæs., v. 3.

[2] "Learn what it is right to wish; what is the true use of coined money; how much it becomes us to give in liberality to our country and our dear relations; whom and what the Deity commanded thee to be; and in what part of the human system thou art placed; what we are and to what purpose engendered."— PERSIUS, iii. 69.

a man may know true and solid contentment; how far death, affliction, and disgrace are to be apprehended:

"Et quo quemque modo fugiatque feratque laborem;"[1]

by what secret springs we move, and the reason of our various agitations and irresolutions; for, methinks, the first doctrine with which one should season his understanding, ought to be that which regulates his manners and his sense; that teaches him to know himself, and how both well to die and well to live. Among the liberal sciences, let us begin with that which makes us free; not that they do not all serve in some measure to the instruction and use of life, as all other things in some sort also do; but let us make choice of that which directly and professedly serves to that end. If we are once able to restrain the offices of human life within their just and natural limits, we shall find that most of the sciences in use are of no great use to us, and even in those that are, that there are many very unnecessary cavities and dilatations which we had better let alone, and follow Socrates' direction, limit the course of our studies to those things only where is a true and real utility.

After having taught him what will make him more wise and good, you may then entertain him with the elements of logic, physics, geometry, rhetoric, and the science which he shall then himself most incline to, his judgment being beforehand formed and fit to choose, he will quickly make his own. The way of instructing him ought to be sometimes by discourse, and sometimes by reading, sometimes his governor shall put the author himself, which he shall think most proper for him, into his hands, and sometimes only the marrow and substance of it; and if himself be

---

[1] "And how you may shun or sustain every hardship."—VIRGIL, *Æneid*, iii. 459.

not conversant enough in books to turn to all the fine discourses the books contain for his purpose, there may some man of learning be joined to him, that upon every occasion shall supply him with what he stands in need of, to furnish it to his pupil. And who can doubt, but that this way of teaching is much more easy and natural than that of Gaza, in which the precepts are so intricate, and so harsh, and the words so vain, lean, and insignificant, that there is no hold to be taken of them, nothing that quickens and elevates the wit and fancy, whereas here the mind has what to feed upon and to digest This fruit, therefore, is not only without comparison, much more fair and beautiful; but will also be much more early ripe.

The soul that lodges philosophy, ought to be of such a constitution of health, as to render the body in like manner healthful too; she ought to make her tranquillity and satisfaction shine so as to appear without, and her contentment ought to fashion the outward behavior to her own mold, and consequently to fortify it with a graceful confidence, an active and joyous carriage, and a serene and contented countenance. The most manifest sign of wisdom is a continual cheerfulness; her state is like that of things in the regions above the moon, always clear and serene. 'Tis Baroco and Baralipton[1] that render their disciples so dirty and ill-favored, and not she; they do not so much as know her but by hearsay. What! It is she that calms and appeases the storms and tempests of the soul, and who teaches famine and fevers to laugh and sing; and that, not by certain imaginary epicycles, but by natural and manifest reasons. She has virtue for her end; which is not, as the schoolmen say, situate upon the summit of a perpendicular, rugged, inaccessible precipice: such as have approached

---

[1] Two terms of the ancient scholastic logic.

her find her, quite on the contrary, to be seated in a fair, fruitful, and flourishing plain, from whence she easily discovers all things below; to which place any one may, however, arrive, if he know but the way, through shady, green, and sweetly flourishing avenues, by a pleasant, easy, and smooth descent, like that of the celestial vault. 'Tis for not having frequented this supreme, this beautiful, triumphant, and amiable, this equally delicious and courageous virtue, this so professed and implacable enemy to anxiety, sorrow, fear, and constraint, who, having nature for her guide, has fortune and pleasure for her companions, that they have gone, according to their own weak imaginations and created this ridiculous, this sorrowful, querulous, despiteful, threatening, terrible image of it to themselves and others, and placed it upon a rock apart, among thorns and brambles, and made of it a hobgoblin to affright people.

Such a tutor will make a pupil digest this new lesson, that the height and value of true virtue consist in the facility, utility, and pleasure of its exercise; so far from difficulty, that boys, as well as men, and the innocent as well as the subtle, may make it their own: it is by order, and not by force, that it is to be acquired. Socrates, her first minion, is so averse to all manner of violence, as totally to throw it aside, to slip into the more natural facility of her own progress: 'tis the nursing mother of all human pleasures, who in rendering them just, renders them also pure and permanent; in moderating them, keeps them in breath and appetite; in interdicting those which she herself refuses, whets our desire to those that she allows; and, like a kind and liberal mother, abundantly allows all that nature requires, even to satiety, if not to lassitude: unless we mean to say, that the regimen which stops the toper before he has drunk himself drunk, the glutton before he has eaten to a surfeit, . . . is an enemy to pleasure. If the ordinary fortune fail, she does without it, and forms another, wholly her own, not so fickle and unsteady as the other. She can be rich, be potent and wise, and knows how to lie upon soft perfumed beds: she loves life, beauty, glory, and health; but her proper and peculiar office is to know how to regulate the use of all these good things, and how to lose them without concern: an office much more noble than troublesome, and without which the whole course of life is unnatural, turbulent, and deformed, and there it is indeed, that men may justly represent those monsters upon rocks and precipices.

If this pupil shall happen to be of so contrary a disposition, that he had rather hear a tale of a tub than the true narrative of some noble expedition or some wise and learned discourse; who at the beat of drum, that excites the youthful ardor of his companions, leaves that to follow another that calls to a morris or the bears; who would not wish, and find it more delightful and more excellent, to return all dust and sweat victorious from a battle, than from tennis or from a ball, with the prize of those exercises; I see no other remedy, but that he be bound prentice in some good town to learn to make minced pies, though he were the son of a duke; according to Plato's precept, that children are to be placed out and disposed of, not according to the wealth, qualities, or condition of the father, but according to the faculties and the capacity of their own souls.

Since philosophy is that which instructs us to live and that infancy has there its lessons as well as other ages, why is it not communicated to children betimes?

"Udum et molle lutum est; nunc, nunc properandus, et acri
Fingendus sine fine rota."[1]

[1] "The clay is moist and soft: now, now make haste, and form the pitcher on the rapid wheel."— PERSIUS, iii. 23.

They begin to teach us to live when we have almost done living. . . . Cicero said, that though he should live two men's ages, he should never find leisure to study the lyric poets; and I find these sophisters yet more deplorably unprofitable. The boy we would breed has a great deal less time to spare; he owes but the first fifteen or sixteen years of his life to education; the remainder is due to action. Let us, therefore, employ that short time in necessary instruction. Away with the thorny subtleties of dialectics, they are abuses, things by which our lives can never be amended: take the plain philosophical discourses, learn how rightly to choose, and then rightly to apply them; they are more easy to be understood than one of Boccaccio's novels; a child from nurse is much more capable of them, than of learning to read or to write. Philosophy has discourses proper for childhood, as well as for the decrepit age of men.

I am of Plutarch's mind, that Aristotle did not so much trouble his great disciple with the knack of forming syllogisms, or with the elements of geometry, as with infusing into him good precepts concerning valor, prowess, magnanimity, temperance, and the contempt of fear; and with this ammunition, sent him, while yet a boy, with no more than thirty thousand foot, four thousand horse, and but forty-two thousand crowns, to subjugate the empire of the whole earth. For the other arts and sciences, he says, Alexander highly indeed commended their excellence and charm, and had them in very great honor and esteem, but not ravished with them to that degree, as to be tempted to affect the practice of them in his own person.

> "Petite hinc, juvenesque senesque,
> Finem animo certum, miserisque viatica canis." [1]

[1] "Young men and old men, derive hence a certain end to the mind, and stores for miserable gray hairs."— PERSIUS, v. 64.

Epicurus, in the beginning of his letter to Meniceus, says, "That neither the youngest should refuse to philosophize, nor the oldest grow weary of it." Who does otherwise, seems tacitly to imply, that either the time of living happily is not yet come, or that it is already past. And yet, for all that, I would not have this pupil of ours imprisoned and made a slave to his book; nor would I have him given up to the morosity and melancholic humor of a sour, ill-natured pedant; I would not have his spirit cowed and subdued, by applying him to the rack, and tormenting him, as some do, fourteen or fifteen hours a day, and so make a pack-horse of him. Neither should I think it good, when, by reason of a solitary and melancholic complexion, he is discovered to be overmuch addicted to his book, to nourish that humor in him; for that renders him unfit for civil conversation, and diverts him from better employments. And how many have I seen in my time totally brutified by an immoderate thirst after knowledge? Carneades was so besotted with it, that he would not find time as so much as to comb his head or to pare his nails. Neither would I have his generous manners spoiled and corrupted by the incivility and barbarism of those of another. The French wisdom was anciently turned into proverb: "early, but of no continuance." And, in truth, we yet see, that nothing can be more ingenious and pleasing than the children of France; but they ordinarily deceive the hope and expectation that have been conceived of them; and grown up to be men, have nothing extraordinary or worth taking notice of: I have heard men of good understanding say, these colleges of ours to which we send our young people (and of which we have but too many) make them such animals as they are.

But to our little monsieur, a closet, a garden, the table, his bed, solitude and company, morning and evening, all hours shall be the same, and all places to him a study; for philosophy, who, as the formatrix of judgment and manners, shall be his principal lesson, has that privilege to have a hand in everything. The orator Isocrates, being at a feast entreated to speak of his art, all the company were satisfied with and commended his answer: " It is not now a time," said he, " to do what I can do; and that which it is now time to do, I cannot do." For to make orations and rhetorical disputes in a company met together to laugh and make good cheer, had been very unseasonable and improper, and as much might have been said of all the other sciences. But as to what concerns philosophy, that part of it at least that treats of man, and of his offices and duties, it has been the common opinion of all wise men, that, out of respect to the sweetness of her conversation, she is ever to be admitted in all sports and entertainments. And Plato, having invited her to his feast, we see after how gentle and obliging a manner, accommodated both to time and place, she entertained the company, though in a discourse of the highest and most important nature.

" Æque pauperibus prodest locupletibus æque;
Et, neglecta, æque pueris senibusque nocebit." [1]

By this method of instruction, my young pupil will be much more and better employed than his fellows of the college are. But as the steps we take in walking to and fro in a gallery, though three times as many, do not tire a man so much as those we employ in a formal journey, so our lesson, as it were accidentally occurring, without any set obligation of time or place, and falling naturally into every action, will insensibly insinuate itself. By which means our very exercises and recreations, running, wres-

---

[1] " It profits poor and rich alike, but, neglected, equally hurts old and young."— HORACE, *Ep.*, i. 1, 25.

tling, music, dancing, hunting, riding, and fencing, will prove to be a good part of our study. I would have his outward fashion and mien and the disposition of his limbs, formed at the same time with his mind. 'Tis not a soul, 'tis not a body that we are training up, but a man, and we ought not to divide him. And, as Plato says, we are not to fashion one without the other, but make them draw together like two horses harnessed to a coach. By which saying of his, does he not seem to allow more time for, and to take more care of, exercises for the body, and to hold that the mind, in a good proportion, does her business at the same time too?

As to the rest, this method of education ought to be carried on with a severe sweetness, quite contrary to the practice of our pedants, who, instead of tempting and alluring children to letters by apt and gentle ways, do in truth present nothing before them but rods and ferules, horror and cruelty. Away with this violence! away with this compulsion! than which, I certainly believe nothing more dulls and degenerates a well-descended nature. If you would have him apprehend shame and chastisement, do not harden him to them: inure him to heat and cold, to wind and sun, and to dangers that he ought to despise; wean him from all effeminacy and delicacy in clothes and lodging, eating and drinking; accustom him to everything, that he may not be a Sir Paris, a carpet-knight, but a sinewy, hardy, and vigorous young man. I have ever from a child to the age wherein I now am, been of this opinion, and am still constant to it. But among other things, the strict government of most of our colleges has evermore displeased me; peradventure, they might have erred less perniciously on the indulgent side. 'Tis a real house of correction of imprisoned youth. They are made debauched, by being punished before they are so. Do but come in when they are about their lesson, and you shall hear nothing but the outcries of boys under execution, with the thundering noise of their pedagogues drunk with fury. A very pretty way this, to tempt these tender and timorous souls to love their book, with a furious countenance, and a rod in hand!

The conduct of our lives is the true mirror of our doctrine. Zeuxidamus, to one who asked him why the Lacedæmonians did not commit their constitutions of chivalry to writing, and deliver them to their young men to read, made answer that it was because they would inure them to action, and not amuse them with words. With such a one, after fifteen or sixteen years' study, compare one of our college Latinists, who has thrown away so much time in nothing but learning to speak. The world is nothing but babble; and I hardly ever yet saw that man who did not rather prate too much, than speak too little. And yet half of our age is embezzled this way: we are kept four or five years to learn words only, and to tack them together into clauses; as many more to form them into a long discourse, divided into four or five parts; and other five years, at least, to learn succinctly to mix and interweave them after a subtle and intricate manner: let us leave all this to those who make a profession of it.

Going one day to Orleans, I met in the plain on this side Clery, two pedants traveling toward Bordeaux, about fifty paces distant from one another; and a good way further behind them, I discovered a troop of horse, with a gentleman at the head of them, who was the late Monsieur le Comte de la Rochefoucauld. One of my people inquired of the foremost of these dominies, who that gentleman was that came after him; he, having not seen the train that followed after, and thinking his companion was meant, pleasantly answered: " He is not a gentleman, he is a grammarian, and I am a logician." Now we who, quite contrary, do not here pretend to breed a grammarian or a logician, but a gentleman, let us leave them to throw away their time at their own fancy: our business lies elsewhere. Let but our pupil be well furnished with things, words will follow but too fast; he will pull them after him if they do not voluntarily follow. I have observed some to make excuses, that they cannot express themselves, and pretend to have their fancies full of a great many very fine things, which yet, for want of eloquence, they cannot utter; 'tis a mere shift, and nothing else. Will you know what I think of it? I think they are nothing but shadows of some imperfect images and conceptions that they know not what to make of within, nor consequently bring out: they do not yet themselves understand what they would be at, and if you but observe how they haggle and stammer upon the point of parturition, you will soon conclude, that their labor is not to delivery, but about conception, and that they are but licking their formless embryo. For my part, I hold, and Socrates commends it, that whoever has in his mind a sprightly and clear imagination, he will express it well enough in one kind of tongue or another, and, if he be dumb, by signs:

"Verbaque prævisam rem non invita sequentur."[1]

I would have things so excelling, and so wholly possessing the imagination of him that hears, that he should have something else to do, than to think of words. The way of speaking that I love, is natural and plain, the same in writing as in speaking, and a sinewy and muscular way of expressing a man's self, short and pithy, not so elegant and artificial as prompt and vehement:

[1] "Once a thing is conceived in the mind, the words to express it soon present themselves."— HORACE, *De Arte Poetica*, v. 311.

"Hæc demum sapiet dictio, quæ feriet;"[1]

rather hard than wearisome; free from affectation; irregular, incontinuous, and bold; where every piece makes up an entire body; not like a pedant, a preacher, or a pleader, but rather a soldier-like style, as Suetonius calls that of Julius Cæsar.

No doubt but Greek and Latin are very great ornaments, and of very great use, but we buy them too dear. I will here discover one way, which has been experimented in my own person, by which they are to be had better cheap, and such may make use of it as will. My late father having made the most precise inquiry that any man could possibly make among men of the greatest learning and judgment, of an exact method of education, was by them cautioned of this inconvenience then in use, and made to believe, that the tedious time we applied to the learning of the tongues of them who had them for nothing, was the sole cause we could not arrive to the grandeur of soul and perfection of knowledge, of the ancient Greeks and Romans. I do not, however, believe that to be the only cause. However, the expedient my father found out for this was, that in my infancy, and before I began to speak, he committed me to the care of a German, who since died a famous physician in France, totally ignorant of our language, but very fluent, and a great critic in Latin. This man, whom he had fetched out of his own country, and whom he entertained with a very great salary for this only end, had me continually with him: to him there were also joined two others, of inferior learning, to attend me, and to relieve him; who all of them spoke to me in no other language but Latin. As to the rest of his family, it was an inviolable rule, that

---

[1] "That has most weight and wisdom which pierces the ear."—Epitaph on Lucan, in Fabricus, Biblioth. Lat., ii. 10.

neither himself, nor my mother, man nor maid, should speak anything in my company, but such Latin words as every one had learned only to gabble with me. It is not to be imagined how great an advantage this proved to the whole family; my father and my mother by this means learned Latin enough to understand it perfectly well, and to speak it to such a degree as was sufficient for any necessary use; as also those of the servants did who were most frequently with me. In short, we Latined it at such a rate, that it overflowed to all the neighboring villages, where there yet remain, that have established themselves by custom, several Latin appellations of artisans and their tools. As for what concerns myself, I was above six years of age before I understood either French or Perigordin, any more than Arabic; and without art, book, grammar, or precept, whipping, or the expense of a tear, I had, by that time, learned to speak as pure Latin as my master himself, for I had no means of mixing it up with any other.

As to Greek, of which I have but a mere smattering, my father also designed to have it taught me by a device, but a new one, and by way of sport; tossing our declensions to and fro, after the manner of those who, by certain games at tables and chess, learn geometry and arithmetic. For he, among other rules, had been advised to make me relish science and duty by an unforced will, and of my own voluntary motion, and to educate my soul in all liberty and delight, without any severity or constraint; which he was an observer of to such a degree, even of superstition, if I may say so, that some being of opinion that it troubles and disturbs the brains of children suddenly to wake them in the morning, and to snatch them violently and over-hastily from sleep (wherein they are much more profoundly involved than we), he caused me to be wakened by the sound of some musical instrument, and was never unprovided of a musician for that purpose. Secondly, like those, who, impatient of a long and steady cure, submit to all sorts of prescriptions and recipes, the good man being extremely timorous of any way failing in a thing he had so wholly set his heart upon, suffered himself at last to be overruled by the common opinions; which always follow their leader as a flight of cranes, and complying with the method of the time, having no more those persons he had brought out of Italy, and who had given him the first model of education, about him, he sent me at six years of age to the College of Guienne, at that time the best and most flourishing in France. And there it was not possible to add anything to the care he had to provide me the most able tutors, with all other circumstances of education, reserving also several particular rules contrary to the college practice; but so it was, that with all these precautions it was a college still. My Latin immediately grew corrupt, of which also by discontinuance I have since lost all manner of use; so that this new way of education served me to no other end, than only at my first coming to prefer me to the first forms; for at thirteen years old, that I came out of the college, I had run through my whole course (as they call it), and, in truth, without any manner of advantage, that I can honestly brag of, in all this time.

XV. ROGER ASCHAM.

BIOGRAPHICAL SKETCH.

Roger Ascham holds an honored place in the long line of English scholars and teachers. He was born in 1515 and died in 1568; thus his life fell in the agitated reigns of Henry VIII., Mary, and Elizabeth. He was graduated from St. John's College, Oxford, in 1537. He was there under the instruction of Sir John Cheke, a man of admirable character and learning, to whom he ever afterwards expressed a sense of deep obligation. After his graduation he became a college tutor and received an appointment to read Greek in the public schools. In 1545 he published a work on archery entitled "Toxophilus, or the School of Shooting." He thought it necessary to apologize for using the mother tongue, in which, as he tells us, he tried to follow the advice of Aristotle "to speake as the common people do, to thinke as wise men do."

In 1848 he became tutor to the lady Elizabeth, afterwards the illustrious queen, to whom for two years he gave instruction in the ancient languages. His position as tutor and Latin secretary introduced him to the society of the nobility. It was at the suggestion of Sir Richard Sackville that he wrote "The Scholemaster," by which his name is chiefly known in English literature and English pedagogy.

The work is not throughout original. Besides the ideas borrowed from Sir John Cheke and John Sturm, the distinguished educator of Strasburg, Ascham naturally drew largely, at this renaissance period, from the ancients, among whom he specifies Plato, Aristotle, and Cicero. The preparation of the work was interrupted by the death of Sir Richard Sackville. "When he was gone," Ascham tells us in the preface, "my heart was dead. There was not one that wore a black gown for him who carried a heavier heart for him than I. When he was gone, I cast this book away; I could not look upon it but with weeping eyes, in remembering him who was the only setter on to do it, and would have been not only a glad commender of it, but also a sure and certain comfort to me and mine for it." The work was published posthumously by his wife.

"The Scholemaster" is a book of nearly three hundred pages. Its general character is fully set forth in the original title page bearing date 1570: "THE SCHOLEMASTER; *or plaine and perfite way of teachyng children to understand, write, and speake in Latin tong, but specially purposed for the private brynging up of youth in Gentlemen and Noble mens houses, and commodious also for all such as have forgot the Latin tonge, and would by themselves, without a Scholemaster, in short tyme, and with small paines, recover a sufficient hability to understand, write, and speake Latin.*"

In teaching Latin Ascham advocates the inductive method which, with variations, has been so often tried since his day. After learning the eight parts of speech and the general principles of agreement, the child is to take up Sturm's collection of Cicero's Letters. "First," continues Ascham, "let the master teach the child, cheerfully and plainly, the cause and matter of the letter; then let him construe it into English so oft as the child may easily carry away the understanding of it. Lastly, parse it over perfectly. This done thus, let the child by and by both construe and parse it over again; so that it may appear that the child doubteth in nothing that his master taught him before. After this, the child must take a paper book, and sitting in some place where no man shall prompt him, by himself let him translate into English his former lesson. Then showing it to his master, let the master take from him his Latin book, and pausing an hour at the least, then let the child translate his own English into Latin again in another paper book. When the child bringeth it turned into Latin, the master must compare it with Tully's book and lay them both together; and where the child doth well, either in choosing or true placing of Tully's words, let the master praise him, and say here ye do well. For I assure you, there is no such whetstone to sharpen a good wit and encourage a will to learning as is praise."

The selection that follows has been chosen for its general pedagogical interest. It will be observed that Ascham is an ardent advocate of gentle methods in teaching, and that he exhibits a rare consideration for the patient, capable plodder.

SELECTION FROM ROGER ASCHAM.

THE SCHOLEMASTER.

I have now wished, twice or thrice, this gentle nature to be in a scholemaster. And, that I have done so, neither by chance, nor without some reason, I will now declare at large, why, in mine opinion, love is fitter than fear, gentleness better than beating, to bring up a child rightly in learning.

With the common use of teaching and beating in common schools of England, I will not greatly contend: which if I did, it were but a small grammatical controversy, neither belonging to heresy nor treason, nor greatly touching God nor the prince; although in very deed, in the rod, the good or ill bringing up of children doth as much serve to the good or ill service of God, our prince, and our whole country, as any one thing doth beside.

I do gladly agree with all good scholemasters in these points: to have children brought to good perfectness in learning; to all honesty in manners; to have all faults rightly amended; to have every vice severely corrected; but for the order and way that leadeth rightly to these points, we somewhat differ. For commonly many scholemasters, some as I have seen, and more as I have heard tell, be of so crooked a nature, as, when they meet with a hard-witted scholar, they rather break him than bow him, rather mar him than mend him. For when the scholemaster is angry with some other matter, then will he soonest fall to beat his scholars; and though he himself should be punished for his folly, yet must he beat some scholar for his pleasure; though there be no cause for him to do so, nor yet fault in the scholar to deserve so. These, we will say, be fond scholemasters; and few they be that be found to be such. They be fond in deed, but surely over many such be found everywhere. But this I will say, that even the wisest of your great beaters do as oft punish nature as they do correct faults. Yea, many times the better nature is over punished. For if one, by quickness of wit, take his lesson readily, another, by hardness of wit, taketh it not so speedily; the first is always commended, the other is commonly punished; when a wise scholemaster should rather discreetly consider the right disposition of both their natures, and not so much weigh what either of them is able to do now, as what either of them is likely to do hereafter. For this I know, not only by reading of books in my study, but also by experience of life abroad in the world, that those which be commonly the wisest, the best learned, and best men also, when they be old, were never commonly the quickest of wit when they were young. The causes why, amongst others which be many, that move me thus to think, be these few, which I will reckon. Quick wits commonly be apt to take, unapt to keep; soon hot, and desirous of this and that; as cold and soon weary of the same again; more quick to enter speedily than able to pierce far; even like over-sharp tools, whose edges be very soon turned. Such wits delight themselves in easy and pleasant studies, and never pass far forward in high and hard sciences. And therefore the quickest wits commonly prove the best poets, but not the wisest orators; ready of tongue to speak boldly, not deep of judgment, either for good counsel or wise writing. Also for manners and life, quick wits commonly be in desire newfangled, in purpose unconstant, light to promise anything, ready to forget everything, both benefit and injury; and thereby neither fast to friend, nor fearful to foe; inquisitive of every trifle, not secret in greatest affairs; bold with any person, busy in every matter; soothing such as be present, nipping any that is absent; of nature also always flattering their betters, envying their equals, despising their inferiors; and by quickness of wit, very quick and ready to like none so well as themselves.

Moreover, commonly men very quick of wit be also very light of conditions, and thereby very ready of disposition to be carried over quickly, by any light company, to any riot and unthriftiness when they be young; and therefore seldom either honest of life or rich in living when they be old. For quick in wit and light in manners be either seldom troubled or very soon weary in carrying a very heavy purse. Quick wits also be, in most part of all their doings, over quick, hasty, rash, heady, and brainsick. These two last words, heady and brainsick, be fit and proper words, rising naturally of the matter, and turned aptly by the condition, of over much quickness of wit. In youth also they be ready scoffers, privy mockers, and ever over light and merry. In age soon testy, very waspish, and always over miserable; and yet few of them come to any great age, by reason of their misordered life when they were young; but a great deal fewer of them come to show any great countenance or bear any great authority abroad in the world, but either live obscurely, men know not how, or die obscurely, men mark not when. They be like trees that show forth fair blossoms and broad leaves in spring time, but bring out small and not long lasting fruit in harvest time; and that only such as fall and rot before they be ripe, and so never or seldom come to any good at all. For this ye shall find most true by experience that, amongst a number of quick wits in youth, few be found in the end either very fortunate for themselves or very profitable to serve the commonwealth, but decay and vanish, men know not which way; except a very few, to whom peradventure blood and happy parentage may perchance purchase a long standing upon the stage. The which felicity, because it cometh by others' procuring, not by their own deserving, and stand by other men's feet, and not by their own, what outward brag so ever is borne by them, is indeed, of itself and in wise men's eyes, of no great estimation.

Some wits, moderate enough by nature, be many times marred by over much study and use of some sciences, namely, music, arithmetic and geometry. These sciences, as they sharpen men's wits over much, so they change men's manners over sore, if they be not moderately mingled, and wisely applied to some good use of life. Mark all mathematical heads, which be only and wholly bent to those sciences, how solitary they be themselves, how unfit to live with others, and how unapt to serve in the world. This is not only known now by common experience, but uttered long before by wise men's judgment and sentence. Galen saith much music marreth men's manners; and Plato hath a notable place of the same thing in his books *de Rep.,* well marked also, and excellently translated by Tully himself. Of this matter I wrote once more at large, twenty years ago, in my book of shooting: now I thought but to touch it, to prove that over much quickness of wit, either given by nature or sharpened by study, doth not commonly bring forth either greatest learning, best manners, or happiest life in the end.

Contrariwise, a wit in youth that is not over dull, heavy, knotty, and lumpish, but hard, rough, and though somewhat staffish, as Tully wisheth *otium, quietum, non languidum,* and *negotium cum labore, non cum periculo,* such a wit I say, if it be at the first well handled by the mother, and rightly smoothed and wrought as it should, not overthwartly and against the wood, by the scholemaster, both for learning and whole course of living, proveth always the best. In wood and stone, not the softest, but hardest be always aptest for portraiture, both fairest for pleasure and most durable for profit. Hard wits be hard to receive, but sure to keep; painful without weariness, heedful without wavering, constant without newfangleness; bearing heavy things, though not lightly, yet willingly; entering hard things, though not easily, yet deeply; and so come to that perfectness of learning in the end, that quick wits seem in hope, but do not indeed, or else very seldom, ever attain unto. Also for manners and life, hard wits commonly are hardly carried either to desire every new thing, or else to marvel at every strange thing; and therefore they be careful and diligent in their own matters, not curious and busy in other men's affairs; and so they become wise themselves, and are also counted honest by others. They be grave, stedfast, silent of tongue, secret of heart. Not hasty in making, but constant in keeping any promise. Not rash in uttering, but wary in considering every matter; and thereby, not quick in speaking, but deep of judgment, whether they write or give counsel in all weighty affairs. And these be the men that become in the end both most happy for themselves, and always best esteemed abroad in the world.

I have been longer in describing the nature, the good or ill success of the quick and hard wit than perchance some will think this place and matter doth require. But my purpose was hereby plainly to utter what injury is offered to all learning, and to the commonwealth also, first by the fond father in choosing, but chiefly by the lewd scholemaster in beating and driving away the best natures from learning. A child that is still, silent, constant, and somewhat hard of wit is either never chosen by the father to be made a scholar, or else, when he cometh to the schole, he is smally regarded, little looked unto, he lacketh teaching, he lacketh couraging, he lacketh all things, only he never lacketh beating, nor any word that may move him to hate learning, nor any deed that may drive him from learning to any other kind of living.

And when this sad-natured and hard-witted child is beat from his book, and becometh after either student of the common law, or page in the court, or serving man, or bound apprentice to a merchant, or to some handicraft, he proveth in the end wiser, happier, and many times honester too, than many of these quick wits do by their learning.

Learning is both hindered and injured, too, by the ill choice of them that send young scholars to the universities. Of whom must needs come all our divines, lawyers, and physicians. These young scholars be chosen commonly, as young apples be chosen by children, in a fair garden about St. James' tide; a child will choose a Sweeting, because it is presently fair and pleasant, and refuse a Runnet, because it is then green, hard, and sour, when the one, if it be eaten, doth breed ill humors; the other, if it stand his time, be ordered and kept as it should, is wholesome of itself, and helpeth to the good digestion of other meats. Sweetings will receive worms, rot, and die on the tree, and never or seldom come to the gathering for good and lasting store.

For very grief of heart I will not apply the similitude; but hereby is plainly seen how learning is robbed of its best wits, first by the great beating, and after by the ill choosing of scholars to go to the universities. Whereof cometh partly that lewd and spiteful proverb, sounding to the great hurt of learning, and shame of learned men, that the greatest clerks be not the wisest men.

And though I, in all this discourse, seem plainly to prefer hard and rough wits, before quick and light wits, both for learning and manners, yet am I not ignorant that some quickness of wit is a singular gift of God, and so most rare amongst men, and namely such a wit as is quick without lightness, sharp without brittleness, desirous of good things without newfangleness, diligent in painful things without wearisomeness, and constant in good will to do all things well, as I know was in Sir John Cheke, and is in some that yet live, in whom all these fair qualities of wit are fully met together.

And speaking thus much of the wits of children for learning, the opportunity of the place, and goodness of the matter might require to have here declared the most special notes of a good wit for learning in a child, after the manner and custom of a good horseman, who is skilful to know, and able to tell others, how by certain sure signs a man may choose a colt that is like to prove another day excellent for the saddle. And it is pity that commonly more care is had, yea, and that amongst very wise men, to find out rather a cunning man for their horse than a cunning man for their children. They say nay in word, but they do so in deed. For to the one they will gladly give a stipend of 200 crowns by the year, and loth to offer to the other 200 shillings. God that sitteth in heaven laugheth their choice to scorn, and rewardeth their liberality as it should; for he suffereth them to have tame and well ordered horse, but wild and unfortunate children; and therefore in the end they find more pleasure in their horse than comfort in their children.

*   *   *   *   *

Yet some will say that children of nature love pastime and mislike learning, because in their kind the one is easy and pleasant, the other hard and wearisome: which is an opinion not so true as some men ween. For the matter lieth not so much in the disposition of them that be young, as in the order and manner of bringing up by them that be old, nor yet in the difference of learning and pastime. For beat a child if he dance not well, and cherish him though he learn not well, ye shall have him unwilling to go to dance, and glad to go to his book. Knock him always when he draweth his shaft ill, and favor him again though he fault at his book, ye shall have him very loth to be in the field, and very willing to be in the schole. Yea, I say more, and not of myself, but by the judgment of those from whom few wise men will gladly dissent, that if ever the nature of man be given at any time more than other to receive goodness, it is in innocency of young years before that experience of evil have taken root in him. For the pure clean wit of a sweet young babe is like the newest wax, most able to receive the best and fairest printing; and like a new bright silver dish never occupied, to receive and keep clean any good thing that is put into it.

And thus will in children, wisely wrought withal, may easily be won to be very well willing to learn. And wit in children by nature, namely memory, the only key and keeper of all learning, is readiest to receive and surest to keep any manner of thing that is learned in youth. This lewd and learned, by common experience, know to be most true. For we remember nothing so well when we be old, as those things which we learned when we were young. Therefore, if to the goodness of nature be joined the wisdom of the teacher in leading young wits into a right and plain way of learning, surely children, kept up in God's fear and governed by his grace, may most easily be brought well to serve God and country both by virtue and wisdom.

There is another discommodity besides cruelty in scholemasters in beating away the love of learning from children, which hindereth learning and virtue, and good bringing up of youth, and namely young gentlemen, very much in England. This fault is clean contrary to the first. I wished before to have love of learning bred up in children; I wish as much now to have young men brought up in good order of living, and in some more severe discipline than commonly they be. We have lack in England of such good order as the old noble Persians so carefully used, whose children, to the age of twenty-one years, were brought up in learning, and exercises of labor, and that in such place where they should neither see that was uncomely nor hear that was unhonest. Yea, a young gentleman was never free to go where he would and do what he list himself, but under the keep and by the counsel of some grave governor, until he was either married or called to bear some office in the commonwealth.

This evil is not common to poor men, as God will have it, but proper to rich and great men's children, as they deserve it. Indeed from seven to seventeen young gentlemen commonly be carefully enough brought up. But from seventeen to seven and twenty (the most dangerous time of all a man's life, and most slippery to stay well in) they have commonly the rein of all license in their own hand, and specially such as do live in the court. And that which is most to be marveled at, commonly the wisest and also best men be found the fondest fathers in this behalf. And if some good father would seek some remedy herein, yet the mother (if the household of our lady) had rather, yea, and will to, have her son cunning and bold, in making him to live trimly when he is young, than by learning and travel to be able to serve his prince and his country both wisely in peace and stoutly in war when he is old.

But nobility, governed by learning and wisdom, is indeed most like a fair ship, having tide and wind at will, under the rule of a skilful master; when contrariwise, a ship carried, yea, by the highest tide and greatest wind, lacking a skilful master, most commonly doth either sink itself upon sands or break itself upon rocks. And even so, how many have been either drowned in vain pleasure or overwhelmed by stout wilfulness the histories of England be able to afford over many examples unto us. Therefore, ye great and noble men's children, if ye will have right fully that praise, and enjoy surely that place which your fathers have, and elders had, and left unto you, ye must keep it as they got it, and that is by the only way of virtue, wisdom and worthiness.

XVI. JOHN MILTON.

BIOGRAPHICAL SKETCH.

Milton is best known as a poet. His "Paradise Lost," one of the world's great epics, has given him a place among the greatest singers of all time. But he was more than a poet. He was a scholar of wide attainments, a controversialist of great force, a patriot of unselfish purpose, and an educator of broad and independent spirit. The Commonwealth, it was said, owed its standing in Europe to Cromwell's battles and Milton's books.

He was born in London, December 9, 1608. He was educated at Cambridge, where he spent seven years and took the usual degrees. But the education of the time did not approve itself to his judgment, and later, as will be seen, he pointed out its defects of subject and method with trenchant force. He left the university in 1632, and spent the next five years in private study at his father's home in Buckinghamshire. Besides reading all the Greek and Latin writers of the classic period, he mastered Italian, and feasted, as he tells us, "with avidity and delight on Dante and Petrarch."

Tiring at length of his country life, Milton left England in 1638 for a tour on the continent. At Paris he met Grotius, one of the most learned men of his age, who resided at the French capital as ambassador from the Queen of Sweden. Afterwards he visited the principal cities of Italy, and was everywhere cordially received by men of learning. In his travels he preserved an admirable and cour-

BIOGRAPHICAL SKETCH

ageous independence; and even under the shadow of St. Peter's he made no effort to conceal his Puritan faith.

He was about to extend his travels to Sicily and Greece when the news of the civil commotion in England caused him to change his purpose. "I thought it base," he said, "to be traveling for amusement abroad, while my fellow-citizens were fighting for liberty at home." Not being called to serve the state in any official capacity on his arrival in London, he opened a private school, in which he tried to exemplify, in some measure at least, his educational theories. He held that languages should be studied, not for verbal drill, but for their literary treasures. At this period in his life he entered upon the religious and political controversies of the time, in which he showed himself a stout champion of Protestantism and the Commonwealth.

In 1644 Milton published two treatises that will long survive; the first is his "Areopagitica, or Speech for the Liberty of Unlicensed Printing," the other is his "Tractate on Education." It is the latter work that places him in the line of modern educational reformers. It was written at the earnest entreaty of Samuel Hartlib, a friend of Milton's, who was interested in educational reform and in the advancement of learning. In this "Tractate" Milton undertakes to "set down in writing," as he states in the opening paragraph, "that voluntary idea, which hath long in silence presented itself to me, of a better education, in extent and comprehension far more large, and yet of time far shorter, and of attainment far more certain, than hath been yet in practice." With the exception of the introductory paragraph, the "Tractate" is here given in its entirety.

SELECTION FROM MILTON.

A TRACTATE ON EDUCATION.

The end, then, of learning is to repair the ruins of our first parents by regaining to know God aright, and out of that knowledge to love him, to imitate him, to be like him, as we may the nearest by possessing our souls of true virtue, which being united to the heavenly grace of faith, makes up the highest perfection. But because our understanding cannot in this body found itself but on sensible things, nor arrive so clearly to the knowledge of God and things invisible, as by orderly conning over the visible and inferior creature; the same method is necessarily to be followed in all discreet teaching. And seeing every nation affords not experience and tradition enough for all kind of learning, therefore we are chiefly taught the languages of those people who have at any time been most industrious after wisdom; so that language is but the instrument conveying to us things useful to be known. And though a linguist should pride himself to have all the tongues that Babel cleft the world into, yet, if he have not studied the solid things in them, as well as the words and lexicons, he were nothing so much to be esteemed a learned man, as any yeoman or tradesman, competently wise in his mother-dialect only. Hence appear the many mistakes which have made learning generally so unpleasing, and so unsuccessful; first, we do amiss to spend seven or eight years merely in scraping together so much miserable Latin and Greek, as might be learned otherwise easily and delightfully in one year. And that which casts our proficiency therein so much behind, is our time lost, partly in too oft idle vacancies given both to schools and universities, partly in a preposterous exaction, forcing the empty wits of children to compose themes, verses and orations, which are the acts of ripest judgment, and the final work of a head filled by long reading and observing, with elegant maxims, and copious invention. These are not matters to be wrung from poor striplings, like blood out of the nose, or the plucking of untimely fruit. Besides the ill habit which they get of wretched barbarizing against the Latin and Greek idiom, with their untutored Anglicisms, odious to be read, yet not to be avoided without a well-continued and judicious conversing among pure authors digested, which they scarce taste; whereas, if after some preparatory grounds of speech, by their certain forms got into memory, they were led to the praxis thereof in some chosen short book lessoned thoroughly to them, they might then forthwith proceed to learn the substance of good things, and arts in due order, which would bring the whole language quickly into their power. This I take to be the most rational and most profitable way of learning languages, and whereby we may best hope to give account to God of our youth spent herein; and for the usual method of teaching arts, I deem it to be an old error of universities, not yet well recovered from the scholastic grossness of barbarous ages, that instead of beginning with arts most easy, (and those be such as are most obvious to the sense,) they present their young unmatriculated novices, at first coming, with the most intellective abstractions of logic and metaphysics: so that they having but newly left those grammatic flats and shallows, where they stuck unreasonably to learn a few words with lamentable construction, and now on the sudden transported under another climate, to be tossed and turmoiled with their unballasted wits, in fathomless and unquiet deeps of controversy, do for the most part grow into hatred and contempt of learning, mocked and deluded all this while with ragged notions and babblements, while they expected worthy and delightful knowledge; till poverty or youthful years call them importunately their several ways, and hasten them, with the sway of friends, either to an ambitious and mercenary, or ignorantly zealous divinity: some allured to the trade of law, grounding their purposes not on the prudent and heavenly contemplation of justice and equity, which was never taught them, but on the promising and pleasing thoughts of litigious terms, fat contentions, and flowing fees. Others betake them to state affairs, with souls so unprincipled in virtue, and true generous breeding, that flattery and court shifts, and tyrannous aphorisms, appear to them the highest points of wisdom; instilling their barren hearts with a conscientious slavery, if, as I rather think, it be not feigned. Others, lastly, of a more delicious and airy spirit, retire themselves, knowing no better, to the enjoyments of ease and luxury, living out their days in feast and jollity; which, indeed, is the wisest and the safest course of all these, unless they were with more integrity undertaken. And these are the errors, and these are the fruits of misspending our prime youth at the schools and universities, as we do, either in learning mere words, or such things chiefly as were better unlearned.

I shall detain you now no longer in the demonstration of what we should not do, but straight conduct you to a hill-side, where I will point you out the right path of a virtuous and noble education; laborious, indeed, at the first ascent, but else so smooth, so green, so full of goodly prospect, and melodious sounds on every side, that the harp of Orpheus was not more charming. I doubt not but ye shall have more ado to drive our dullest and laziest youth, our stocks and stubs, from the infinite desire of such a happy nurture, than we have now to hale and drag our choicest and hopefullest wits to that asinine feast of sow-thistles and brambles, which is commonly set before them, as all the food and entertainment of their tenderest and most docible age. I call therefore a complete and generous education, that which fits a man to perform justly, skilfully, and magnanimously, all the offices both private and public, of peace and war. And how all this may be done between twelve, and one-and-twenty, (less time than is now bestowed in pure trifling at grammar and sophistry), is to be thus ordered.

First, To find out a spacious house, and ground about it, fit for an academy, and big enough to lodge a hundred and fifty persons, whereof twenty, or thereabout, may be attendants, all under the government of one, who shall be thought of desert sufficient, and ability either to do all, or wisely to direct and oversee it done. This place should be at once both school and university, not needing a remove to any other house of scholarship, except it be some peculiar college of law, or physic, where they mean to be a practitioner; but as for those general studies, which take up all our time from Lilly to the commencing, as they term it, Master of Art, it should be absolute. After this pattern as many edifices may be converted to this use, as shall be needful in every city throughout this land, which would tend much to the increase of learning and civility everywhere. This number, less or more, thus collected to the convenience of a foot company, or interchangeably two troops of cavalry, should divide their day's work into three parts, as it lies orderly; their studies, their exercise, and their diet.

For their studies: First, they should begin with the chief and necessary rules of some good grammar, either that now used, or any better; and while this is doing, their speech is to be fashioned to a distinct and clear pronunciation, as near as may be to the Italian, especially in vowels: for we Englishmen being far northerly, do not open our mouths in the cold air, wide enough to grace a southern tongue; but are observed by all other nations to speak exceeding close and inward: so that to smatter Latin with an English mouth, is as ill a hearing as Law-French. Next, to make them expert in the usefullest points of grammar, and withal to season them, and win them early to the love of virtue and true labor, ere any flattering seducement, or vain principle seize them wondering, some easy and delightful book of education should be read to them; whereof the Greeks have store, as Cebes, Plutarch, and other Socratic discourses. But in Latin, we have none of classic authority extant, except the two or three first books of Quintilian, and some select pieces elsewhere. But here the main skill and ground-work will be to temper them such lectures and explanations upon every opportunity, as may lead and draw them in willing obedience, enflamed with a study of learning, and the admiration of virtue; stirred up with high hopes of living to be brave men, and worthy patriots, dear to God, and famous to all ages, that they may despise and scorn all their childish, and ill-taught qualities, to delight in manly and liberal exercises; which he who hath the art, and proper eloquence to catch them with, what with mild and effectual persuasions, and what with the intimation of some fear, if need be, but chiefly by his own example, might in a short space gain them to an incredible diligence and courage; infusing into their young breasts such an ingenuous and noble ardor, as would not fail to make many of them renowned and matchless men. At the same time, some other hour of the day, might be taught them the rules of arithmetic, and soon after the elements of geometry, even playing, as the old manner was. After evening repast till bedtime, their thoughts will be best taken up in the easy grounds of religion, and the story of Scripture. The next step would be to the authors on agriculture, Cato, Varro, and Columella, for the matter is most easy, and if the language be difficult, so much the better, it is not a difficulty above their years. And here will be an occasion of inciting and enabling them hereafter to improve the tillage of their country, to recover the bad soil, and to remedy the waste that is made of good; for this is one of Hercules' praises. Ere half these authors be read, (which will soon be with plying hard and daily), they cannot choose but be masters of any ordinary prose. So that it will be then seasonable for them to learn in any modern author the use of the globes, and all the maps; first, with the old names, and then with the new: or they might be then capable to read any compendious method of natural philosophy; and at the same time might be entering into the Greek tongue, after the same manner as was prescribed in the Latin; whereby the difficulties of grammar being soon overcome, all the historical physiology of Aristotle and Theophrastus are open before them, and as I may say, under contribution. The like access will be to Vitruvius, to Seneca's natural questions, to Mela, Celsus, Pliny, or Solinus. And having thus passed the principles of arithmetic, geometry, astronomy, and geography, with a general compact of physics, they may descend in mathematics to the instrumental science of trigonometry, and from thence to fortification, architecture, enginery or navigation. And in natural philosophy they may proceed leisurely from the history of meteors, minerals, plants, and living creatures, as far as anatomy. Then also in course might be read to them out of some not tedious writer the institution of physic; that they may know the tempers, the humors, the seasons, and how to manage a crudity: which he who can wisely and timely do, is not only a great physician to himself, and to his friends, but also may at some time or other save an army by this frugal and expenseless means only; and not let the healthy and stout bodies of young men rot away under him for want of this discipline; which is a great pity, and no less a shame to the commander. To set forward all these proceedings in nature and mathematics, what hinders, but that they may procure, as oft as shall be needful, the helpful experiences of hunters, fowlers, fishermen, shepherds, gardeners, apothecaries; and in the other sciences, architects, engineers, mariners, anatomists; who doubtless will be ready, some for reward, and some to favor such a hopeful seminary? And this will give them such a real tincture of natural knowledge, as they shall never forget, but daily augment with delight. Then also those poets which are now counted most hard, will be both facile and pleasant, Orpheus, Hesiod, Theocritus, Aratus, Nicander, Oppian, Dionysius, and in Latin, Lucretius, Manilius and the rural part of Virgil.

By this time, years and good general precepts will have furnished them more distinctly with that act of reason which in ethics is called Proairesis: that they may with some judgment contemplate upon moral good and evil. Then will be required a special reinforcement of constant and sound indoctrinating, to set them right and firm, instructing them more amply in the knowledge of virtue, and the hatred of vice: while their young and pliant affections are led through all the moral works of Plato, Xenophon, Cicero, Plutarch, Laertius, and those Locrian remnants; but still to be reduced in their nightward studies, wherewith they close the day's work, under the determinate sentence of David or Solomon, or the evangelists and apostolic Scriptures. Being perfect in the knowledge of personal duty, they may then begin the study of economics: and either now, or before this, they may have easily learned, at any odd hour, the Italian tongue. And soon after, but with wariness and good antidote, it would be wholesome enough to let them taste some choice comedies, Greek, Latin, or Italian: those tragedies also that treat of household matters, as Trachiniæ, Alcestis, and the like. The next remove must be to the study of politics; to know the beginning, end, and reasons of political societies; that they may not in a dangerous fit of the commonwealth be such poor, shaken, uncertain reeds, of such a tottering conscience as many of our great counselors have lately shown themselves, but steadfast pillars of the state. After this, they are to dive into the grounds of law, and legal justice; delivered first, and with best warrant, by Moses; and as far as human prudence can be trusted, in those extolled remains of Grecian lawgivers, Lycurgus, Solon, Zaleucus, Charondas, and thence to all the Roman edicts and tables, with their Justinian; and so down to the Saxon and common laws of England, and the statutes. Sundays also, and every evening, may be now understandingly spent in the highest matters of theology, and church history, ancient and modern: and ere this time the Hebrew tongue at a set hour might have been gained, that the Scriptures may be now read in their own original; whereto it would be no impossibility to add the Chaldee, and the Syrian dialect. When all these employments are well conquered, then will the choice histories, heroic poems, and Attic tragedies of stateliest and most regal argument, with all the famous political orations, offer themselves; which, if they were not only read, but some of them got by memory, and solemnly pronounced with right accent and grace, as might be taught, would endue them even with the spirit and vigor of Demosthenes or Cicero, Euripides or Sophocles. And now, lastly, will be the time to read with them those organic arts which enable men to discourse and write perspicuously, elegantly, and according to the fitted style of lofty, mean, or lowly. Logic therefore, so much as is useful, is to be referred to this due place, with all her well-couched heads and topics, until it be time to open her contracted palm, into a graceful and ornate rhetoric, taught out of the rule of Plato, Aristotle, Phalerius, Cicero, Hermogenes, Longinus. To which poetry would be made subsequent, or, indeed, rather precedent, as being less subtile and fine, but more simple, sensuous, and passionate. I mean not here the prosody of a verse, which they could not but have hit on before among the rudiments of grammer; but that sublime art which in Aristotle's poetics, in Horace, and the Italian commentaries of Castelvetro, Tasso, Mazzoni, and others, teaches what the laws are of a true epic poem, what of a dramatic, what of a lyric, what decorum is, which is the grand master-piece to observe. This would make them soon perceive what despicable creatures our common rhymers and play writers be, and show them what religious, what glorious and magnificent use might be made of poetry, both in divine and human things. From hence, and not till now, will be the right season of forming them to be able writers and composers in every excellent matter, when they shall be thus fraught with an universal insight into things. Or whether they be to speak in parliament or council, honor and attention would be waiting on their lips. There would then also appear in pulpits other visages, other gestures, and stuff otherwise wrought, than what we now sit under, oft-times to as great a trial of our patience, as any other that they preach to us. These are the studies wherein our noble and our gentle youth ought to bestow their time in a disciplinary way, from twelve to one-and-twenty; unless they rely more upon their ancestors dead, than upon themselves living. In which methodical course it is so supposed they must proceed by the steady pace of learning onward, as at convenient times, for memory's sake, to retire back into the middle ward, and sometimes into the rear of what they have been taught, until they have confirmed and solidly united the whole body of their perfected knowledge, like the last embattling of a Roman legion. Now will be worth the seeing what exercises and recreations may best agree and become these studies.

The course of study hitherto briefly described, is, what I can guess by reading, likest to those ancient and famous schools of Pythagoras, Plato, Isocrates, Aristotle, and such others, out of which were bred up such a number of renowned philosophers, orators, historians, poets and princes, all over Greece, Italy, and Asia, besides the flourishing studies of Cyrene and Alexandria. But herein it shall exceed them, and supply a defect as great as that which Plato noted in the commonwealth of Sparta; whereas that city trained up their youth most for war, and these in their academies and lyceum, all for the gown; this institution of breeding which I here delineate, shall be equally good, both for peace and war; therefore about an hour and a half ere they eat at noon, should be allowed them for exercise, and due rest afterwards: but the time for this may be enlarged at pleasure, according as their rising in the morning shall be early. The exercise which I commend first, is the exact use of their weapon, to guard and to strike safely with edge or point; this will keep them healthy, nimble, strong, and well in breath; is also the likeliest means to make them grow large and tall, and to inspire them with a gallant and fearless courage, which being tempered with seasonable lectures and precepts to them of true fortitude and patience, will turn into a native and heroic valor, and make them hate the cowardice of doing wrong. They must be also practiced in all the locks and gripes of wrestling, wherein Englishmen were wont to excel, as need may often be in fight to tug or grapple, and to close. And this, perhaps, will be enough, wherein to prove and heat their single strength. The interim of unsweating themselves regularly, and convenient rest before meat, may both with profit and delight be taken up in recreating and composing their travailed spirits, with the solemn and divine harmonies of music heard or learnt; either while the skilful organist plies his grave and fancied descants in lofty fugues, or the whole symphony with artful and unimaginable touches adorn and grace the well-studied chords of some choice composer; sometimes the lute, or soft organ-stop, waiting on elegant voices, either to religious, martial, or civil ditties; which, if wise men and prophets be not extremely out, have a great power over dispositions and manners; to smooth and make them gentle from rustic harshness and distempered passions. The like also would not be unexpedient after meat, to assist and cherish nature in her first concoction, and send their minds back to study in good tune and satisfaction; where having followed it close under vigilant eyes, till about two hours before supper, they are by a sudden alarum or watch-word, to be called out to their military motions under sky or covert, according to the season, as was the Roman wont; first on foot, then, as their age permits, on horseback, to all the art of cavalry: that, having in sport, but with much exactness, and daily muster, served out the rudiments of their soldiership in all the skill of embattling, marching, encamping, fortifying, besieging and battering, with all the helps of ancient and modern stratagems, tactics and warlike maxims, they may as it were out of a long war come forth renowned and perfect commanders in the service of their country. They would not then, if they were trusted with fair and hopeful armies, suffer them, for want of just and wise discipline, to shed away from about them like sick feathers, though they be never so oft supplied; they would not suffer their empty and unrecruitable colonels of twenty men in a company, to quaff out, or convey into secret hoards, the wages of a delusive list, and a miserable remnant: yet in the meanwhile to be over-mastered with a score or two of drunkards, the only soldiery left about them, or else to comply with all rapines and violences. No, certainly, if they knew aught of that knowledge which belongs to good men or good governors, they would not suffer these things. But to return to our own institute, besides these constant exercises at home, there is another opportunity of gaining experience, to be won from pleasure itself abroad. In those vernal seasons of the year, when the air is calm and pleasant, it were an injury and sullenness against nature not to go out and see her riches, and partake in her rejoicing with heaven and earth. I should not therefore be a persuader to them of studying much then, after two or three years that they have well laid their grounds, but to ride out in companies with prudent and staid guides, to all the quarters of the land; learning and observing all places of strength, all commodities of building and of soil, for towns and tillage, harbors and ports for trade. Sometimes taking sea as far as to our navy, to learn there also what they can in the practical knowledge of sailing, and of seafight. These ways would try all their peculiar gifts of nature, and if there were any secret excellence among them, would fetch it out, and give it fair opportunities to advance itself by, which could not but mightily redound to the good of this nation, and bring into fashion again those old admired virtues and excellencies, with far more advantage, now in this purity of Christian knowledge. Nor shall we then need the Monsieurs of Paris to take our hopeful youth into their slight and prodigal custodies, and send them over back again transformed into mimics, apes and kick-shoes. But if they desire to see other countries at three or four-and-twenty years of age, not to learn principles, but to enlarge experience, and make wise observations, they will by that time be such as shall deserve the regard and honor of all men where they pass, and the society and friendship of those in all places who are best and most eminent. And perhaps then other nations will be glad to visit us for their breeding, or else to imitate us in their own country.

Now, lastly, for their diet, there cannot be much to say, save only that it would be best in the same house; for much time else would be lost abroad, and many ill habits got; and that it should be plain, healthful and moderate, I suppose is out of controversy. Thus, Mr. Hartlib, you have a general view in writing, as your desire was, of that which at several times I had discoursed with you concerning the best and noblest way of education; not beginning, as some have done, from the cradle, which yet might be worth many considerations, if brevity had not been my scope. Many other circumstances also I could have mentioned, but this to such as have the worth in them to make trial, for light and direction, may be enough. Only, I believe that this is not a bow for every man to shoot in, that counts himself a teacher, but will require sinews almost equal to those which Homer gave Ulysses; yet I am withal persuaded, that it may prove much more easy in the essay, than it now seems at distance, and much more illustrious: howbeit, not more difficult than I imagine, and that imagination presents me with nothing but very happy and very possible, according to best wishes; if God hath so decreed, and this age hath spirit and capacity enough to apprehend.

XVII. JOHN AMOS COMENIUS.

BIOGRAPHICAL SKETCH.

John Amos Comenius, one of the most influential of modern educators, was born at Komna in Moravia, March 28, 1592. His family belonged to the earnest Protestant organization known as Moravian Brethren, in which he subsequently became a distinguished preacher and bishop. In youth he displayed an eager thirst for knowledge; but his experience in the schcols of the time opened his eyes to many defects in method and discipline, which later in life he earnestly endeavored to remedy. After studying at the College of Herborn and the University of Heidelberg, he took charge, in 1616, of the Moravian congregation at Fulneck, and in connection with his pastoral duties assumed direction of the recently established school there. But the busy and happy life which he had thus entered upon, was disturbed by the outbreak of the Thirty Years' War. In 1621 Fulneck was sacked by the Spaniards. Comenius lost all his property, including his library; and owing to the intolerance of the Austrian government, he was compelled at length to seek refuge at Lissa in Poland.

At Lissa he was placed at the head of the Moravian gymnasium, and he turned his attention anew to the theory and practice of education. He perused with deep interest the works of Ratich and Bacon, but observed " here and there," to use his own words, " some defects and gaps. . . . Therefore, after many workings and tossings of my thoughts, by reducing everything to the immovable law of nature, I lighted upon my 'Great Didactic,' which shows the art of readily and solidly teaching all men all things." This work, which remained in manuscript till 1649, is one of the greatest of all books on educational theory and method; and though, after a temporary vogue, it was neglected for some two hundred years, its principles in recent decades have done much to reform the schools of Christendom.

Comenius next set about reforming the teaching of Latin, which was then carried on in the most unscientific manner. Schools were little short of a terror to boys; instruction in unintelligible Latin grammars was accompanied with an inconsiderate and sometimes cruel use of the rod. Comenius emphasized the teaching of *things* as well as of *words*. As he states it in his "Gate of Tongues Unlocked" (*Janua Linguarum Reserata*), which was published in 1631, "My fundamental principle — an irrefragable law of didactics — is that the understanding and the tongue should advance in parallel lines always." This book had an immense success, and was translated into no fewer than a dozen European languages.

The fame of Comenius was now well established throughout Europe. In 1641 he was invited to England to reform education and to establish a "universal college." But the time was not propitious. The excitement and uncertainty connected with the approaching civil war threw all his plans into confusion. At this juncture he accepted an invitation to visit Sweden. There he elaborately discussed with Oxenstiern, "the eagle of the North," his great educational schemes. His cherished pansophic plans were not encouraged; and as a result of this conference, he withdrew to Elbing in Prussia and devoted the next four years to the preparation of his "Latest Method with Languages" (*Methodus Linguarum Novissima*), in which he laid down the principle that words and things should be learned together; that theory should not be divorced from practice; and that study should advance by easy gradations. This work appeared in 1648.

In 1650 Comenius established a model school at Patak in Hungary, where he produced his "World Illustrated" (*Orbis Pictus*), the most famous of all his writings. This work contains, as stated on the title-page, "the pictures and names of all the principal things in the world, and of all the principal occupations of man." It was designed to lay a solid foundation of knowledge in accurate sense-perception. "The foundation of all knowledge," as Comenius explained, "consists in representing clearly to the senses sensible objects, so that they can be apprehended easily."

In 1654 Comenius returned to Lissa, where one more misfortune awaited him. Two years later the town was plundered by the Poles, and he lost his house, books, and above all, his manuscripts. "This loss," he said, "I shall cease to lament only when I cease to breathe." After several months' wandering in Germany, he was offered an asylum at Amsterdam by Laurence de Geer. Here he spent the remaining years of his life, devoting himself to teaching as a means of support, and to the promulgation and defense of his educational views. His last days were somewhat imbittered by envious attacks upon his character and methods, but in all his trials he exhibited a meek, forbearing Christian spirit. He died in 1671 at the advanced age of eighty years.

The following selection is taken from Keatinge's translation of "The Great Didactic." The opening paragraphs present important or fundamental views from the earlier chapters. The sixteenth chapter is given in full for two reasons: 1. It exhibits the process, not always convincing perhaps, by which the great Moravian arrives at his conclusions; and 2, The principles he lays down as the foundation upon which the imposing superstructure of his educational system is based.

SELECTION FROM COMENIUS.

THE GREAT DIDACTIC.

1. The seeds of knowledge, of virtue, and of piety are naturally implanted in us; but the actual knowledge, virtue, and piety are not so given. These must be acquired by prayer, by education, and by action. He gave no bad definition who said that man was a "teachable animal." And indeed it is only by a proper education that he can become a man.

2. All who have been born to man's estate have been born with the same end in view, namely, that they may be men, that is to say, rational creatures, the lords of other creatures, and the images of their Creator. All, therefore, must be brought on to a point at which, being properly imbued with wisdom, virtue, and piety, they may usefully employ the present life and be worthily prepared for that to come. God himself has frequently asserted that with him there is no respect of persons, so that if, while we admit some to the culture of the intellect, we exclude others, we commit an injury not only against those who share the same nature as ourselves, but against God himself, who wishes to be acknowledged, to be loved, and to be praised by all upon whom he has impressed his image. In this respect the fervor of all men will increase in proportion to the flame of knowledge that has been kindled. For our love is in direct ratio to our knowledge.

3. Nor can any sufficient reason be given why the weaker sex (to give a word of advice on this point in particular)

should be altogether excluded from the pursuit of knowledge, whether in Latin or in their mother-tongue. They also are formed in the image of God, and share in his grace and in the kingdom of the world to come. They are endowed with equal sharpness of mind and capacity for knowledge (often with more than the opposite sex), and they are able to attain the highest positions, since they have often been called by God himself to rule over nations, to give sound advice to kings and princes, to the study of medicine and of other things which benefit the human race, even to the office of prophesying and of inveighing against priests and bishops. Why, therefore, should we admit them to the alphabet, and afterwards drive them away from books? Do we fear their folly? The more we occupy their thoughts, so much the less will the folly that arises from emptiness of mind find a place.

4. Things themselves, as far as they concern us, can be divided into three classes only: 1, Objects that we can observe, such as the heavens, the earth, and all that is in them; 2, Objects that we can imitate, such as the marvelous order which pervades all things, and which man ought to imitate in his actions; 3, Objects that we can enjoy, such as the grace of God and his manifold blessing here and for eternity. If man is to acquit himself creditably when brought into contact with this order of nature, he must be trained to know the things that are spread out for his observation in this marvelous amphitheatre, to do the things that it is right for him to do, and finally, to enjoy those things of which the most benign Creator, treating him as a guest in his house, has with liberal hand given him the fruition.

5. I call a school that fulfils its function perfectly, one which is a true forging-place of men; where the minds of those who learn are illuminated by the light of wisdom, so

as to penetrate with ease all that is manifest and all that is secret, where the emotions and the desires are brought into harmony with virtue, and where the heart is filled with and permeated by divine love, so that all who are handed over to Christian schools to be imbued with true wisdom, may be taught to live a heavenly life on earth; in a word, where all men are taught all things thoroughly.

CHAPTER XVI.

The universal requirements of teaching and of learning; that is to say, a method of teaching and of learning with such certainty that the desired result must of necessity follow.

1. Exceptionally fine is that comparison made by our Lord Jesus Christ in the gospel, " So is the kingdom of God, as if a man should cast seed upon the earth; and should sleep and rise night and day, and the seed should spring up and grow, he knoweth not how. The earth beareth fruit of herself; first the blade, then the ear, then the full corn in the ear. But when the fruit is ripe, straightway he putteth forth the sickle, because the harvest is come." (Mark iv. 26).

2. The Savior here shows that it is God who operates in everything, and that nothing remains for man but to receive the seeds of instruction with a devout heart; the processes of growth and of ripening will then continue of themselves, unperceived by him. The duty of the teachers of the young, therefore, is none other than skilfully to scatter the seeds of instruction in their minds, and carefully to water God's plants. Increase and growth will come from above.

3. Is there any who denies that sowing and planting

need skill and experience? If an unpracticed gardener plant an orchard with young trees, the greater number of them die, and the few that prosper do so rather through chance than through skill. But the trained gardener goes to work carefully, since he is well instructed, where, when, and how to act and what to leave alone, that he may meet with no failure. It is true that even an experienced man meets with failure occasionally (indeed it is scarcely possible for a man to take such careful forethought that no error can arise); but we are now discussing, not the abstract question of circumspection and chance, but the art of doing away with chance by means of circumspection.

4. Hitherto the method of instruction has been so uncertain that scarcely any one would dare to say: "In so many years I will bring this youth to such and such a point, I will educate him in such and such a way." We must therefore see if it be possible to place the art of intellectual discipline on such a firm basis that sure and certain progress may be made.

5. Since this basis can be properly laid only by assimilating the processes of art as much as possible to those of nature, we will follow the method of nature, taking as our example a bird hatching out its young; and, if we see with what good results gardeners, painters, and builders follow in the track of nature, we shall have to recognize that the educator of the young should follow in the same path.

6. If any think this course of action petty or commonplace, let him consider that from that which is of daily occurrence and universal notoriety and which takes place with good results in nature and in the arts (the teaching art excepted), we are seeking to deduce that which is less known and which is necessary for our present purpose. Indeed, if the facts from which we derive the principles that form the basis for our precepts are known, we can

entertain hopes that our conclusions will be the more evident.

First Principle.

7. *Nature observes a suitable time.*— For example: a bird that wishes to multiply its species, does not set about it in winter, when everything is stiff with cold, nor in summer when everything is parched and withered by the heat; nor in autumn, when the vital force of all creatures declines with the sun's declining rays, and a new winter with hostile mien is approaching; but in spring, when the sun brings back life and strength to all. Again, the process consists of several steps. While it is yet cold the bird conceives the eggs and warms them inside its body, where they are protected from the cold; when the air grows warmer it lays them in its nest, but does not hatch them out until the warm season comes, that the tender chicks may grow accustomed to light and warmth by degrees.

8. *Imitation.*— In the same way the gardener takes care to do nothing out of season. He does not, therefore, plant in the winter (because the sap is then in the roots, preparing to mount and nourish the plant later on); nor in summer (when the sap is already dispersed through the branches); nor in autumn (when the sap is retiring to the roots once more); but in spring, when the moisture is beginning to rise from the roots and the upper part of the plant begins to shoot. Later on, too, it is of great importance to the little tree that the right time be chosen for the various operations that are needful, such as manuring, pruning, and cutting. Even the tree itself has its proper time for putting forth shoots and blossoms, for growing, and for coming to maturity.

In the same manner the careful builder must choose the right time for cutting timber, burning bricks, laying foundations, building and plastering walls, etc.

9. *Deviation.*— In direct opposition to this principle, a twofold error is committed in schools.

(i.) The right time for mental exercise is not chosen.

(ii.) The exercises are not properly divided, so that all advance may be made through the several stages needful, without any omission. As long as the boy is still a child he cannot be taught, because the roots of his understanding are still too deep below the surface. As soon as he becomes old, it is too late to teach him, because the intellect and the memory are then failing. In middle age it is difficult, because the forces of the intellect are dissipated over a variety of objects and are not easily concentrated. The season of youth, therefore, must be chosen. Then life and mind are fresh and gathering strength; then everything is vigorous and strikes root deeply.

10. *Rectification.*— We conclude, therefore, that

(i.) The education of men should be commenced in the springtime of life, that is to say, in boyhood (for boyhood is the equivalent of spring, youth of summer, manhood of autumn, and old age of winter).

(ii.) The morning hours are the most suitable for study (for here again the morning is the equivalent of spring, midday of summer, the evening of autumn, and the night of winter).

(iii.) All the subjects that are to be learned should be arranged so as to suit the age of the students, that nothing which is beyond their comprehension be given them to learn.

Second Principle.

11. *Nature prepares the material, before she begins to give it form.*— For example: the bird that wishes to produce a creature similar to itself first conceives the embryo from a drop of its blood; it then prepares the nest in which

it is to lay the eggs, but does not begin to hatch them until the chick is formed and moves within the shell.

12. *Imitation.*— In the same way the prudent builder, before he begins to erect a building, collects a quantity of wood, lime, stones, iron, and the other things needful, in order that he may not have to stop the work later on from lack of materials, nor find that its solidity has been impaired. In the same way, the painter who wishes to produce a picture, prepares the canvas, stretches it on a frame, lays the ground on it, mixes his colors, places his brushes so that they may be ready to hand, and then at last commences to paint.

In the same way the gardener, before he commences operations, tries to have the garden, the stocks, the grafts, and the tools in readiness, that he may not have to fetch the necessary appliances while at work, and so spoil the whole operation.

13. *Deviation.*— Against this principle schools are offenders: firstly, because they take no care to prepare beforehand the mechanical aids such as books, maps, pictures, diagrams, etc., and to have them in readiness for general use, but at the moment that they need this or that, they make experiments, draw, dictate, copy, etc., and when this is done by an unskilled or careless teacher (and their number increases daily), the result is deplorable. It is just as if a physician, whenever he wishes to administer a medicine, had to wander through gardens and forests, and collect and distil herbs and roots, though medicaments to suit every case should be ready to his hand.

14. Secondly, because even in school-books, the natural order, that the matter come first and the form follow, is not observed. Everywhere the exact opposite is to be found. The classification of objects is unnaturally made to precede a knowledge of the objects themselves, although it is im-

possible to classify, before the matter to be classified is there.

I will demonstrate this by four examples:

15. (1) Languages are learned in schools before the sciences, since the intellect is detained for some years over the study of languages, and only then allowed to proceed to the sciences, mathematics, physics, etc. And yet things are essential, words only accidental; things are the body, words but the garment; things are the kernel, words the shells and husks. Both should therefore be presented to the intellect at the same time, but particularly the things, since they are as much objects of the understanding as are languages.

16. (2) Even in the study of languages the proper order is reversed, since the students commence, not with some author or with a skilfully-compiled phrase-book, but with the grammar; though the authors (and in their own way the phrase-books) present the material of speech, namely, words, while the grammars on the other hand, only give the form; that is to say, the laws of the foundation, order, and combination of words.

17. (3) In the encyclopædic compilations of human knowledge, the arts are always placed first, while the sciences follow after, though the latter teach of the things themselves, the former how to manipulate the things.

18. (4) Finally: it is the abstract rules that are first taught and then illustrated by dragging in a few examples; though it is plain that a light should precede him whom it lights.

19. *Rectification.*—It follows, therefore, that in order to effect a thorough improvement in schools it is necessary:

(i.) That books and the materials necessary for teaching be held in readiness.

(ii.) That the understanding be first instructed in things, and then taught to express them in language.

(iii.) That no language be learned from a grammar, but from suitable authors.

(iv.) That the knowledge of things precede the knowledge of their combinations.

(v.) And that examples come before rules.

Third Principle.

20. *Nature chooses a fit subject to act upon, or first submits one to a suitable treatment in order to make it fit.*— For example: a bird does not place any object in the nest in which it sits, but an object of such a kind that a chicken can be hatched from it; that is to say, an egg. If a small stone or anything else falls into the nest, it throws it out as useless. But when the process of hatching takes place, it warms the material contained in the egg, and looks after it until the chicken makes its way out.

21. *Imitation.*— In the same way the builder cuts down timber, of as good quality as possible, dries it, squares it, and saws it into planks. Then he chooses a spot to build on, clears it, lays a new foundation, or repairs the old one so that he can make use of it.

22. In the same way, if the canvas or the surface do not suit his colors, the painter tries to make them more suitable, and, by rubbing them and polishing them, fits them for his use.

23. The gardener too (1) chooses from a fruit-bearing stock a shoot that possesses as much vitality as possible; (2) transplants it to a garden, and places it carefully in the earth; (3) does not burden it with a new graft unless he sees that it has taken root; (4) before he inserts the new graft, removes the former shoot, and even cuts a piece away round the stock in order that none of the sap may

perform any function other than that of vivifying the graft.

24. *Deviation.*— Against this principle the schools are offenders; not because they include the weak of intellect (for in our opinion all the young should be admitted into the schools) but far more because:

(1) These tender plants are not transplanted into the garden, that is to say, are not entirely entrusted to the schools, so that none, who are to be trained as men, shall be allowed to leave the workshop before their training is complete.

(2) The attempt is generally made to engraft that noblest graft of knowledge, virtue and piety, too early, before the stock itself has taken root; that is to say, before the desire to learn has been excited in those who have no natural bent in that direction.

(3) The side-shoots or root-suckers are not removed before the grafting takes place; that is to say, the minds are not freed from all idle tendencies by being habituated to discipline and order.

25. *Rectification.*— It is therefore desirable:

(i.) That all who enter schools persevere in their studies.

(ii.) That, before any special study is introduced, the mind of the student be prepared and made receptive of it.

(iii.) That all obstacles be removed out of the way of schools.

"For it is of no use to give precepts," says Seneca, "unless the obstacles that stand in the way be removed."

Fourth Principle.

26. *Nature is not confused in its operations, but in its forward progress advances distinctly from one point to another.*— For example: if a bird is being produced, its bones, veins, and nerves are formed at separate and distinct periods;

at one time its flesh becomes firm, at another it receives its covering of skin or feathers, and at another it learns how to fly, etc.

27. *Imitation.*— When a builder lays foundations, he does not build the walls at the same time, much less does he put on the roof, but does each of these things at the proper time and in the proper place.

28. In the same way a painter does not work at twenty or thirty pictures at once, but occupies himself with one only. For, though he may from time to time put a few touches to some others or give his attention to something else, it is on one picture and one only that he concentrates his energies.

29. In the same way the gardener does not plant several shoots at once, but plants them one after the other, that he may neither confuse himself nor spoil the operations of nature.

30. *Deviation.*— Confusion has arisen in the schools through the endeavor to teach the scholars many things at one time. As, for example, Latin and Greek grammar, perhaps rhetoric and poetic as well, and a multitude of other subjects. For it is notorious that in the classical schools the subject-matter for reading and for composition is changed almost every hour throughout the day. If this be not confusion I should like to know what is. It is just as if a shoemaker wished to make six or seven new shoes at once, and took them up one by one in turn, only to lay them aside in a few minutes; or as if a baker, who wished to place various kinds of bread in his oven, were to take them out again immediately, removing one kind as he put in another. Who would commit such an act of folly? The shoemaker finishes one shoe before he begins to make another. The baker places no fresh bread in the oven until that already in it is thoroughly baked.

31. *Rectification.*— Let us imitate these people and take care not to confuse scholars who are learning grammar by teaching them dialectic, or by introducing rhetoric into their studies. We should also put off the study of Greek until Latin is mastered, since it is impossible to concentrate the mind on any one thing, when it has to busy itself with several things at once.

That great man, Joseph Scaliger, was well aware of this. It is related of him that (perhaps on the advice of his father) he never occupied himself with more than one branch of knowledge at once, and concentrated all his energies on that one. It was owing to this that he was able to master not only fourteen languages, but also all the arts and sciences that lie within the province of man. He devoted himself to these one after the other with such success that in each subject his learning excelled that of men who had given their whole lives to it. And those who have tried to follow in his footsteps and imitate his method, have done so with considerable success.

32. Schools, therefore, should be organized in such a manner that the scholar shall be occupied with only one object of study at any given time.

Fifth Principle.

33. *In all the operations of nature development is from within.*— For example: in the case of the bird it is not the claws, or the feathers, or the skin that is first formed, but the inner parts; the outer parts are formed later, at the proper season.

34. *Imitation.*— In the same way the gardener does not insert his graft into the outer bark nor into the outside layer of wood, but making an incision right into the pith, places the graft as far in as it will go.

In this way he makes the joint so firm that the sap cannot escape, but is forced right into the shoot, and uses all its strength in vivifying it.

35. So too, a tree, that is nourished by the rain of heaven and the moisture of the earth, assimilates its nutriment, not through its outer bark, but the pores of its inmost parts. On this account the gardener waters, not the branches, but the roots. Animals also convey their food, not to their outer limbs, but to the stomach, which assimilates it and nourishes the whole body. If, therefore, the educator of the young give special attention to the roots of knowledge, the understanding, these will soon impart their vitality to the stem, that is, to the memory, and finally blossoms and fruits, that is to say, a facile use of language and practical capacity, will be produced.

36. *Deviation.*— It is on this point that those teachers fall into error who, instead of thoroughly explaining the subjects of study to the boys under their charge, give them endless dictations, and make them learn their lessons off by heart. Even those who wish to explain the subject-matter do not know how to do so; that is to say, do not know how to tend the roots or how to engraft the graft of knowledge. Thus they fatigue their pupils, and resemble a man who uses a club or a mallet, instead of a knife, when he wishes to make an incision in a plant.

37. *Rectification.*— It therefore follows:

(i.) That the scholar should be taught first to understand things, and then to remember them, and that no stress should be laid on the use of speech or pen, till after a training on the first two points.

(ii.) That the teacher should know all the methods by which the understanding may be sharpened, and should put them into practice skilfully.

Sixth Principle.

38. *Nature, in its formative processes, begins with the universal and ends with the particular.*— For example: a bird is to be produced from an egg. It is not the head, an eye, a feather, or a claw that is first formed, but the following process takes place. The whole egg is warmed, the warmth produces movement, and this movement brings into existence a system of veins, which mark in outline the shape of the whole bird (defining the parts that are to become the head, the wings, the feet, etc.). It is not until this outline is complete that the individual parts are brought to perfection.

39. *Imitation.*— The builder takes this as his model. He first makes a general plan of the building in his head, or on paper, or in wood. Then he lays the foundations, builds the walls, and lays on the roof. It is not until he has done this that he gives his attention to the small details that are necessary to complete a house, such as doors, windows, staircases, etc.; while last of all he adds ornamentation such as paintings, sculptures, and carpets.

40. An artist proceeds in the same way. He does not begin by drawing an ear, an eye, a nose, or a mouth, but first makes a charcoal sketch of the face or of the whole body. If he be satisfied that this sketch resembles the original, he paints it with light strokes of the brush, still omitting all detail. Then, finally, he puts in the light and shade, and, using a variety of colors, finishes the several parts in detail.

41. The procedure of the sculptor is the same. When he wishes to carve a statue, he takes a block of marble and shapes it roughly. Then he sets to work more carefully and outlines the most important features. Finally, he chisels the

individual parts with the greatest accuracy and colors them artistically.

42. In the same way the gardener takes the most simple and universal part of a tree, namely, a shoot. Later on, this can put forth as many branches as it possesses buds.

43. *Deviation.*— From this it follows that it is a mistake to teach the several branches of science in detail before a general outline of the whole realm of knowledge has been placed before the student, and that no one should be instructed in such a way as to become proficient in any one branch of knowledge without thoroughly understanding its relation to all the rest.

44. It follows also that arts, sciences, and languages are badly taught unless a general notion of the elements be first given. I remember well that, when we began to learn dialectic, rhetoric, and metaphysics, we were, at the very beginning, overburdened with long-winded rules, with commentaries and notes on commentaries, with comparison of authors and with knotty questions. Latin grammar was taught us with all the exceptions and irregularities; Greek grammar with all its dialects, and we, poor wretches, were so confused that we scarcely understood what it was all about.

45. *Rectification.*—The remedy for this want of system is as follows: At the very commencement of their studies, boys should receive instruction in the first principles of general culture, that is to say, the subjects learned should be arranged in such a manner that the studies that come later introduce nothing new, but only expand the elements of knowledge that the boy has already mastered. Just as a tree, even if it live for a hundred years, puts no new branches, but only suffers those that already exist to develop and to spread.

(i.) Each language, science, or art must be first taught in its most simple elements, that the student may obtain a general idea of it. (ii.) His knowledge may next be developed further by placing rules and examples before him. (iii.) Then he may be allowed to learn the subject systematically with the exceptions and irregularities; and (iv.), last of all, may be given a commentary, though only where it is absolutely necessary. For he who has thoroughly mastered a subject from the beginning will have little need of a commentary, but will soon be in the position to write one himself.

Seventh Principle.

46. *Nature makes no leaps, but proceeds step by step.*— The development of a chicken consists of certain gradual processes which cannot be omitted or deferred, until finally it breaks its shell and comes forth. When this takes place, the mother does not allow the young bird to fly and seek its food (indeed it is unable to do so), but she feeds it herself, and by keeping it warm with her body promotes the growth of its feathers. When the chick's feathers have grown she does not thrust it forth from the nest immediately and make it fly, but teaches it first to move its wings in the nest itself or perching on its edge, then to try to fly outside the nest, though quite near it, by fluttering from branch to branch, then to fly from tree to tree, and later on from hill to hill, till finally it gains sufficient confidence to fly right out in the open. It is easy to see how necessary it is that each of these processes should take place at the right time; that not only the time should be suitable but that the processes should be graduated; and that there should be not graduation merely, but an immutable graduation.

47. *Imitation.*— The builder proceeds in the same manner. He does not begin with the gables or with the walls, but with the foundations. When the foundations are laid he

does not go on with the roof, but builds the walls. In a word, the order in which the several stages are combined depends on the relation that they mutually bear to one another.

48. The gardener likewise has to adopt the principle of graduation. The wild-stock must be found, dug up, transplanted, pruned, and cut; the graft must be inserted and the joint made firm, etc., and none of these processes can be omitted or taken in a different order. But, if these processes are carried out properly and in the right order, it is scarcely possible, in fact it is impossible, for the result to be unsuccessful.

49. *Deviation.*— It is an evident absurdity, therefore, if teachers for their own sake and that of their pupils, do not graduate the subjects which they teach in such a way that, not only one stage may lead on directly to the next, but also that each shall be completed in a given space of time. For unless goals are set up, means provided for reaching them, and a proper system devised for the use of those means, it is easy for something to be omitted or perverted, and failure is the result.

50. *Rectification.*— It follows therefore:

(i.) That all studies should be carefully graduated throughout the various classes, in such a way that those that come first may prepare the way for and throw light on those that come after.

(ii.) That the time should be carefully divided, so that each year, each month, each day, and each hour may have its appointed task.

(iii) That the division of the time and of the subjects of study should be rigidly adhered to, that nothing may be omitted or perverted.

Eighth Principle.

51. *If nature commences anything, it does not leave off until the operation is completed.*— If a bird, urged by the impulse of nature, begins to sit on eggs, she does not leave off until she has hatched out the chickens. If she sat on them for a few hours only, the embryo in the egg would become cold and die. Even when the chickens are hatched she does not cease to keep them warm, but continues to do so until they have grown strong, are covered with feathers, and can endure the cold air.

52. *Imitation.*— The painter, also, who has begun a picture, will produce his work best if he finish it without any interruption. For in this case the colors blend better and hold faster.

53. For this reason it is best to finish the erection of a building without any interruption; otherwise the sun, the wind, and the rain spoil the work, the later additions will not be so firm, and on every side there will be cracks, weak spots, and loose joints.

54. The gardener, too, acts with wisdom, for when once he has begun to work at a graft he does not cease until the operation is completed. Since, if the sap dry in the stock or in the graft, owing to a delay in completing the process, the plant is ruined.

55. *Deviation.*— It is therefore injurious if boys are sent to school for months or years continuously, but are then withdrawn for considerable periods and employed otherwise; equally so if the teacher commences now one subject, now another, and finishes nothing satisfactorily; and lastly, it is equally fatal if he does not fix a certain task for each hour, and complete it, so that in each period his pupil can make an unmistakable advance towards the desired goal. Where

such a fire is wanting, everything grows cold. Not without reason does the proverb say, "Strike while the iron is hot." For if it be allowed to cool it is useless to hammer it, but it must once more be placed in the fire, and thus much time and iron are wasted. Since every time that it is heated, it loses some of its mass.

56. *Rectification.*— It follows therefore:

(i.) That he who is sent to school must be kept there until he becomes well informed, virtuous, and pious.

(ii.) That the school must be situated in a quiet spot, far from noise and distractions.

(iii.) That whatever has to be done, in accordance with the scheme of study, must be done without any shirking.

(iv.) That no boys, under any pretext whatever, should be allowed to stay away or to play truant.

Ninth Principle.

57. *Nature carefully avoids obstacles and things likely to cause hurt.*— For example, when a bird is hatching eggs it does not allow a cold wind, much less rain or hail to reach them. It also drives away snakes, birds of prey, etc.

58. *Imitation.*—In the same way the builder, so far as is possible, keeps dry his wood, bricks, and lime, and does not allow what he has built to be destroyed or to fall down.

59. So, too, the painter protects a newly-painted picture from wind, from violent heat, and from dust, and allows no hand but his own to touch it.

60. The gardener also protects a young plant by a railing or by hurdles, that hares or goats may not gnaw it or root it up.

61. *Deviation.*—It is therefore folly to introduce a student to controversial points when he is just beginning a subject; that is to say, to allow a mind that is mastering

something new to assume an attitude of doubt. What is this but to tear up a plant that is just beginning to strike root? (Rightly does Hugo say: "He who starts by investigating doubtful points will never enter into the temple of wisdom.") But this is exactly what takes place if the young are not protected from incorrect, intricate, and badly written books as well as from evil companions.

62. *Rectification.*—Care should therefore be taken

(i.) That the scholars receive no books but those suitable for their classes.

(ii.) That these books be of such a kind that they can rightly be termed sources of wisdom, virtue, and piety.

(iii.) That neither in the school nor in its vicinity the scholars be allowed to mix with bad companions.

63. If all these recommendations are observed, it is scarcely possible that schools should fail to attain their object.

XVIII. JOHN LOCKE.

BIOGRAPHICAL SKETCH.

John Locke, distinguished as a philosopher and educator, was born at Wrington in Somersetshire, August 29, 1632. His father served as captain in the Parliamentary army during the Civil War. After receiving a preparatory training at Westminster School, he proceeded to Oxford, where he took his bachelor's degree in 1655. He was endowed with a penetrating and practical mind, and, like Milton at Cambridge, he early found fault with the university on account of its extreme conservative tendencies. In after-life he expressed regret that so much of his time had been wasted in what he regarded as profitless studies.

After taking his degree Locke studied medicine, in which he made noteworthy attainments. In 1664 he went to Berlin as secretary to the English envoy Sir William Swan. Returning to Oxford at the end of a year, he made the acquaintance of the Earl of Shaftesbury, by whom he was introduced into the society of the most eminent political leaders of the day. He superintended the education of the Earl of Shaftesbury's son; and it was while acting as tutor in this distinguished family, that he developed the comprehensive and independent views embodied in his great educational treatise presently to be noticed.

Having become involved in the political troubles of his generous patron, who had been charged with treason, Locke deemed it prudent to go to Holland in voluntary exile. This was in 1682. In 1688 he returned to England in the fleet that conveyed the Princess of Orange. The year following he published his great philosophical work, "An Essay Concerning Human Understanding," which was designed to establish the capabilities and the limitations of the human mind. It had a wide circulation not only in England, but also in France and Germany; and everywhere it exerted an immense influence upon philosophic thought.

In 1693, after he had achieved a European reputation as a philosopher, he published a treatise entitled, "Some Thoughts Concerning Education." It is not very careful in style nor methodical in its arrangement; but it is especially noteworthy as the first attempt in England to discuss education in a comprehensive and practical way. Though primarily designed to direct the education of a gentleman, or nobleman, the work, in large measure, is applicable to general education. It has influenced educational thought in no small degree, Rollin and Rousseau, in particular, borrowing from it in large measure.

"Locke is a thorough Englishman," says Karl Schmidt, "and the principle underlying his education is the principle according to which the English people have developed. Hence his theory of education has in the history of pedagogy the same value that the English nation has in the history of the world. He stood in strong opposition to the scholastic education current in his time, a living protest against the prevailing pedantry; in the universal development of pedagogy he gives impulse to the movement which grounds education upon sound psychological principles, and lays stress upon breeding and the formation of character."

Locke's treatise covers more than two hundred octavo pages. The following extracts, in every case the language of the original, are designed to exhibit his views on all essential points, and will be read with interest.

SELECTIONS FROM JOHN LOCKE.

SOME THOUGHTS CONCERNING EDUCATION.

1. A sound mind in a sound body is a short but full description of a happy state in this world; he that has these two has little more to wish for; and he that wants either of them will be but little the better for anything else. Men's happiness or misery is most part of their own making. He whose mind directs not wisely will never take the right way; and he whose body is crazy and feeble will never be able to advance in it. I confess there are some men's constitutions of body and mind so vigorous, and well framed by nature that they need not much assistance from others; but, by the strength of their natural genius, they are, from their cradles, carried towards what is excellent; and, by the privilege of their happy constitutions, are able to do wonders. But examples of this kind are but few; and I think I may say that of all the men we meet with, nine parts of ten are good or evil, useful or not, by their education. It is that which makes the great difference in mankind.

2. I imagine the minds of children as easily turned this or that way as water itself; and though this be the principal part, and our main care should be about the inside, yet the clay cottage is not to be neglected. How necessary health is to our business and happiness, and how requisite a strong constitution, able to endure hardships and fatigue, is to one that will make any figure in the world, is too obvious to need any proof. What concerns the body and health reduces itself to these few and easily observable rules. Plenty of open air, exercise, and sleep; plain diet, no wine or strong drink, and very little or no physic; not too warm and strait clothing; especially the head and feet

kept cold, and the feet often used to cold water and exposed to wet.

3. The great mistake I have observed in people's breeding their children has been that this has not been taken care enough of in its due season; that the mind has not been made obedient to discipline, and pliant to reason, when at first it was most tender, most easy to be bowed. Parents being wisely ordained by nature to love their children, are very apt, if reason watch not that natural affection very warily — are apt, I say, to let it run into fondness. They love their little ones, and it is their duty: but they often with them cherish their faults too. They must not be crossed, forsooth; they must be permitted to have their wills in all things: and they being in their infancies not capable of great vices, their parents think they may safely enough indulge their little irregularities, and make themselves sport with that pretty perverseness, which they think well enough becomes that innocent age. But to a fond parent, that would not have his child corrected for a perverse trick, but excused it, saying it was a small matter, Solon very well replied: "Aye, but custom is a great one."

4. He that has not a mastery over his inclinations, he that knows not how to resist the importunity of present pleasure or pain, for the sake of what reason tells him is fit to be done, wants the true principle of virtue and industry, and is in danger of never being good for anything. This temper, therefore, so contrary to unguided nature, is to be got betimes; and this habit, as the true foundation of future ability and happiness, is to be wrought into the mind as early as may be, even from the first dawnings of any knowledge or apprehension in children; and so to be confirmed in them, by all the care and ways imaginable, by those who have the oversight of their education.

5. On the other hand, if the mind be curbed and hum-

bled too much in children; if their spirits be abased and broken much by too strict a hand over them, they lose all their vigor and industry, and are in a worse state than the former. For extravagant young fellows, that have liveliness and spirit, need sometimes to be set right, and so make able and great men: but dejected minds, timorous and tame, and low spirits, are hardly ever to be raised, and very seldom attain to anything. To avoid the danger that is on either hand is the great art: and he that has found a way how to keep up a child's spirit, easy, active, and free, and yet, at the same time, to restrain him from many things he has a mind to, and to draw him to things that are uneasy to him — he, I say, that knows how to reconcile these seeming contradictions, has, in my opinion, got the true secret of education.

6. He therefore that is about children should well study their natures and aptitudes, and see, by often trials, what turn they easily take, and what becomes them; observe what their native stock is, how it may be improved, and what it is fit for; he should consider what they want, whether they be capable of having it wrought into them by industry, and incorporated there by practice; and whether it be worth while to endeavor it. For in many cases all that we can do or should aim at, is to make the best of what nature has given, to prevent the vices and faults to which such a constitution is most inclined, and give it all the advantages it is capable of. Every one's natural genius should be carried as far as it could; but to attempt the putting another upon him will be but labor in vain; and what is so plaistered on will at best sit but untowardly, and have always hanging to it the ungracefulness of constraint and affectation.

7. It is virtue, direct virtue, which is the hard and valuable part to be aimed at in education, and not a forward

pertness or any little arts of shifting. All other considerations and accomplishments should give way and be postponed to this. This is the solid and substantial good, which tutors should not only read lectures and talk of, but the labor and art of education should furnish the mind with, and fasten there, and never cease till the young man had a true relish to it, and placed his strength, his glory, and his pleasure in it.

The more this advances, the easier way will be made for other accomplishments in their turns. For he that is brought to submit to virtue will not be refractory or resty in anything that becomes him. And therefore I can not but prefer breeding of a young gentleman at home in his father's sight, under a good governor, as much the best and safest way to this great and main end of education, when it can be had, and is ordered as it should be.

8. It will perhaps be wondered that I mention reasoning with children; and yet I can not but think that the true way of dealing with them. They understand it as early as they do language; and if I misobserve not, they love to be treated as rational creatures sooner than is imagined. It is a pride should be cherished in them, and as much as can be, made the greatest instrument to turn them by.

But when I talk of reasoning, I do not intend any other but such as is suited to the child's capacity and apprehension. Nobody can think a boy of three or seven years old should be argued with as a grown man. Long discourses and philosophical reasonings at best amaze and confound, but do not instruct children. When I say therefore that they must be treated as rational creatures, I mean that you should make them sensible, by the mildness of your carriage, and the composure, even in your correction of them, that what you do is reasonable in you, and useful and necessary for them; and that it is not out of caprice, passion, or fancy that you command or forbid them anything. This they are capable of understanding; and there is no virtue they should be excited to, nor fault they should be kept from, which I do not think they may be convinced of; but it must be by such reasons as their age and understanding are capable of, and those proposed always in very few and plain words.

9. Beating is the worst, and therefore the last means to be used in the correction of children; and that only in cases of extremity, after all gentler ways have been tried, and proved unsuccessful: which, if well observed, there will be very seldom any need of blows. For, it not being to be imagined that a child will often, if ever, dispute his father's present command in any particular instance; and the father not interposing his absolute authority, in peremptory rules, concerning either childish or indifferent actions, wherein his son is to have his liberty; or concerning his learning or improvement, wherein there is no compulsion to be used: there remains only the prohibition of some vicious actions, wherein a child is capable of obstinacy, and consequently can deserve beating; and so there will be but very few occasions of that discipline to be used by any one who considers well, and orders his child's education as it should be.

10. The character of a sober man and a scholar is what every one expects in a tutor. This generally is thought enough, and is all that parents commonly look for. But when such an one has emptied out into his pupil all the Latin and logic he has brought from the university, will that furniture make him a fine gentleman? Or can it be expected that he should be better bred, better skilled in the world, better principled in the grounds and foundations of true virtue and generosity than his young tutor is?

The great work of a governor is to fashion the carriage and form the mind; to settle in his pupil good habits, and the principles of virtue and wisdom; to give him, by little and little, a view of mankind; and work him into a love and imitation of what is excellent and praiseworthy; and, in the prosecution of it, to give him vigor, activity, and industry. The studies which he sets him upon are but, as it were, the exercises of his faculties, and employment of his time, to keep him from sauntering and idleness, to teach him application, and accustom him to take pains, and to give him some little taste of what his own industry must perfect. For who expects that under a tutor a young gentleman should be an accomplished critic, orator, or logician; go to the bottom of metaphysics, natural philosophy, or mathematics; or be a master in history or chronology? though something of each of these is to be taught him: but it is only to open the door that he may look in, and, as it were, begin an acquaintance, but not to dwell there; and a governor would be much blamed that should keep his pupil too long, and lead him too far in most of them. But of good breeding, knowledge of the world, virtue, industry, and a love of reputation, he can not have too much; and if he have these, he will not long want what he needs or desires of the other.

11. That which every gentleman (that takes any care of his education) desires for his son, besides the estate he leaves him, is contained, I suppose, in these four things, *virtue, wisdom, breeding,* and *learning.* I place virtue as the first and most necessary of those endowments that belong to a man or a gentleman, as absolutely requisite to make him valued and beloved by others, acceptable or tolerable to himself. Without that, I think, he will be happy neither in this nor the other world.

Wisdom I take, in the popular acceptation, for a man's

managing his business ably, and with foresight, in this world. This is the product of a good natural temper, application of mind, and experience together; and so above the reach of children. The greatest thing that in them can be done towards it, is to hinder them, as much as may be, from being cunning; which, being the ape of wisdom, is the most distant from it that can be. To accustom a child to have true notions of things, and not to be satisfied till he has them; to raise his mind to great and worthy thoughts; and to keep him at a distance from falsehood and cunning, which has always a broad mixture of falsehood in it, is the fittest preparation of a child for wisdom.

The next good quality belonging to a gentleman is good-breeding. There are two sorts of ill-breeding: the one, a sheepish bashfulness; and the other, a misbecoming negligence and disrespect in our carriage — both which are avoided by only observing this one rule: Not to think meanly of ourselves, and not to think meanly of others.

12. You will wonder, perhaps, that I put learning last, especially if I tell you I think it the least part. This may seem strange in the mouth of a bookish man: and this making usually the chief, if not only bustle and stir about children, this being almost that alone which is thought on, when people talk of education, makes it the greater paradox. When I consider what ado is made about a little Latin and Greek, how many years are spent in it, and what a noise and business it makes to no purpose, I can hardly forbear thinking that the parents of children still live in fear of the schoolmaster's rod, which they look on as the only instrument of education; as if a language or two were its whole business. How else is it possible that a child should be chained to the oar seven, eight, or ten of the best years of his life, to get a language or two, which

I think might be had at a great deal cheaper rate of pains and time, and be learned almost in playing?

13. The great skill of a teacher is to get and keep the attention of his scholar: whilst he has that, he is sure to advance as fast as the learner's abilities will carry him; and without that, all his bustle and pother will be to little or no purpose. To attain this, he should make the child comprehend (as much as may be) the usefulness of what he teaches him; and let him see, by what he has learned, that he can do something which he could not do before; something which gives him some power and real advantage above others, who are ignorant of it. To this he should add sweetness in all his instructions; and by a certain tenderness in his whole carriage, make the child sensible that he loves him, and designs nothing but his good; the only way to beget love in the child, which will make him hearken to his lessons, and relish what he teaches him.

14. When, by interlining Latin and English one with another, he has got a moderate knowledge of the Latin tongue, he may then be advanced a little further to the reading of some other easy Latin book, such as Justin, or Eutropius; and to make the reading and understanding of it the less tedious and difficult to him, let him help himself, if he please, with the English translation. Nor let the objection, that he will then know it only by rote, fright any one. This, when well considered, is not of any moment against, but plainly for, this way of learning a language; for languages are only to be learned by rote; and a man, who does not speak English or Latin perfectly by rote, so that having thought of the thing he would speak of, his tongue of course, without thought of rule or grammar, falls into the proper expression and idiom of that language, does not speak it well, nor is master of it. And I would fain have any one name to me that tongue, that

any one can learn or speak as he should do, by the rules of grammar. Languages were made not by rules or art, but by accident, and the common use of the people. And he that will speak them well, has no other rule but that; nor anything to trust to but his memory, and the habit of speaking after the fashion learned from those that are allowed to speak properly, which, in other words, is only to speak by rote.

It will possibly be asked here, Is grammar then of no use? And have those who have taken so much pains in reducing several languages to rules and observations, who have writ so much about declensions and conjugations, about concords and syntaxis, lost their labor, and been learned to no purpose? I say not so; grammar has its place too. But this I think I may say, there is more stir a great deal made with it than there needs, and those are tormented about it, to whom it does not at all belong; I mean children, at the age wherein they are usually perplexed with it in grammar-schools.

15. Since it is English that an English gentleman will have constant use of, that is the language he should chiefly cultivate, and wherein most care should be taken to polish and perfect his style. To speak or write better Latin than English may make a man be talked of; but he would find it more to his purpose to express himself well in his own tongue, that he uses every moment, than to have the vain commendation of others for a very insignificant quality. This I find universally neglected, and no care taken anywhere to improve young men in their own language, that they may thoroughly understand and be masters of it. If any one among us have a facility or purity more than ordinary in his mother-tongue, it is owing to chance, or his genius, or anything, rather than to his education, or any care of his teacher. To mind what English his pupil speaks

or writes, is below the dignity of one bred up amongst Greek and Latin, though he have but little of them himself. These are the learned languages, fit only for learned men to meddle with and teach; English is the language of the illiterate vulgar; though yet we see the policy of some of our neighbors hath not thought it beneath the public care to promote and reward the improvement of their own language.

16. This is, in short, what I have thought concerning a young gentleman's studies; wherein it will possibly be wondered, that I should omit Greek, since amongst the Grecians is to be found the original, as it were, and foundation of all that learning which we have in this part of the world. I grant it so; and will add, that no man can pass for a scholar that is ignorant of the Greek tongue. But I am not here considering the education of a professed scholar, but of a gentleman, to whom Latin and French, as the world now goes, is by every one acknowledged to be necessary. When he comes to be a man, if he has a mind to carry his studies further, and look into the Greek learning, he will then easily get that tongue himself; and if he has not that inclination, his learning of it under a tutor, will be but lost labor, and much of his time and pains spent in that, which will be neglected and thrown away, as soon as he is at liberty. For how many are there of an hundred, even amongst scholars themselves, who retain the Greek they carried from school; or ever improve it to a familiar reading, and perfect understanding of Greek authors?

17. Order and constancy are said to make the great difference between one man and another; of this I am sure, nothing so much clears a learner's way, helps him so much on in it, and makes him go so easy and so far in any inquiry, as a good method. His governor should take pains to make him sensible of this, accustom him to order, and teach him

method in all the applications of his thought; show him wherein it lies, and the advantages of it; acquaint him with the several sorts of it, either from general to particulars, or from particulars to what is more general; exercise him in both of them; and make him see in what cases each different method is most proper, and to what ends it best serves.

In history the order of time should govern; in philosophical inquiries, that of nature, which in all progression is to go from the place one is then in, to that which joins and lies next to it; and so it is in the mind, from the knowledge it stands possessed of already, to that which lies next, and is coherent to it; and so on to what it aims at, by the simplest and most uncompounded parts it can divide the matter into. To this purpose, it will be of great use to his pupil to accustom him to distinguish well, that is, to have distinct notions, wherever the mind can find any real difference; but as carefully to avoid distinctions in terms, where he has not distinct and different clear ideas.

XIX. FÉNELON.

BIOGRAPHICAL SKETCH.

This celebrated ecclesiastic and teacher was born in the province of Périgord, August 6, 1651. From an early age he was remarkable for his industry, his amiable disposition, and his thirst for knowledge. Up to the age of twelve his education was conducted at home; he was then sent to Cahors, and two years later to Paris, where his course of instruction was completed. Destined to the clerical office by his family, and inclined toward it by natural gifts and disposition, he entered the theological seminary of Saint-Sulpice, and won general esteem by his application, ability, and exemplary character. He was ordained priest at the age of twenty-four, and four years later he was placed over an institution in Paris designed for the instruction of young women who had renounced the Protestant faith. He spent ten years of his life as director of this institution, and it was while in charge of it that he wrote his excellent and famous treatise on the " Education of Girls."

After the revocation of the Edict of Nantes, Fénelon was placed at the head of a mission that was sent to Poitou to labor among the Protestant portion of the population. He fulfilled the trying duties of this office with gentleness and toleration; and such was the affability of his manners and the charm of his discourse that his labors were not unattended with success. In the words of Antonin Roche, " No person was more capable than he of rendering virtue attractive by that touching and effective language which addresses itself to the heart and inspires confidence. To this precious gift he joined the merit of giving his instructions that simple, clear, and agreeable form that placed them within reach of all minds."

In 1689 he was appointed tutor to the young Duke of Burgundy, grandson of Louis XIV. This young prince was endowed with fine natural abilities, but possessed of an inordinate pride and a furious temper. This rendered Fénelon's task exceedingly difficult, but he discharged its duties with rare wisdom and surprising success. Under his skilful and affectionate instruction, the young prince developed the virtues of patience, self-control, and kindly consideration. As aids to his instruction Fénelon composed fables, compiled histories, and wrote fiction, particularly "Telemachus," which holds a permanent place in the classic literature of France. A brilliant future was predicted for this young duke, but unfortunately death intervened to prevent its realization.

In 1695 Fénelon was elevated to the archbishopric of Cambray in recognition of his distinguished ability and service. He devoted himself conscientiously to the duties of his diocese. He led a life of great simplicity, and divided his time between the administration of affairs and the personal instruction of his flock. Though he had delighted the French court by his eloquence, and had embarrassed Bossuet by his learning and force of argument, yet he found pleasure in going through the villages of his diocese to teach the simple peasantry the catechism in language suited to their uncultured condition.

The later years of his life were rendered unhappy by theological controversies, by the displeasure of the king, and by the loss of his dearest friends. His disappointments and sorrows were grievous, but he bore them with touching resignation. "He died," says Lamartine, "like a saint and poet, listening to the sweetest and sublimest hymns, which carried at the same time his imagination and his soul to heaven." His death occurred January 7, 1715.

Fénelon's "Education of Girls," which was published in 1681, has the distinction of being the first systematic and comprehensive treatise ever written on the subject. It consists of thirteen chapters, the first two of which here follow without abridgment. From the remaining chapters such passages are given as will present Fénelon's views in tolerable completeness. As will be seen, he may be regarded as an advocate of the higher education of woman, "fully recognizing the influence she exerts in the home and in society." In this he belongs to the list of modern educational reformers. But his views are somewhat limited by his belief that woman is intellectually inferior to man, and by his fundamental principle that her education should be restricted to the practical needs of domestic life. In addition to specific recommendations as to study and methods, the treatise is rich in general pedagogical principles of great insight and wisdom.

"We have today," says Paroz in his *Histoire Universelle de la Pédagogie,* "educational works that are more complete and systematic, but this one will live because of its excellent spirit and beautiful style. In all ages and in every land it will be read with pleasure and profit. Of all the Catholic clergy who have engaged in educational work, Fénelon has perhaps approached nearest to the rational principles which form the basis of modern pedagogy. The order of nature has a place in his theology, and he knows how to reconcile the needs of temporal life with the spirit of Christianity. This characteristic will always assign him a high rank among educators."

SELECTION FROM FÉNELON.

THE EDUCATION OF GIRLS.

The Importance of the Education of Girls.

1. Nothing is more neglected than the education of girls. Custom and the caprice of mothers frequently decide everything: people suppose that they ought to give but little instruction to this sex. The education of boys passes for one of the principal concerns of life through its relation to the public weal; and although scarcely fewer mistakes are made than in the education of girls, people are at least persuaded that much intelligence is needed to succeed in it. The cleverest people have endeavored to give rules in this matter. How many teachers and colleges we see! What expense for the printing of books, for the researches of science, for methods of learning the languages, for the choice of professors! All this great preparation often has more superficiality than solidity; but it indicates the high conception people have of the education of boys. As for girls, they say, it is not necessary that they be learned, curiosity renders them vain and affected; it is enough if they know how to govern some day their households, and to obey their husbands without question. People do not fail to refer to many women whom science has rendered ridiculous: after which they believe themselves justified in blindly abandoning girls to the management of ignorant and indiscreet mothers.

2. It is true that we should fear making ridiculous scholars. Women ordinarily have minds weaker and more inquisitive than men; thus it is not expedient to engage them in studies that might turn their heads. They are not to govern the state, make war, or enter the sacred ministry;

accordingly they can dispense with certain branches of knowledge which belong to statecraft, the art of war, jurisprudence, philosophy, and theology. The greater part of the mechanic arts does not suit them: they are constituted for moderate exertion. Their bodies, as well as their minds, are less strong and robust than those of men; in return, nature has given them industry, neatness, and economy, to occupy them tranquilly in their homes.

3. But what follows from this natural weakness of women? The more they are weak, the more important is it to make them strong. Have they not duties to perform, even duties which form the foundation of all human life? Is it not women that ruin or uphold families, that regulate all the details of domestic life, and that decide, consequently, what touches most closely the whole human race? In that way they have the principal part in the good or the bad manners of almost the entire world. A judicious, diligent, and pious wife is the soul of a great household; she introduces order there for temporal welfare and future salvation. Even men, who have all authority in public, can not, by their deliberations, establish any efficient good, if women do not aid them to execute it.

4. The world is not a phantom; it is the union of all the families: and who can govern them with a nicer care than women who, besides their natural authority and their diligence in the household, have still the advantage of being born painstaking, attentive to details, industrious, winning, and persuasive? Can men themselves hope for any happiness in life, if their most intimate relation, which is that of marriage, turns to bitterness? And what will become of the children, who are later to constitute the human race, if their mothers spoil them from infancy?

5. These, then, are the occupations of women, which are scarcely less important to the public than those of men,

since they have households to regulate, husbands to make happy, and children to bring up well. Add to this that virtue is no less for women than for men; without speaking of the good or ill they can do to the public, they are the half of the human race, redeemed by the blood of Jesus Christ, and destined to eternal life.

6. Finally, we must consider, besides the good which women do when they are well brought up, the evil which they cause in the world when they lack an education which inspires them with virtue. It is unquestionable that the bad education of women does more harm than that of men, since the disorders of men often come both from the evil training which they have received from their mothers, and from the passions which other women have inspired in them at a more advanced age. What intrigues are presented to us in history, what overturnings of laws and manners, what bloody wars, what innovations in religion, what revolutions in the state, caused by the profligacy of women! These are the considerations that prove the importance of giving girls a good education: let us seek the means of doing so.

Defects of the Prevailing Education.

7. A girl's ignorance is the cause that she grows weary, and that she does not know how to employ herself innocently. When she has reached a certain age without applying herself to solid things, she has neither a taste nor regard for them; all that is serious appears to her sad, all that demands sustained attention fatigues her; the inclination to pleasure, which is strong in youth, the examples of persons of the same age who are plunged in amusements — all serves to make her fear a regular and laborious life. At this early age she lacks the experience and authority to manage anything in the house of her parents; she does not even know the im-

portance of applying herself to it, unless her mother has taken care to instruct her in detail. If she is of rank, she is exempt from the work of her hands: she will work therefore only some hour of the day, because people say, without knowing why, that it is proper for women to work; but often it will be only a pretense, and she will not become accustomed to continuous employment.

8. In this condition what will she do? The companionship of a mother who watches her, who scolds her, who thinks she is bringing her up properly by overlooking nothing, who is reconciled with her, who makes her endure her whims, and who always appears burdened with domestic cares, offends and repels her; she has around her flattering women, who seek to insinuate themselves into her regard by base and dangerous attentions, follow all her idle fancies, and entertain her with all that can disgust her with the good: piety seems to her a tiresome business — a rule hostile to every pleasure. With what will she occupy herself? With nothing useful. This heedlessness will even turn into an incurable habit.

9. Meanwhile there is a great vacancy, which one can not hope to fill with solid things; it is necessary, therefore, that frivolous things take their place. In this inactivity a girl gives herself up to idleness; and idleness, which is a languor of the soul, is an inexhaustible source of weariness. She accustoms herself to sleep a third more than would be needful to keep her in perfect health; this large amount of sleep serves only to enervate her, to make her more delicate, more exposed to bodily ills: while moderate sleep, accompanied by regular exercise, renders a person cheerful, vigorous and strong — a thing which undoubtedly tends to the true perfection of the body, not to speak of its advantages to the mind. This effeminacy and indolence, being joined to ignorance, beget a pernicious desire for diversions and

plays; they excite an inconsiderate and insatiable curiosity.

10. Persons who are educated and engaged in serious employments, have ordinarily only a moderate curiosity: what they know gives them a contempt for many things that they do not know; they see the uselessness and folly of most of the things which little minds that know nothing and have nothing to do, are eager to learn.

On the contrary, girls who are badly educated and indolent, always have a wandering imagination. For lack of solid nourishment, their curiosity ardently turns toward vain and dangerous objects. Those who have cleverness often become affected, and read all the books that can feed their vanity; they become passionately fond of novels, comedies, and fantastic adventures, in which sexual love has a place. They develop a visionary spirit of accustoming themselves to the magniloquent language of romantic heroes: they are even spoiled in that way for society; for all those beautiful, high-flown sentiments, all those generous passions, all those adventures which the author of the novel has invented for pleasure, have no connection with the true motives that operate in the world and decide its affairs, nor with the disappointments that one finds in all that one undertakes.

A poor girl, full of the tender and marvelous incidents that have charmed her in her reading, is astonished not to find in society real persons resembling these heroes: she would like to live as imaginary princesses, who in novels are always charming, always adored, and always above every need. What disgust for her to descend from this heroism to the smallest details of housekeeping!

11. Some women push their inquisitiveness still further, and meddle in the decision of religious questions, although they lack the requisite knowledge. But those who have not sufficient openness of mind for these matters, have others that are suited to them: they ardently desire to know what

is said, what is done, a song, a bit of news, an intrigue; to receive letters, to read those that others receive; they wish to be told all, and also to tell all; they are vain, and vanity talks a great deal; they are frivolous, and frivolity prevents the thoughtfulness which would often keep silent.

Various Principles and Recommendations.

12. It is necessary to be content with following and aiding nature. Children know but little, we should not urge them to talk: but since they do not know many things, they have many questions to ask. It is sufficient to answer them precisely, and to add sometimes little comparisons in order to render more intelligible the explanations that one is to give them. If they express a judgment of something without knowing it well, it is needful to embarrass them by some new question, in order to make them feel their error, without rudely putting them to confusion. At the same time we should let them see, not by vague praises, but by some practical mark of esteem, that we approve them much more when they doubt and when they ask what they do not know, than when they decide the best. This is the true means of imparting to their minds, with much politeness, a genuine modesty, and a great contempt for the wranglings that are so common with young people of little intelligence.

13. The curiosity of children is a natural inclination which goes out to meet instruction; do not fail to take advantage of it. In the country, for example, they see a mill, and wish to know what it is; we should show them how the food that nourishes man is prepared. They observe some harvesters, and it is necessary to explain to them what they are doing, how grain is sowed, and how it multiplies in the earth. In the city they see shops where different arts are practiced, and where different articles of merchandise are

sold. We should never be annoyed by their questions; these are openings which nature offers in order to facilitate instruction: express a pleasure in them; in that way you will gradually teach them how all the things are made which are of use to man, and with which commerce is concerned. Little by little, without special study, they will learn the best way to make everything they need, and the just value of it, which is the true foundation of economy. This knowledge, which ought to be despised by no one, since everybody has need to estimate his expense, is chiefly necessary to girls.

14. We have remarked that the brain of children is altogether warm and moist, a fact that gives them continual movement. By reason of this softness of the brain everything is easily impressed upon it, and the images of all sensible objects are very vivid: hence we should make haste to write on their minds while the characters are easily formed there. But we should chose well the images that we are to engrave there; for we should pour into so small and precious a receptacle only exquisite things: we should remember that we ought, at that age, to pour into minds only what we desire to remain there for life. The first impressions made while the brain is still soft, and nothing is written there, are the most profound. Besides they harden as age dries the brain; hence they become ineffaceable: whence it happens that when one is old, one distinctly remembers the things of youth, although far distant, while one recollects less clearly what has been seen at a more advanced age, because the impressions have been made upon the brain when it was hardened and full of other images.

15. At the same time it is necessary to seek every means to render agreeable to the child what you demand of her. If you have something unpleasant to propose, let her understand that the pain will be soon followed by pleasure; show her always the utility of the things you teach her; make her

see their use in relation to society and the duties of her station. Without that, study will seem to her an abstract, fruitless, and painful toil. Of what use is it, they will say to themselves, to learn all these things which people do not talk about in conversation, and which have no relation to what we are obliged to do? It is necessary, therefore, to give them a reason for what we teach them. It is to enable you, you will say to them, to do well what you will have to do some day; it is to form your judgment; it is to accustom you to reason correctly about all the affairs of life. We should always show them a substantial and agreeable end which will sustain them in their labor, and never pretend to bring them into subjection by a base and absolute authority.

16. Note a great fault in the prevailing education: we put all the pleasure on one side, and all the irksomeness on the other; all the irksomeness in study, and all the pleasure in amusement. What can a child do but bear this rule impatiently, and ardently run after games?

Let us endeavor then to change this order: let us render study agreeable, let us conceal it under the appearance of liberty and pleasure; let us allow children sometimes to interrupt their studies with little flights of amusement; they have need of these distractions in order to rest their minds.

17. Let us come now to the things in which a woman ought to be instructed. What are her employments? She is charged with the education of her children; with the boys up to a certain age, with the girls till they are married or enter a convent; with the management of servants, with their manners and duties; with the details of expense, with the means of doing everything economically and honorably; and ordinarily even with directing the estate and receiving its revenues.

The learning of women, as that of men, ought to be restricted to knowledge relating to their duties; the difference of their employments should make that of their studies. It is necessary therefore to limit the instruction of women to the things we have just mentioned. But an acquisitive woman will find that this is giving very narrow bounds to her desire for knowledge; she is mistaken; it is because she does not know the importance and the extent of the things in which I propose to have her instructed.

18. Though the difficulty of finding governesses is great, we must confess that there is another still greater; it is that of the irregularity of parents: all the rest is useless, unless they are willing to coöperate themselves in the work. The foundation of all is that they give their children only correct maxims and edifying examples. It is what one can hope for only in a very small number of families. In most homes we see only confusion, change, a crowd of wrong-headed servants, and disagreement of master and mistress. What a frightful school for children! Often a mother who passes her life at cards, at the theater, and in unbecoming conversation, complains in a grave tone that she can not find a governess capable of educating her daughters. But what can the best education do with girls in view of such a mother?

XX. CHARLES ROLLIN.

BIOGRAPHICAL SKETCH.

Charles Rollin was a distinguished historian and educator. He is known in America chiefly through his "Ancient History," which a few decades ago was widely disseminated among our people. Though exhibiting a wide acquaintance with ancient writers, who are freely quoted, this work has been superseded in recent years by more critical histories.

Rollin was born in Paris, January 30, 1661. He was the son of a poor cutler, who intended to train up his son to the same trade; but happily the boy's talents were discovered by a Benedictine friar, who had him sent to the Collége du Plessis. He made rapid progress in his studies, especially in rhetoric and literature. Later he studied theology at the Sorbonne, the most celebrated of the Roman Catholic seminaries of France.

In 1688 he became professor of eloquence in the College of France. He encouraged the study of the French language and literature, and revived an interest in the ancient tongues, particularly in Greek. In 1694 he was appointed rector of the University of Paris, and signalized his brief tenure of two years by the introduction of salutary reforms. A few years later he was placed at the head of the College of Beauvais, where his great reputation soon filled the deserted halls with students. But his life, notwithstanding his eminence and piety, was not suffered to run smoothly. His adherence to Jansenism brought upon him the persecution of the Jesuits, and in 1712 he was forced to resign his office.

In 1720 he was called from his modest and busy retirement to assume again the management of the University as rector. Six years later he published his famous "Treatise on Studies," or, as the title of the book reads, "The Method of Teaching and Studying the Belles-Lettres." Apart from his own varied experience, Rollin drew his materials largely from Plato, Aristotle, and especially from Quintilian and Seneca; but he profited also from the pedagogical labors of his contemporaries. Fénelon in particular is frequently quoted.

The four volumes of the "Treatise on Studies" discusses in successive books the education of young children, the learning of languages, poetry, rhetoric, eloquence, history, and philosophy. It is the most comprehensive work on pedagogy that was written in the eighteenth century. Its great value was soon recognized, and translations of it were made into several foreign languages, including the English.

The following extract, with some unimportant omissions, constitutes Part First of Book VI., which is devoted to a discussion of "the government of classes and colleges." Part Second of this book is devoted to "particular duties relating to the education of youth," such as the diet of students, their studies, college discipline, religion, etc. The extract is remarkable for the emphasis it places on the moral and religious side of education, while its lofty aims and noble spirit are worthy of the high commendation the "Treatise on Studies" has received.

SELECTION FROM ROLLIN.

GENERAL INSTRUCTIONS UPON THE EDUCATION OF YOUTH.

The education of youth has been always considered by the great philosophers and the most famous lawgivers as the most certain source of the tranquillity and happiness both of private families and of states and empires. For what else, in short, is a republic or kingdom, but a large body, whose health and strength depend upon those of private families, which are the members and parts of it, and none of which can fail in the discharge of their function, but the whole body must be sensible of it? Now what is it but good education which enables all the citizens and great men, and princes above the rest, to perform their different functions in a deserving manner? Is it not evident that youth are as the nursery of the state? That it is renewed and perpetuated by them? That from among them all the fathers of families, all magistrates and ministers, in a word, all persons placed in authority and power are taken? And is it not certain that the good education of those who are one day to fill those places, will have an influence over the whole body of the state, and become, in a manner, the spirit and general character of the whole nation?

ARTICLE I.—*What End We Should Propose to Ourselves in Education.*

If we consult our reason ever so little, it is easy to discern that the end which masters should have in view is not barely to teach their scholars Greek and Latin, to teach them to make exercises and verses, to charge their memory with facts and historical dates, to draw up syllogisms in form, or to trace lines and figures upon paper. These branches of learning I own are useful and valuable, but as means and not as the end; when they conduct us to other things, and not when we stop at them; when they serve us as preparation and instruments for better knowledge, without which the rest would be useless. Youth would have cause to complain, if they were condemned to spend eight or ten of the best years of their life in learning, at a great expense and with incredible pains, one or two languages, and some other matters of a like nature, which perhaps they would seldom have occasion to use. The end of masters in the long course of their studies is to habituate their scholars to serious application of mind, to make them love and value the sciences, and to cultivate in them such a taste as shall make them thirst after them when they have gone from school; to point out the method of attaining them, and to make them thoroughly sensible of their use and value; and by that means dispose them for the different employments to which it shall please God to call them. Besides this, the end of masters should be to improve their hearts and understandings, to protect their innocence, to inspire them with principles of honor and probity, to train them up to good habits, to correct and subdue in them by gentle means the ill inclinations they shall be observed to have, such as pride, insolence, an high opinion of themselves, and a saucy vanity continually employed in depreciating others, a blind self-love, solely attentive to its own advantage, a spirit of raillery which is pleased with offending and insulting others, an indolence and sloth which render all the good qualities of the mind useless.

ARTICLE II.—*To Study the Character of Children in Order to be Able to Manage Them Well.*

Education, properly speaking, is the art of managing and forming the mind. Of all sciences it is the most difficult, the most extraordinary, and at the same time the most important, but yet not sufficiently studied. To judge of it by common experience one would say that of all animals man is the most untractable.

The master's first care is thoroughly to study and search into the genius and character of the children, for by this he must regulate his conduct. There are some who are lazy and remiss, unless they are continually called upon, and others can not bear to be treated imperiously; some will be restrained by fear, and others on the contrary discouraged. We can gain nothing out of some but by mere labor and application; and others will study only by fits and starts: to endeavor to bring them all to a level, and make them submit to one and the same rule is to attempt to force nature. The prudence of the master will consist in keeping a medium, equally removed from the two extremes; for here the ill so closely borders upon the good, that it is easy to mistake the one for the other, and it is this which renders the management of youth so difficult. Too much liberty makes way for licentiousness; and too much constraint makes them stupid; commendation excites and encourages, but it also inspires vanity and presumption. We must therefore keep a just temper, and hold an even hand between these two extremes.

Children carry within them the principles, and in a manner the seeds of all virtues and vices; and the principal point is thoroughly to study at first their genius and character, to become acquainted with their humor, their disposition, and talents; and above all, to discover their passions and prevailing inclinations; not with a view or expectation of entirely changing their temper, of making him gay, for instance, who is naturally grave, or him serious who is of a lively and cheerful disposition. It is with certain characters, as with personal defects, they may be somewhat improved, but not absolutely cured. Now the way of growing acquainted in this manner with children is to give them great liberty to discover their inclinations whilst young, to let them follow their natural bent, in order to discern it the better; to comply with their little infirmities, to encourage them to let us see them; to observe them whilst they think least of it, especially at their play, when they show their tempers most; for children are naturally plain and without reserve; but as soon as they think themselves taken notice of, they throw themselves under a restraint, and keep upon their guard.

Article III.—*To Assume an Immediate Authority over Children.*

This maxim is of the utmost moment during their whole education, and for all persons who are charged with it. By authority I mean a certain air and ascendant which imprint respect and procure obedience. It is neither age nor stature, the tone of the voice, nor threatening, by which this authority is to be obtained: but an even, firm, moderate disposition of mind, which is always master of itself, is guided only by reason, and never acts by fancy or passion.

It is this qualification and talent which keeps all in order, establishes an exact discipline, sees what commands are observed, saves the trouble of reprimands, and prevents almost all punishments. Now it is from the very first entrance upon their government that parents and masters should assume this ascendant. If they do not seize upon this favorable moment, and possess themselves early of this authority, they will have all the pains in the world to do it afterwards, and the child will domineer at last.

The first care of a pupil who is put under a new master, is to study and sound him. There is nothing he does not attempt, he spares no industry or artifice to get the better of him if he can. When he sees all his pains and cunning are to no purpose, and that the master calmly and quietly opposes them with a gentle and reasonable resolution, which always ends in making himself obeyed, he then yields, and cheerfully submits, and this kind of little war, or rather skirmish, where on both sides they have tried each other's forces, is happily concluded with a peace and good understanding which make them easy all the rest of the time they are to live together.

ARTICLE IV.—*To Make Oneself Beloved and Feared.*

The respect, upon which the authority I have spoken of is founded, includes two things, fear and love, which lend each other a mutual assistance, and are the two great springs and hinges of all government in general, and of the conduct of children in particular. As they are of an age wherein reason, instead of having the superiority, scarce begins to show itself, it is requisite that fear should sometimes be called in to its assistance and take its place; but if it comes alone, and the allurement of pleasure does not follow close at its heels, it is not long regarded, and its instructions produce but a slight effect, which the hope of impunity soon removes. Hence it comes to pass that in point of education the greatest skill lies in knowing how to blend discreetly together a force, which shall keep children within due bounds without discouragement, and a mildness which shall gain upon them without indulging them too much.

But some will say, though this manner of governing children by kindness and gentleness is easy perhaps to a private tutor, is it practicable in the case of a principal of a college, a regent of a class, or a master who has a great many scholars in one common chamber? And how is it possible in all these places to keep up an exact discipline, without which no good is to be expected, and at the same time to gain the love of the scholars? I own that nothing is more difficult in this circumstance than to keep up a just medium betwixt too great severity and an excessive indulgence; but the thing is not impossible, since we see it practiced by persons who have the uncommon talent of making themselves feared, and still more beloved. The whole depends upon the behavior of the masters. If they are such as they should be, their success will answer their desires.

Article V.— *Of Correction.*

The most common and shortest way of correcting children is by the rod, which is almost the only remedy that is known or made use of by those who are entrusted with the education of youth. But this remedy becomes often a more dangerous evil than those they would cure, if employed out of season or beyond measure. For besides that the corrections of the rod and the lash we are now speaking of, have something unbecoming, mean, and servile in them, they have nothing in themselves to remedy any fault committed, nor is it likely that such a correction may become useful to a child, if the shame of suffering for having done ill has not a greater power over his mind than the punishment itself. Besides, these corrections give an incurable aversion to the things we should endeavor to make them love. They do not change the humor nor work any reformation in the natural disposition, but only restrain it for a time, and serve to make the passions break out with more violence, when they are at liberty. They often stupefy the mind, and harden it in evil. For a child that has so little honor as to be insensible to reproof, will accustom himself to blows like a slave, and grow obstinate against punishment.

Must we therefore conclude that we ought never to make use of this sort of correction? That is not my meaning. For I am far from condemning in general the use of the rod, after what has been said of it in several places of Scripture, and especially in the Book of Proverbs; . . . but it ought to be employed very seldom, and for faults of consequence. These corrections are like the violent remedies which are used in violent diseases: they purge, but alter the constitution and wear out the organs. A mind conducted by fear is always the weaker for it. Whoever, therefore, has the direction of others, if he would heal, should first use gentle remonstrances, try what he can do by persuasion, make honesty and justice grateful if possible, and inspire a hatred for vice, and a passion for virtue. If this first attempt does not succeed, he may pass to stronger methods and sharper reproaches; and lastly, when all this has been employed to no purpose, he may then proceed to corrections, but by degrees, still leaving the hopes of pardon in view, and reserving the greatest for extreme faults and those he despairs of.

Article VI.— *Of Reproofs.*

To make reproofs useful, there are in my opinion three things principally to be considered, *the subject, the time,* and *the manner* of making them.

1. It is a very common mistake to use reprimand for the slightest faults, and such as are almost unavoidable in children, which takes away all their force, and frustrates all their advantage. For they accustom themselves to them, are no longer affected by them, and even make a jest of them.

But I make a great difference between *admonitions* and *reprimands.* The first savor less of the authority of a master than of the affection of a friend. They are always attended with an air and tone of gentleness, which gives them a more agreeable reception; and for this reason they may be more frequently used. But as reprimands always shock self-love, and often assume an air and a language of severity, they should be reserved for more considerable faults, and consequently be more seldom used.

2. The master's prudence consists in carefully studying and watching for the favorable moment, when the mind of the child shall be most disposed to improve by correction. Do not, therefore, reprimand a child, says Fénelon, in his first emotion, or your own. If you do it in yours, he will find that you have been governed by humor and inclination, and not by reason and friendship, and you will inevitably lose your authority. If you chide him immediately, his mind is not at liberty enough to own his faults, to conquer his passion and perceive the importance of your advice. You likewise expose the child to losing the respect he owes you. Show him always that you are master of yourself; and nothing will let him see it better than your patience. Watch a favorable opportunity for several days, if necessary, to time a correction well.

3. Corrections and reprimands set before men what they care not for seeing, and attack self-love in the dearest and most sensible part, where it never gives way without great reluctance and opposition. We love ourselves as we are, and would have reason for doing so. Thus we are careful to justify ourselves in our faults by various deceitful colors; and it must not seem strange that men should be displeased with being contradicted and condemned, as it is an attack at the same time upon the reason which is deceived, and the heart which is corrupted.

This is properly the foundation of the care and caution which are required in correction and reprimand. We must leave nothing for a child to discern in us that may hinder the effect of it. We must avoid raising his ill will by the severity of our expressions, his anger by exaggerations, or his pride by expressions of contempt.

We must not heap upon him such a multitude of reproofs,

as may deprive him of the hope of being able to correct the faults he is reproached with. It might be advisable likewise not to tell a child his faults without adding some means of amending it. For correction when it is sharp, is apt to occasion chagrin and discouragement.

We must avoid giving him any occasion to think that we are prejudiced, lest he should thence take occasion to defend the faults laid to his charge, and to attribute our admonitions to our prejudice. Neither must there be any room left for him to believe that they are occasioned by any interest or particular passion, or indeed any other motive than that of his good.

ARTICLE VII.—*To Reason with Children; to Prompt Them by the Sense of Honor; to Make Use of Praises, Rewards, and Caresses.*

I call reasoning with boys the acting always without passion and humor, and giving them the reason of our behavior toward them. It is requisite, says Fénelon, to pursue all possible means to make the things you require of them agreeable to children. Have you anything displeasing to propose to them? Let them know that the pain will soon be followed by pleasure; show them always the usefulness of what you teach them; let them see its advantage in regard to the commerce of the world and the duties of particular stations. This, say to them, is to enable you to do well what you are one day to do; it is to form your judgment, it is to accustom you to reason well upon all the affairs of life. It is requisite to show them a solid and agreeable end, which may support them in their labor, and never pretend to oblige them to the performance by a dry, absolute authority.

Children are capable of hearing reason sooner than is imagined, and they love to be treated like reasonable creatures from their infancy. We should keep up in them this good opinion and sense of honor, upon which they pique themselves, and make use of it, as much as possible, as a universal means to bring them to the end we propose.

They are likewise very much affected with praise. It is our duty to make an advantage of this weakness, and to endeavor to improve it into a virtue in them. We should run a risk of discouraging them, were we never to praise them when they do well; and though we have reason to apprehend that commendations may inflame their vanity, we must strive to use them for their encouragement without making them conceited.

For of all the motives that affect a reasonable soul, there are none more powerful than honor and shame; and when we have once brought children to be sensible of these feelings, we have gained everything.

Rewards for children are not to be neglected; and though they are not, any more than praises, the principal motive upon which they should act, yet both of them may become useful to virtue, and be a powerful incentive to it. Is it not an advantage for them to know that the doing well will, in every respect, be their advantage, and that it is as well their interest as their duty to execute faithfully what is required of them either in point of study or behavior.

ARTICLE VIII.—*To Accustom Children to a Strict Observance of Truth.*

One of the vices we must carefully correct in children is lying, for which we can not excite in them too great an aversion and horror. It must always be represented to them as mean, base, and shameful; as a vice which entirely dishonors a man, disgraces him, and places him in the most contemptible light, and is not to be suffered even in slaves.

Dissimulation, cunning, and bad excuses come very near it, and infallibly lead to it.

Everything that the children see or hear from their parents or masters must conduce to make them in love with truth, and give them a contempt for all double dealing. Thus they must never make use of any false pretenses to appease them, or to persuade them to do as they would have them, or either promise or threaten any thing without their being sensible that the performance will soon follow. For by this means they will be taught deceit, to which they have already too much inclination.

To prevent it, they must be accustomed not to stand in need of it, and be taught to tell ingenuously what pleases them or what makes them uneasy. They must be told that tricking always proceeds from a bad disposition; for nobody uses it but with a view to dissemble; as not being such a one as he ought to be, or from desiring such things as are not to be permitted; or if they are, from taking dishonest means to come at them. Let the children be made to observe how ridiculous such arts are, as they see practiced by others, which have generally a bad success, and serve only to make them contemptible. Make them ashamed of themselves, when you catch them in any dissimulation. Take from them from time to time what they are fond of, if they have endeavored to obtain it by any deceit, and tell them they shall have it, when they ask for it plainly and without artifice.

ARTICLE IX.—*To Accustom Boys to be Polite, Cleanly, and Punctual.*

Good breeding is one of the qualities which parents most desire in their children, and it usually affects them more than any other. The value they set upon it arises from their conversation with the world, where they find that almost everything is judged by its outside. In short, the want of politeness takes off very much from the most solid merit, and makes virtue itself seem less estimable and lovely. A rough diamond can never serve as an ornament; it must be polished before it can be shown to advantage. We can not, therefore, take care too early to make children civil and well bred.

It is also to be wished that children should be accustomed to neatness, order, and exactness; that they take care of their dress, especially on Sundays and holidays, and such days as they go abroad; that everything should be set in order in their chambers and upon their tables, and every book put in its place, when they have done with it; that they should be ready to discharge their different duties precisely at the time appointed. This exactness is of great importance at all times and in every station of life.

ARTICLE X.—*To Make Study Agreeable.*

This is one of the most important points in education, and at the same time one of the most difficult: for among a great number of masters, who in other respects are very deserving, there are very few to be found who are happy enough to make their scholars fond of study. Success in this point depends very much on the first impressions, and it should be the great care of masters, who teach children their letters, to do it in such a manner that a child who is not yet capable of being fond of his book, should not take an aversion to it, and the dislike continue when he grows up.

The great secret, says Quintilian, to make children love their books is to make them fond of their master. In this case they willingly give ear to him, become docile, strive to please him and take a pleasure in his lessons. They readily receive his advice and correction, are much affected by his commendation, and strive to merit his friendship by a proper discharge of their duty. There is implanted in children, as in all mankind, a natural spirit of curiosity, or desire of knowledge and information, of which a good use may be made towards rendering their study agreeable. As everything is new to them, they are continually asking questions, and inquiring the name and use of everything they see. And they should be answered without expressing any pain or uneasiness. Their curiosity should be commended and satisfied by clear and express answers, without anything in them deceitful or illusory; for they will soon find it out and take offense at it.

This great principle must be always in view: that study depends upon the will, which admits of no constraint. We may confine the body, make a scholar sit at his desk against his inclination, double his labor by way of punishment, force him to finish a task imposed on him, and for that end deprive him of his play and recreation; but can laboring thus from force be properly called study? And what will follow upon it but the hatred both of books, learning, and masters too, very often as long as they live? The will, therefore, must be gained; and this can only be by mildness, affectionate behavior, and persuasion, and above all by the allurement of pleasure.

ARTICLE XI.—*To Grant the Boys Rest and Recreation.*

A great many reasons oblige us to grant rest and recreation to children; first, the care of their health, which should go before that of knowledge. Now nothing is more prejudicial to it than too long and constant an application, which insensibly wears and weakens the organs, which in that age are very tender, and incapable of taking great pains. And this gives me an opportunity of advising and entreating parents not to push their children too much in study in their early years, but to deny themselves the pleasure of seeing them make a figure before their time. For besides that these ripe fruits seldom come to maturity, and their early progress resembles those seeds that are cast upon the surface of the earth, which spring up immediately, but take no root, nothing is more pernicious to the health of children than these untimely efforts, though the ill effect be not immediately perceived.

If they are prejudicial to the body, they are no less dangerous to the mind, which exhausts itself and grows dull by a continual application, and, like the earth, stands in need of a stated alternation of labor and rest, in order to preserve its force and vigor. Besides, the boys, after they have refreshed themselves a while, return to their studies with more cheerfulness and a better heart; and this little relaxation animates them with fresh courage; whereas constraint shocks and disheartens them. I add with Quintilian, and the boys will doubtless agree to it, that a moderate inclination to play should not displease in them, as it is often a mark of vivacity. In short, can we expect much ardor for study in a child who at an age that is naturally brisk and gay, is always heavy, pensive, and indifferent even to its play?

But in this, as in everything else, we must use discretion, and observe a medium, which consists in not refusing them diversion, lest they should grow out of love with study; and in not granting too much, lest they should contract a habit of idleness.

ARTICLE XII.—*To Train up Boys to Virtue by Discourse and Example.*

What I have said shows that this is the indispensable duty of teachers. As it is often requisite to fortify children beforehand against the example and discourses of their parents, as well as against the false prejudices and false principles advanced in common conversation, and authorized by an almost general practice, they should be to them that guardian and monitor which Seneca so often speaks of, to preserve or deliver them from popular errors, and to inspire them with such principles as are conformable to right and sound reason.

It is requisite, therefore, that they have a perfect sense of them themselves, and think and talk always with wisdom and truth. For nothing can be said before children without effect, and they regulate their fears and desires by the discourses they hear.

There is still another shorter and surer way of conducting boys to virtue, and this is by example. For the language of actions is far stronger and more persuasive than that of words. It is a great happiness for boys to have masters, whose lives are a continual instruction to them, whose actions never contradict their lessons, who do what they advise, and shun what they blame, and who are still more admired when seen than when they are heard.

ARTICLE XIII.—*Piety, Religion, and Zeal for the Children's Salvation.*

Christianity is the soul and sum of all the duties I have hitherto spoken of. It is Christianity which animates them, which exalts and ennobles them, which brings them to perfection, and gives them a merit, whereof God alone is the principle and motive, and of which God alone can be the just reward.

What then is a Christian teacher, who is entrusted with the education of youth? He is a man, into whose hands Christ has committed a number of children whom he has redeemed with his blood, and for whom he has laid down his life, in whom he dwells, as in his house and temple; whom he considers as his members, as his brethren and coheirs, of whom he will make so many kings and priests, who shall reign and serve God with him and by him to all eternity. And for what end has he committed them to his care? Is it barely to make them poets, orators, and men of learning? Who dares presume to say or even to think so? He has committed them to the master's care in order to preserve in them the precious and inestimable deposit of innocence, which he has imprinted in their souls by baptism, in order to make them true Christians. This is the true end and design of the education of children, to which all the rest are but means. Now how great and noble an addition does the office of a master receive from so honorable a commission? But what care, what attention and vigilance, and above all, how great a dependence upon Christ does it require!

XXI. JEAN JACQUES ROUSSEAU.

BIOGRAPHICAL SKETCH.

There are few men who have exerted a greater influence upon education than the celebrated French author, Jean Jacques Rousseau. He was born in Geneva June 28, 1712, and died at Ermenonville, near Paris, July 2, 1778. As a child he was very fond of reading, a disposition that was encouraged by his father; and among other works, many of which were worthless, he early devoured Bossuet, Ovid, and Plutarch. "Thus began to be formed within me," he says, "that heart, at once so proud and so tender, that effeminate but yet indomitable character which, ever oscillating between weakness and courage, between indulgence and virtue, has to the last placed me in contradiction with myself, and has brought it to pass that abstinence and enjoyment, pleasure and wisdom, have alike eluded me." In these few words Rousseau has admirably sketched the main features of his character.

It is not worth while to follow him through the unimportant events of his life. His boyhood was characterized by a singular waywardness; and in his "Confessions," a work written with the utmost frankness, he does not attempt to conceal lying and theft. He ran away from an engraver to whom he had been apprenticed, and during the remainder of his life he was a wanderer who enjoyed but temporary seasons of repose. His life was a singular paradox. "Full of enthusiasm for the beautiful and the good," says a French writer, "he defended with invincible logic and passionate eloquence the eternal principles of justice and morality, and he committed the most shameful and culpable acts. This man, who wrote admirable pages upon domestic affection, friendship, and gratitude, chose a companion unworthy of him, placed his children in a foundling hospital, and showed himself unjust and harsh toward his friends, and ungrateful toward his benefactors."

Rousseau has exerted his influence upon educational development through a single work, half treatise and half romance, to which all subsequent educators — Basedow, Pestalozzi, Richter, Kant, and even Herbert Spencer — have been more or less indebted. It is, as he himself says, "a collection of thoughts and observations, without order and almost without connection." It is entitled "Émile, or concerning Education." In many respects a radical book, it is flung defiantly in the face of prevalent usage. "Go directly contrary to custom," he says, "and you will nearly always be right." The work was condemned by parliament, and to escape arrest, Rousseau fled to Switzerland. The work abounds in mingled truth and error, and needs to be read with great discrimination; but many of its truths are fundamental, and ever since their publication have been gradually forcing an entrance into educational practice. "Not Rousseau's individual rules," says the great German Richter, "many of which may be erroneous without injury to the whole, but the spirit of education which fills and animates the work, has shaken to their foundations and purified all the schoolrooms, and even the nurseries, in Europe. In no previous work on education was the ideal so richly and beautifully combined with actual observation as in his."

Rousseau was largely indebted to his predecessors, especially to Locke, whom he frequently quotes, but with whom he does not always agree. The two fundamental principles which have perhaps exerted the widest influence are these: 1. Nature is to be studied and followed. 2. Education is an unbroken unity, extending from early childhood to maturity. It is true that both these principles had been advocated by Comenius, but it was through the charm of Rousseau's work that they made a deep impression upon the educational thinking of Europe. Along with positions wholly indefensible, he urges, in admirable style, many of the reforms that have become commonplaces in the education of to-day.

With the intention of following nature, Rousseau carries Émile, his hero, through five periods of development: the first embraces his infancy, the second extends to his twelfth year, the third to his fifteenth, the fourth to his twentieth, and the fifth includes his marriage. To each of these periods a book, sufficient for a small volume, is devoted, setting forth principles and methods in detail. The following extracts consist of such paragraphs from the different books as will give a clear and comprehensive view of Rousseau's system of pedagogy.

SELECTIONS FROM ROUSSEAU.

ÉMILE, OR CONCERNING EDUCATION.

BOOK I.

1. We are born weak, we need strength; we are born destitute of all things, we need assistance; we are born stupid, we need judgment. All that we have not at our birth, and that we need when grown up, is given us by education.

This education comes to us from nature itself, or from other men, or from circumstances. The internal development of our faculties and of our organs is the education nature gives us; the use we are taught to make of this development is the education we get from other men; and what we learn, by our own experience, about things that interest us, is the education of circumstances.

2. In the natural order of things, all men being equal, the vocation common to all is the state of manhood; and whoever is well trained for that, cannot fulfil badly any vocation which depends upon it. Whether my pupil be destined for the army, the church, or the bar, matters little to me. Before he can think of adopting the vocation of his parents, nature calls upon him to be a man. How to live is the business I wish to teach him. On leaving my hands he will not, I admit, be a magistrate, a soldier, or a priest; first of all he will be a man. All that a man ought to be he can be, at need, as well as any one else can. Fortune will in vain alter his position, for he will always occupy his own.

Our real study is that of the state of man. He among us who best knows how to bear the good and evil fortunes of this life is, in my opinion, the best educated; whence it follows that true education consists less in precept than in practice. We begin to instruct ourselves when we begin to live; our education commences with the commencement of our life; our first teacher is our nurse. For this reason the word "education" had among the ancients another meaning which we no longer attach to it; it signified nutriment.

To live is not merely to breathe, it is to act. It is to make use of our organs, of our senses, of our faculties, of all the powers which bear witness to us of our own existence. He who has lived most is not he who has numbered the most years, but he who has been most truly conscious of what life is. A man may have himself buried at the age of a hundred years, who died from the hour of his birth. He would have gained something by going to his grave in youth, if up to that time he had only lived.

3. But let mothers only vouchsafe to nourish their chil-

dren, and our manners will reform themselves; the feelings of nature will re-awaken in all hearts. The State will be repeopled; this chief thing, this one thing will bring all the rest into order again. The attractions of home life present the best antidote to bad morals. The bustling life of little children, considered so tiresome, becomes pleasant; it makes the father and the mother more necessary to one another, more dear to one another; it draws closer between them the conjugal tie. When the family is sprightly and animated, domestic cares form the dearest occupation of the wife and the sweetest recreation of the husband. Thus the correction of this one abuse would soon result in a general reform; nature would resume all her rights. When women are once more true mothers, men will become true fathers and husbands.

4. A father, when he brings his children into existence and supports them, has, in so doing, fulfilled only a third part of his task. To the human race he owes men; to society, men fitted for society; to the State, citizens. Every man who can pay this triple debt, and does not pay it is a guilty man; and if he pays it by halves, he is perhaps more guilty still. He who cannot fulfil the duties of a father has no right to be a father. Not poverty, nor severe labor, nor human respect can release him from the duty of supporting his children and of educating them himself. Readers, you may believe my words. I prophesy to any one who has natural feeling and neglects these sacred duties,— that he will long shed bitter tears over this fault, and that for those tears he will find no consolation.

5. The qualifications of a good tutor are very freely discussed. The first qualification I should require in him, and this one presupposes many others, is, that he shall not be capable of selling himself. There are employments so noble that we cannot fulfil them for money without showing our-

selves unworthy to fulfill them. Such an employment is that of a soldier; such a one is that of a teacher. Who, then, shall educate my child? I have told you already,—yourself. I cannot! Then make for yourself a friend who can. I see no other alternative.

A teacher! what a great soul he ought to be! Truly, to form a man, one must be either himself a father, or else something more than human. And this is the office you calmly entrust to hirelings!

6. In this outset of life, while memory and imagination are still inactive, the child pays attention only to what actually affects his senses. The first materials of his knowledge are his sensations. If, therefore, these are presented to him in suitable order, his memory can hereafter present them to his understanding in the same order. But as he attends to his sensations only, it will at first suffice to show him very clearly the connection between these sensations, and the objects which give rise to them. He is eager to touch everything, to handle everything. Do not thwart this restless desire; it suggests to him a very necessary apprenticeship. It is thus he learns to feel the heat and coldness, hardness and softness, heaviness and lightness of bodies; to judge of their size, their shape, and all their sensible qualities, by looking, by touching, by listening; above all, by comparing the results of sight with those of touch, estimating with the eye the sensation a thing produces upon the fingers.

BOOK II.

7. Far from taking care that Émile does not hurt himself, I shall be dissatisfied if he never does, and so grows up unacquainted with pain. To suffer is the first and most necessary thing for him to learn. Children are little and weak,

apparently that they may learn these important lessons. If a child fall his whole length, he will not break his leg; if he strike himself with a stick, he will not break his arm; if he lay hold of an edged tool, he does not grasp it tightly, and will not cut himself very badly.

Our pedantic mania for instructing constantly leads us to teach children what they can learn far better for themselves, and to lose sight of what we alone can teach them. Is there anything more absurd than the pains we take in teaching them to walk? As if we had ever seen one, who, through his nurse's negligence, did not know how to walk when grown! On the contrary, how many people do we see moving awkwardly all their lives because they have been badly taught how to walk!

8. O men, be humane! it is your highest duty; be humane to all conditions of men, to every age, to everything not alien to mankind. What higher wisdom is there for you than humanity? Love childhood; encourage its sports, its pleasures, its lovable instincts. Who among us has not at times looked back with regret to the age when a smile was continually on our lips, when the soul was always at peace? Why should we rob these little innocent creatures of the enjoyment of a time so brief, so transient, of a boon so precious, which they cannot misuse? Why will you fill with bitterness and sorrow these fleeting years which can no more return to them than to you? Do you know, you fathers, the moment when death awaits your children? Do not store up for yourselves remorse, by taking from them the brief moments nature has given them. As soon as they can appreciate the delights of existence, let them enjoy it. At whatever hour God may call them, let them not die without having tasted life at all.

9. The surest way to make a child unhappy is to accustom him to obtain everything he wants to have. For since

his wishes multiply in proportion to the ease with which they are gratified, your inability to fulfil them will sooner or later oblige you to refuse in spite of yourself, and this unwonted refusal will pain him more than withholding from him what he demands. At first he will want the cane you hold; soon he will want your watch; afterward he will want the bird he sees flying, or the star he sees shining. He will want everything he sees, and without being God himself how can you content him?

10. Treat your pupil as his age demands. From the first, assign him to his true place, and keep him there so effectually that he will not try to leave it. Then, without knowing what wisdom is, he will practice its most important lesson. Never, absolutely never, command him to do a thing, whatever it may be. Do not let him even imagine that you claim any authority over him. Let him know only that he is weak and you are strong: that from his condition and yours he is necessarily at your mercy. Let him know this — learn it and feel it. Let him early know that upon his haughty neck is the stern yoke nature imposes upon man, the heavy yoke of necessity, under which every finite being must toil.

In this way you will make him patient, even-tempered, resigned, gentle, even when he has not what he wants. For it is in our nature to endure patiently the decrees of fate, but not the ill will of others. "There is no more," is an answer against which no child ever rebelled unless he believed it untrue. Besides, there is no other way; either nothing at all is to be required of him, or he must from the first be accustomed to perfect obedience. The worst training of all is to leave him wavering between his own will and yours, and to dispute incessantly with him as to which shall be master. I should a hundred times prefer his being master in every case.

11. Reverse the common practice, and you will nearly always do well. Parents and teachers desiring to make of a child not a child, but a learned man, have never begun early enough to chide, to correct, to reprimand, to flatter, to promise, to instruct, to discourse reason to him. Do better than this: be reasonable yourself, and do not argue with your pupil, least of all, to make him approve what he dislikes. For if you persist in reasoning about disagreeable things, you make reasoning disagreeable to him, and weaken its influence beforehand in a mind as yet unfitted to understand it. Keep his organs, his senses, his physical strength, busy; but, as long as possible, keep his mind inactive. Guard against all sensations arising in advance of judgment, which estimates their true value. Keep back and check unfamiliar impressions, and be in no haste to do good for the sake of preventing evil. For the good is not real unless enlightened by reason. Regard every delay as an advantage; for much is gained if the critical period be approached without losing anything. Let childhood have its full growth. If indeed a lesson must be given, avoid it to-day, if you can without danger delay it until to-morrow.

12. I do not intend to enter fully into details, but to lay down some general maxims and to illustrate difficult cases. I believe it impossible, in the very heart of social surroundings, to educate a child up to the age of twelve years, without giving him some ideas of the relations of man to man, and of morality in human actions. It will suffice if we put off as long as possible the necessity for these ideas, and when they must be given, limit them to such as are immediately applicable. We must do this only lest he consider himself master of everything, and so injure others without scruple, because unknowingly. There are gentle, quiet characters who, in their early innocence, may be led a long way without danger of this kind. But others, naturally violent, whose wildness

is precocious, must be trained into men as early as may be, that you may not be obliged to fetter them outright.

13. We are now within the domain of morals, and the door is open to vice. Side by side with conventionalities and duties spring up deceit and falsehood. As soon as there are things we ought not to do, we desire to hide what we ought not to have done. As soon as one interest leads us to promise, a stronger one may urge us to break the promise. Our chief concern is how to break it and still go unscathed. It is natural to find expedients; we dissemble and we utter falsehood. Unable to prevent this evil, we must nevertheless punish it. Thus the miseries of our life arise from our mistakes.

I have said enough to show that punishment, as such, should not be inflicted upon children, but should always happen to them as the natural result of their own wrong-doing. Do not, then, preach to them against falsehood, or punish them confessedly on account of a falsehood. But if they are guilty of one, let all its consequences fall heavily on their heads. Let them know what it is to be disbelieved even when they speak the truth, and to be accused of faults in spite of their earnest denial.

14. The only moral lesson suited to childhood and the most important at any age is, never to injure any one. Even the principle of doing good, if not subordinated to this, is dangerous, false, and contradictory. For who does not do good? Everybody does, even a wicked man who makes one happy at the expense of making a hundred miserable: and thence arise all our calamities. The most exalted virtues are negative: they are hardest to attain, too, because they are unostentatious, and rise above even that gratification dear to the heart of man,— sending another person away pleased with us. If there be a man who never injures one of his fellow-creatures, what good must he achieve for them!

What fearlessness, what vigor of mind he requires for it! Not by reasoning about this principle, but by attempting to carry it into practice, do we find out how great it is, how hard to fulfil.

15. Respect children, and be in no haste to judge their actions, good or evil. Let the exceptional cases show themselves such for some time before you adopt special methods of dealing with them. Let nature be long at work before you attempt to supplant her, lest you thwart her work. You say you know how precious time is, and do not wish to lose it. Do you not know that to employ it badly is to waste it still more, and that a child badly taught is farther from being wise than one not taught at all? You are troubled at seeing him spend his early years in doing nothing. What! is it nothing to be happy? Is it nothing to skip, to play, to run about all day long? Never in all his life will he be so busy as now.

16. Pedagogues, who make such an imposing display of what they teach, are paid to talk in another strain than mine, but their conduct shows that they think as I do. For after all, what do they teach their pupils? Words, words, words. Among all their boasted subjects, none are selected because they are useful; such would be the sciences of things, in which these professors are unskillful. But they prefer sciences; we seem to know when we know their nomenclature, such as heraldry, geography, chronology, languages; studies so far removed from human interests, and particularly from the child, that it would be wonderful if any of them could be of the least use at any time in life.

17. In any study, words that represent things are nothing without the ideas of the things they represent. We, however, limit children to these signs, without ever being able to make them understand the things represented. We think we are teaching a child the description of the earth, when he is

merely learning maps. We teach him the names of cities, countries, rivers; he has no idea that they exist anywhere but on the map we use in pointing them out to him. I recollect seeing somewhere a text-book on geography which began thus: "What is the world? A pasteboard globe." Precisely such is the geography of children. I will venture to say that after two years of globes and cosmography no child of ten, by rules they give him, could find the way from Paris to St. Denis. I maintain that not one of them, from a plan of his father's garden, could trace out its windings without going astray. And yet these are the knowing creatures who can tell you exactly where Pekin, Ispahan, Mexico, and all the countries of the world are.

18. The memory of which a child is capable is far from inactive, even without the use of books. All he sees and hears impresses him, and he remembers it. He keeps a mental register of people's sayings and doings. Everything around him is the book from which he is continually but unconsciously enriching his memory against the time his judgment can benefit by it. If we intend rightly to cultivate this chief faculty of the mind, we must choose these objects carefully, constantly acquainting him with such as he ought to understand, and keeping back those he ought not to know. In this way we should endeavor to make his mind a storehouse of knowledge, to aid in his education in youth, and to direct him at all times. This method does not, it is true, produce phenomenal children, nor does it make the reputation of their teachers; but it produces judicious, robust men, sound in body and in mind, who, although not admired in youth, will make themselves respected in manhood.

19. Man's first natural movements are for the purpose of comparing himself with whatever surrounds him and finding in each thing those sensible qualities likely to affect himself. His first study is, therefore, a kind of experimental physics

relating to his own preservation. From this, before he has fully understood his place here on earth, he is turned aside to speculative studies. While yet his delicate and pliable organs can adapt themselves to the objects upon which they are to act, while his senses, still pure, are free from illusion, it is time to exercise both in their peculiar functions, and to learn the perceptible relations between ourselves and outward things. Since whatever enters the human understanding enters by the senses, man's primitive reason is a reason of the senses, serving as foundation for the reason of the intellect. Our first teachers in philosophy are our own feet, hands, and eyes. To substitute books for these is teaching us not to reason, but to use the reason of another; to believe a great deal, and to know nothing at all.

20. All children, being natural imitators, try to draw. I would have my pupil cultivate this art, not exactly for the sake of the art itself, but to render the eye true and the hand flexible. In general, it matters little whether he understands this or that exercise, provided he acquires the mental insight, and the manual skill furnished by the exercise. I should take care, therefore, not to give him a drawing-master, who would give him only copies to imitate, and would make him draw from drawings only. He shall have no teacher but nature, no models but real things. He shall have before his eyes the originals, and not the paper which represents them. He shall draw a house from a real house, a tree from a tree, a human figure from the man himself. In this way he will accustom himself to observe bodies and their appearances, and not mistake for accurate imitations those that are false and conventional.

BOOK III.

21. In general, never show the representation of a thing unless it be impossible to show the thing itself; for the sign

absorbs the child's attention, and makes him lose sight of the thing signified.

The two starting-points in his geography shall be the town in which he lives, and his father's house in the country. Afterward shall come the places lying between these two; then the neighboring rivers; lastly, the aspect of the sun, and the manner of finding out where the east is. This last is the point of union. Let him make himself a map of all these details; a very simple map, including at first only two objects, then by degrees the others, as he learns their distance and position. You see now what an advantage we have gained beforehand, by making his eyes serve him instead of a compass.

22. Bear in mind always that the life and soul of my system is, not to teach the child many things, but to allow only correct and clear ideas to enter his mind. I do not care if he knows nothing, so long as he is not mistaken. To guard him from errors he might learn, I furnish his mind with truths only. Reason and judgment enter slowly; prejudices crowd in; and he must be preserved from these last. Yet if you consider science in itself, you launch upon an unfathomable and boundless sea, full of unavoidable dangers. When I see a man carried away by his love for knowledge, hastening from one alluring science to another, without knowing where to stop, I think I see a child gathering shells upon the seashore. At first he loads himself with them; then, tempted by others, he throws these away, and gathers more. At last, weighed down by so many, and no longer knowing which to choose, he ends by throwing all away, and returning empty-handed.

23. Let the child take nothing for granted because some one says it is so. Nothing is good to him but what he feels to be good. You think it far sighted to push him beyond his understanding of things, but you are mistaken. For the

sake of arming him with weapons he does not know how to use, you take from him one universal among men, common sense: you teach him to allow himself always to be led, never to be more than a machine in the hands of others. If you will have him docile while he is young, you will make him a credulous dupe when he is a man. You are continually saying to him, "All I require of you is for your own good, but you cannot understand it yet. What does it matter to me whether you do what I require or not? You are doing it entirely for your own sake." With such fine speeches you are paving the way for some kind of trickster or fool,— some visionary babbler or charlatan,— who will entrap him or persuade him to adopt his own folly.

Obliged to learn by his own effort, he employs his own reason, not that of another. Most of our mistakes arise less within ourselves than from others; so that if he is not to be ruled by opinion, he must receive nothing upon authority. Such continual exercise must invigorate the mind as labor and fatigue strengthen the body.

The mind as well as the body can bear only what its strength will allow. When the understanding fully masters a thing before intrusting it to the memory, what it afterward draws therefrom is in reality its own. But if instead we load the memory with matters the understanding has not mastered, we run the risk of never finding there anything that belongs to it.

24. Since we must have books, there is one which, to my mind, furnishes the finest of treatises on education according to nature. My Émile shall read this book before any other; it shall for a long time be his entire library, and shall always hold an honorable place. It shall be the text on which all our discussions of natural science shall be only commentaries. It shall be a test for all we meet during our progress toward a ripened judgment, and so long as our taste is un-

spoiled, we shall enjoy reading it. What wonderful book is this? Aristotle? Pliny? Buffon? No; it is "Robinson Crusoe."

The story of this man, alone on his island, unaided by his fellow-men, without any art or its implements, and yet providing for his own preservation and subsistence, even contriving to live in what might be called comfort, is interesting to persons of all ages. It may be made delightful to children in a thousand ways. Thus we make the desert island, which I used at the outset for a comparison, a reality.

25. In a word, Émile has every virtue which affects himself. To have the social virtues as well, he only needs to know the relations which make them necessary; and this knowledge his mind is ready to receive. He considers himself independently of others, and is satisfied when others do not think of him at all. He exacts nothing from others, and never thinks of owing anything to them. He is alone in human society, and depends solely upon himself. He has the best right of all to be independent, for he is all that any one can be at his age. He has no errors but such as a human being must have; no vices but those from which no one can warrant himself exempt. He has a sound constitution, active limbs, a fair and unprejudiced mind, a heart free and without passions. Self-love, the first and most natural of all, has scarcely manifested itself at all. Without disturbing any one's peace of mind he has led a happy, contented life, as free as nature will allow. Do you think a youth who has thus attained his fifteenth year has lost the years that have gone before?

BOOK IV.

26. Respect your species; consider that it is composed essentially of a collection of peoples; that even if all the kings and all the philosophers were taken away, they would

scarcely be missed, and that things would not go worse. In a word, teach your pupil to love all men, even those who despise them; let him not belong to any class, but be at home in all. Speak before him of the human race with tenderness, even with pity, but never with contempt. Man, do not dishonor man!

27. When the critical age approaches, bring before young people scenes that will restrain and not excite them; give a change to their nascent imagination by objects which, far from inflaming their senses, will repress the activity of them. Remove them from great cities where the dress and immodesty of women will hasten and anticipate the lessons of nature, where everything presents to their eyes pleasures which they ought to be acquainted with only when they know how to choose them. Take them back to their first dwelling-place, where rural simplicity lets the passions of their age develop less rapidly; or if their taste for the arts still attaches them to the city, prevent in them, by this taste itself, a dangerous idleness. Carefully choose their associations, their occupations, and their pleasures; show them only touching but modest pictures, which will move without demoralizing them, and which will nourish their sensibilities without stirring their senses.

28. When I see that young people, at the age of greatest activity, are restricted to studies purely speculative, and that afterwards, without the slightest experience, they are suddenly thrown into society and business, I find that reason no less than nature is offended, and I am no longer surprised that so few persons know how to act. By what strange perversity of mind are we taught so many useless things, while the art of doing counts for nothing? People pretend to form us for society, and instruct us as if each one were to pass his life in thinking alone in his cell, or in treating subjects with indifference. You think you are teaching

your children to live by instructing them in certain contortions of the body and in certain forms of words, which have no meaning. I too have taught my Émile to live; for I have taught him to live with himself, and besides to know how to earn his bread. But that is not enough. To live in society, we must know how to deal with men, how to recognize the means of influencing them; how to calculate the action and reaction of individual interests in civil society, and to foresee events so clearly that we are rarely deceived, or at least always take the best means to succeed.

29. I foresee how many of my readers will be surprised to see me let the early years of my pupil pass without speaking to him of religion. At fifteen he did not know whether he had a soul, and perhaps at eighteen it is not yet time for him to learn it; for if he learns it sooner than is necessary, he runs the risk of never knowing it.

30. If there is nothing of morality in the human soul, whence come those transports of admiration for heroic deeds, those raptures of love for great souls? What relation has this enthusiasm for virtue with our private interests? Why should I rather be Cato who thrusts a dagger into his heart, than Cæsar with all his triumphs? Take away from our hearts this love of the beautiful, and you take away all the charm of life. He whose vile passions have stifled in his narrow soul these delightful sentiments; he who, by always centering his thoughts upon himself, comes at length to love only himself, has no more transports; his icy heart no longer palpitates with joy; a sweet tenderness never moistens his eyes; he no longer enjoys anything; the wretch no longer feels, no longer lives; he is already dead.

31. Be sincere and true without pride; know how to be ignorant: you will deceive neither yourself nor others. If ever your cultivated talents put you in a position to speak to men, speak to them always according to your conscience.

without being embarrassed if they do not applaud. The abuse of knowledge begets incredulity. Every learned man disdains the common sentiment; each one wishes to have an opinion of his own. A proud philosophy leads to scepticism, as a blind devotion leads to fanaticism. Avoid these extremes; always remain firm in the path of truth, or of what seems to be so in the simplicity of your heart, without ever turning aside through vanity or weakness. Dare to confess God among philosophers; dare to preach humanity to the intolerant. You will be alone in your position perhaps; but you will have within yourself a testimony that will enable you to do without that of men. Whether they love you or hate you, whether they read or despise your writings, makes no difference. Speak what is true, do what is right; that which is important for man is to fulfil his duties upon the earth; and it is by forgetting one's self that one works for one's self. My child, selfish interests deceive us; it is only the hope of the just that never deceives.

BOOK V.

32. On the good constitution of mothers depends that of children; on the care of woman depends the first education of men; on woman depend again their manners, their passions, their tastes, their pleasures, and even their happiness. Thus all the education of women ought to be relative to men. To please them, to be useful to them, to make themselves loved and honored by them, to bring them up when young, to care for them when grown, to counsel and console them, to render their life agreeable and sweet — these are the duties of women in every age, and what they ought to learn from their childhood. So long as we do not recognize this principle, we shall miss the end, and all the precepts we give them will be of no service either for their happiness or ours.

XXII. IMMANUEL KANT.

BIOGRAPHICAL SKETCH.

This illustrious philosopher was born at Königsberg, April 22, 1724, and died there February 12, 1804. He was educated in the University of his native city, where, after serving as a tutor in private families for several years, and afterwards acting as *Privatdocent,* he was appointed professor in the philosophical faculty in 1770. His life was given to study with great singleness of purpose; he never married, and it is said that he never traveled beyond the limits of the small province in which he was born. His philosophic system, known as the *critical philosophy,* marks a turning point in the history of speculative thought. He proved himself one of the profoundest thinkers of all time.

With his philosophical system, which had no immediate or determining influence upon his educational system, we have here nothing to do. As professor of philosophy Kant was required to deliver courses of lectures on pedagogy, a subject in which he had become deeply interested. He had read Rousseau's "Émile" with delighted attention, and observed Basedow's experiments with hopeful interest. Unfortunately he did not prepare an elaborate work on education. What we have are the notes of his lectures, which, not long before his death, were revised and arranged by his pupil Rink. They were published in 1803 under the title "Immanuel Kant über Pädagogik." It is a comparatively brief treatise, covering only seventy pages of Kant's collective works, in which it is now included.

The treatise is divided into three parts, namely, *the introduction, physical education,* and *practical or moral education.* In spite of its lack of careful, systematic development, it is notable for the lofty spirit in which it is written, and for the profound pedagogical principles which here and there appear. The introduction which, with a few minor omissions, is here given, presents pretty fully the various phases of Kant's system of education. He assigns a high aim to education — the perfection of the individual — and lays great stress upon the importance of moral training. His pedagogy was not without influence. A number of prominent German educators, among whom may be mentioned Niemeyer, Schwarz, and Rosenkranz, were stimulated and directed by the teachings of the Königsberg philosopher.

SELECTION FROM KANT.

PEDAGOGY.

1. Man is the only creature that needs to be educated. By education we understand *nurture* (attention, food), *discipline,* and *instruction* together with *culture.* Accordingly man is infant, child, and pupil.

Animals use their powers, as soon as they are possessed of them, according to a regular plan, that is, in a way not to injure themselves. It is indeed wonderful, for example, that young swallows, newly hatched and still blind, are careful not to defile their nest. Animals therefore need no nurture, but at the most food, warmth, and guidance, or a kind of protection. It is true most animals need feeding, but they do not require nurture. For by nurture we mean the tender care that parents exercise in order to prevent their children from using their powers in a way to be harmful to them. For instance, should an animal cry at birth, as children do, it would surely fall a prey to wolves and other wild animals, which would be attracted by its cry.

2. Discipline or training transforms animal nature into human nature. An animal is by instinct all that it ever can be; some other reason has already provided everything for it. But man needs a reason of his own. Having no instinct, he has to work out a plan of conduct himself. Since, however, he is not able to do this at once, but comes into the world undeveloped, others must do it for him.

Through its own efforts the human race is by degrees to develop all the natural endowments of man. One generation educates the next. The beginning of this process may be looked for either in a rude and unformed, or in a perfect and cultivated condition. If we assume the latter, man must afterwards have degenerated and lapsed into barbarism.

Discipline prevents man from being turned aside by his animal impulses from humanity, his appointed end. It must restrain him, for example, from venturing wildly and thoughtlessly into danger. Discipline thus is merely negative, namely, the process by which man is deprived of his brutality. Instruction, on the contrary, is the positive part of education.

Brutality is independence of law. Discipline subjects man to the laws of mankind, and lets him feel their constraint. But this must take place early. Thus children are at first sent to school, not so much to learn anything, as to become accustomed to sitting still and obeying promptly what they are told, to the end that later in life they may not actually and instantly follow all their impulses.

3. The love of freedom is naturally so strong in man that when he has once grown accustomed to it, he will sacrifice everything for it. For this very reason discipline must be brought into exercise early; for when this has not been done, it is difficult afterwards to change the character.

He will then follow every caprice. We see this also among savage nations which, though they may live in subjection to Europeans a long time, yet never adopt European customs. With them, however, this is not a noble love of freedom, as Rousseau and others imagine, but a kind of savagery, in which the animal, so to speak, has not yet developed its humanity. Man should therefore accustom himself early to submit to the dictates of reason. If a man in his youth is allowed to follow his own will without opposition, he will retain a certain lawlessness through life. And it is no advantage to such a man to be spared in his youth through a superabundant motherly tenderness, for later on he will meet with all the more opposition on every side and everywhere encounter rebuffs, when he enters into the business of the world.

It is a common mistake in the education of the great that, because they are destined to rule, they should never meet with opposition in their youth. Owing to his love of freedom, man needs to have his native roughness smoothed down; but with animals instinct renders this unnecessary.

4. Man needs *nurture* and *culture*. Culture includes discipline and instruction. These, so far as we know, no animal needs; for none of them learn anything from their elders, except the birds, which are taught by them to sing. It is a touching sight to watch the mother bird singing with all her might to her young ones, which like children at school, try to produce the same tones out of their tiny throats.

Man can become man only by education. He is nothing but what education makes him. It is to be noted that man is educated only by men who have themselves been educated. Hence lack of discipline and instruction on the part of some men makes them in turn bad educators of their pupils. Were some being of a higher nature than man to undertake our education, we should then be able to see what man might become. Since some things are imparted to man by education, and others only developed, it is difficult for us to estimate accurately his native capabilities. If, by the help of the great and the coöperative efforts of many persons, the experiment were made, we might gain some idea of the eminence which it is possible for man to attain. But it is just as important for the philosopher, as it is sad for the philanthropist, to see how the great generally care only for their own interests, and take no part in the weighty experiments of education, which might bring our nature one step nearer to perfection.

5. A theory of education is a glorious ideal, and it matters little, if we are not able to realize it at once. Only we must not look upon the idea as chimerical, nor decry it as a beautiful dream, though difficulties stand in the way of its realization.

An idea is nothing else than the conception of a perfection that has not yet been realized. For instance, the idea of a perfect republic governed by the principles of justice — is it impossible because it has never existed? First of all our idea must be correct, and then, in spite of all the hindrances that stand in the way of its realization, it is by no means impossible. If, for example, lying became universal, would veracity on that account be merely a whim? And the idea of an education which will develop all man's natural gifts is certainly a true one.

6. Under the present system of education man does not fully attain the object of his being. For how differently men live! Uniformity can prevail among them, only when they act according to the same principles, which have become to them a second nature. We can work out a better system of education, and hand down to posterity such directions as will enable them by degrees to bring it to realization.

There are many undeveloped powers in man; and it is our task to unfold these natural gifts in due proportion, to develop humanity from its germinal state, and to lead man to a realization of his destiny. Animals unconsciously fulfil their destiny themselves. Man must strive to attain it, but this he can not do, unless he has a conception as to the object of his existence. The fulfilment of his destiny is absolutely impossible to the individual. In times past men had no conception of the perfection to which human nature might attain. We ourselves have not yet become perfectly clear on the subject. This much, however, is certain: no individual man, whatever may be the culture of his pupils, can insure the fulfilment of their destiny. To succeed in this high end, not the work of individuals, but that of the whole human race, is necessary.

7. Education is an art, the practice of which can become perfect only through many generations. Each generation, provided with the knowledge of the preceding one, can more and more bring about an education, which will develop man's natural gifts in due proportion and relation to their end, and thus advance the whole human race towards its destiny. Providence has willed that man shall develop the good that lies hidden in his nature, and has spoken, as it were, thus to him: " Go forth into the world, I have equipped thee with all the potencies of good. It is for thee to develop them, and thus thy happiness and unhappiness depend upon thyself alone."

Man must develop his talents for the good; Providence has not placed a fully formed goodness in him, but merely capabilities without moral distinction. Man's duty is to improve himself; to cultivate his mind, and when he is evil, to develop moral character. Upon reflection we shall find this very difficult. Hence education is the greatest and most difficult problem to which man can devote himself. For insight depends on education, and education in its turn depends on insight. Hence it follows that education can advance only by degrees, and that a true conception of the method of education can arise only when one generation transmits its stores of experience and knowledge to the following one, which in turn adds something of its own before handing them down to its successor. What vast culture and experience does not this conception presuppose! Accordingly it can originate only at a remote period, and we ourselves have not fully realized it. The question arises whether the education of the individual should be conformed to the education of the human race through its successive generations?

There are two inventions of man which may be regarded as the most difficult of all, namely, the art of government and the art of education; and people are still divided as to their true idea.

8. Since the development of man's natural gifts does not take place of itself, all education is an art. Nature has placed no instinct in him for that purpose. The origin as well as the progress of this art is either mechanical and without plan, ordered according to given circumstances, or it involves the exercise of intelligent judgment. Education is mechanical when on only chance occasions we learn by experience whether anything is useful or harmful to man. All education which is merely mechanical must carry with it many mistakes and deficiencies because it rests on no basal principle. If education is to develop human nature so that it may attain its destiny, it must involve the exercise of judgment. Educated parents are models which children use for imitation. But if children are to progress beyond their parents, pedagogy must become a study; otherwise we can hope nothing from it, and men of defective education will become the educators of others. Mechanism in education

must be changed into a science; otherwise it will never become a consistent pursuit, and one generation may pull down what another had built up.

9. One principle of education which those men especially who form educational schemes should keep before their eyes is this — children ought to be educated, not for the present, but for a possibly improved condition of man in the future; that is, in a manner which is adapted to the idea of humanity and the whole destiny of man. This principle is of great importance. Parents usually educate their children in such a manner that they may be adapted to the present conditions, however degenerate the world may be. But they ought to give them a better education, in order that a better condition of things may thereby be brought about in the future.

10. Here, however, we encounter two difficulties: (1) Parents usually care only that their children make their way in the world, and (2) Princes consider their subjects only as instruments for their own purposes. Parents care for the home, princes for the state. Neither have as their aim the universal good and the perfection to which man is destined and for which he has also the natural gifts. But the basis of a scheme of education must be cosmopolitan. And is, then, the idea of the universal good hurtful to us as individuals? Never! for though it may appear that something must be sacrificed with this idea, nevertheless it furthers the best interests of the individual under his present conditions. And then what splendid results follow! It is through good education that all the good in the world arises. The germs which lie hidden in man need only to be more and more developed. For the elements of evil are not to be found in the natural endowments of man. The failure to bring nature under control — this is the cause of evil. In man there are only germs of good.

11. But by whom is this better condition of the world to be brought about? By rulers, or by their subjects? Shall the latter improve themselves so that they meet a good government half way? If this better condition is to be established by princes, then their own education must first be improved, for their training has long suffered the great mistake of not allowing them to meet with opposition in their youth.

Accordingly the management of schools should entirely depend upon the judgment of the most enlightened experts. All culture begins with the individual, and radiates from him as a center. It is only through the efforts of people of broader views, who take an interest in the general good, and who are capable of entertaining the idea of a better condition of things in the future, that the gradual progress of human nature towards its goal is possible.

12. Thus, in education, man must in the first place, be made the subject of *discipline*. Discipline means the effort to restrain the animal side of our nature, in the individual as well as in social life, from working harm. It is thus nothing but the subjugation of our brutality. In the second place, man must acquire *culture*. Culture includes information and instruction. It is culture that brings out ability. Ability is the possession of a faculty which is capable of being adapted to all desired ends. It does not determine ends, but leaves that to subsequent circumstances. On account of the multitude of ends, ability is in some sense infinite. In the third place, man must acquire *discretion* and be able to conduct himself in society so that he may be esteemed, and possess influence. To this end there is needed a kind of culture which we call *refinement*. This includes manners, courtesy, and a certain discretion, which will enable their possessor to use all men for his own ends. This refinement changes according to the varying taste of successive ages.

Thus, some decades ago, ceremonies were the fashion in social intercourse. In the fourth place, *moral training* must form a part of education. It is not enough that a man be fitted for any end, but he must also acquire the disposition to choose only good ends. Good ends are those which are necessarily approved by everyone, and which may at the same time be the aim of everyone.

13. Man may be either broken in, trained, and mechanically taught, or he may be really enlightened. Horses and dogs are broken in, and man, too, may be broken in. But it is not enough that children should be merely broken in; it is eminently important that they learn to think. That leads to the principle from which all transactions proceed. Thus we see that a real education involves a great deal. But as a rule, in private education, the fourth and most important point is still too much neglected, for children are substantially educated in such a way that moral training is left to the preacher. And yet how infinitely important it is that children be taught from youth up to detest vice, not merely on the ground that God has forbidden it, but because it is in itself detestable.

14. Experimental schools must be established before we can establish normal schools. Education and instruction must not be merely mechanical; they must be based on fixed principles. Yet education must be not entirely theoretical, but at the same time, in a certain sense, mechanical.

People commonly imagine that experiments in education are not necessary, and that we can judge from our reason whether anything is good or not. But this is a great mistake, and experience teaches that the results of our experiments are often entirely different from what we expected. Thus we see that, since we must be guided by experiments, no one generation can set forth a complete scheme of education.

15. Education is either *private* or *public*. The latter is concerned only with instruction, and this can always remain public. The practice of what is taught is left to private education. A complete public education is one which unites instruction and moral culture. Its aim is to promote a good private education.

Education in the home is conducted either by the parents themselves, or, should the parents not have the time, aptitude, or inclination, by others who are paid to assist them. But in education carried on by these assistants, one very great difficulty arises, namely, the division of authority between parent and tutor. The child must obey the regulations of his teacher, and at the same time follow the whims of his parents. The only way out of this difficulty is for parents to surrender entirely their authority to the tutor.

16. How far, then, has private education an advantage over public education, or *vice versa?* In general it seems to me that, not merely for the development of ability but also for the cultivation of civic character, public education is to be preferred. Private education, in many cases, not only fosters family failings, but transmits them to the new generation.

17. One of the greatest problems of education is how to unite submission to legal restraint with the exercise of freewill. For restraint is necessary! How am I to develop freedom in the presence of restraint? I am to accustom my pupil to endure a restraint of his freedom, and at the same time I am to guide him to use his freedom aright. Without this all education is merely mechanical, and the child, when his education is over, does not know how to make a proper use of his freedom. He must be made to feel early the inevitable opposition of society, that he may learn the difficulty of supporting himself, enduring privation, and acquiring what is necessary to make him independent.

XXIII. JOHN HENRY PESTALOZZI.

BIOGRAPHICAL SKETCH.

This great educational reformer, the greatest perhaps since the Reformation of the sixteenth century, was born January 12, 1746, in the beautiful town of Zürich. He was lacking in administrative ability, but possessed a deep love and noble enthusiasm for humanity. Intellectual force was subordinate in him to imagination and sensibility. He engaged in several famous educational experiments, all which, in spite of their failure, were fruitful in blessings to mankind. It was through his efforts, unselfish and self-sacrificing, that what was best in educational theory up to his time obtained permanent recognition. He gave a new impulse to popular education, from which he expected great improvement in the moral, intellectual, and social condition of Europe.

Having failed as a farmer, Pestalozzi turned his farm, to which he had given the name of Neuhof, into an industrial school for the poor. He soon had fifty children under his charge to provide for. His plan was to combine study with remunerative labor; but after five years the school was closed in 1780, leaving him heavily involved in debt, but greatly enriched in educational experience.

The next few years were devoted chiefly to authorship as a means of earning a livelihood. He turned his pedagogical studies and experience to good account. "The Evening Hour of a Hermit," an educational treatise in the form of aphorisms, appeared in 1780. In 1782 he edited for a few months the *Swiss News,* a weekly newspaper, in which from time to time he touched upon educational matters. In 1787 he published the fourth and last volume of "Leonard and Gertrude," an educational novel descriptive of humble scenes and conditions in his native land.

In 1798, upon the recommendation of the Swiss directors, Pestalozzi took charge of nearly a hundred destitute and homeless children at Stanz. They composed a heterogeneous mass that would have been appalling to any one with less enthusiasm than Pestalozzi. With almost superhuman zeal he addressed himself to the work of improving their condition, and in the space of a few months wrought so great a change in them that they no longer seemed the same beings. But in less than a year the school was broken up by the return of the French army, which had previously devastated the district. In 1799 Pestalozzi wrote a letter to his friend Gessner, in which he gave a detailed account of the work at Stanz. This letter, a large part of which follows this sketch, is interesting for the light it throws on the character and pedagogy of Pestalozzi.

In 1805 he opened a school at Yverdun, where he attained his greatest triumphs. He achieved a European reputation, and kings and philosophers united in showing him regard. Yverdun became a place of pilgrimage for philanthropists and educators from all parts of Europe. For a time the progress, happiness, and high moral tone of its pupils made the school at once a model and an inspiration in education; but at length in 1825 internal dissension brought the work to an ignominious end. The following year Pestalozzi published "The Song of the Swan," in which he gave a clear statement of his educational labors and principles. He died February 17, 1827.

The following extracts present Pestalozzi's educational system with clearness and fulness. The following summary however, prepared by his biographer Morf, will be found very helpful:

" 1. Sense-impression is the foundation of instruction.

" 2. Language must be connected with sense-impression.

" 3. The time for learning is not the time for judgment and criticism.

" 4. In each branch instruction must begin with the simplest elements, and proceed gradually by following the child's developments; that is, by a series of steps which are psychologically connected.

" 5. A pause must be made at each stage of the instruction sufficiently long for the child to get the new matter thoroughly into his grasp and under his control.

" 6. Teaching must follow the path of development, and not that of dogmatic exposition

" 7. The individuality of the pupil must be sacred for the teacher.

" 8. The chief aim of elementary instruction is not to furnish the child with knowledge and talents, but to develop and increase the powers of his mind.

" 9. To knowledge must be joined power; to what is known, the ability to turn it to account

" 10. The relations between master and pupil, especially so far as discipline is concerned, must be established and regulated by love.

" 11. Instruction must be subordinated to the higher end of education."

SELECTIONS FROM VARIOUS WRITINGS OF PESTALOZZI.

I. DIARY, 1774.

No education would be worth a jot that resulted in a loss of manliness and lightness of heart. So long as there is joy in the child's face, ardor and enthusiasm in all his games, so long as happiness accompanies most of his impressions, there is nothing to fear. Short moments of self-subjugation quickly followed by new interests and new joys do not dishearten. To see peace and happiness resulting from habits of order and obedience is the true preparation for social life.

Be in no hurry to get on, but make the first step sound before moving; in this way you will avoid confusion and waste. Order, exactness, completion — alas, not thus was my character formed. And in the case of my own child in particular, I am in great danger of being blinded by his quickness, and rapid progress, and, dazzled by the unusual extent of his knowledge, of forgetting how much ignorance lurks behind this apparent development, and how much has yet to be done before we can go farther. Completeness, orderliness, absence of confusion — what important points!

Lead your child out into Nature, teach him on the hilltops and in the valleys. There he will listen better, and the sense of freedom will give him more strength to overcome difficulties. But in these hours of freedom let him be taught by Nature rather than by you. Let him fully realize that she is the real teacher and that you, with your art, do nothing more than walk quietly at her side. Should a bird sing or an insect hum on a leaf, at once stop your talk; bird and insect are teaching him; you may be silent.

I would say to the teacher, Be thoroughly convinced of the immense value of liberty; do not let vanity make you anxious to see your efforts producing premature fruit; let your child be as free as possible, and seek diligently for every means of ensuring his liberty, peace of mind, and good humor. Teach him absolutely nothing by words that you can teach him by the things themselves; let him see for himself, hear, find out, fall, pick himself up, make mistakes; no word, in short, when action is possible. What he can do for himself, let him do it; let him be always occupied, always active, and let the time you leave him to himself represent by far the greatest part of his childhood. You will then see that Nature teaches him better than men.

2. THE EVENING HOUR OF A HERMIT, 1780.

1. Man! in thyself, in the inward consciousness of thine own strength, is the instrument intended by Nature for thy development.

2. The path of Nature, which develops the forces of humanity, must be easy and open to all; education, which brings true wisdom and peace of mind, must be simple and within everybody's reach.

3. Nature develops all the forces of humanity by exercising them; they increase with use.

4. The exercise of a man's faculties and talents, to be profitable, must follow the course laid down by Nature for the education of humanity.

5. This is why the man who, in simplicity and innocence, exercises his forces and faculties with order, calmness, and steady application, is naturally led to true human wisdom; whereas he who subverts the order of Nature, and thus breaks the due connection between the different branches of his knowledge, destroys in himself not only the true basis of knowledge, but the very need of such a basis, and becomes incapable of appreciating the advantages of truth.

6. Thou who wouldst be a father to thy child, do not expect too much of him till his mind has been strengthened by practice in the things he can understand; and beware of harshness and constraint.

7. When men are anxious to go too fast, and are not satisfied with Nature's method of development, they im-

peril their inward strength, and destroy the peace and harmony of their souls.

8. When men rush into the labyrinth of words, formulas, and opinions, without having gained a progressive knowledge of the realities of life, their minds must develop on this one basis, and can have no other source of strength.

9. The schools hastily substitute an artificial method of words for the truer method of Nature, which knows no hurry, and is content to wait.

In this way a specious form of development is produced, hiding the want of real inward strength, but satisfying times like our own.

10. Man! if thou seekest the truth in this natural order, thou wilt find it as thou hast need of it for thy position and for the career which is opening before thee.

11. The pure sentiment of truth and wisdom is formed in the narrow circle of our personal relations, the circumstances which suggest our actions, and the powers we need to develop.

12. The performance of acts which are contrary to our inward sense of right, takes from us the power of recognizing truth, and our principles and impressions lose in nobleness, simplicity, and purity.

13. And thus all human wisdom rests on the strength of a heart that follows truth, and all human happiness on this feeling of simplicity and innocence.

14. A man's domestic relations are the first and most important of his nature.

15. A man works at his calling, and bears his share of the public burdens, that he may have undisturbed enjoyment of his home.

16. Thus the education which fits a man for his profession and position in the state must be made subordinate to that which is necessary for his domestic happiness.

17. The home is the true basis of the education of humanity.

18. It is the home that gives the best moral training, whether for private or public life.

19. A man's greatest need is the knowledge of God.

20. The purest pleasures of his home do not always satisfy him.

21. His weak, impressionable nature is powerless without God to endure constraint, suffering, and death.

22. God is the Father of humanity, and his children are immortal.

23. Sin is both the cause and effect of want of faith, and is an act opposed to what a man's inmost sense of good and evil tells him to be right.

24. It is because humanity believes in God that I am contented in my humble dwelling.

25. I base all liberty on justice, but I see no certainty of justice in the world so long as men are wanting in uprightness, piety, and love.

26. The source of justice and of every other blessing in the world, the source of all brotherly love amongst men, lies in the great conception of religion that we are the children of God.

27. That man of God who, by his sufferings and death, restored to men the sense that God is their Father, is indeed the Saviour of the world. His teaching is justice itself, a simple philosophy of practical value for all, the revelation of God the Father to his erring children.

3. SWISS NEWS, 1782.

1. The child at its mother's breast is the weakest and most dependent of human creatures, and yet it is already receiving the first moral impressions of love and gratitude.

2. Morality is nothing but a result of the development in the child of these first sentiments of love and gratitude.

3. The first development of the child's powers should come from his participation in the work of his home, for this work is necessarily what the parents understood best, what most absorbs their attention, and what they are most competent to teach.

4. But even if this were not so, work undertaken to supply real needs would be just as truly the surest foundation of a good education.

5. To engage the attention of the child, to exercise his judgments, to open his heart to noble sentiments, is, I think, the chief end of education; and how can this end be reached so surely as by training the child as early as possible in the various daily duties of domestic life.

6. Nothing makes a greater call on the attention than work in general, because without close attention no work can be well done; but this is especially true of work which children can do in a house, for it varies continually, and in a thousand ways, and compels them to fix their attention on a great number of different objects.

7. Further, it is by doing all sorts of work at an early age that a man acquires a sound judgment; for if his work is to succeed, the difficult circumstances under which it has to be done, must be thoroughly understood; nor can the child help being struck by the fact that failure results from errors in judgment.

8. Finally, work is also the best means of ennobling the heart of man, and of preparing him for all the domestic and social virtues. For, to teach a child obedience, unselfishness, and patience I do not think that anything can be better than work in which he engages regularly with the rest of the family.

*9. As a general rule, art and books would not replace

it in any way. The best story, the most touching picture the child finds in a book is but a sort of dream for him, something unreal, and in a sense untrue; whereas what takes place before his eyes, in his own house, is associated with a thousand similar occurrences, with all his own experience as well as that of his parents and neighbors, and brings him without fail to a true knowledge of men, and develops in him a thoroughly observant mind.

4. LETTER ON HIS WORK AT STANZ, 1799.

I wanted to prove by my experiment that if public education is to have any real value, it must imitate the methods which make the merit of domestic education; for it is my opinion that if public education does not take into consideration the circumstances of family life, and everything else that bears on a man's general education, it can only lead to an artificial and methodical dwarfing of humanity.

In any good education, the mother must be able to judge daily, nay hourly, from the child's eyes, lips, and face, of the slightest change in his soul. The power of the educator, too, must be that of a father, quickened by the general circumstances of domestic life.

Such was the foundation upon which I built. I determined that there should not be a minute in the day when my children should not be aware from my face and my lips that my heart was theirs, that their happiness was my happiness, and their pleasures my pleasures.

Man readily accepts what is good, and the child readily listens to it; but it is not for you that he wants it, master and educator, but for himself. The good to which you would lead him must not depend on your capricious humor or passion; it must be a good which is good in itself and by the nature of things, and which the child can recognize as good. He must feel the necessity of your will in things which concern his comfort before he can be expected to obey it.

Whenever he does anything gladly, anything that brings him honor, anything that helps to realize any of his great hopes, or stimulates his powers, and enables him to say with truth, *I can,* then he is exercising his will.

The will, however, can not be stimulated by mere words; its action must depend upon those feelings and powers which are the result of general culture. Words alone can not give us a knowledge of things; they are only useful for giving expression to what we have in our mind.

The first thing to be done was to win the confidence and affection of the children. I was sure that if I succeeded in doing that, all the rest would follow of itself. Think for a moment of the prejudices of the people, and even of the children, and you will understand the difficulties with which I had to contend.

And yet, however painful this want of help and support was to me, it was favorable to the success of my undertaking, for it compelled me to be always everything for my children. I was alone with them from morning till night. It was my hand that supplied all their wants, both of body and soul. All needful help, consolation, and instruction they received direct from me. Their hands were in mine, my eyes were fixed on theirs.

We wept and smiled together. They forgot the world and Stanz; they only knew that they were with me and I with them. We shared our food and drink. I had neither family, friends, nor servants; nothing but them. I was with them in sickness and health, and when they slept. I was the last to go to bed, and the first to get up. In the bedroom I prayed with them, and, at their own request, taught them till they fell asleep.

This is how it was that these children gradually became so attached to me, some indeed so deeply that they contradicted their parents and friends when they heard evil things said about me. They felt that I was being treated unfairly, and loved me, I think, the more for it. But of what avail is it for the young nestlings to love their mother, when the bird of prey that is bent on destroying them is constantly hovering near?

For most of them study was something entirely new. As soon as they found that they could learn, their zeal was indefatigable, and in a few weeks children who had never before opened a book, and could hardly repeat a *Pater Noster* or an *Ave,* would study the whole day long with the keenest interest. Even after supper, when I used to say to them, " Children, will you go to bed, or learn something? " they would generally answer, especially in the first month or two, " Learn something." It is true that afterwards, when they had to get up very early, it was not quite the same.

But this first eagerness did much towards starting the establishment on the right lines, and making the studies the success they ultimately were — a success, indeed, which far surpassed my expectations. And yet the difficulties in the way of introducing a well-ordered system of studies were at that time almost unsurmountable.

My one aim was to make their new life in common, and their new powers, awaken a feeling of brotherhood amongst the children, and make them affectionate, just and considerate. I reached this end without much difficulty. Amongst these seventy wild beggar-children there soon existed such peace, friendship, and cordial relations as are rare even between actual brothers and sisters.

The principle to which I endeavored to conform all my conduct was as follows: Endeavor, first, to broaden your children's sympathies, and, by satisfying their daily needs, to bring love and kindness into such unceasing contact with their impressions and their activity, that these sentiments may be engrafted in their hearts; then try to give them such judgment and tact as will enable them to make a wise, sure, and abundant use of these virtues in the circle which surrounds them.

In the last place, do not hesitate to touch on the difficult questions of good and evil, and the words connected with them. And you must do this especially in connection with the ordinary events of every day, upon which your whole teaching in these matters must be founded, so that the children may be reminded of their own feelings, and supplied, as it were, with solid facts upon which to base their conception of the beauty and justice of the moral life.

The pedagogical principle which says that we must win the hearts and minds of our children by words alone, without having recourse to corporal punishment, is certainly good, and applicable under favorable conditions and circumstances; but with children of such widely different ages as mine, children for the most part beggars, and all full of deeply-rooted faults, a certain amount of corporal punishment was inevitable, especially as I was anxious to arrive surely, speedily, and by the simplest means, at gaining an influence over them all, for the sake of putting them all in the right road. I was compelled to punish them, but it would be a mistake to suppose that I thereby, in any way, lost the confidence of my pupils.

Elementary moral education, considered as a whole, includes three distinct parts: the children's moral sense must first be aroused by their feelings being made active and pure; then they must be exercised in self-control, and taught to take interest in whatever is just and good; finally, they must be brought to form for themselves, by reflection and comparison, a just notion of the moral rights and duties which are theirs by reason of their position and surroundings.

I have generally found that great, noble, and high thoughts are indispensable for developing wisdom and firmness of character. Such instruction must be complete in the sense that it must take account of all our aptitudes and all our circumstances; it must be conducted, too, in a truly psychological spirit, that is to say, simply, lovingly, energetically, and calmly. Then, by its very nature, it produces an enlightened and delicate feeling for everything true and good, and brings to light a number of accessory and dependent truths, which are forthwith accepted and assimilated by the human soul, even in the case of those who could not express those truths in words.

I believe that the first development of thought in the child is very much disturbed by a wordy system of teaching, which is not adapted either to his faculties or the circumstances of his life. According to my experience, success depends upon whether what is taught to children commends itself to them as true, through being closely connected with their own personal observation and experience. Without this foundation truth must seem to them to be little better than a plaything, which is beyond their comprehension, and therefore a burden.

Human knowledge derives its real advantages from the solidity of the foundations on which it rests. The man who knows a great deal must be stronger and must work harder than others, if he is to bring his knowledge into harmony with his nature and with the circumstances of his life. If he does not do this, his knowledge is but a delusive will-o'-the-wisp, and will often rob him of such ordinary pleasures of life as even the most ignorant man, if he have but common sense, can make quite sure of.

5. THE SONG OF THE SWAN, 1826.

The idea of elementary education, to which I have devoted my life, consists in re-establishing the course of Nature, and in developing and improving the tendencies and powers of humanity.

But what is human nature? It is, at bottom, that which distinguishes the man from the animal, that which should predominate and control whatever they have in common. Thus elementary education must aim at developing heart, mind, and body in such a way as to bring the flesh into subjection to the spirit.

Now it is evident that this development must follow a certain course, that this course must be the course of Nature, and that it is regulated by immutable laws.

Indeed, however great the diversities of men may be, they do not in any way affect either the unity of human nature or the universality of the laws which govern its development.

These laws apply to the whole of man's nature, and serve to maintain the necessary harmony between his heart, his intellect, and his physical powers. Any educational method which neglects either of these three sides, does but encourage a partial development. False to Nature, it produces no real and lasting results; it is as sounding brass or a tinkling cymbal, and exercises a fatal influence on the harmony of the natural development.

The idea of elementary education involves the equilibrium of a man's powers, and the equilibrium of the powers involves the natural development of each of them. Each power develops according to the particular laws of its nature, which laws are not the same for heart, mind, and body.

And yet all human powers may be developed in the simplest way by use. Thus a man lays the foundation of his moral life of love and faith, by the practice of these virtues; of his intellectual life of thought, by thinking; of his industrial life, by making use of his physical powers.

Indeed, man is impelled by the very nature of the powers he possesses to use and train them, and thus to develop and improve them, as far at least as they are susceptible of development and improvement. These powers exist at first but in germ, but the desire to use them increases with every successful attempt, though it decreases and sometimes disappears with failure, especially if the failure should cause suffering.

Further, the idea of elementary education consists in so regulating the use of the different powers that every effort shall succeed, and none fail; and this must be the case no less with the intellectual and the physical than with the moral powers.

The natural means for this early education are to be looked for in the enlightened love, faith, and tenderness of parents, made wise by a knowledge of all the conquests humanity has won.

The method of Nature is, in its principle, holy and divine, but if left to itself, it is often disturbed and perverted by the predominance of the animal instincts. Our duty, our heart's chief desire, the aim of our faith and wisdom, should be to keep it truly human, to quicken it by means of the divine element within us.

The first cares of a mother for her child are for its physical needs; she satisfies these with unfailing tenderness, enjoys the child's contentment, smiles at it with love, and receives an answering smile of love, trust, and gratitude. These are the first manifestations of the moral and religious development.

But the child must also feel the peace which proceeds from satisfied needs; this peace of the soul is indeed an essential condition of the moral development. It is no sooner replaced by anxiety and trouble than love, trust, and gratitude give way to selfishness, pride, and other evil passions.

When the mother succeeds in keeping the child contented, the benefit is felt by every member of the family. The home becomes a center of moral and religious life, and the child, whose trust in its parents nothing can shake, loves what they love, believes what they believe, and worships the same God and Savior.

But when this peace is wanting from the very cradle, the home, troubled in every part, is no longer a sanctuary of peace and happiness, and its good influence on the moral and religious development disappears.

The starting-point of thought is sense-perception, that is to say, the direct impression produced by the world on our internal and external senses.

Thus the power of thinking is formed and developed first of all by the impressions of the moral world upon our moral sense and by those of the physical world upon our bodily senses.

These impressions, acting on the understanding of the child, give him his first ideas, and at the same time awaken in him the desire to express them, first by signs, then by words.

To speak we must have not only ideas, but practiced and supple organs. And further, we can only speak clearly and exactly of those things from which we have received clear and exact impressions.

To teach a child to talk, then, we must first make him see, hear, and touch many things, and especially things which please him, so that he may readily give his attention to them; we must also make him observe them in order, observing each thoroughly before he proceeds to another At the same time he must have constant practice in putting his impressions into words. All this is what a good mother does for her child when it is beginning to speak.

Afterwards a foreign or dead language may be learned differently; partly because the organs of speech have already been trained, partly because most of the fundamental ideas are already there, and lastly, because the mother-tongue supplies the child with a point of comparison.

But before a child can compare things and exercise his judgment about them, his thought must also have practice in the two other chief elements of human knowledge, number and form.

The fundamental elements, then, that serve to develop the force of thought are language, number, and form, and it is the business of education to present these elements to the child's mind in the simplest possible manner, and in psychological and progressive order.

Art, practical knowledge, bodily skill, whatever in short enables a man to make what he has conceived in his mind, is what we call the industrial life. What are its fundamental elements? How may they be developed?

Its fundamental elements are two: the power of the thought within, the practical skill of the senses and limbs without. To be completely useful, it must be the outcome of the harmonious development of heart, mind, and body. We have already spoken of the two first; it remains for us now to consider the fundamental elements of physical development.

Just as elementary exercises in number and form are necessary as training for the intellectual life, so elementary exercises in art and practical work are a necessary part of that physical training which is essential to success in the industrial life. Technical apprenticeship is but one particular form of this training.

And further, just as our moral and intellectual powers are

naturally inclined to be active, and attract us to whatever exercises them, so our industrial powers have a similar natural tendency, and attract us to whatever exercises and develops them.

The physical instinct which leads us to use our senses and limbs is generally connected with our animal nature, and needs no assistance from us. But this instinct must be subordinated to the moral and intellectual elements which constitute the superiority of human nature. To bring about this subordination is the essential work of education.

It consists in developing, according to the natural law, the child's various powers, moral, intellectual, and physical, with such subordination as is necessary to their perfect equilibrium.

This equilibrium alone can produce a peaceful, happy life, and one likely to profit the general welfare. Piety, faith, and love bring a man peace, and are indeed its conditions, for without these virtues the highest development of intellect, art or industry brings no rest, but leaves the man full of trouble, uneasiness, and discontent.

XXIV. FREDERICK FROEBEL

BIOGRAPHICAL SKETCH.

The most illustrious disciple of Pestalozzi was Frederick Froebel, who was born in Thuringia, April 21, 1782. Owing to the early death of his mother, his childhood training was sadly neglected. At the village school, which he entered in due time, he received religious impressions that never left him. At the age of ten years he went to live with an uncle, in whose home he found the kindness and sympathy that his earlier childhood had missed. He entered the town school of Stadt-Ilm, but the teacher, an old-time mechanical driller, failed to reach the inner nature of his gifted pupil.

At the age of fifteen Froebel became a forester's apprentice. Not receiving the instruction he had a right to expect, he was thrown upon his own resources, and by means of the books at hand he made considerable attainments in the forester's art. He was especially fond of botany. "My church religion," he wrote, "changed into a religious life in Nature, and in the last half-year I lived entirely in and with plants, which attracted me wonderfully, without however the meaning of the inner life of the plant-world yet dawning on me."

In 1799 he entered the University of Jena, where he attended lectures on mathematics, botany, natural history, physics, chemistry, and architecture. Several years were spent in various employments without yielding him either much profit or peace of mind. In 1805 we find him in Frankfort with an architect. Then the turning point in his life came. He was offered a position as teacher; and the ecstasy he felt, as he stood for the first time in the presence of the school, convinced him that he had found his place. To use his own expression, " The fish was in the water."

In 1808 he went to Yverdun, and spent two years with Pestalozzi. He took with him three pupils, of whom he had charge as tutor. Thus he became thoroughly acquainted with Pestalozzi's system, which in its essential features he cordially adopted, but which he also supplemented and improved. Afterward feeling the necessity of increasing his store of knowledge, he studied at the universities of Göttingen and Berlin. In 1813 he joined the Prussian army, and took an active part in the campaign against Napoleon. After the close of the war he established a school at Keilhau in 1817, in which he followed " the principle of cultivating the self-activity of the pupil by connecting manual labor with every study." After a temporary success, the enterprise, on political and religious grounds, was opposed by the Prussian government, and in 1831 Froebel was forced to abandon it.

It was during his work at Keilhau that Froebel published his great work, from which the following extracts are taken. The full title of the work is as follows: " The Education of Man, the Art of Education, Instruction and Training, Aimed at in the German Educational Institute at Keilhau, set forth by its Principal, F. W. A. Froebel." It is a work of profound thought, requiring and repaying repeated perusal. " His great word," to adopt the judgment of Dr. W. T. Harris, " is *inner connection*. There must be an inner connection between the pupil's mind and the objects which he studies, and this shall determine what to study. There must be an inner connection in those objects among themselves which determines their succession and the order in which they are to be taken up in the course of instruction. Finally, there is an inner connection within the soul that unites the faculties of feeling, perception, phantasy, thought, and volition, and determines the law of their unfolding. Inner connection is in fact the law of development, the principle of evolution, and Froebel is the educational reformer who has done more than all the rest to make valid in education what the Germans call the ' developing method.' "

After a varied experience at Keilhau, extending through nearly fifteen years, Froebel came to the conclusion that a change in the methods of early instruction was necessary to a thorough educational reform. Carefully considering the ways of children, he saw that they delight in movement; that they use their senses; that they observe; that they invent and construct. All this activity he proposed to turn to account in the interest of education. This led to the founding of the kindergarten — a school which receives children at a very early age, and by systematizing their plays, directing their activity, and giving order to their ideas, develops their faculties harmoniously, and prepares them for the work of the ordinary school.

Froebel died June 21, 1852. " The fame of knowledge," it was said over his grave, " was not his ambition. Glowing love for mankind, for the people, left him neither rest nor quiet. After he had offered his life for his native land in the wars of freedom, he turned with the same enthusiasm which surrenders and sacrifices for the highest thought, to the aim of cultivating the people and youth. And how many brave men he has educated, who honor his memory and bless his name!"

SELECTION FROM FROEBEL.

THE EDUCATION OF MAN.

1. In all things there lives and reigns an eternal law. This all-controlling law is necessarily based on an all-pervading, energetic, living, self-conscious, and hence eternal unity. This Unity is God. All things have come from the divine Unity, from God, and have their origin in the divine Unity, in God alone. God is the sole source of all things. In all things there lives and reigns the divine Unity, God. All things live and have their being in and through the divine Unity, in and through God. All things are only through the divine effluence that lives in them. The divine effluence that lives in each thing is the essence of each thing.

2. It is the destiny and lifework of all things to unfold their essence, hence their divine being, and therefore the divine Unity itself — to reveal God in their external and transient being. It is the special destiny and life-work of man, as an intelligent and rational being, to become fully, vividly, and clearly conscious of his essence, of the divine effluence in him, and therefore, of God; to become fully, vividly, and clearly conscious of his destiny and life-work; and to accomplish this, to render it (his essence) active, to reveal it in his own life with self-determination and freedom. *Education consists in leading man, as a thinking, intelligent being, growing into self-consciousness, to a pure and unsullied, conscious and free representation of the inner law of divine Unity, and in teaching him ways and means thereto.*

3. The knowledge of that eternal law, the insight into its origin, into its essence, into the totality, the connection, and intensity of its effects, the knowledge of life in its totality, constitute *science, the science of life;* and, referred by the

self-conscious, thinking, intelligent being to representation and practice through and in himself, this becomes *the science of education.*

The system of directions, derived from the knowledge and study of that law, to guide thinking, intelligent beings in the apprehension of their life-work and in the accomplishment of their destiny, is *the theory of education.* The self-active application of this knowledge in the direct development and cultivation of rational beings toward the attainment of their destiny, is *the practice of education.* The object of education is the realization of a faithful, pure, inviolate, and hence holy life. Knowledge and application, consciousness and realization in life, united in the service of a faithful, pure, and holy life, constitute the *wisdom of life,* pure wisdom.

4. By education, then, the divine essence of man should be unfolded, brought out, lifted into consciousness, and man himself raised into free, conscious obedience to the divine principle that lives in him, and to a free representation of this principle in his life. Education as a whole, by means of instruction and training, should bring to man's consciousness, and render efficient in his life, the fact that man and nature proceed from God and are conditioned by him — that both have their being in God. *Education should lead and guide man to clearness concerning himself and in himself, to peace with nature, and to unity with God;* hence, it should lift him to a knowledge of himself and of mankind, to a knowledge of God and of nature, and to the pure and holy life to which such knowledge leads.

5. Education in instruction and training, originally and in its first principles, should necessarily be *passive, following with due protection, not prescriptive, categorical, or interfering.* Indeed, in its very essence, education should have these characteristics; for the undisturbed operation of the divine Unity is necessarily good — can not be otherwise than

good. This necessity implies that the young human being — as it were, still in process of creation — would seek, although still unconsciously, as a product of nature, yet decidedly and surely, that which is in itself best; and, moreover, in a form wholly adapted to his condition, as well as to his disposition, his powers, and means. Thus the duckling hastens to the pond and into the water, while the young chicken scratches the ground, and the young swallow catches its food upon the wing and scarcely ever touches the ground.

6. The prescriptive, interfering education, indeed, can be justified only on two grounds; either because it teaches the clear, living thought, self-evident truth, or because it holds up a life whose ideal value has been established in experience. But, where self-evident, living, absolute truth rules, the eternal principle itself reigns, as it were, and will on this account maintain a passive, following character. For the living thought, the eternal divine principle as such demands and requires free self-activity and self-determination on the part of man, the being created for freedom in the image of God.

7. Again, a life whose ideal value has been perfectly established in experience never aims to serve as model in its form, but only in its essence, in its spirit. It is the greatest mistake to suppose that spiritual, human perfection can serve as model in its form. This accounts for the common experience that the taking of such external manifestations of perfection as examples, instead of elevating mankind, checks, nay, represses, its development.

8. In good education, in genuine instruction, in true training, necessity should call forth freedom; law, self-determination; external compulsion, inner free-will; external hate, inner love. Where hatred brings forth hatred; law, dishonesty and crime; compulsion, slavery; necessity, serviture; where oppression destroys and debases; where severity and harshness give rise to stubbornness and deceit — all educa-

tion is abortive. In order to avoid the latter and to secure the former, all prescription should be adapted to the pupil's nature and needs, and secure his coöperation. This is the case when all education in instruction and training, in spite of its necessarily categorical character, bears in all details and ramifications the irrefutable and irresistible impress that the one who makes the demand is himself strictly and unavoidably subject to an eternally ruling law, to an unavoidable eternal necessity, and that, therefore, all despotism is banished.

9. All true education in training and instruction should, therefore, at every moment, in every demand and regulation, be simultaneously double-sided — giving and taking, uniting and dividing, prescribing and following, active and passive, positive yet giving scope, firm and yielding; and the pupil should be similarly conditioned; but between the two, between educator and pupil, between request and obedience, there should invisibly rule a third something, to which educator and pupil are equally subject. The third something is the *right,* the *best,* necessarily conditioned and expressed without arbitrariness in the circumstances. The calm recognition, the clear knowledge, and the serene, cheerful obedience to the rule of this third something is the particular feature that should be constantly and clearly manifest in the bearing and conduct of the educator and teacher, and often firmly and sternly emphasized by him. The child, the pupil, has a very keen feeling, a very clear apprehension, and rarely fails to distinguish whether what the educator, the teacher, or the father says or requests is personal or arbitrary, or whether it is expressed by him as a general law and necessity.

10. The representation of the infinite in the finite, of the eternal in the temporal, of the celestial in the terrestrial, of the divine in and through man, in the life of man by the *nursing* of his originally divine nature, confronts us unmis-

takably on every side as the only object, the only aim of all education, in all instruction and training. Therefore man should be viewed from this only true standpoint immediately with his appearance on earth; nay, as in the case of Mary, immediately with his annunciation, and he should be thus heeded and nursed while yet invisible, unborn.

11. The debasing illusion that man works, produces, creates only in order to preserve his body, in order to secure food, clothing, and shelter, may have to be endured, but should not be diffused and propagated. Primarily and in truth man works only that his spiritual, divine essence may assume outward form, and that thus he may be enabled to recognize his own spiritual, divine nature and the innermost being of God. Whatever food, clothing, and shelter he obtains thereby comes to him as an insignificant surplus. Therefore Jesus says, "Seek ye first the kingdom of heaven," that is, the realization of the divine spirit in your life and through your life, and whatever else your finite life may require, will be added unto you.

Yet human power should be developed, cultivated, and manifested, not only in inner repose, as religion and religious spirit; not only in outward efficiency, as work and industry; but also — withdrawing upon itself and its own resources — in abstinence, temperance, and frugality. Is it needful to do more than indicate this to a human being not wholly at variance with himself? Where *religion, industry* and *temperance,* the truly undivided trinity, rule in harmony, in true pristine unity, there, indeed, is heaven upon earth — peace, joy, salvation, grace, blessedness.

12. *Play* is the highest phase of child-development — of human development at this period; for *it is self-active representation of the inner — representation of the inner from inner necessity and impulse*. Play is the purest, most spiritual activity of man at this stage, and, at the same time,

typical of human life as a whole — of the inner hidden natural life in man and all things. It gives, therefore, joy, freedom, contentment, inner and outer rest, peace with the world. It holds the sources of all that is good. A child that plays thoroughly, with self-active determination, perseveringly until physical fatigue forbids, will surely be a thorough, determined man, capable of self-sacrifice for the promotion of the welfare of himself and others. Is not the most beautiful expression of child-life at this time a playing child?— a child wholly absorbed in his play?— a child that has fallen asleep while so absorbed?

13. The aim and object of parental care, in the domestic and family circle, is to awaken and develop, to quicken all the powers and natural gifts of the child, to enable all the members and organs of man to fulfill the requirements of the child's powers and gifts. The natural mother does all this instinctively, without instruction and direction; but this is not enough: it is needful that she should do it consciously, as a conscious being acting upon another being which is growing into consciousness, and consciously tending toward the continuous development of the human being, in a certain inner living connection.

14. The child — your child, ye fathers — follows you wherever you are, wherever you go, in whatever you do. Do not harshly repel him; show no impatience about his ever-recurring questions. Every harshly repelling word crushes a bud or shoot of his tree of life. Do not, however, tell him in words much more than he could find himself without your words. For it is, of course, easier to hear the answer from another, perhaps to only half hear and understand it, than it is to seek and discover it himself. To have found one fourth of the answer by his own effort is of more value and importance to the child than it is to half hear and half understand it in the words of another; for this causes mental in-

dolence. Do not, therefore, always answer your children's questions at once and directly; but, as soon as they have gathered sufficient strength and experience, furnish them with the means to find the answers in the sphere of their own knowledge.

15. On the part of parents and educators the period of infancy demands chiefly *fostering care*. During the succeeding period of childhood, which looks upon man predominantly as a unit, and would lead him to unity, *training* prevails. The period of boyhood leads man chiefly to the consideration of particular relationships and individual things, in order to enable him later on to discover their inner unity. The inner tendencies and relationships of individual things and conditions are sought and established.

Such a process constitutes the *school* in the widest sense of the word. The school, then, leads man to a knowledge of external things, and of their nature in accordance with the particular and general laws that lie in them; by the presentation of the external, the individual, the particular, it leads man to a knowledge of the internal, of unity, of the universal. Therefore, on entering the period of boyhood, man becomes at the same time a *school-boy*. With this period school begins for him, be it in the home or out of it, and taught by the father, the members of the family, or a teacher. School, then, means here by no means the school-room, nor school-keeping, but *the conscious communication of knowledge, for a definite purpose and in definite inner connection*.

16. On the other hand, as it has appeared and continues to appear in every aspect, the development and cultivation of man, for the attainment of his destiny and the fulfillment of his mission, constitute an unbroken whole, steadily and continuously progressing, gradually ascending. The feeling of community, awakened in the infant, becomes in the child impulse, inclination; these lead to the formation of the dis-

position and of the heart, and arouse in the boy his intellect and will. *To give firmness to the will, to quicken it, and to make it pure, strong, and enduring, in a life of pure humanity, is the chief concern, the main object in the guidance of the boy, in instruction and the school.*

17. Will is the mental activity, ever consciously proceeding from a definite point in a definite direction toward a definite object, in harmony with the man's nature as a whole. This statement contains everything, and indicates all that parent and educator, teacher and school, should be or should give to the boy in example and precept during these years. The starting-point of all mental activity in the boy should be energetic and sound; the source whence it flows, pure, clear, and ever-flowing; the direction, simple, definite; the object, fixed, clear, living and life-giving, elevating, worthy of the effort, worthy of the destiny and mission of man, worthy of his essential nature, and tending to develop it and give it full expression.

Instruction in example and in words, which later on become precept and example, furnishes the means for this. Neither example alone nor words alone will do: not example alone, for it is particular and special, and the word is needed to give to particular individual examples universal applicability; not words alone, for example is needed to interpret and explain the word which is general, spiritual, and of many meanings. But instruction and example alone and in themselves are not sufficient: they must meet a good, pure heart, and this is an outcome of proper educational influences in childhood.

18. In the family the child sees the parents and other members at work, producing, doing something; the same he notices with adults generally in life and in those active interests with which his family is concerned. Consequently the child, at this stage, would like himself to represent what

he sees. He would like to represent — and tries to do so — all he sees his parents and other adults do and represent in work, all which he thus sees represented by human power and human skill.

What formerly the *child* did only *for the sake of the activity,* the *boy* now does *for the sake of the result* or product of his activity; the child's instinct of activity has in the boy become a *formative instinct,* and this occupies the whole outward life, the outward manifestation of boy-life at this period. How cheerfully and eagerly the boy and the girl at this age begin to share the work of father and mother — not the easy work, indeed, but the difficult work, calling for strength and labor!

19. By no means, however, do all the plays and occupations of boys at this age aim at the representation of things; on the contrary, many are predominantly mere practice and trials of strength, and many aim simply at display of strength. Nevertheless, the play of this period always bears a peculiar character, corresponding with its inner life. For, while during the previous period of childhood the aim of play consisted simply in *activity* as such, its aim lies now in a *definite, conscious purpose;* it seeks *representation* as such, or the thing to be represented in the activity. This character is developed more and more in the free boyish games as the boys advance in age.

It is the sense of rare and reliable power, the sense of its increase, both as an individual and as a member of the group, that fills the boy with all-pervading, jubilant joy during these games. It is by no means, however, only the physical power that is fed and strengthened in these games; intellectual and moral power, too, is definitely and steadily gained and brought under control. Indeed, a comparison of the relative gains of the mental and of the physical phases would scarcely yield the palm to the body. Justice, moderation, self-control, truthfulness, loyalty, brotherly love, and, again, strict impartiality — who, when he approaches a group of boys engaged in such games, could fail to catch the fragrance of these delicious blossomings of the heart and mind, and of a firm will; not to mention the beautiful, though perhaps less fragrant blossoms of courage, perseverance, resolution, prudence, together with the severe elimination of indolent indulgence? Whoever would inhale a fresh, quickening breath of life should visit the play-grounds of such boys.

20. The existence of the present teaches man the existence of the past. This, too, which was before he was, he would know. Then there is developed in the boy at this age the desire and craving for tales, for legends, for all kinds of stories, and later on for historical accounts. This craving, especially in its first appearance, is very intense; so much so, that, when others fail to gratify it, the boys seek to gratify it themselves, particularly on days of leisure, and in times when the regular employments of the day are ended.

21. Man is by no means naturally bad, nor has he originally bad or evil qualities and tendencies; unless, indeed, we consider as naturally evil, bad, and faulty the *finite,* the *material,* the *transitory,* the *physical* as such, and the logical consequences of the existing of these phenomena, namely, that man must have the possibility of failure in order to be good and virtuous, that he must be able to make himself a slave in order to be truly free. Yet these things are the necessary concomitants of the manifestation of the eternal in the temporal, of unity in diversity, and follow necessarily from man's destiny to become a conscious, reasonable, and free being.

A suppressed or perverted good quality — a good tendency, only repressed, misunderstood, or misguided — lies originally at the bottom of every shortcoming in man. Hence the only and infallible remedy for counteracting any shortcoming and even wickedness is to find the originally good source, the originally good side of the human being that has been repressed, disturbed, or misled into the shortcoming, and then to foster, build up, and properly guide this good side. Thus the shortcoming will at last disappear, although it may involve a hard struggle *against habit, but not against original depravity* in man; and this is accomplished so much the more rapidly and surely because man himself tends to abandon his shortcomings, for man prefers right to wrong.

XXV. HORACE MANN.

BIOGRAPHICAL SKETCH.

The state of Massachusetts has been the pioneer in American education. It was the first of the colonies to establish public schools and to found a college. From 1642, when the selectmen of every town were enjoined to see that the young were instructed in "the English tongue and a knowledge of the capital laws," Massachusetts has shown an interest in education by the passage of many laws designed to give greater efficiency to the public schools. But it was due principally to the efforts of one person that between 1837 and 1848 the public school system was unified and brought to a higher degree of efficiency than had prevailed before. This person was Horace Mann, one of the most distinguished of American educators. To natural endowments of a high order he added an invincible zeal in behalf of popular education, and a sublime faith in its possibilities as a means of uplifting and regenerating society.

Horace Mann was born in Franklin, Massachusetts, May 4, 1796. With admirable energy he overcame in early manhood the deficiencies in his childhood education which poverty and constant toil had rendered inevitable. Having learned the elements of Latin and Greek from an itinerant school-master, he entered the sophomore class of Brown University in 1816, from which he graduated three years later with the highest honors of his class. He studied law, was admitted to the bar in 1823, and four years later was elected to the legislature. In the legislature, to which he was re-elected for a number of terms, he displayed the same integrity, energy, and eloquence, which had previously promised a bright career at the bar. His moral sense was largely developed, and he showed an especial interest in temperance, charity and education.

In 1835 he entered upon the work with which his name is chiefly associated and in which he rendered the greatest service to his native state and to the American union. In that year the legislature appointed a Board of Education to revise and reorganize the common school system of the state. Owing to various forms of opposition, it was a work of great magnitude and peculiar difficulty. The Board, which was composed of able and distinguished men, called Horace Mann to be its secretary — a position that made him practically the state superintendent of education. Recognizing at once the responsibilities and opportunities of the office, he gave up his legal and political career, and devoted himself with great singleness of purpose to the duties of his new position. He visited all parts of the state, and delivered able and enthusiastic addresses; he established *The Common School Journal* for the discussion of educational questions; but above all other agencies for reaching and molding public opinion must be placed his "Annual Reports," in which he treated the various phases of education in a practical and masterful manner. To a comprehensive grasp of the subject he joined the charm of an eloquent style and the force of a deep conviction.

In 1848 he was elected to Congress to fill the vacancy caused by the death of John Quincy Adams. To this new field he carried his moral enthusiasm and his interest in education. In 1853, giving up a political life, he accepted the presidency of Antioch College; and during his brief administration of six years, he gave the institution a wise, progressive, and liberal policy. His death, which occurred August

2, 1859, cut short a career which would otherwise, no doubt, have exerted a far-reaching influence in the field of higher education.

The following extract is taken from his twelfth and last "Annual Report," which was made in 1848. It may be regarded as presenting the matured convictions resulting from his work as secretary of the Board of Education. He does not discuss education in the abstract, but in its relations to the material, intellectual, and moral welfare of society. He had been charged with a purpose to exclude religion from education; and in vindicating himself from this charge, he lays great stress upon the importance of religious training. The extracts given, though but a small part of the Report, present its essential features, and will serve to show his fundamental views, and the masterful grasp and the splendid energy with which he asserted and maintained them.

SELECTION FROM HORACE MANN.

PHYSICAL, INTELLECTUAL, MORAL, AND RELIGIOUS EDUCATION.

Without undervaluing any other human agency, it may be safely affirmed that the common school, improved and energized as it can easily be, may become the most effective and benignant of all the forces of civilization. Two reasons sustain this position. In the first place, there is a universality in its operation, which can be affirmed of no other institution whatever. If administered in the spirit of justice and conciliation, all the rising generation may be brought within the circle of its reformatory and elevating influences. And, in the second place, the materials upon which it operates are so pliant and ductile as to be susceptible of assuming a greater variety of forms than any other earthly work of the Creator. The inflexibility and ruggedness of the oak, when compared with the lithe sapling or the tender germ, are but feeble emblems to typify the docility of childhood when contrasted with the obduracy and intractableness of man. It is these inherent advantages of the common school, which, in our own state, have produced results so striking, from a system so imperfect, and an administration so feeble. In teaching the blind and the deaf and dumb, in kindling the latent spark of intelligence that lurks in an idiot's mind, and in the more holy work of reforming abandoned and outcast children, education has proved what it can do by glorious experiments. These wonders it has done in its infancy, and with the lights of a limited experience; but when its faculties shall be fully developed, when it shall be trained to wield its mighty energies for the protection of society against the giant vices which now invade and torment it, — against intemperance, avarice, war, slavery, bigotry, the woes of want, and the wickedness of waste,— then there will not be a height to which these enemies of the race can escape which it will not scale, nor a Titan among them all whom it will not slay.

I proceed, then, in endeavoring to show how the true business of the schoolroom connects itself, and becomes identical, with the great interests of society. The former is the infant, immature state of those interests; the latter their developed, adult state. As "the child is father to the man," so may the training of the schoolroom expand into the institutions and fortunes of the state. . . .

Physical Education.

My general conclusion, then, under this head is that it is the duty of all the governing minds in society — whether in office or out of it — to diffuse a knowledge of these beautiful and beneficent laws of health and life throughout the length and breadth of the state; to popularize them; to make them, in the first place, the common acquisition of all, and through education and custom the common inheritance of all, so that the healthful habits naturally growing out of their observance shall be inbred in the people, exemplified in the personal régime of each individual, incorporated into the economy of every household, observable in all private dwellings, and in all public edifices, especially in those buildings which are erected by capitalists for the residence of their work-people, or for renting to the poorer classes; obeyed by supplying cities with pure water; by providing public baths, public walks, and public squares; by rural cemeteries; by the drainage and sewerage of populous towns, and by whatever else may promote the general salubrity of the atmosphere: in fine, by a religious observance of all those sanitary regulations with which modern science has blessed the world.

For this thorough diffusion of sanitary intelligence, the common school is the only agency. It is, however, an adequate agency. Let human physiology be introduced as an indispensable branch of study into our public schools; let no teacher be approved who is not master of its leading principles, and of their applications to the varying circumstances of life; let all the older classes in the schools be regularly and rigidly examined upon this study by the school-committees, —and a speedy change would come over our personal habits, over our domestic usages, and over the public arrangements of society. Temperance and moderation would not be such strangers at the table. Fashion, like European sovereigns, if not compelled to abdicate and fly, would be forced to compromise for the continual possession of her throne by the surrender to her subjects of many of their natural rights. A sixth order of architecture would be invented,— the hygienic, — which, without subtracting at all from the beauty of any other order, would add a new element of utility to them all. The "health regulations" of cities would be issued in a revised code,— a code that would bear the scrutiny of science. And, as the result and reward of all, a race of men and women, loftier in stature, firmer in structure, fairer in form, and better able to perform the duties and bear the burdens of life, would revisit the earth. The minikin specimens of the race, who now go on dwindling and tapering from parent to child, would reascend to manhood and womanhood. Just in proportion as the laws of health and life were discovered and obeyed, would pain, disease, insanity, and untimely death, cease from among men. Consumption would remain; but it would be consumption in the active sense.

Intellectual Education.

Another cardinal object which the government of Massachusetts, and all the influential men in the state, should propose to themselves, is the physical well-being of all the people,— the sufficiency, comfort, competence, of every individual in regard to food, raiment, and shelter. And these necessaries and conveniences of life should be obtained by each individual for himself, or by each family for themselves, rather than accepted from the hand of charity or extorted by poor laws. It is not averred that this most desirable result can, in all instances, be obtained; but it is, nevertheless, the end to be aimed at.

True statesmanship and true political economy, not less than true philanthropy, present this perfect theory as the goal, to be more and more closely approximated by our imperfect practice. The desire to achieve such a result cannot be regarded as an unreasonable ambition; for, though all mankind were well fed, well clothed, and well housed, they might still be but half civilized.

Our ambition as a state should trace itself to a different origin, and propose to itself a different object. Its flame should be lighted at the skies. Its radiance and its warmth should reach the darkest and the coldest abodes of men. It should seek the solution of such problems as these: To what extent can competence displace pauperism? How nearly can we free ourselves from the low-minded and the vicious, not by their expatriation, but by their elevation? To what extent can the resources and powers of nature be converted into human welfare, the peaceful arts of life be advanced, and the vast treasures of human talent and genius be developed? How much of suffering, in all its forms, can be relieved? or, what is better than relief, how much can be prevented? Cannot the classes of crimes be lessened and the number of criminals in each class be diminished? Our exemplars, both for public and for private imitation, should be the parables of the lost sheep and of the lost piece of silver.

When we have spread competence through all the abodes of poverty, when we have substituted knowledge for ignorance in the minds of the whole people, when we have reformed the vicious and reclaimed the criminal, then may we invite all neighboring nations to behold the spectacle, and say to them, in the conscious elation of virtue, "Rejoice with me," for I have found that which was lost. Until that day shall arrive, our duties will not be wholly fulfilled, and our ambition will have new honors to win. . . .

Surely nothing but universal education can counterwork this tendency to the domination of capital and the servility of labor. If one class possesses all the wealth and education, while the residue of society is ignorant and poor, it matters not by what name the relation between them may be called; the latter, in fact and in truth, will be the servile dependants and subjects of the former. But, if education be equally diffused, it will draw property after it by the strongest of all attractions; for such a thing never did happen, and never can happen, as that an intelligent and practical body of men should be permanently poor. Property and labor in different classes are essentially antagonistic; but property and labor in the same class are essentially fraternal. The people of Massachusetts have, in some degree, appreciated the truth, that the unexampled prosperity of the state — its comfort, its competence, its general intelligence and virtue — is attributable to the education, more or less perfect, which all its people have received; but are they sensible of a fact equally important, namely, that it is to this same education that two-thirds of the people are indebted for not being to-day the vassals of as severe a tyranny, in the form of capital, as the lower classes of Europe are bound to in the form of brute force?

Education, then, beyond all other devices of human origin, is the great equalizer of the conditions of men,— the balance-wheel of the social machinery. I do not here mean that it so elevates the moral nature as to make men disdain and abhor the oppression of their fellow-men. This idea pertains to another of its attributes. But I mean that it gives each man the independence and the means by which he can resist the selfishness of other men. It does better than to disarm the poor of their hostility towards the rich: it prevents being poor. Agrarianism is the revenge of poverty against wealth. The wanton destruction of the property of others — the burning of hay-ricks and corn-ricks, the demolition of machinery because it supersedes hand-labor, the sprinkling of vitriol on rich dresses — is only agrarianism run mad. Education prevents both the revenge and the madness. On the other hand, a fellow-feeling for one's class or caste is the common instinct of hearts not wholly sunk in selfish regards for person or family. The spread of education, by enlarging the cultivated class or caste, will open a wider area over which the social feelings will expand; and, if this education should be universal and complete, it would do more than all things else to obliterate factitious distinctions in society. . . .

I hold all past achievements of the human mind to be rather in the nature of prophecy than of fulfilment,— the first-fruits of the beneficence of God in endowing us with the faculties of perception, comparison, calculation, and causality, rather than the full harvest of their eventual development. For look at the magnificent creation into which we have been brought, and at the adaptation of our faculties to understand, admire, and use it. All around us are works worthy of an infinite God; and we are led, by irresistible evidence, to believe that, just so far as we acquire this knowledge, we shall be endued with his power. From history and from consciousness, we find ourselves capable of ever-onward improvement: and therefore it seems to be a denial of first principles — it seems no better than impiety — to suppose that we shall ever become such finished scholars, that the works of the All-wise will have no new problem for our solution, and will, therefore, be able to teach us no longer.

Nor is it any less than impiety to suppose that we shall ever so completely enlist the powers of Nature in our service, that exhausted Omnipotence can reward our industry with no further bounties. This would be to suppose that we shall arrive at a period when our active and progressive natures will become passive and stationary; when we shall have nothing to do but to sit in indolent and inglorious contemplation of past achievements; and when, all aspirations having been lost in fruition, we shall have outlived the joys of hope and the rewards of effort, and no new glories will beckon us onward to new felicities.

Moral Education.

Moral education is a primal necessity of social existence. The unrestrained passions of men are not only homicidal, but suicidal; and a community without a conscience would soon extinguish itself. Even with a natural conscience, how often has evil triumphed over good! From the beginning of time, wrong has followed right, as the shadow, the substance. As the relations of men become more complex, and the business of the world more extended, new opportunities and new temptations for wrong-doing have been created. With the endearing relations of parent and child came also the possibility of infanticide and parricide; and the first domestic altar that brothers ever reared was stained with fratricidal blood. Following close upon the obligations to truth came falsehood and perjury, and closer still upon the duty of obedience to the divine law came disobedience. With the existence of private relations between men came fraud; and with the existence of public relations between nations came aggression, war, and slavery. And so, just in proportion as the relations of life became more numerous, and the interests of society more various and manifold, the range of possible and of actual offenses has been continually enlarging. As for every new substance there may be a new shadow, so for every new law there may be a new transgression. . . .

The race has existed long enough to try many experiments for the solution of this greatest problem ever submitted to its hands; and the race has experimented, without stint of time or circumscription of space to mar or modify legitimate results. Mankind have tried despotisms, monarchies, and republican forms of government. They have tried the extremes of anarchy and of autocracy. They have tried Draconian codes of law, and for the lightest offenses have extinguished the life of the offender. They have established theological standards, claiming for them the sanction of divine authority, and the attributes of a perfect and infallible law; and then they have imprisoned, burnt, massacred, not individuals only, but whole communities at a time, for not bowing down to idols which ecclesiastical authority had set up. These and other great systems of measures have been adopted as barriers against error and guilt: they have been extended over empires, prolonged through centuries, and administered with terrible energy; and yet the great ocean of vice and crime overleaps every embankment, pours down upon our heads, saps the foundations under our feet, and sweeps away the securities of social order, of property, liberty, and life. . . .

But to all doubters, disbelievers, or despairers in human progress, it may still be said, there is one experiment which has never yet been tried. It is an experiment which, even before its inception, offers the highest authority for its ultimate success. Its formula is intelligible to all; and it is as legible as though written in starry letters on an azure sky. It is expressed in these few and simple words: "*Train up a child in the way he should go; and when he is old, he will not depart from it.*" This declaration is positive. If the conditions are complied with, it makes no provision for a failure. Though pertaining to morals, yet, if the terms of the direction are observed, there is no more reason to doubt the result than there would be in an optical or a chemical experiment.

But this experiment has never yet been tried. Education has never yet been brought to bear with one-hundredth part of its potential force upon the natures of children, and through them upon the character of men and of the race. In all the attempts to reform mankind which have hitherto been made, whether by changing the frame of government, by aggravating or softening the severity of the penal code, or by substituting a government — created for a God-created religion — in all these attempts, the infantile and youthful mind, its amenability to influences, and the enduring and self-operating character of the influences it receives, have been almost wholly unrecognized. Here, then, is a new agency, whose powers are but just beginning to be understood, and whose mighty energies hitherto have been but feebly invoked; and yet, from our experience, limited and imperfect as it is, we do know that, far beyond any other earthly instrumentality, it is comprehensive and decisive. . . .

Is any high-minded, exemplary, and conscientious man disposed to believe that this substantial extirpation of social vices and crimes is a Utopian idea, is more than we have any reason to expect while human nature remains as it is, let me use the *ad hominem* argument to refute him. Let me refer him to himself, and ask him why the same influences which have saved him from gaming, intemperance, dissoluteness, falsehood, dishonesty, violence, and their kindred offenses, and have made him a man of sobriety, frugality, and probity, why the same influences which have saved him from ruin, might not, if brought to bear upon others, save them also. So far as human instrumentalities are concerned, we have abundant means for surrounding every child in the state with preservative and moral influences as extensive and as efficient as those under which the present industrious, worthy, and virtuous members of the community were reared. And as to all those things in regard to which we are directly dependent upon the divine favor, have we not the promise, explicit and unconditional, that the men *shall not* depart from the way in which they should go, if the children are trained up in it? It has been overlooked that this promise is not restricted to parents, but seems to be addressed indiscriminately to all, whether parents, communities, states, or mankind.

Religious Education.

But it will be said that this grand result in practical morals is a consummation of blessedness that can never be attained without religion, and that no community will ever be religious without a religious education. Both these propositions I regard as eternal and immutable truths. Devoid of religious principles and religious affections, the race can never fall so low but that it may sink still lower; animated and sanctified by them, it can never rise so high but that it may ascend still higher. And is it not at least as presumptuous to expect that mankind will attain to the knowledge of truth, without being instructed in truth, and without that general expansion and development of faculty which will enable them to recognize and comprehend truth in any other department of human interest as in the department of religion? No creature of God of whom we have any knowledge has such a range of moral oscillation as a human being. He may despise privileges, and turn a deaf ear to warnings and instructions such as evil spirits may never have known, and therefore be more guilty than they; or, ascending through temptation and conflict along the radiant pathway of duty, he may reach the sublimest heights of happiness, and may there experience the joys of a contrast such as ever-perfect beings can never feel. And can it be that our nature in this respect is taken out of the law that governs it in every other respect,— the law, namely, that the teachings which supply it with new views, and the training that leads it to act in conformity with those views, are ineffective and nugatory?

Indeed, the whole frame and constitution of the human

soul show that, if man be not a religious being, he is among the most deformed and monstrous of all possible existences. His propensities and passions need the fear of God as a restraint from evil; and his sentiments and affections need the love of God as a condition and preliminary to every thing worthy of the name of happiness. Without a capability or susceptibility, therefore, of knowing and reverencing his Maker and Preserver, his whole nature is a contradiction and a solecism: it is a moral absurdity, as strictly so as a triangle with but two sides, or a circle without a circumference, is a mathematical absurdity. The man, indeed, of whatever denomination or kindred or tongue he may be, who believes that the human race, or any nation, or any individual in it, can attain to happiness, or avoid misery, without religious principle and religious affections, must be ignorant of the capacities of the human soul, and of the highest attributes in the nature of man. . . .

There is not a faculty nor a susceptibility in the nature of man, from the lightning-like intuitions that make him akin to the cherubim, or the fire and fervor of affection that assimilate him to seraphic beings, down to the lowest appetites and desires by which he holds brotherhood with beast and reptile and worm — there is not one of them all that will ever be governed by its proper law, or enjoy a full measure of the gratification it was adapted to feel, without a knowledge of the true God, without a sense of acting in harmony with his will and without spontaneous effusions of gratitude for his goodness. Convictions and sentiments such as these can alone supply the vacuity in the soul of man, and fill with significance and loveliness what would otherwise be a blank and hollow universe. . . .

Among the infinite errors and enormities resulting from systems of religion devised by man, and enforced by the terrors of human government, have been those dreadful reactions which have abjured all religion, spurned its obligations, and voted the Deity into non-existence. This extreme is, if possible, more fatal than that by which it was produced. Between these extremes, philanthropic and godly men have sought to find a medium, which should avoid both the evils of ecclesiastical tyranny and the greater evils of atheism. And this medium has at length been supposed to be found. It is promulgated in the great principle that government should do all that it can to facilitate the acquisition of religious truth, but shall leave the decision of the question, what religious truth is, to the arbitrament, without human appeal, of each man's reason and conscience; in other words, that government shall never, by the infliction of pains and penalties, or by the privation of rights or immunities, call such decision either into pre-judgment or into review. The formula in which the constitution of Massachusetts expresses it is in these words: "All religious sects and denominations demeaning themselves peaceably and as good citizens shall be equally under the protection of law; and no subordination of one sect or denomination to another shall ever be established by law." . . .

Beyond our western frontier, another and a wider realm spreads out, as yet unorganized into governments, and uninhabited by civilized man. The western is still broader than the eastern expanse. It stretches through thirty degrees of longitude,— one-twelfth part of the circumference of the globe. Half the population of Continental Europe might be transplanted to it, find subsistence on it, and leave room to spare. It is now a waste more dreary than desolation itself; for it is filled only with savage life. Yet soon will every rood of its surface be explored by the centrifugal force of the Saxon soul; and whatever of vegetable wealth is spread upon it, or of mineral wealth is garnered beneath it, will be appropriated by the vehemence of Saxon enterprise. Shall this new empire, wider than that of the Ptolemies, and almost as extensive as that of the Cæsars, be reclaimed to humanity, to a Christian life, and a Christian history? or shall it be a receptacle where the avarice, the profligacy, and the licentiousness of a corrupt civilization shall cast its criminals and breed its monsters? If it is ever to be saved from such a perdition, the mother states of this Union, those states where the institutions of learning and religion are now honored and cherished, must send out their hallowing influences to redeem it. And if, in the benignant providence of God, the tree of Paradise is ever to be planted and to flourish in this new realm; if its branches are to spread, and its leaves to be scattered for the healing of the people — will not the heart of every true son of Massachusetts palpitate with desire — not a low and vainglorious ambition, but such a high and holy aspiration as angels might feel — that her name may be engraved upon its youthful trunk, there to deepen and expand with its immortal growth?

XXVI. HERBERT SPENCER.

BIOGRAPHICAL SKETCH.

Herbert Spencer, one of the greatest philosophers of all time, was born in Derby, England, April 27, 1820. In early life he was a civil engineer, and later interested himself in economics. He devoted the later years of his life to working out a comprehensive system of philosophy based on the theory of evolution. Among his best known philosophical works, which have been widely read in this country, are the "Data of Ethics," and "First Principles of Psychology." He died December 8, 1903, "the last of the great thinkers of the Victorian age."

In 1860 he published a volume entitled "Education: Intellectual, Moral, and Physical"—a work of rare pedagogical insight and argumentative power. It is thoroughly utilitarian in spirit and contains the most forcible arraignment to which the older education was ever subjected. It is noteworthy that the changes made in the last twenty-five years in our courses of study have been chiefly in the line pointed out by Spencer.

The following extract is, with a few unimportant omissions, the first chapter of Spencer's "Education." His discussion of the question "What Knowledge is of Most Worth?" is the most original part of the work and lays the foundation of his system. It is a powerful presentation of the claims of science, and in its uncompromising criticism of the current education, and in its confident advocacy of scientific studies it gives Spencer a high place among educational reformers.

SELECTION FROM HERBERT SPENCER.

WHAT KNOWLEDGE IS OF MOST WORTH?

It has been truly remarked that, in order of time, decoration precedes dress. Among people who submit to great physical suffering that they may have themselves handsomely tattooed, extremes of temperature are borne with but little attempt at mitigation. Humboldt tells us that an Orinoco Indian, though quite regardless of bodily comfort, will yet labor for a fortnight to purchase pigment wherewith to make himself admired; and that the same woman who would not hesitate to leave her hut without a fragment of clothing on, would not dare to commit such a breach of decorum as to go out unpainted. Voyagers uniformly find that colored beads and trinkets are much more prized by wild tribes than are calicoes or broadcloths. And the anecdotes we have of the ways in which, when shirts and coats are given, they turn them to some ludicrous display, show how completely the idea of ornament predominates over that of use. Nay, there are still more extreme illustrations: witness the fact narrated by Captain Speke of his African attendants, who strutted about in their goat-skin mantles when the weather was fine, but when it was wet, took them off, folded them up, and went about naked, shivering in the rain! Indeed, the facts of aboriginal life seem to indicate that dress is developed out of decorations. And when we remember that even among ourselves most think more about the fineness of the fabric than its warmth, and more about the cut than the convenience — when we see that the function is still in great measure subordinated to the appearance — we have further reason for inferring such an origin.

It is not a little curious that the like relations hold with the mind. Among mental as among bodily acquisitions, the ornamental comes before the useful. Not only in times past, but almost as much in our own era, that knowledge which conduces to personal well-being has been postponed to that which brings applause. In the Greek schools, music, poetry, rhetoric, and a philosophy which, until Socrates taught, had but little bearing upon action, were the dominant subjects; while knowledge aiding the arts of life had a very subordinate place. And in our own universities and schools at the present moment the like antithesis holds. We are guilty of something like a platitude when we say that throughout his after-career a boy, in nine cases out of ten, applies his Latin and Greek to no practical purposes. The remark is trite that in his shop, or his office, in managing his estate or his family, in playing his part as director of a bank or a railway, he is very little aided by this knowledge he took so many years to acquire — so little, that generally the greater part of it drops out of his memory; and if he occasionally vents a Latin quotation or alludes to some Greek myth, it is less to throw light on the topic in hand than for the sake of effect. If we inquire what is the real motive for giving boys a classical education, we find it to be simply conformity to public opinion. Men dress their children's minds as they do their bodies, in the prevailing fashion. As the Orinoco Indian puts on his paint before leaving his hut, not with a view to any direct benefit, but because he would be ashamed to be seen without it; so a boy's drilling in Latin and Greek is insisted on, not because of their intrinsic value, but that he may not be disgraced by being found ignorant of them — that he may have "the education of a gentleman" — the badge marking a certain social position, and bringing a consequent respect.

This parallel is still more clearly displayed in the case of the other sex. In the treatment of both mind and body, the decorative element has continued to predominate in a greater degree among women than among men. Originally personal adornment occupied the attention of both sexes equally. In these latter days of civilization, however, we see that in the dress of men the regard for appearance has, in a considerable degree, yielded to the regard for comfort; while in their education the useful has of late been trenching on the ornamental. In neither direction has this change gone so far with women. The wearing of ear-rings, finger-rings, bracelets; the elaborate dressings of the hair; the still occasional use of paint; the immense labor bestowed in making habiliments sufficiently attractive; and the great discomfort that will be submitted to for the sake of conformity, show how greatly, in the attiring of women, the desire of approbation overrides the desire for warmth and convenience. And similarly in their education, the immense preponderance of "accomplishments" proves how here, too, use is subordinated to display. Dancing, deportment, the piano, singing, drawing — what a large space do these occupy! If you ask why Italian and German are learned, you will find that, under all the sham reasons given, the real reason is, that a knowledge of those tongues is thought ladylike. It is not that the books written in them may be utilized, which they scarcely ever are; but that Italian and German songs may be sung, and that the extent of attainment may bring whispered admiration. The births, deaths, and marriages of kings, and other like historic trivialities, are committed to memory, not because of any direct benefits that can possibly result from knowing them, but because society considers them parts of a good education — because the absence of such knowledge may bring the contempt of others. When we have named reading, writing, spelling, grammar, arithmetic, and sewing, we have named about all the things a girl is taught with a view to their direct uses in life; and even some of these have more reference to the good opinion of others than to immediate personal welfare.

Thoroughly to realize the truth that with the mind as with the body the ornamental precedes the useful, it is needful to glance at its rationale. This lies in the fact that, from the far past down even to the present, social needs have subordinated individual needs, and that the chief social need has been the control of individuals. It is not, as we commonly suppose, that there are no governments but those of monarchs, and parliaments, and constituted authorities. These acknowledged governments are supplemented by other unacknowledged ones, that grow up in all circles, in which every man or woman strives to be king or queen or lesser dignitary. To get above some and be reverenced by them, and to propitiate those who are above us, is the universal struggle in which the chief energies of life are expended. By the accumulation of weath, by style of living, by beauty of dress, by display of knowledge or intellect, each tries to subjugate others, and so aids in weaving that ramified network of restraints by which society is kept in order. It is not the savage chief only who, in formidable warpaint, with scalps at his belt, aims to strike awe into his inferiors; it is not only the belle who, by elaborate toilet, polished manners, and numerous accomplishments, strives to "make conquests," but the scholar, the historian, the philosopher, use their acquirements to the same end. We are none of us content with quietly unfolding our own individualities to the full in all directions, but have a restless craving to impress our individualities upon others, and in some way subordinate them. And this it is which determines the character of our education. Not what knowledge is of most real worth is the consideration, but what will bring most applause, honor, respect — what will most conduce to social position and influence — what will be most imposing. As throughout life not what we are, but what we shall be thought, is the question; so in education, the question is, not the intrinsic value of knowledge, so much as its extrinsic effects on others. And this being one dominant idea, direct utility is scarcely more regarded than by the barbarian when filing his teeth and staining his nails.

If there needs any further evidence of the rude, undeveloped character of our education, we have it in the fact that the comparative worths of different kinds of knowledge have been as yet scarcely even discussed — much less discussed in a methodic way with definite results. Not only is it that no standard of relative values has yet been agreed upon, but the existence of any such standard has not been conceived in any clear manner. And not only is it that the existence of any such standard has not been clearly conceived, but the need for it seems to have been scarcely even felt. Men read books on this topic, and attend lectures on that; decide that their children shall be instructed in these branches of knowledge, and shall not be instructed in those; and all under the guidance of mere custom, or liking, or prejudice, without ever considering the enormous importance of determining in some rational way what things are really most worth learning. It is true that in all circles we have occasional remarks on the importance of this or the other order of information. But whether the degree of its importance justifies the expenditure of the time needed to acquire it, and whether there are not things of more importance to which the time might be better devoted, are queries which, if raised at all, are disposed of quite summarily, according to personal predilections. It is true, also, that from time to time we hear revived the standing controversy respecting the comparative merits of classics and mathematics. Not only, however, is this controversy carried on in an empirical manner, with no reference to an ascertained criterion, but the question at issue is totally insignificant when compared with the general question of which it is part. To suppose that deciding whether a mathematical or a classical education is the best, is deciding what is the proper *curriculum,* is much the same thing as to suppose that the whole of dietetics lies in determining whether or not bread is more nutritive than potatoes.

The question which we contend is of such transcendent moment, is, not whether such or such knowledge is of worth, but what is its *relative* worth? When they have named certain advantages which a given course of study has secured them, persons are apt to assume that they have justified themselves; quite forgetting that the adequateness of the advantages is the point to be judged. There is, perhaps, not a subject to which men devote attention that has not *some* value. A year diligently spent in getting up heraldry would very possibly give a little further insight into ancient manners and morals, and into the origin of names. Any one who should learn the distances between all the towns in England might, in the course of his life, find one or two of the thousand facts he had acquired of some slight service when arranging a journey. Gathering together all the small gossip of a county, profitless occupation as it would be, might yet occasionally help to establish some useful fact — say, a good example of hereditary transmission. But in these cases every one would admit that there was no proportion between the required labor and the probable benefit. No one would tolerate the proposal to devote some years of a boy's time to getting such information, at the cost of much more valuable information which he might else have got.

And if here the test of relative value is appealed to and held conclusive, then should it be appealed to and held conclusive throughout. Had we time to master all subjects we need not be particular. To quote the old song:

> "Could a man be secure
> That his days would endure
> As of old, for a thousand long years,
> What things might he know!
> What deeds might he do!
> And all without hurry or care."

"But we that have but span-long lives" must ever bear in mind our limited time for acquisition. And remembering how narrowly this time is limited, not only by the shortness of life but also still more by the business of life, we ought to be especially solicitous to employ what time we have to the greatest advantage. Before devoting years to some subject which fashion or fancy suggests, it is surely wise to weigh with great care the worth of various alternative results which the same years might bring if otherwise applied.

In education, then, this is the question of questions, which it is high time we discussed in some methodic way. The first in importance, though the last to be considered, is the problem how to decide among the conflicting claims of various subjects on our attention. Before there can be a rational *curriculum,* we must settle which things it most concerns us to know; or, to use a word of Bacon's, now unfortunately obsolete, we must determine the relative values of knowledges.

To this end a measure of value is the first requisite. And happily, respecting the true measure of value, as expressed in general terms, there can be no dispute. Every one in contending for the worth of any particular order of information, does so by showing its bearing upon some part of life. In reply to the question, "Of what use is it?" the mathematician, linguist, naturalist, or philosopher explains the way in which his learning beneficially influences action — saves from evil or secures good — conduces to happiness. When the teacher of writing has pointed out how great an aid writing is to success in business — that is, to the obtaining of sustenance — that is, to satisfactory living — he is held to have proved his case. And when the collector of dead facts (say a numismatist) fails to make clear any appreciable effects which these facts can produce on human welfare, he is obliged to admit that they are comparatively valueless. All then, either directly or by implication, appeal to this as the ultimate test.

How to live? — that is the essential question for us. Not how to live in the mere material sense only, but in the widest sense. The general problem which comprehends every special problem is, the right ruling of conduct in all directions under all circumstances. In what way to treat the body; in what way to treat the mind; in what way to manage our affairs; in what way to bring up a family; in what way to behave as a citizen; in what way to utilize all those sources of happiness which nature supplies — how to use our faculties to the greatest advantage of ourselves and others — how to live completely? And this being the great thing needful for us to learn, is, by consequence, the great thing which education has to teach. To prepare us for complete living is the function which education has to discharge; and the only rational mode of judging of any educational course is, to judge in what degree it discharges such function.

This test, never used in its entirety, but rarely even partially used, and used then in a vague, half-conscious way, has to be applied consciously, methodically, and throughout all cases. It behooves us to set before ourselves, and ever to keep clearly in view, complete living as the end to be achieved; so that in bringing up our children we may choose subjects and methods of instruction with deliberate reference to this end. Not only ought we to cease from the mere unthinking adoption of the current fashion in education, which has no better warrant than any other fashion, but we must also rise above that rude, empirical style of judging displayed by those more intelligent people who do bestow some care in overseeing the cultivation of their children's minds. It must not suffice simply to *think* that such or such information will be useful in after life, or that this kind of knowledge is of more practical value than that; but we must seek out some process of estimating their respective values, so that as far as possible we may positively *know* which are most deserving of attention.

Doubtless the task is difficult — perhaps never to be more than approximately achieved. But considering the vastness of the interests at stake, its difficulty is no reason for pusillanimously passing it by, but rather for devoting every energy to its mastery. And if we only proceed systematically, we may very soon get at results of no small moment.

Our first step must obviously be to classify, in the order of their importance, the leading kinds of activity which constitute human life. They may naturally be arranged into, 1. Those activities which directly minister to self-preservation; 2. Those activities which, by securing the necessaries of life, indirectly minister to self-preservation; 3. Those activities which have for their end the rearing and discipline of offspring; 4. Those activities which are involved in the maintenance of proper social and political relations; 5. Those miscellaneous activities which make up the leisure part of life, devoted to the gratification of the tastes and feelings.

That these stand in something like their true order of subordination, it needs no long consideration to show. The actions and precautions by which, from moment to moment, we secure personal safety must clearly take precedence of all others. Could there be a man, ignorant as an infant of all surrounding objects and movements, or how to guide himself among them, he would pretty certainly lose his life the first time he went into the street, notwithstanding any amount of learning he might have on other matters. And as entire ignorance in all other directions would be less promptly fatal than entire ignorance in this direction, it must be admitted that knowledge immediately conducive to self-preservation is of primary importance.

That next after direct self-preservation comes the indirect self-preservation, which consists in acquiring the means of living, none will question. That a man's industrial functions must be considered before his parental ones is manifest from the fact that, speaking generally, the discharge of the parental functions is made possible only by the previous discharge of the industrial ones. The power of self-maintenance necessarily preceding the power of maintaining offspring, it follows that knowledge needful for self-maintenance has stronger claims than knowledge for family welfare — is second in value to none save knowledge needful for immediate self-preservation.

As the family comes before the state in order of time — as the bringing up of children is possible before the state exists, or when it has ceased to be, whereas the state is rendered possible only by the bringing up of children — it follows that the duties of the parent demand closer attention than those of the citizen. Or, to use a further argument, since the goodness of a society ultimately depends on the nature of its citizens, and since the nature of its citizens is more modifiable by early training than by anything else, we must conclude that the welfare of the family underlies the welfare of society. And hence knowledge directly conducing to the first must take precedence of knowledge directly conducing to the last.

Those various forms of pleasurable occupation which fill up the leisure left by graver occupations — the enjoyments of music, poetry, painting, etc.— manifestly imply a pre-existing society. Not only is a considerable development of them impossible without a long-established social union, but their very subject-matter consists in great part of social sentiments and sympathies. Not only does society supply the conditions to their growth, but also the ideas and sentiments they express. And consequently that part of human conduct which constitutes good citizenship is of more moment than that which goes out in accomplishments or exercise of the tastes; and, in education, preparation for the one must rank before preparation for the other.

Such then, we repeat, is something like the rational order of subordination: That education which prepares for direct self-preservation; that which prepares for indirect self-preservation; that which prepares for parenthood; that which prepares for citizenship; that which prepares for the miscellaneous refinements of life. We do not mean to say that these divisions are definitely separable. We do not deny that they are intricately entangled with each other in such way that there can be no training for any that is not in some measure a training for all. Nor do we question that of each division there are portions more important than certain portions of the preceding divisions: that, for instance, a man of much skill in business, but little other faculty, may fall farther below the standard of complete living than one of but moderate power of acquiring money but great judgment as a parent; or that exhaustive information bearing on right social action, joined with entire want of general culture in literature and the fine arts, is less desirable than a more moderate share of the one joined with some of the other. But after making all qualifications, there still remain these broadly-marked divisions: and it still continues substantially true that these divisions subordinate one another in the foregoing order, because the corresponding divisions of life make one another *possible* in that order.

Of course the ideal of education is complete preparation

in all these divisions. But failing this ideal, as in our phase of civilization every one must do more or less, the aim should be to maintain *a due proportion* between the degrees of preparation in each. Not exhaustive cultivation in any one, supremely important though it may be — not even an exclusive attention to the two, three, or four divisions of greatest importance; but an attention to all — greatest where the value is greatest, less where the value is less, least where the value is least. For the average man (not to forget the cases in which peculiar aptitude for some one department of knowledge rightly makes that one the bread-winning occupation) — for the average man, we say, the desideratum is a training that approaches nearest to perfection in the things which most subserve complete living, and falls more and more below perfection in the things that have more and more remote bearings on complete living.

In regulating education by this standard there are some general considerations that should be ever present to us. The worth of any kind of culture, as aiding complete living, may be either necessary or more or less contingent. There is knowledge of intrinsic value, knowledge of quasi-intrinsic value, and knowledge of conventional value. Such facts as that sensations of numbness and tingling commonly precede paralysis, that the resistance of water to a body moving through it varies as the square of the velocity, that chlorine is a disinfectant — these, and the truths of science in general, are of intrinsic value: they will bear on human conduct ten thousand years hence as they do now. The extra knowledge of our own language, which is given by an acquaintance with Latin and Greek, may be considered to have a value that is quasi-intrinsic; it must exist for us and for other races whose languages owe much to these sources, but will last only as long as our languages last. While that kind of information which, in our schools, usurps the name History — the mere tissue of names and dates and dead unmeaning events — has a conventional value only, it has not the remotest bearing upon any of our actions, and it is of use only for the avoidance of those unpleasant criticisms which current opinion passes upon its absence. Of course, as those facts which concern all mankind throughout all time must be held of greater moment than those which concern only a portion of them during a limited era, and of far greater moment than those which concern only a portion of them during the continuance of a fashion, it follows that in a rational estimate, knowledge of intrinsic worth must, other things equal, take precedence of knowledge that is of quasi-intrinsic or conventional worth.

One further preliminary. Acquirement of every kind has two values — value as *knowledge* and value as *discipline*. Besides its use for guidance in conduct, the acquisition of each order of facts has also its use as mental exercise; and its effects as a preparative for complete living have to be considered under both these heads.

These, then, are the general ideas with which we must set out in discussing a *curriculum:* Life as divided into several kinds of activity of successively decreasing importance; the worth of each order of facts as regulating these several kinds of activity, intrinsically, quasi-intrinsically, and conventionally; and their regulative influences estimated both as knowledge and discipline.

* * * * *

[In the paragraphs omitted Spencer argues that physiology should have a place in our courses of study for its direct relation to self-preservation; that mathematics, physics, chemistry, biology and social science should be taught for their relation to indirect self-preservation; that instruction should be provided in relation to parenthood — an important subject at present wholly neglected; and that more adequate arrangements should be made for instruction in the duties of citizenship.]

And now we come to that remaining division of human life which includes the relaxations, pleasures, and amusements filling leisure hours. After considering what training best fits for self-preservation, for the obtaining of sustenance, for the discharge of parental duties, and for the regulation of social and political conduct, we have now to consider what training best fits for the miscellaneous ends not included in these — for the enjoyments of nature, of literature, and of the fine arts, in all their forms. Postponing them as we do to things that bear more vitally upon human welfare, and bringing everything, as we have, to the list of actual value, it will perhaps be inferred that we are inclined to slight these less essential things. No greater mistake could be made, however. We yield to none in the value we attach to æsthetic culture and its pleasures. Without painting, sculpture, music, poetry, and the emotions produced by natural beauty of every kind, life would lose half its charm. So far from thinking that the training and gratification of the tastes are unimportant, we believe that the time will come when they will occupy a much larger share of human life than now. When the forces of nature have been fully conquered to man's use — when the means of production have been brought to perfection — when labor has been economized to the highest degree — when education has been so systematized that a preparation for the more essential activities may be made with comparative rapidity — and when, consequently, there is a great increase of spare time, then will the poetry, both of art and nature, rightly fill a large space in the minds of all.

But it is one thing to admit that æsthetic culture is in a high degree conducive to human happiness, and another thing to admit that it is a fundamental requisite to human happiness. However important it may be, it must yield precedence to those kinds of culture which bear more directly upon the duties of life. As before hinted, literature and the fine arts are made possible by those activities which make individual and social life possible; and manifestly, that which is made possible must be postponed to that which makes it possible. A florist cultivates a plant for the sake of its flower, and regards the roots and leaves as of value chiefly because they are instrumental in producing the flower. But while, as an ultimate product, the flower is the thing to which everything else is subordinate, the florist very well knows that the root and leaves are intrinsically of greater importance, because on them the evolution of the flower depends. He bestows every care in rearing a healthy plant, and knows it would be folly if, in his anxiety to obtain the flower, he were to neglect the plant. Similarly in the case before us. Architecture, sculpture, painting, music, poetry, etc., may be truly called the efflorescence of civilized life. But even supposing them to be of such transcendent worth as to subordinate the civilized life out of which they grow (which can hardly be asserted), it will still be admitted that the production of a healthy civilized life must be the first consideration, and that the knowledge conducing to this must occupy the highest place.

And here we see most distinctly the vice of our educational system. It neglects the plant for the sake of the flower. In anxiety for elegance it forgets substance. While it gives no knowledge conducive to self-preservation — while of knowledge that facilitates gaining a livelihood it gives but the rudiments, and leaves the greater part to be picked up anyhow in after life — while for the discharge of parental functions it makes not the slightest provision — and while for the duties of citizenship it prepares by imparting a mass of facts, most of which are irrelevant, and the rest without a key, it is diligent in teaching everything that adds to refinement, polish, eclat. However fully we may admit that extensive acquaintance with modern languages is a valuable accomplishment, which, through reading, conversation, and travel, aids in giving a certain finish, it by no means follows that this result is rightly purchased at the cost of that vitally important knowledge sacrificed to it. Supposing it true that classical education conduces to elegance and correctness of style, it can not be said that elegance and correctness of style are comparable in importance to a familiarity with the principles that should guide the rearing of children. Grant that the taste may be greatly improved by reading all the poetry written in extinct languages, yet it is not to be inferred that such improvement of taste is equivalent in value to an acquaintance with the laws of health. Accomplishments, the fine arts, *belles-lettres,* and all those things which, as we say, constitute the efflorescence of civilization, should be wholly subordinate to that knowledge and discipline in which civilization rests. *As they occupy the leisure part of life, so should they occupy the leisure part of education.*

* * * * *

Thus far our question has been the worth of knowledge of this or that kind for purposes of guidance. We have now to judge the relative values of different kinds of knowledge for purposes of discipline. This division of our subject we are obliged to treat with comparative brevity; and happily no very lengthened treatment of it is needed. Having found what is best for the one end, we have by implication found what is best for the other. We may be quite sure that the acquirement of those classes of facts which are most useful for regulating conduct involves a mental exercise best fitted for strengthening the faculties. It would be utterly contrary to the beautiful economy of nature if one kind of culture were needed for the gaining of information and another kind were needed as a mental gymnastic. Everywhere throughout creation we find faculties developed through the performance of those functions which it is their office to perform, not through the performance of artificial exercises devised to fit them for these functions. The red Indian acquires the swiftness and agility which make him a successful hunter by the actual pursuit of animals; and by the miscellaneous activities of his life he gains a better balance of physical powers than gymnastics ever give. That skill in tracking enemies and prey which he has reached by long practice implies a subtlety of perception far exceeding anything produced by artificial training. And similarly throughout. From the Bushman, whose eye, which being habitually employed in identifying distant objects that are to be pursued or fled from, has acquired a quite telescopic range, to the accountant whose daily practice enables him to add up several columns of figures simultaneously, we find that the highest power of a faculty results from the discharge of those duties which the conditions of life require it to discharge. And we may be certain, *a priori*, that the same law holds throughout education. The education of most value for guidance must at the same time be the education of most value for discipline.

*   *   *   *   *

We conclude, then, that for discipline as well as for guidance, science is of chiefest value. In all its effects, learning the meaning of things is better than learning the meaning of words. Whether for intellectual, moral, or religious training, the study of surrounding phenomena is immensely superior to the study of grammars and lexicons.

Thus to the question with which we set out, What knowledge is of most worth? the uniform reply is — science. This is the verdict on all the counts. For direct self-preservation, or the maintenance of life and health, the all-important knowledge is — science. For that indirect self-preservation which we call gaining a livelihood, the knowledge of greatest value is — science. For the due discharge of parental functions, the proper guidance is to be found only in — science. For that interpretation of national life, past and present, without which the citizen can not rightly regulate his conduct, the indispensable key is — science. Alike for the most perfect production and highest enjoyment of art in all its forms, the needful preparation is still — science. And for purposes of discipline — intellectual, moral, religious — the most efficient study is, once more — science. The question which at first seemed so perplexed has become, in the course of our inquiry, comparatively simple. We have not to estimate the degrees of importance of different orders of human activity, and different studies as severally fitting us for them, since we find that the study of science, in its most comprehensive meaning, is the best preparation for all these orders of activity. We have not to decide between the claims of knowledge of great though conventional value, and knowledge of less though intrinsic value, seeing that the knowledge which we find to be of most value in all other respects is intrinsically most valuable: its worth is not dependent upon opinion, but is as fixed as is the relation of man to the surrounding world. Necessary and eternal as are its truths, all science concerns all mankind for all time. Equally at present and in the remotest future must it be of incalculable importance for the regulation of their conduct that men should understand the science of life, physical, mental, and social, and that they should understand all other science as a key to the science of life.

And yet the knowledge which is of such transcendent value is that which, in our age of boasted education, receives the least attention. While this which we call civilization could never have arisen had it not been for science, science forms scarcely an appreciable element in what men consider civilized training. Though to the progress of science we owe it that millions find support where once there was food only for thousands, yet of these millions but a few thousands pay any respect to that which has made their existence possible. Though this increasing knowledge of the properties and relations of things has not only enabled wandering tribes to grow into populous nations, but has given to the countless members of those populous nations comforts and pleasures which their few naked ancestors never even conceived, or could have believed, yet is this kind of knowledge only now receiving a grudging recognition in our highest educational institutions. To the slowly growing acquaintance with the uniform coexistences and sequences of phenomena — to the establishment of invariable laws — we owe our emancipation from the grossest superstitions. But for science we should be still worshipping fetishes, or, with hecatombs of victims, propitiating diabolical deities.

Paraphrasing an Eastern fable, we may say that in the family of knowledges, science is the household drudge, who, in obscurity, hides unrecognized perfections. To her has been committed all the work; by her skill, intelligence, and devotion have all the conveniences and gratifications been obtained; and while ceaselessly occupied ministering to the rest, she has been kept in the background, that her haughty sisters might flaunt their fripperies in the eyes of the world. The parallel holds yet further. For we are fast coming to the *dénouement,* when the positions will be changed; and while these haughty sisters sink into merited neglect, science, proclaimed as highest alike in worth and beauty, will reign supreme.

INDEX

Activities, the leading, of life, 408.
Alphabet, how to be taught, 110; how to be learned, 144.
Alexander, taught by Aristotle, 109, 219.
Anger, to be avoided, 138.
Apostolical Constitution, described, 150; forbid pagan books, 151; parents should bring up children religiously, 152; corporal punishment, 152; catechumens, 153; preparation for baptism, 154.
Aristotle, sketch of, 33; principal books, 34; virtue dependent on nature, habit, and reason, 35; character of rulers, 36; the soul divided into two parts, 37; Spartan education, 38; education for peace rather than for war, 39; virtues of a state, 39; reason and appetite, 41; early training, 41, 42; Plato criticised, 42; prohibition of indecency, 42, 43; education a civic duty, 44; should be public, 44; diverse aims of, 45; what should be taught, 45; branches of education, 46; music, 46, 47; liberal and utilitarian culture, 48; athletics should not be brutal, 49; not excessive, 50; music in education, 50–54; musical instruments, 56; Plato's views criticised, 59; three principles of education, 60.
Arithmetic defined, 164; its relation to the Scriptures, 165.
Ascham, Roger, sketch of, 228; "The Schole-master," 228; method with Latin, 229; on method, 231; precocious children, 232; brilliant men, 232; on mathematics, 233; persistent plodders, 234; bad choice of university students, 235; supervision of youth, 238.
Associations, influence of evil, 140; bad, to be avoided, 277.
Astronomy, defined and explained, 167.
Athletics, see Gymnastics.

Baptism, preparation for, 154.
Books, should be collected, 134; different classes of, 184; injurious, to be excluded from schools, 191; good, to be provided, 192; excessive devotion to, 220; sources of wisdom and piety, 277.

Catechumens, instruction of, 153.
Censors, in Jesuit schools, 200.
Charlemagne, sketch of, 155; efforts in behalf of education, 155; "Capitulary of 787," 156; study of letters in monasteries, 156; who should teach, 157.
Children, nature of, 28; early training of, 41; protected from evil influences, 42, 43; quick to learn, 104; should be accustomed to correct speech, 105; to be taught early, 108, 109; to be cared for by mothers, 127; easily molded, 127; fond of learning, 180; precocious, 232; ready to learn, 237; not to be broken, 282; dispositions to be studied, 282; to be reasoned with, 283; seldom need whipping, 284; desirous of instruction, 299; easily impressed, 300; characters to be weighed, 306, 307; authority over, to be assumed, 308; fear and love to be called forth, 309; correction of, 310; appeal to reason,

313; trained in truthfulness, 314; in good habits, 315; should have recreation, 317; trained in virtue, 319; should be loved, 327; indulgence of, 327; not to be commanded, 328; how to be trained, 329; the only moral lesson suited to, 330; should be respected, 331; memory of, 332; not to be taught many things, 334; taught to love all men, 337; trained in morals, 349; their confidence to be won, 360; eagerness to learn, 361; not to be repelled, 377.

Christianity, relation to education, 319; the Christian teacher, 320.

Church, the, attitude of, to pagan literature, 151.

Cicero, sketch of, 83; ideal of orator, 84; orator and poet, 86; studies for the orator, 88; rhetorical study, 89; nature of eloquence, 90; five parts of oratory, 91; elements of discourse, 92; writing as aid to speaking, 93; utility of declamation and translation, 95; the orator's knowledge, 96.

Clergy, education of, 159.

Comenius, John Amos, sketch of, 255; "Gate of Tongues Unlocked," 256; "Orbis Pictus," 257; "Great Didactic," 257; end of education, 258; woman to be educated, 258; classes of objects, 259; purpose of schools, 259; office of teachers, 260; nature observes a suitable time, 262; common errors, 265; examples before rules, 266; premature instruction, 267; too many studies, 268; comprehension before memorizing, 270; the general before the particular, 272; gradual progress, 273, 274; education should be continuous, 276; on books, 277.

Compulsory education, 23.

Cornelia, learning of, 106.

Culture, nature of, 348.

Cyrus, character of, 62.

Decoration precedes dress, 400.

Dialectic, defined and explained, 164.

Discipline, nature of, 342; subduing brutality, 348.

Discipline and knowledge, 412.

Disputations, how conducted in Jesuit schools, 192; emulation encouraged, 201.

Dittes, quoted on Luther, 170.

Drawing, to be taught, 333.

Education, two branches of, 9; gymnastics, 11; of woman, 23, 24; scope and periods of, 28; order of, 41; a civic duty, 44; should be public, 44; diverse aims of, 45; utilitarian, 45; liberal arts, 45; branches of, 46; three principles of, 60; in Persia, 62, 67; a difficult task, 98; certain moral virtues, 99; utility, 100; moral aims of, 101; should begin early, 107, 108; in public schools, 113; inferior ability helped by, 126; importance of, 130; universal, 135; memory in, 136; religious, 144; manual, 148; catechetical, 153; Charlemagne's efforts for, 155; clerical, 159; the world concerned in, 173; shame of neglecting, 174; relation to civic welfare, 175; liberal studies in, 176; relation to civil government, 178; necessity of, 179; united with work, 181; aim of, 193; emulation in, 201; purpose of, 204; bookish learning, 208; uses of travel in, 208; physical, 209; right use of, 210; what the scholar should know, 214; age for, 219; nature of, 222; should be made pleasant, 222; excessive language study in, 223; harsh methods, 231; end of, 242; Spartan, criticised, 251; traveling in, 253; purpose aimed at, 258; time for, 263; to be continuous, 276; ideal of, 280; virtue as the end of, 282; fourfold aim of, 285; of girls, neglected, 294; for woman, 301; source of happiness, 305; object of, 306; definition of, 306; fear and love in, 309; to be made agreeable, 316;

relation of Christianity to, 319; what it gives, 323; sense, perception in, 326; authority in, 334; religious, to be deferred, 338; what it includes, 341; develops manhood, 343; as development, 345; progressive, 346; an art, 346; adapted to the idea of humanity, 347; moral training in, 349; experiments in, 349; private and public, 350; a problem of, 350; Pestalozzian principles of, 353; hurry to be avoided in, 354; study of nature in, 354; exercising faculties in, 355; study of words in, 356; value of work in, 358; domestic, 359; moral, 362; solid foundation for, 363; elementary, 364; complete, 364; the senses in, 366; fundamental elements in, 367; essential work of, 368; defined, 372; theory and practice of, 373; results of good instruction, 374; as giving and taking, 375; material and spiritual ends in, 376; uninterrupted, 378; precept and example in, 379; of the body, 386; of the intellect, 388; and plutocracy, 389; an equalizer, 390; a source of power, 391; moral side of, 392; religious, 395; a controlling principle of, 403; present rude character of, 404; preparation for complete living, 407; symmetrical, 411; esthetic, 413; error of, 414; science in, 416.

Egypt, dancing and music in, 15.

Eloquence, see Orator.

Emulation, recommended, 145; in Jesuit schools, 201.

English, importance of, 288.

Epicurus, quoted on philosophy, 220.

Example, influence of, 142.

FAMILY, the, relation to the state, 409.

Fénelon, sketch of, 291; as tutor, 292; "Education of Girls," 293; neglect of girls' education, 294; sphere and influence of woman, 295; defects in her education, 296; frivolity and idleness of, 297; her reading, 298; children fond of instruction, 299; easily impressed, 300; studies for woman, 301.

Froebel, Frederick, sketch of, 369; with Pestalozzi, 370; fundamental thought of, 370; tribute to, 371; the divine unity, 372; definition of education, 372, 379; theory and practice of education, 373; effects of good education, 374; education as giving and taking, 375; supremacy of right, 375; material and spiritual ends, 376; play, 376, 380; children not to be repelled, 378; nature of schools, 378; example and precept, 379; craving for tales, 381; man not bad by nature, 381.

GEOGRAPHY, starting points of, 334.

Geometry, defined, 165.

God, as worthy object of endeavor, 20; man's greatest need, 357; the unity of all things, 372; a knowledge of necessary, 396.

Grammar, the study of, 123; defined, 162; relation to the Scriptures, 162.

Greek, a language for scholars, 289. (See Languages, The ancient.)

Gymnastics, two parts, 11; should be employed, 49; should not be excessive, 50; nor neglected, 134.

HARRIS, Dr. W. T., quoted on Froebel, 370.

Health, laws of, 280.

History, proper study of, 212; conventional value of, 412.

Housekeeper, a model, described, 81.

Humboldt, referred to, 400.

Hunting, a preparation for war, 65.

JEROME, sketch of, 143; letter to Laeta, 143; religious education, 144; learning the alphabet, 144; writing, 145; emulation, 145; teacher to be moral and learned, 145; early impressions, 146; dress and ornament, 146; study of the Scriptures, 146; religious exercises, 147; manual training, 148; monastic education, 149.

Jesuits, the, sketch of, 187; Constitutions of, 187; *Ratio Studiorum,* 188; selection of teachers, 188; study of the Scriptures, 189; innovating opinions discouraged, 189; examinations, 189, 199; different schools or grades, 190; lifelong teachers, 190; injurious books to be excluded, 191; use of Latin language, 191; prizes, 191; disputations, 192, 198; useful books, 192; the teacher's aim, 193; rules for quoting authorities, 194; directions for the teacher, 195; the Vulgate to be defended, 195; Thomas Aquinas to be followed, 196; rules for various studies, 197; religious study of the sciences, 199; appointment of censors, 200; religious lectures, 201; emulation, 201.

KANT, Immanuel, sketch of, 340; his "Pedagogy," 341; nature of education, 341; office of discipline, 342, 348; love of freedom, 343; culture, 343, 348; theory of education, 344; development of latent powers, 345; education progressive, 346; as an art, 346; a mistake of parents, 347; moral training, 349; experimental schools, 349; private and public education, 350; an educational problem, 350.

Knowledge, relative worth of, 405; intrinsic and conventional value of, 411; and discipline, 412.

LANGUAGES, the ancient, 176, 177; excessive study of, 223; too dearly bought, 225; how learned by Montaigne, 225, 226; why studied, 242; studied too long, 286; of no practical utility, 401; quasi-intrinsic value of, 411.

Latin, in Jesuit schools, 191.

Liberal Arts, 45; not to be pursued for profit, 100; enumerated, 162.

Libraries, to be established, 183; different kinds of books for, 184.

Life, divided into two parts, 37; its nature, 324.

Locke, John, sketch of, 278; "Thoughts Concerning Education," 279; ideal of education, 280; rules for health, 280; mistakes of parents, 281; self-control, 281; children not to be broken, 282; their aptitudes studied, 282; reasoning with, 283; whipping to be avoided, 284; character of teacher, 284; four ends in education, 285; ancient languages, 286; gaining the attention, 287; pre-eminence of English, 288.

Luther, Martin, sketch of, 169; principal educational writings, 170; fundamental conception of education, 170; Letter to Mayors and Aldermen, 171; decline of schools, 171; the devil's purpose, 172; importance of education, 173; shame of neglecting, 174; civic welfare dependent on education, 175; liberal studies, 176; the languages and the gospel, 177; schools required for civil government, 178; necessity of education, 179; children delight in learning, 180; music, 180; work and study, 181; appeal to city authorities, 182; on libraries, 183; defects of schools, 183, 184; different classes of books, 184.

MANN, Horace, sketch of, 383; secretary of Board of Education, 384; last Annual Report, 385; schools a civilizing force, 385; physical education, 386; intellectual, 388; education and plutocracy, 389; education an equalizer, 390; a source of power, 391; moral education, 392; effect of right training, 393; religious education, 395.

Manual training, inculcated, 148; honest trades to be learned, 152.

Marriage, effects of, 141.

Mathematics, influence of, 233.

Maurus, Rhabanus, sketch of, 158; principal works, 159; education of the clergy, 159; character of the Scriptures, 160; how to be read,

INDEX

161; liberal arts, 162; grammar defined, 162; rhetoric defined, 163; dialectic explained, 164; arithmetic, 164; geometry, 165; music, 166; astronomy, 167.

Memory, a sign of ability, 119; should be cultivated, 136.

Method, the developing, 205; truth to be assimilated, 206; nothing to be imparted by mere authority, 206; teaching by rote, 208; right method of instruction, 215; Aristotle's 219; severe sweetness in, 222; Ascham's, in Latin, 229; harsh, in English, 231, 235; order of studies, 243; with languages, 245, 246; traveling, 253; basis of, 261; subjects suited to pupil's age, 263; errors of, 265; examples before rules, 266; premature instruction, 267; too many studies, 268; comprehension should precede memorizing, 270; the general should precede the particular, 272; gradual progress, 273, 274; holding the attention, 287; with Latin, 287; succession of studies, 290; instruction to be made pleasant, 300; studies for women, 301; in domestic education, 359.

Milton, John, sketch of, 240; school in London, 241; "Tractate on Education," 241; end of learning, 242; purpose of language study, 242; too difficult tasks exacted, 243; professional pursuits, 244; school arrangements, 245; method with Latin and Greek, 245, 246; range of studies, 247; moral training, 248; on poetry, 250; physical culture, 251; travel, 253.

Mimicry, an unfavorable sign, 120.

Monasteries, urged to give instruction, 156.

Montaigne, sketch of, 203; "Essays," 204; purpose of education, 204; developing method, 205; truth to be assimilated, 206; nothing by mere authority, 206; bookish learning, 208; uses of travel, 208; physical training, 209; how to use learning, 210; sincerity, 211; acquisitive disposition, 212; study of history, 212; the world a great book, 213; what the scholar should know, 214; various studies, 215; effects of philosophy, 216; Aristotle's teaching, 219; book-worm study, 220; times and places of study, 220, 221; best style of expression, 224; learning Latin and Greek, 225, 226; at the College of Guienne, 227.

Music, conformed to right models, 17; how regulated, 19; for men and women, 20; in education, 46; why taught, 50, 51; for social enjoyment, 53; different kinds, 54; should be taught to children, 54; instruments of, 56; why studied, 58; nature and utility of, 166; should be taught, 180.

Orator, Cicero's ideal of, 84; definition of, 85; and poet, 86; studies of, 88; five parts of his art, 91; should write speeches, 93; various exercises, 94, 95; comprehensive knowledge, 96; should make preparation, 131; his style, 132.

Order, utility of, 76–79; in the household, 79.

Parents, should be educated, 105; conduct of, 141; should set good example, 142; should be models, 147; should bring up children in religion, 152; mistakes of, 281; influence of, 302; their obligations, 325; an error of, 347; aim of, 377.

Paroz, quoted on Fénelon, 293.

Pedagogues. See Teachers.

Pestalozzi, John Henry, sketch of, 351; at Stanz, 352, 360; at Yverdun, 352; summary of principles, 353; avoid hurry, 354; study of nature, 354; development by exercise, 355; study of words, 356; truth a source of strength, 356; man's need of God, 357; work, 358; domestic education, 359; winning confidence, 360; eagerness of children to learn, 361; moral education, 362; solid foundation, 363; complete development, 364; impulse of development, 365; sense-perception, 366; fundamental elements, 367; essential work of education, 368.

Philosophy, nature of, 100; importance of, 133; utility of, 197; value of, 214; effects of, 216; early inculcated, 219; suited to all occasions, 221.

Physiology, to be taught, 387.

Plato, sketch of, 7; principal works, 8; early training of children, 9; training both hands, 10; two branches of education, 11; influence of play, 13; dancing in Egypt, 15; music, 17; poetry, 18; God as object of endeavor, 21; right way to live, 22; gymnasia, 23; compulsory education, 23; female education, 23, 34; life of virtue, 26; boys insubordinate, 28; scope and periods of education, 29; different kinds of poets, 31; teachers, 32.

Play, influence of, 13; significance of, 376; relation to inner life, 380.

Plutarch, sketch of, 125; three needs in development, 126; inferior ability helped by training, 126; care of children, 127; teachers of blameless life, 128; philosophy, 133; universal education, 135; children to be encouraged, 135; memory to be cultivated, 136; self-control, 137; anger to be avoided, 138; faults of young men, 138; evil associations, 140; conduct of parents, 141; marriage, 141.

Poets, should be heedful, 18; different kinds, 31; allied to orators, 86; study of, 250.

Punishment, corporal, condemned, 122; inculcated, 132; to be avoided, 284; use of rod in, 310; reproof, 311; should come as a natural result, 330; bodily chastisement, 362.

Pythagoras, enigmatical precepts of, 140.

QUINTILIAN, sketch of, 103; his "Institutes," 103; children quick to learn, 104; trained to correct speech, 105; parents should be educated, 105; character of teachers, 106; Greek should precede Latin, 107; education should begin early, 108; should be made pleasant, 109; the alphabet, 110; learning to write, 110; reading, 111; kind of copies, 112; public schools, 113; evil influences, 114; emulation, 117; pupil's disposition to be ascertained, 119; mimicry, 120; school management, 120; recreation, 121; corporal punishment, 122; study of grammar, 123.

READING, how to be taught, 111.
Recreation, to be allowed, 121, 317.
Refinement, nature of, 348.
Rhetoric, study of, 89, 90; defined, 163; its utility, 163.
Rollin, Charles, sketch of, 303; "Treatise on Studies," 304; education a source of happiness, 305; purpose of teaching, 306; definition of education, 306; children's character to be studied, 307; authority in teaching, 308; fear and love, 309; punishment, 310; reproof, 311; reasoning with children, 313; truthfulness, 314; good habits, 315; study to be made agreeable, 316; rest and recreation, 317; training in virtue, 319; Christianity, 319.

Rousseau, Jean Jacques, sketch of, 321; "Confessions," 321; "Émile," 322; two fundamental principles, 323; what education is, 323; the best educated man, 324; mothers should nourish children, 324; a father's obligation, 325; the teacher, 325, 326; use of the senses, 326; love for childhood, 327; indulgence of children, 327; not to be com-

INDEX

manded. 328; right training, 329; punishment, 330; injuring others, 330; respect for children, 331; right teaching, 331; words and ideas, 331; memory, 332; drawing, 333; geography, 334; nothing by authority, 334; "Robinson Crusoe," 336; results of Émile's training, 336; rural surroundings, 337; religion, 338; woman's education to be relative to man, 339.

Rulers, character of, 36.

SCHOOLS, buildings for, 23; public and private, 113; management of, 120; cathedral and cloister, 181; size and arrangement of, 245; forging-place of men, 259; location of, 276; experimental, 349; explained, 378; as civilizing force, 385.

Science, value of, 416.

Scriptures, the, to be studied, 147; order of study, 148; superior to pagan literature, 151; character of, 160; require learning, 161; relation of grammar to, 162; the Vulgate to be defended, 195; studied in the original tongues, 249.

Self-control, instance of, 137; importance of, 281.

Seneca, sketch of, 97; education difficult, 98; recreation moderate, 99; virtues to be inculcated, 99; nature of philosophy, 100; morality the end of education, 101.

Sense-perception, 326, 366.

Socrates, instance of self-control, 137.

Sparta, education in, 38; brutalizing, 49; defects of, 251.

Spencer, Herbert, sketch of, 399; his "Education," 399; what knowledge is of most worth, 400; decoration and dress, 400; ornamental studies, 401; feminine accomplishments, 402; determining principle of education, 403; rude character of, 404; relative worth of knowledge, 405; limited time of acquisition, 406; measure of value, 406; education a preparation for life, 407; leading activities of life, 408; self-preservation, 409; symmetrical training, 411; esthetic education, 413; vice of current education, 414; worth of science, 416.

State, the, how rendered virtuous, 34; what its virtues should be, 39, 40.

Studies, liberal and utilitarian, 45, 48; not to be pursued for money, 100; moral side of, 101; Milton's list of, 247; in morals, 248; how determine course of, 412.

Style, in discourse, 132; Montaigne on, 224.

TEACHERS, qualifications of, 32; character of Persian, 63; even-tempered, 100; learned, 106; influence of numbers on, 119; blameless, 128; desirable traits of, 145; office of, 260; character of, 284; Christian, 320; qualifications of, 325.

Travel, in education, 208.

Truth, a source of strength, 356; supremacy of, 375.

UNIVERSITIES, criticised, 243.

VIRTUE, on what dependent, 35; political virtues, 39, 40; in what it consists, 53; relation of music to, 53.

WOMAN, to be educated as man is, 23; her domestic sphere, 71; distinctive virtues of, 72; should be educated, 258; sphere and influence of, 295; defects in her education, 296; idleness and frivolity of, 297; what she should study, 301; educated relatively to man, 339.

Words, without ideas, 331; study of, 356.

Work, value of, 358.

Writing, how to be taught, 110, 144.

XENOPHON, sketch of, 61; "Cyropaedia" "Economics," 61; character of Cyrus, 62; Persian education, 62; its methods, 63; study of justice, 64; hunting, 65; practice of abstinence, 66; duties of husband and wife, 70; different duties of, 71; virtues of each, 72; utility of order, 76–79; household arrangement, 79, 80; model housekeeper, 81.

YOUTH, to be guarded against temptation, 139.

Important Pedagogical Works

By RURIC N. ROARK

Dean of the Department of Pedagogy, Kentucky State College

ROARK'S PSYCHOLOGY IN EDUCATION, $1.00

This new work is designed for use as a text-book in Secondary and Normal Schools, Teachers' Training Classes, and Reading Circles. The general purpose of the book is to give teachers a logical and scientific basis for their daily work in the schoolroom. It makes a distinct departure from the methods heretofore in vogue in the treatment of Psychology, and is justly regarded as the most important contribution to pedagogical science and literature in recent years.

ROARK'S METHOD IN EDUCATION - $1.00

The second book of Roark's Pedagogical Series is designed for Normal Schools and Teachers' Reading Circles, and for private reading by every teacher who seeks a key to the solution of the problems that present themselves in the schoolroom. By its practical application and illustration of sound pedagogical principles, it presents a working manual of great helpfulness to all teachers, both to the experienced and the inexperienced.

ROARK'S ECONOMY IN EDUCATION, $1.00

This book deals with the problems confronting the individual teacher in the successful administration of his school, and also with the larger problems of the school as a part of the institutional life and growth of modern society. The book is not only invaluable to the individual teacher in any grade of work, but it is especially adapted for use as a text in Normal Schools, Teachers' Reading Courses, and College Departments of Pedagogy.

AMERICAN BOOK COMPANY

NEW YORK   CINCINNATI   CHICAGO

A Complete System of Pedagogy

IN THREE VOLUMES

BY EMERSON E. WHITE, A.M., LL.D.

THE ART OF TEACHING. Cloth, 321 pages . . Price, $1.00

This new work in Pedagogy is a scientific and practical consideration of *teaching as an art*. It presents in a lucid manner the fundamental principles of teaching, and then applies them in generic and comprehensive methods. The closing chapters discuss in a masterly way the teaching of reading, language, arithmetic, geography, and other elementary branches. The author also considers most helpfully the various problems connected with teaching, including oral instruction, book study, class instruction and management, examinations, promotion of pupils, etc.

ELEMENTS OF PEDAGOGY. Cloth, 336 pages . . Price, $1.00

This treatise, by unanimous verdict of the teachers' profession, has been accepted as the leading standard authority on the subject. From its first publication it has met with the greatest favor, and its wide circulation ever since has been phenomenal. It has been adopted in more Normal Schools, Teachers' Institutes, and State Reading Circles, than any other book of its class. This wide circulation and popularity is directly attributable to the intrinsic value and merit of the book itself and the reputation of its author, who is everywhere recognized as preeminently qualified to speak or write with authority on educational subjects.

SCHOOL MANAGEMENT. Cloth, 320 pages . . Price, $1.00

The first part of this work is devoted to school organization and discipline, and the second part to moral training. Principles are clearly stated and aptly illustrated by examples drawn largely from the author's own wide experience. A clear light is thrown on the most important problems in school management. The necessity for moral training, which, in the minds of many, also involves religious instruction, will make the second part of this book a welcome contribution to pedagogical literature. The subject is thoroughly and wisely treated, and the materials which are provided for moral lessons will be highly appreciated by all teachers who feel the importance of this work.

Copies sent, prepaid, to any address on receipt of the price.

American Book Company

New York • Cincinnati • Chicago

Seeley's History of Education

BY DR. LEVI SEELEY
Professor of Pedagogy, State Normal School, Trenton, N. J.

Cloth, 12mo, 350 pages.   Price, $1.25

Nearly 400,000 active teachers in the United States are required to pass an examination in the History of Education. Normal schools, and colleges with pedagogical departments lay particular stress upon this subject and the Superintendents of Education in most states, counties, and cities, now expect their teachers to possess a knowledge of it.

This book is not based on theory, but is the practical outgrowth of Dr. Seeley's own class-work after years of trial. It is therefore a working book, plain, comprehensive, accurate, and sufficient in itself to furnish all the material on the subject required by any examining board, or that may be demanded in a normal or college course.

It arranges the material in such a manner as to appeal to the student and assist him to grasp and remember the subject.

It gives a concise summary of each system discussed, pointing out the most important lessons.

It lays stress upon the development of education, showing the steps of progress from one period to another.

It begins the study of each educational system or period with an examination of the environment of the people, their history, geography, home conditions, etc.

It gives a biographical sketch of the leading educators, and their systems of pedagogy, including those of Horace Mann and Herbart.

It treats of the systems of education of Germany, France, England, and the United States,—bringing the study of education down to the present time.

It furnishes the literature of each subject and gives an extensive general bibliography for reference.

Copies of Seeley's History of Education will be sent, prepaid, to any address on receipt of the price by the Publishers.

American Book Company

New York   •   Cincinnati   •   Chicago

For Teachers and School Officers

KING'S SCHOOL INTERESTS AND DUTIES

Developed from "Page's Mutual Duties of Parents and Teachers," from various Public Records and Documents, and from the Bulletins of the National Bureau of Education. By ROBERT M. KING.

Cloth, 12mo, 336 pages $1.00

This new work, original in its scope and plan, presents in one volume interesting and valuable expositions of the modern demands, best methods, and most important interests of our Public School Systems. Its central idea is to show the importance and value of co-operation in school work and the mutual duties of teachers, school officers, and parents. It also embodies synopses of the discussions on leading educational topics from the various fugitive reports and manuals issued, from time to time, by school officials and State Departments of Education. It will be found an invaluable manual and guide for school superintendents, officers, and patrons, and, indeed, for every one interested in educational work.

MANN'S SCHOOL RECREATIONS AND AMUSEMENTS

By CHARLES W. MANN, A.M., Dean of the Chicago Academy.

Cloth, 12mo, 352 pages $1.00

This volume not only opens up a new field of much needed information and direction in the matter of physical training of pupils, but also furnishes suggestions for intellectual recreations which will greatly add to the interest and value of school work and lend a charm to school life in all its phases. Some of the subjects treated in this work are: Morning Exercises, Care and Equipment of Schoolrooms, Singing Games and Songs, Indoor Exercises and Outdoor Games, Experiments in Physics and Chemistry, Recreations in Latin, Outline for Reading Circles, etc.

Copies of the above books will be sent, prepaid, to any address on receipt of the price by the Publishers:

American Book Company

New York • Cincinnati • Chicago

The Ideal Language Series

Steps In English

By **A. C. McLean**, A. M., Principal of Luckey Schools, Pittsburg; **Thomas C. Blaisdell**, A. M., Professor of English, Fifth Avenue Normal High School, Pittsburg; and **John Morrow**, Supt. of Schools, Allegheny, Pa.

BOOK I - $0.40 BOOK II - $0.60

THESE books constitute a distinct innovation in teaching language in elementary schools, which is at once sensible, practical, and modern. They teach the child how to express his thoughts in his own language, and do not furnish an undue amount of grammar and rules. They mark out the work for the teacher in a clearly defined manner by telling him what to do and when to do it. From the start lessons in writing language are employed simultaneously with those in conversation; and picture study, study of literary selections, and letter writing are presented at frequent intervals. The lessons are of a proper length, well arranged and well graded.

This series is free from the many faults found in other books of a similar nature. The work is not based on an antiquated plan, but is particularly suited to modern conditions. It does not shoot over the heads of pupils, nor does it show a marked effort in writing down to the supposed level of young minds. The books do not contain too much technical grammar, nor are they filled with sentimental twaddle and gush.

AMERICAN BOOK COMPANY
NEW YORK   CINCINNATI   CHICAGO

Spencers' Practical Writing

By PLATT R. SPENCER'S SONS

Books 1, 2, 3, 4, 5, and 6   Per Dozen, 60 Cents

THIS new system of writing has been devised because of the distinct and wide-spread reaction from the use of vertical writing in the schools. It is thoroughly up-to-date, embodying all the advantages of the old and of the new. Each word can be written by one continuous movement of the pen.

The books teach a plain, practical hand, moderate in slant, and free from ornamental curves, shade, and meaningless lines. The stem letters are long enough to be clear and unmistakable. The capitals are about two spaces in height. In each of the six numbers composing this series there are twenty-four copies, and the space for practice is about the same as in other series, although the number of lines is greater because the books open on the long side.

The copies begin with words and gradually develop into sentences. The letters, both large and small, are taught systematically. In the first two books the writing is somewhat larger than is customary because it is more easily learned by young children, while in the succeeding books the writing is more nearly the normal size. Books One and Two contain many illustrations in outline. Each succeeding book presents more work and in greater variety.

The ruling of the books is very simple and will in no way unduly confine or hamper the movements of the pen. Instruction is afforded showing how the pupil should sit at the desk and hold the pen and paper. A series of drill movement exercises, thirty-three in number, with directions for their use, accompanies each book.

AMERICAN BOOK COMPANY

NEW YORK   CINCINNATI   CHICAGO

NORTHERN ILLINOIS UNIVERSITY
3 1211 01814329 3